D1795619

JEWS IN UKRAINIAN LITERATURE

Jews in Ukrainian Literature

Representation and Identity

Myroslav Shkandrij

Yale University Press   NEW HAVEN & LONDON

Published with assistance from the Mary Cady Tew Memorial Fund.

Copyright © 2009 by Yale University.
All rights reserved.
This book may not be reproduced, in whole or in part, including illustrations, in any form
(beyond that copying permitted by Sections 107 and 108 of the U.S. Copyright Law and except
by reviewers for the public press), without written permission from the publishers.

Set in Ehrhardt Roman types by The Composing Room of Michigan, Inc.
Printed in the United States of America.

Library of Congress Cataloging-in-Publication Data
Shkandrij, Myroslav, 1950–
    Jews in Ukrainian literature : representation and identity / Myroslav Shkandrij.
       p. cm.
    Includes bibliographical references and index.
    ISBN 978-0-300-12588-7 (pbk. : alk. paper)
    1. Jews in literature. 2. Ukrainian literature—History and criticism.   I. Title.
    PG3906.J49S55   2009
    891.7′9093529924—dc22

                          2009007813

A catalogue record for this book is available from the British Library.

This paper meets the requirements of ANSI/NISO Z39.48–1992 (Permanence of Paper).

10 9 8 7 6 5 4 3 2 1

For Alexandra and Helena

Contents

Acknowledgments

A mong the colleagues and friends who read various drafts of this book and shared their comments and insights, I would like to thank John-Paul Himka, Yohanan Petrovsky-Shtern, Serhy Yekelchyk, Orest Martynowych, Elena Baraban, and Zina Gimpelevich. Several individuals directed my attention to sources and helped me find materials, among them Viktoria Khiterer, Yurii Shapoval, Vira Aheieva, Viacheslav Aheiev, Mykola Klymchuk, Yaryna Tsymbal, Robert Klymasz, Jars Balan, Serhy Cipko, Bohdan Harasymiw, and Denys Volkov. Oksana Oliferovych and Adriana Choptiany helped with translations and tracking down difficult references. The following individuals and institutions were invaluable in finding materials: Leonid Finberh and the Judaica Institute in Kyiv; Sophia Kachor, Bohdana Bashuk, and the archival staff of the Ukrainian Cultural and Educational Centre (Oseredok) in Winnipeg; James Kominowski in the Slavic Collection and staff in Document Delivery at the University of Manitoba's Dafoe Library. A special thanks goes to my wife Natalka, who was a first reader, commentator, and supporter of the project throughout.

I would like to acknowledge the *Ukrainian Quarterly* for permission to reproduce sections of the text that appeared in the journal as "The Jewish Voice in Ukrainian Literature," 62.1 (2006): 69–94; the Social Sciences and Humanities Research Council of Canada for a grant that allowed me to conduct research; and the University of Manitoba for research-study time.

Finally, I would like to point out that I alone am responsible for the views expressed in this book.

Note on Transliteration

A modified version of the Library of Congress transliteration system has been used for proper names in the text. Hard and soft signs have been omitted, and in order to approximate English usage and pronunciation Ya- and Yu- have replaced Ia- and Iu- as the initial syllable in names, while -y has replaced -yi or -ii in surname endings. The full system has been used to transliterate Slavic text, author-date citations, and the reference list. The rule of thumb has been to transliterate Ukrainian place names from the Ukrainian language, and Russian from the Russian. A few exceptions were made in cases where established English usage was considered preferable because of its familiarity and acceptableness to all parties (Galicia, Volhynia), or because of its closeness to the Slavic pronunciation (Ignatiev).

Abbreviations

Cheka	Extraordinary Commission. Short for VChK or the All-Russian Extraordinary Commission for Fighting Counterrevolution and Sabotage (1917–22), the Soviet secret police. The term is often applied to all the organization's later incarnations under their various names: GPU, OGPU, NKVD, MVD, MGD,KGB
CP(B)U	Communist Party (Bolshevik) of Ukraine
EIEO	Jewish Historical-Ethnographic Society
GPU	State Political Administration (1922–30), successor of the Cheka
KGB	Committee for State Security (1954–91), successor of the MVD
KOMZET	Committee for Rural Placement of Jewish Laborers
MAUP	Interregional Academy for Personnel Management
MGD	Ministry of State Security (1946–62) (a branch of the secret police), successor of the NKVD
MUR	Ukrainian Artistic Movement
MVD	Ministry of Internal Affairs (1946–62) (a branch of the secret police), successor of the NKVD
NDP	National Democratic Party
NKVD	People's Commissariat for Internal Affairs (1917–46) (at various points controlled the GPU and OGPU), successor of the Cheka
OGPU	Unified State Political Administration (1923–34) (the central agency that controlled all republican GPUs), successor of the Cheka
OPE	Society for Spreading Enlightenment Among Jews in Russia
OUN	Organization of Ukrainian Nationalists
OZET	Society for Settlement on Land of Working Jews

SVU	League for the Liberation of Ukraine
VAPLITE	The Free Academy of Proletarian Literature (1925–28)
VUFKU	All-Ukrainian Photo-Cinema Management
UGA	Ukrainian Galician Army
UNA-UNSO	Ukrainian National Assembly—Ukrainian National Self-Defense
UNR	Ukrainian National Republic (also known as Ukrainian People's Republic)
USDP	Ukrainian Social Democratic Party
WUNR	Western Ukrainian National Republic

Introduction

Jews have lived for many centuries on the territory of what is today Ukraine. Their interaction with the local population is recorded in the earliest East Slavic written records, such as the *Paterik* of the Kyivan Caves Monastery, which reports a dialogue between Kyiv's Christians and Jews in the eleventh century. The Jewish presence has been large—at the beginning of the twentieth century almost a third of all world Jewry lived in Ukraine—and it has played a significant role in Ukrainian life. The rich imprint left by this presence on Ukrainian literature is the subject of this book.

The focus is on key works in modern writing, roughly from the 1840s to the present. The crystallization of literary narratives and myths (the latter term understood here as powerful, iconic ways of imaginatively ordering experience) is described within both the historical context and the contemporary discourse concerning Ukrainian-Jewish relations. Changing literary conventions have also shaped the depiction of Jews, especially the period-styles of romanticism, populism-realism, modernism, socialist realism, the vogue for national heroism in the 1930s, and postmodernism, all of which have influenced characterization and the generation of plots, imagery, and tropes. Some narrative elements, such as the Jewish "leaseholder" (*orendar* in Ukrainian) who rents the Orthodox church from the Polish Catholic landowner and makes worshipers pay to hold their services, or characters such as Ahasuerus and Marko Prokliaty, appear in several periods, receiving a different treatment in each. While recognizing the importance of period-styles, this account also situates the literature within the history of Jewish-Ukrainian relations, and of the identity-building projects of both Jews and Ukrainians.

There is much that is not included. In the first place no attempt is made to cover the depiction of Ukrainian-Jewish relations in Yiddish, Russian, Polish, German, or other literatures. References are made to texts in these literatures only to illustrate a particular point, or to throw into relief perceptions of Jews in Ukrainian literature. Studies of texts in these and other languages, although they form a part of Ukraine's multilingual literary environment and heritage, await future scholars. The focus here, it should also be stressed, is on the mainstream Ukrainian literary tradition. Aspects of popular culture are referenced, but this book is not a study of popular culture or attitudes—another subject of enormous scope and potential that awaits serious researchers.

The questions this account tries to answer are as follows: What does Ukrainian literature teach its readers? Does it reflect, as some have argued, a deeply anti-Semitic culture? Or does it portray, as others have reasoned, an insufficiently acknowledged side of Jewish history—the close and enriching interaction with Ukrainian life? The following pages suggest that both propositions require careful qualification. The first because it denies that there were many varied strands within the literature and culture: anti-Semitism competed with philo-Semitism, with one or the other becoming dominant at different times and in different places. And the second because, for one thing, it should be recognized that literary narratives are often myths in the other meaning of the term— inaccurate and biased versions of historical or contemporary events that must be examined with reference to the contexts and the cultural codes that generated them.

This having been said, this book nonetheless attempts to challenge some settled opinions. The retrospective produced by the horrors of the Holocaust and the Second World War has cast a pall over the entire history of Ukrainian-Jewish relations and has shaped attitudes to the past. Partly as a result of this, one point of view—widely accepted today—holds that Jews and Ukrainians lived apart, in self-imposed isolation, interacting only for economic purposes. The model of "two solitudes," or of cultures engaged in mutually exclusive monologues, pays little attention to complexities in the relationship between peoples. There have been calls for the recovery of a fuller, more textured picture of mutual relations. Peter Potichnyj has noted that a thousand years of contact produced Hasidism, a rich literature in Yiddish, and, for many, a relatively prosperous life. He prefers the perspective of two communities living parallel lives, with dramatic conflicts rare and short-lived phenomena that have nonetheless played a large role in collective memory and the construction of literary narratives. (Potichnyj 1985, 93– 94.) Historians have recently begun turning their attention to some of the details of interaction. Viktoria Khiterer, for example, has recorded reports of the weddings of tzaddiks (Jewish holy men) in 1865 and 1900, which contain descriptions of peasants drinking together with Jews and "in spite of prohibition by local authorities, stealthily presenting bread and salt to the bride and groom." (Khiterer 1999, 273, 283.) Such examples of fellowship should, perhaps, not come as a surprise when one considers the long time-frame and the close proximity in which Jews and Ukrainians lived together.

Ukrainian literature provides many such moments of discovery. It sheds light on mutual relations and goes some distance to undermining the "two solitudes" paradigm. Not all periods and not all depictions are dominated by a sense of a tragic impasse, mutual isolation, or inescapable antagonism. The literature of the last two centuries also provides examples of intimacy and mutual understanding. Perhaps most importantly, this literature demonstrates a marked evolution. Certainly, in the first half of the nineteenth century the dominant narratives stressed conflict and resentment. However, in the century's last two decades descriptions of mutually felt suffering, the search for common ground and for respectful dialogue became the norm. The first two decades of the twentieth century were almost entirely philo-Semitic. Partly this was a result of the fact that the emancipation of the Jews became a rallying cry of all liberals in the Russian empire. But the Ukrainian intelligentsia at the time also began to hope for a great alliance between the two peoples. The rise of anti-Semitism during the thirties revived conflictual paradigms from the early nineteenth century. The sixties and seventies then re-created the idea of two communities allied in the struggle for civil and national rights. After 1991, in Ukraine's postindependence period, new ironic narratives emerged to challenge old myths. Most recently, while a vocal minority has attempted to revive stereotypes from the early nineteenth century, a greater awareness of the Holocaust has led to some new soul-searching among many writers. This evolution suggests the need for a model of cultural dynamics that simultaneously takes account of dominant currents and of countertendencies that work to disrupt them. For this reason the literary texts have been viewed through the discourse of Ukrainian-Jewish relations.

Writings of Jewish authors often corroborate the need for a more textured interpretation of these relations. The literature written in Yiddish or Hebrew that has been produced in Ukraine and has dealt with Ukrainian-Jewish relations often suggests a degree of interaction than the "two solitudes" model is not prepared to contemplate. It also alerts readers to the fact that another widely accepted view, the supposed chasm between urban Jews and village Ukrainians, requires some rethinking. Sholem Aleichem's work, for instance, recognizes and celebrates the rural. In his autobiography *From the Fair* he describes growing up in Ukraine in Voronko near Pereiaslav, and how he spent "the best, the most blissful years of his life" in the village, where he was "closer to nature, to God's world, and to God's earth." (Sholem Aleichem 1985, 237.) He describes the wealthy old Jewish landowner Loyev, who conducted an "aristocratic house-hold," loved the soil, and devoted himself to farming:

> He took part in every phase of the work himself: plowing, sowing, weeding, dig-ging, reaping and processing the grain; he was with the horses, the oxen and all the domestic animals. He worked everywhere.
>
> If we ever had to show other people an exemplar of a Jewish landowner, an authentic farmer, old Loyev could have been chosen. Christians said openly that people ought to learn from this Jew how to manage a farm, work the soil in the best possible fashion, and make poor workers content. All the village peasants, without exception, would have done anything in the world for him. Not only did they fear him and stand in awe of him—they loved him. They simply loved him because he treated them like human beings, like friends, like children. These gentiles had never experienced such good treatment from previous landlords— the Polish noblemen. One should remember that the older generation of peas-ants had not yet forgotten the feel of serfdom on their bodies; they still bore the marks of beatings and blows. And now they were being treated like human be-ings, not like animals. (Ibid., 236.)

This passage, which challenges many stereotypes of the rural, the Jewish, and the Ukrainian, could give many contemporary readers pause for thought. East European Jewish literature written in Yiddish and Hebrew, as researchers have indicated, examines various points of contact between Jews and their non-Jewish environment. (Bartal 1988, 313–24.)

Joseph Roth's German-language writings provide more recent examples that disturb the concept of settled, binary oppositions. In his *Wandering Jews* he describes the Jewish community of Ukraine as differing from others precisely because it formed an integral part of rural society. One in three Jews lived among or close to the rural population. Jews even resembled rural Ukrainians:

> The rustic Jew of Eastern Europe is a type completely unknown in the West. No wonder: He has never gotten there. No less "a son of the soil" than the peasant, he is half peasant himself. He is a sharecropper or a miller or a village innkeeper. He has never learned a trade. Often he is completely illiterate. At most he is ca-pable of doing little deals. He's barely any cleverer than the peasant. He is big and strong and of an improbably sound constitution. He is physically brave, doesn't mind a fistfight, and is afraid of nothing. Many take advantage of their superior-ity to the peasants, something that provoked local pogroms in old Russia and anti-Semitic campaigns in Galicia. But many are of a peasant-like meekness and

great-heartedness. Many have the healthy common sense that one tends to find in the countryside, and that develops wherever a sensible race is immediately subject to the laws of nature. (Roth 2001, 48–49.)

Roth suggests that the long history of interaction has led to conversions and intermarriage. Speaking of water carriers and furniture movers, he says: "Some Slav peasants who converted to Judaism also live by such casual labor. Such conversions are relatively frequent in the East, even though official Judaism opposes them, and of all the religions in the world the Jewish faith is the one that doesn't set out to make converts. No question, the Eastern Jews have a much greater admixture of Slav blood in their veins than the German Jews have of German." (Ibid., 53.) By the same token, the author accepts the Ukrainian influence on Jewish culture: "You are probably all familiar with Jewish melodies from the East, but I want to try to give you a sense of that music. I think I can best describe it as a mixture of Russia and Jerusalem, of popular song and psalm. It is music that blends the pathos of the synagogue with the naiveté of folk songs." (Ibid., 77.) Roth was one of the *Ostjuden* (East European Jews) who migrated to Germany in the early twentieth century and were viewed with scorn, even by many Westernized Jews. His account, like Sholem Aleichem's stories, might lead readers to suspect the existence of a richer interaction between Ukrainian and Jewish cultures than conventional wisdom often admits.

In dealing with a still more recent reality, Shimon Redlich has written that the retrospectives of the Holocaust and Second World War produced among Jews, Poles, and Ukrainians a conviction of "exclusive victimhood," which has resulted in "self-centered memories." The notion took root among many Jewish writers that ordinary Poles, or Ukrainians, were naturally inclined, by virtue of their congenital anti-Semitism, to participate in genocide and that even today they should be viewed with profound suspicion and condemned as guilty for the fate of Jews in their countries. He has pointed out that the "return to one's roots is usually a mono-ethnic experience" and has cautioned that the traumas of the war have led people to interpret all the past in the light of subsequent events. He offers the following suggestion: "Each period should be viewed separately. This is particularly necessary when a collective trauma casts its long shadow both backward and forward." (Redlich 2002, 163.)

The dominance of conflict narratives that have cast each as the brutal Other has been a painful reality—for both Jews and Ukrainians. This account shows how the Jewish Other has been constructed in Ukrainian literature, but it is important to realize that for generations there has been a corresponding, often unconscious, construction of the Ukrainian Other. Long a stateless nation,

Ukrainians have often found themselves portrayed in neighboring literatures in ways that diminish or deny their voice, the legitimacy of their concerns, or even their existence. Perceptions and misperceptions of the Ukrainian nation have been filtered through dominant narrative paradigms in Russian, Polish, German, and other literatures. In the following passage by the already-quoted Joseph Roth, written in the 1930s in German but widely translated since then, anti-Semitism in the Russian empire is described as a product of imperial power: "In Russia anti-Semitism was a pillar of government. The simple peasant, the muzhyk, was not anti-Semitic. The Jew was not a friend to him, but a stranger. Russia, which had so much room for strangers, was also open to them. In contrast, it was the half-educated and the middle classes who were anti-Semites, who became so because the nobility was. The nobility was because the court was. The court was because the czar, for whom it was not acceptable to fear his own Orthodox 'children,' could only claim to be afraid of the Jews." (Roth 2001, 105–6.) Roth provides an overview of imperial society (peasants, middle class, nobles), but his use of the term "Russia" to homogenize its inhabitants is problematic. Like so many other narratives, this one ignores the Ukrainian dimension. Today's reader might wonder whether there was a difference between the Russian and Ukrainian peasantry, or gentry, or middle class. Were Russian and Ukrainian realities the same, or did observers fail to see and record any differences?

A similar question arises while reading Shimon Redlich's already quoted Polish-language memoir *Together and Apart in Brzezany*, which has also been widely read in English translation. In describing the interaction of Poles, Jews, and Ukrainians in interwar Eastern Galicia (then part of the Polish state), he makes no mention of the Ukrainian drive for national emancipation, or the rise of nationalism and the growth of the OUN (Organization of Ukrainian Nationalists), or the famine of 1933 and the impact this had on both Galicia and Soviet Ukraine. Consequently, for Redlich the appearance of politically active Ukrainians at a time of upheaval comes as an incomprehensible bolt from the blue. However, Redlich at least mentions Ukrainians, the majority population in Eastern Galicia. A contemporary reader who picks up some other memoirs of Jewish life in small-town Eastern Galicia might wonder whether Ukrainians were invisible. The perspectives provided by Ukrainian literature act as a counterpoint and a corrective to such accounts.

After Ukraine's independence, many formerly taboo topics were opened up to writers and researchers. In the 1990s Marten Feller did much to stimulate interest in the neglected subject of Ukrainian Jewish identity. He complained of the refusal to accept such an identity in some quarters, where it was considered axiomatic that Jews served Russian or Polish interests, but never Ukrainian—an attitude that unwittingly supported the "cultural colonizer's" practice of incorporating Jews into a dominant Russian or Polish narrative while denying their Ukrainianness. (Feller 2001, 4.) His own sense of identity had to overcome this view by bridging stories. He describes how, as a Ukrainian Jew, he found himself dealing with two counterposed truths, two narrative threads that required interweaving. He had to combine, for example, the story of "those Ukrainians who were accessories to the pogroms and Holocaust," and of "those Jews who took part in the dekulakization and collectivization." Both stories are a part of the Ukrainian reality. And yet, depending on a given narrator's predisposition or identity choice, one tends to receive great prominence, while the other is avoided or repressed. Others have also expressed the need to provide a wider perspective that would allow both stories to be told. The memoirist Lev Chykalenko at the time of the 1918–20 pogroms wrote despairingly of his fellow Ukrainians who were pogromists: "They will drown Ukrainian freedom in Jewish blood." (Kleiner 2000, 121.) He saw clearly that the Jewish tragedy was simultaneously a Ukrainian one, and realized that it would have both immediate and long-term repercussions. Feller and Chykalenko are only two of a number of writers who have expressed regrets over the loss of this wider perspective—one that is able to bear in mind both viewpoints, empathize with both identities, and share their pain.

Feller also laments the fact that so little research has been done on the interconnectedness of Ukrainian and Jewish cultures. He has stimulated interest in Ukrainian philo-Semitism and in Jewish culture in Ukraine, which, according to him, was focused on the "patriarchal culture of Ukrainian Jewry, the culture of the kahal [internal governing body] and Hasidism, and also of those secular Jews who sometimes subconsciously inherited it. This culture was treated with contempt not only by some prominent figures of European culture (including, among others, Drahomanov), but also by assimilated Jews, and even more so by Jewish assimilators. At the same time, this culture was most widespread in Ukraine, and, unexpectedly for Austrian and Western European Jews, it produced the Zionist movement . . . a fact that T. Herzl noted with astonishment." (Feller 1998, 106.)

An analogous position to Feller's has been voiced by Jews who lived in a Polish cultural context. Alexander Hertz examined the cultural interpenetration of Poles and Jews. Writing in 1961 in the United States, where he was influenced by the black emancipation movement, he showed an awareness that hatreds embedded in cultures can be transmitted to future generations: "Even if there were not a single Jew in Poland today or if no Jew were playing the slightest part in Polish life, it is likely that some forms of anti-Semitism would still exist. The living would be replaced by their own ghosts. In Poland the traditions of anti-Semitism have left such deep traces that the Jew as symbol could suffice entirely." (Hertz 1988, 1.) He challenged the view that Jews were culturally isolated and alien, pointing out that in the nineteenth century many Poles were convinced that Jews would soon undergo a complete "kindredification." (Ibid., 19.) This tendency was pronounced after the 1863 uprising in which Jews acquitted themselves admirably in the eyes of Polish patriots and were often referred to as "Poles of the Mosaic faith." Later in the century, according to Hertz, as national emancipation movements took hold, ideologues of the Jewish national rebirth began emphasizing the separateness of the Jews: "Jewish historians like Simon Dubnov were in agreement with the majority of Polish historians that the Polish Jews had always constituted an isolated community whose contacts with the surrounding world were sporadic," and "Zionists in particular were willing to refer to the Jews' alienness in the diaspora." (Ibid., 27–28.) Hertz did not deny Jewish separateness in matters of language, religion, and custom. His point was that Jews, for all their uniqueness, were an integral part of Polish life. This is also Feller's view concerning Jews in Ukraine. For both writers Jews constituted not an alien, but a kindred culture. Both writers protest the denial of this kindredness by anti-Semites and some Jewish nationalists alike. Hertz rejects the romantic mystical conception of a homogeneous national culture. Instead he holds that "within every national group there exists a multitude of specific cultures connected with class, region, profession, and so on. They do not necessarily fit into the framework of what we recognize as the official national culture. In reality, every national culture is a multiplicity to which writers, and in recent times propagandists and journalists, strive to lend a homogeneous appearance." (Ibid., 44.)

Although it does not ignore the tragic moments in modern history, the present account, like much research into Ukrainian-Jewish cultural relations since 1991, is sympathetic to the kind of perspective outlined by Feller and Hertz. It draws on work done by scholars in Ukraine and on Western research into Jewish-Ukrainian relations, literary representation, and identity formation. The main focus throughout is on the representation of Jews as seen through the prism of Ukrainian writing and on the way this prism has itself been shaped and reshaped.

CHAPTER I

Confronting the Other, 1800–1880

After the partitions of Poland in the late eighteenth century, around 600,000 Jews found themselves within the Russian empire. Catherine the Great decreed in 1791 that they could not enter Russia proper but were restricted to the western territories. Here, imperial authorities gradually established the Pale of Settlement, which remained in force until 1915. It included eight out of nine Ukrainian gubernias (provinces) and what is today Belarus and Lithuania. In the 1880s the population of Jews in the Ukrainian part of the Pale was over 1.5 million. If one adds to this figure the almost half-million Jews in territories then under Austrian rule, the number of Jews who at the dawn of the twentieth century lived within the boundaries of to-day's Ukraine constituted one-third of all world Jewry.

About 30 percent lived in, or close to, villages. In the nineteenth century, they began to settle the southern steppe, mainly in colonies near Kherson and Ekaterynoslav (today's Dnipropetrovsk), where tsarist authorities offered tax relief to encourage farming. More frequently, they managed various parts of manorial estates, kept shops or taverns, traded, or were artisans. Some did well economically. By 1872 they owned 89 percent of all distilleries on the three Right Bank gubernias (those on the right or western bank of the Dnipro River) of Kyiv, Volhynia, and Podillia. By 1897 they worked 33.9 percent of the food industry (flour, sugar, oil, and tobacco), light industry (footwear and furniture), construction (bricks and timber). (Liubchenko 2005, 73.) The Brodskys, Halperins, and Zaitsivs owned 24 percent of the Right Bank's sugar factories, and Jews were owners or leaseholders of 90 percent of the mills, 96 percent of the distilleries, and 80 percent of the breweries. Seventy percent of the traffic on the Dnipro

River was conducted by David Margolin's Kyiv firm. Jewish merchants dominated the export of grain from Odesa, Mykolaiv, and Kherson. Margolin helped Kyiv obtain the empire's first electric tramway in 1892, while Brodsky helped finance the building of the city's Polytechnic and Bacteriological Institutes. The Jewish population of Kyiv grew from 500 in 1862 to an estimated 87,240, or 15 percent of the population in 1917. By 1911 Jews comprised 17 percent of the students at Kyiv University and about 44 percent of the city's merchants. However, most of the population remained desperately poor. In the second half of the nineteenth century, 40 percent of the Jewish population of Kyiv's Podil area, where most artisans lived, depended on charity. (Ibid., 73–74.) One-fifth of the inhabitants of Berdychiv lived in charitable institutions, while in 1900 nearly two-thirds of the dead in Odesa had to be buried at the community's expense.

The reforming tsar, Alexander II (whose rule began in 1855) allowed wealthy Jewish merchants to leave the Pale. By 1864 government schools, which had been offered to Jews in 1841, contained nearly six thousand students. A Jewish middle class appeared and began to acculturate and assimilate. Western education and European culture were accepted by the *maskilim,* or supporters of the Haskala (Jewish Enlightenment), who had strong centers in Uman and Odesa. Russian-language periodicals like *Rassvet* (Dawn, 1860–61), *Sion* (Zion, 1861–62), and the daily newspaper *Den', organ russkikh evreev* (Day, Organ of Russian Jews, 1869–71) appeared in the latter city. Jewish intellectuals, who had previously been drawn to German culture, now began to see themselves as Russians "of the Mosaic persuasion." However, not all *maskilim* defined themselves this way. The Ukrainian movement was beginning its gradual development and it too was attracting supporters.

Anxieties in official circles about Jews produced expressions of anti-Semitism like the *Knigi kagala* (Books of the Kahal, 1869 and 1875). Written by a Christianized Jew, Yakov Brafman, it falsified evidence of an international Jewish conspiracy. The climate of suspicion eventually ignited the pogrom wave of 1880–81.

Jews in the Austro-Hungarian empire suffered far fewer restrictions. The predominantly Ukrainian territories of Eastern Galicia and Bukovyna were occupied by Austria in 1772 and 1774. By 1869 there were 428,077 Jews in Eastern Galicia, a figure that constituted over 12 percent of the population. Sixty percent of Jews lived in towns. The liberalization of the 1860s gave them full citizenship, the right to own land within what is now Western Ukraine (Galicia, Bukovyna, and Transcarpathia), and full access to universities, higher educational institutions, and all professions. The Constitution of 1867 made them full citizens. In the same year the government transferred power in Galicia to the Poles. Jews and Ukrainians often formed a voting bloc in elections, but when Jews supported the Poles, this often led to conflicts with Ukrainians. There were two other major sources of conflict: the Polish gentry's leasing to Jews of its monopoly on the production and sale of alcohol, and the practice of usury, which was often conducted by Jews.

The Jewish presence has always been reflected in Ukrainian literature. The first great work of the modern vernacular, Ivan Kotliarevsky's *Eneida* (Aeneid, 1798–1842), a product of the cultural revival on the Left Bank, includes Jews in its great comic panorama of Ukrainian society, but the space devoted to them is small and they attract no particular attention. The term "leaseholder" (*orendar*—used here to describe the innkeeper who rented from the landowner the right to produce and sell alcohol) gives no indication that he might be Jewish, nor are there any negative connotations attached to the establishment or the profession. If anything, the opposite is the case:

> Then she dressed up finely
> As though going to the tavern for a dance. (Kotliarevs'kyi 1969, 17.)

Jews find themselves listed as denizens of hell, alongside every other race, religion, and profession in the ebullient, fun-loving and carnivalized world created by the writer.

The "Keys to the Church" Theme

In the early nineteenth century a stereotype of the Jew developed in modern Ukrainian literature. A key influence on its emergence was played by a text written in Russian, *Istoriia Rusov ili Maloi Rossii* (History of the Rus or Little Russia, 1846). Already known in 1825, and perhaps composed two decades earlier, it argues the case for a restoration of Cossack rights, and describes how grievances against the Poles—in particular the violation of Cossack rights and the mistreatment of the Orthodox Church—ignited the great revolution of 1648 and created a new body politic, the Hetmanate. The book is mainly concerned with the achievement of statehood, the Pereiaslav treaty with Muscovy (which it sees as an agreement between equals), and the struggle to regain rights to independent action after the empire had gradually abolished these.

As Polish magnates attempted to enserf the population and ban the Orthodox Church, many Cossacks turned to revolt. Jews, on the other hand, played an important role in maintaining the established order: "In the new society of estates being established in Ukraine, Jews functioned as a corporate order. Whether they were powerful leaseholders or petty craftsmen, they were linked as a group to a declining royal power and more directly to the magnate landowning order." (Sysyn 2003, 133.) The socio-economic conflict—magnates versus Cossacks—took on a religious appearance when the Catholic Poles were accused of allowing religious freedom to Jews while denying it to Orthodox Christians. Although early historical accounts had barely mentioned the Jews, when the story of 1648 was retold 150 later in *Istoriia Rusov,* they were given much greater prominence.

This account gave the "keys to the church" theme a powerful resonance, one that would make the image of the Jew holding the keys to a Christian church "the defining topos in both Ukrainian and Russian literary works on the historical theme." (Grabowicz 1988, 331.) Here is how the theme is presented:

> The churches of those parishioners who did not accept the Union [with Rome] were leased to the Jews, and for each service a fee of one to five talers was set, and for christenings and funerals a fee of one to four zloty. The Jews, relentless enemies of Christianity, universal wanderers and a parable for humanity, eagerly took to this vile source of gain and immediately removed the church keys and bell ropes to their taverns. For every Christian need, the cantor was obliged to go to the Jews, haggle with him, and, depending on the importance of the service, pay for it and beg for the keys. And the Jew, meanwhile, having ridiculed the Christian service to his heart's content, and having reviled all that Christians hold dear, calling it pagan, or, in their language, goyish, would order the cantor to return the keys with an oath that no services had been celebrated without payment. (*Istoriia Rusov* 1846, 40–41)

The reader learns that during Easter a tax was collected by Jews on the paska, or traditional Easter bread. Parishioners who baked their own were taxed as though they had bought it at the market and the loaves were then marked with chalk and coal: "In this way the Jews insulted Christians in their own land, while they themselves could celebrate their own feasts freely, and they cursed the Christians and their faith in their synagogues, built on Rus land, freely. The Poles rejoiced in this and helped the Jews in every possible way." (Ibid., 49.)

The theme then merges with the national issue: Jews are described as protégés and spies of the Poles, and contemporary Poles and Jews are accused of hiding the original texts of the Cossack treaties with Muscovy, in which it is made clear that the union between the Cossack state (the Hetmanate) and the empire was between equals. Poles and Jews, in other words, are accused of suppressing Ukraine's rights in the present day.

The narrator indicates that "those Poles and Jews who did not own Rus people, who were useful to it and worked only in free industries and trades, were left alone without any animosity." Accordingly, the reader learns, the large commercial center of Brody, which was almost entirely Jewish, was left in its former free state and untouched, since it was recognized by the Rus population as useful for its trade and income, "and only a small contribution was taken from the Jews in clothing materials and furs for the sewing of uniforms and footwear for the registered army, and some provisions for the army."(Ibid, 80.) On the other hand, the taking of Bar by Kryvonos is described as a "terrible massacre, especially of the Jews and their families, that left not one living; about fifteen thousand corpses were thrown out of the town and buried in a wooded ravine." (Ibid., 76.)

Competition for status and rank in the contemporary period is added to the list of grievances. The narrator complains that present-day Poles and Jewish converts to Christianity who have been given gentry status are taking leading administrative positions. It describes these "newcomers" as the "scourge" of Cossacks and Little Russians, because they enrich themselves through "various schemes," and take gentry status from Ukrainians while giving it to their own people. (Ibid., 121.)

Why was the Polish-Jewish theme voiced so vehemently in the early nineteenth century? Kohut speculates that it was likely a response to developments that followed the Second Partition of Poland in 1793, which brought Ukraine's Right Bank territories into the Russian empire. Poles assumed a dominant cultural position in Kyiv and large numbers of Jews appeared for the first time on the Left Bank (the former territory of the Hetmanate). The families of the old Cossack elite reacted by making the Jewish issue a lightning rod for their economic fears and cultural hostilities. Kohut describes how the typical Cossack descendant might have seen matters:

> On the Right Bank the Polish magnates still ruled, the Jews held a monopoly on taverns and tax collection, and the Uniate Church continued to exist. To complete the humiliation, his Left-Bank homeland was now included in the Pale of Settlement. It was this constellation of developments, I contend, that gave rise to the author's virulent anti-Polish, anti-Uniate, and anti-Jewish views and his almost fanatical devotion to Orthodoxy. At the same time, the author of *Istoriia Rusov* is still a child of the Enlightenment and distinguishes between "good" and "bad" Jews, Poles, and even Tatars. Thus, neither all Poles nor all Jews—nor all Tatars, either—are considered perpetual enemies of Ukraine, and there is hope of achieving harmony with the "good" elements of those nations. The author does not extend similar consideration to Ukrainian Uniates. (Kohut 2003, 154.)

In short, anti-Jewish animus provided an outlet for discontent over the loss of Cossack autonomy, the influx of Polish noblemen, the appearance of Jewish leaseholders who rented monopolies on taverns and tax collection from the lords, and the return of the Uniate Church.

In Ukrainian writings, this sharpening of the focus on Jews as exploitative leaseholders, trade monopolists, and tax farmers was a recent development. The "keys to the church" theme had initially appeared in Polish writing, in Fr. Pawel Ruszel's *Fawor niebieski* (Heaven's Favor, 1649). A Catholic priest from Lublin, he presented the revolution as God's punishment for Poland's failure to prevent Jewish exploitation, and asserted that Jewish leaseholders had been paid by both Catholics and Orthodox for the use of churches. Later historians have suggested that Polish writers needed to shift blame for the disaster of losing Ukraine onto greedy magnates and their Jewish estate managers in order to alleviate their feelings of guilt. (Hrushevs'kyi 1956, 120–25.)

Ukrainian writing picked up the theme much later. It is given one sentence in Hryhorii Hrabianka's chronicle (1710). The author informs reader that the Poles "sold the Lord's churches to the Jews, and infants were baptized with the Jews' permission, and various religious customs and the pious [Christians] were at the mercy of Jewish leaseholders." (Hrabjanka 1990, 30.) The theme then reappeared in Stefan Lukomsky's postscript to his compilation *Sobranie istoricheskoe* (Historical Collection, 1770). Here the reader is informed that the Jews kept the keys, preventing Christians from celebrating "baptisms, weddings, or anything else," and charged a special tax, while "insulting and beating priests, tearing out their hair and beards." (Lukoms'kyi 1972, 371–72.) It is significant that in this account, written 120 years after the events, the accusation begins to "materialize" with the addition of details that provide a strong emotional coloring and stimulate the reader's sense of outrage.

The evidence of folklore has often been enlisted in support of the veracity of the "keys to the church" theme. However, several prominent academics have reviewed this evidence and reached the conclusion that the folklore collected in the nineteenth century had been influenced by later events and literary accounts, and therefore should be treated with care. The Jewish theme figures prominently in two dumas, or lyrical epics: the "Duma of the Oppression of Ukraine by Jewish Leaseholders" and the "Duma of the Battle of Korsun." The first was recorded in the late 1840s and early 1850s by Panteleimon Kulish, who described national history to the kobzar (*kobza*-player or minstrel) in the process. It is therefore unclear how much of the text was inspired by Kulish, how much by the performer, and how much by the original composer or composers. Given Kulish's practice of tampering with original materials, his credentials as an ethnographer do not inspire confidence. He approached all cultural production in an anti-individualistic manner. In 1846 he wrote to Shevchenko: "Your works do not belong to you alone or to your time alone; they belong to all Ukraine and will speak to her eternally. This gives me the right to intrude into your fantasy and creativity and firmly demand of them that they be brought to the highest level of perfection." (Petrov 1929, 324.) Since he viewed literature as a collective national endeavor, Kulish felt that it was quite proper for him to alter works, even Shevchenko's, in order to better reflect what he considered to be the authentic popular spirit. Moreover, determined to provide his nation with the epic narratives that his own research had failed to uncover, he wrote imitations of the dumas, presenting in them the national memory that heroic songs of the past ought, in his estimation, to have demonstrated. In fact in the nineteenth century there were numerous writers who falsified "ancient" dumas in the belief that they were merely completing lost pages from the great epics of the past and in this way serving to develop the national culture. The idea that such oral accounts can be treated as unadulterated records of past events is therefore untenable, and the most authoritative scholars have repeatedly warned that caution is required in assigning the views expressed in these accounts to the 1640s and 1650s. This is particularly true of the two dumas mentioned above, which were recorded in very few variants and two hundred years after the events of 1648. (Hrushevs'ka 1931, 147, 163.) Apart from the above-mentioned dubious role of Kulish in recording the first of them, both show evidence of literary influences. A number of commentators have observed that sections of the first duma appear to have been borrowed from Samiilo Velychko's chronicle (1720). The folklorist Filaret Kolessa has remarked on the parallels between this duma's plot and a Polish poem about the battle of Zhovti Vody. Jacob Shatzky has shown that the duma displays a resemblance to a Polish literary work of 1648 by Jan Kmita. (Kohut 2003, 155.) Even Volodymyr Antonovych and Mykhailo Drahomanov, who include both dumas in volume 2 of their *Istoricheskiia pesni* (Historical Songs, 1874), are circumspect. They offer corroborative information concerning the renting of churches from three sources. (Antonovych and Drahomanov 1895, 30.) However, they inform readers that a number of the dumas have been tampered with or falsified, and that the invention of epic songs is a widespread phenomenon. For this reason they omit all dumas dealing with events earlier that 1648. (Antonovych and Drahomanov 1874, xviii, and 1895, ii–iii.)

Ivan Franko, the leading Ukrainian literary figure of the late nineteenth century, thought that the two dumas were reflections of post-1768 events, by which time the literary tradition, especially the chronicles of Hrabianka, Lukomsky, and Velychko, had influenced the oral tradition. He pointed out that enlisting

folklore in the study of political and social relations, particularly when it was collected much later than the events it purports to describe, fails to allow for the
likelihood of contamination by later performers. (Franko 1986,14.) He reached
the following conclusion: "The role of Jews in the history of the Polish occupation, or, as the Poles say, the civilization of Ukraine, has not been explained by
historians of Ukraine as carefully as it should be, so as to, for one thing, overturn
many legends and exaggerations of an anti-Jewish character that have been su-
perimposed on the real facts by a later tradition. This later tradition found its
vivid, usually humorous and satirical expression in the dumas and episodes from
the dumas dealing with Khmelnytsky, and also a significant expression in the
Cossack chronicles, which tried to compose an entire register of Jewish crimes
and injustices said to have called forth the nationwide Jewish pogroms in the
summer of 1648." (Ibid., 171.)

Mykhailo Hrushevsky, the historian who would become head of the Ukrainian state in 1917, could also find no documentary evidence of churches being
rented and found it suspicious that the accusation appeared so late. (Hrushevs'kyi
1956, 126.) The Russian Jewish historian Ilia Galant argued the same, pointing
out that the most anti-Jewish text of the seventeenth century, *Mesia pravdyvyi*
(The True Messiah, 1669) by Ioaniki Galiatovsky (Joannicyusz Galatowski)
failed to mention this accusation. (Galant 1909, 9–10.)

Nonetheless, two leading historians and writers of the romantic period, Pan-
telemon Kulish and Mykola (Nikolai) Kostomarov, used the dumas and songs as
primary sources to describe the Khmelnytsky period. Kostomarov reproduced
both above-mentioned dumas in an appendix to his history, *Bogdan Khmel'nitskii* (Bohdan Khmelnytsky, 1857), and his *Istoricheskoe znachenie iuzhnorusskago
narodnago pesennago tvorchestva* (Historical Importance of South Russian Folk
Songs, 1906) drew heavily on poems and songs to describe events. Moreover,
Kostomarov used only the evidence that suited his purpose, rejecting, for example, songs that gave a different picture of events, on the grounds that they were
of Polish gentry origin and therefore unrepresentative of popular attitudes. He
accepted only what he considered "undoubtedly popular compositions of that
epoch," citing their humor as "typical of the period." (Kostomarov 1967a, 804.)
However, as Franko has indicated, a humorous treatment of the issue was in fact
characteristic not of the seventeenth century, as Kostomarov thought, but of the
late eighteenth century. According to Kostomarov, both dumas provide evidence
of the persecution of Ukrainians. He generalizes from the incidents described to
conclude that Jews created taverns along the main roads and forced people to pay
for alcohol, whether they wanted to or not, collected taxes from passersby, and

leased churches. In the description of a Jew who disarms a Cossack, he detects the echo of another historical event—a preventative measure taken by the Poles, and executed by the Jews on their behalf, to forestall the expected revolution. Kostomarov's romantic faith in folklore as a mirror of the popular soul leads him to state confidently: "Not the chronicles, whose character has to be examined in order to define the truthfulness of their views, not the acts, whose authenticity and accuracy are sometimes difficult to prove . . . but the people itself, the whole people, in the words of several generations proclaim to us and bear witness that the economic constraints in the hands of the Jews were one of the main reasons for the uprising of the South Russian [i.e. Ukrainian: iuzhnorusskago] people." (Ibid., 809.)

When Franko analyzed the same dumas and songs, and compared them to the historical documents that have come down to us, he reached the conclusion that the oral evidence was in fact the least reliable. There are two versions of the "Duma of the Oppression of Ukraine," one recorded by Kulish from the kobzar Andrii Shuta and the second recorded by Toma Shtanhei. According to Franko, there can be no doubt that Shtanhei's version has been colored by eighteenth-century realities. In it the Polish king is called an emperor, the Cossack proclamations known as universals are called ukases (tsarist decrees), the Cossacks themselves are described merely as brewers and hunters, and the long, difficult war for Cossack freedoms is nothing but a three-day riot. (Franko 1986, 149.) Franko comments that in Kulish's version, which was the one Kostomarov reprinted, the phrase "Poles, eminent gentlemen" (*liakhiv, mostyvykh paniv*) has been changed throughout to "Jews-orendars" (*zhydiv-randariv*). As for the "Duma of the Battle of Korsun," it appeared to Franko to be a much later product and even less reliable as a historical record.

Regrettably, the dumas are still often uncritically accepted as authentic and irrefutable eyewitness evidence. A recent anti-Semitic publication, for example, states that there is "unanimous feeling among contemporaries, the chroniclers, and historians" concerning the facts of Jewish exploitation of Ukrainians, and presents the dumas as "the most eloquent and truthful evidence of this." (Shestopal 2002, 49.)

Did the accusation have any factual basis? Judith Kalik of the Hebrew University of Jerusalem has studied the archival evidence. She indicates how the perception that Catholic and Orthodox churches were being leased might have arisen. Sometimes noble leaseholders of various kinds of seigneurial monopolies, who were usually Catholic, would seal a church if a debt owed by parishioners remained unpaid. Jews were often responsible for collecting such debts, and generally for dues owing to magnates from local churches. At the same time, many parish priests were forbidden from producing alcohol, but were obliged to purchase it from the Jewish tavern leaseholder, just as they were obliged to grind their grain at the leaseholder's mill (another lordly monopoly), along with others. (Kalik 2003, 232.) When debts went unpaid, the situation could turn violent, and sometimes the violence was initiated by the Jew. Kalik describes one instance of a leaseholder entering a priest's house and turning it upside down looking for homemade vodka. Although nothing was found, he later returned to the home with armed servants, confiscated all the priest's property and sealed the church. Kalik suggests that this is probably how the issue of locked churches and fees for holding services arose. Although rare, references to actual church leasings do occur in the archives, but cases of nonrepayment of debts, as a result of which the leaseholder "might delay the sacrament being administered," are more common. (Ibid., 233.) She continues: "In addition, Jewish lease-holders sealed Orthodox churches as a sanction against the violation of propination rights [the sale of alcohol], the prohibition on fishing in the lord's river, or the non-payment by the priest of taxes, and so forth. This, however, was much the same procedure as that which led Roman Catholic, Uniate, and Orthodox officials to seal synagogues when Jews failed to pay interest on *wyderkaf* loans [mortgages on property]." (Ibid.)

The most salient issue here, Kalik suggests, was perhaps the self-confident behavior of Jewish leaseholders, who could rely on the protection of anti-Orthodox lords and magnates, and on the violent enforcement of the law if this was required. As a result, the Orthodox clergy identified "Jesuits, Uniates, and Jews" as a single oppressor in the eastern parts of the Polish Commonwealth. Although technically, it was not the churches that were being leased but the lord's rights (which included services performed in churches on his estate), and although the leaseholder's demand for overdue payment in return for unsealing a church was also technically not a leasing of churches, it would have been interpreted as such, and the use of violence would have magnified the sense of outrage. In fact, it was common practice for Jews to borrow money at a favorable interest rate from Catholic and Orthodox churches, and to be sometimes unwilling or slow to repay these debts. This would inevitably have been seen as another example of unfair privilege. Kalik concludes that violence, often initiated by Jews, characterized relations between Jews and the Orthodox Church. (Ibid, 232, 234–35.)

The "keys to the church" theme therefore has some basis in reality. This reality was, however, much more prevalent in Catholic and Uniate churches—information that is not made available in Ukrainian sources, because this would undermine the argument that the Poles let the Jews control Orthodox churches out of contempt for the Orthodox faith. In the final analysis, the crucial factor here is not whether such leasing occurred or how many instances can be uncovered, but the theme's strong emotive impact, its use as a mobilizing tactic, and the productive literary life it was to lead.

The theme was central to the construction of a Jewish stereotype in the historical fiction of the early nineteenth century. This stereotype differs somewhat from the stock image of the Jew in the popular eighteenth-century puppet dramas known as Vertep, religious school dramas, and mystery plays, or carols dealing with Christ's passion, which are primarily vehicles for Christian teaching and sometimes focus on Judas's treachery and Pilate's decision to crucify Jesus, assigning to Jews a collective guilt for these acts. By contrast, the "keys to the church" theme is more concerned with social and national oppression. According to this stereotype, the Jew serves the Polish magnate by ruthlessly exploiting the Ukrainian people and inventing all manner of taxes; he despises the Orthodox Church and its traditions, and humiliates its congregations; and he acts as an informer, reporting all subversive activities to the magnates. In the 1830s and 1840s this stereotype entered Russian literature primarily through Nikolai Gogol's *Taras Bul'ba* (1834, 1843) and the five-volume *Istoriia Malorossii* (History of Little Russia, 1842–43) by Nikolai Markevich (Mykola Markevych), which was the first of a number of histories that tell of Jews levying duties on the blessing of bread at Easter. It was simultaneously developed in Ukrainian literature by Kulish and Kostomarov.

Taras Shevchenko

Shevchenko's attitude toward Jews has been the subject of some ill-informed controversy. He has often been misread. In the early twentieth century, Vladimir Purishkevich, a member of the State Duma of the Russian empire and a leader of the Black Hundreds, "solidarized" with Shevchenko's supposed belief in the blood libel. In support of this he quoted the lines

> The *kutia* [a sweet grain dish served in the Christmas Eve supper] is on
>   the table,
> The children are by the hearth.
> She brought them into the world
> But does not know what to do with them:
> Drown them?
> Suffocate them?

Sell them to the Jew for blood
And drink away the money? (Shevchenko 1983, 293.)

Critics immediately pointed out that these lines from "Vid'ma" (The Witch, 1847–58) are the words of a madwoman, and no previous reader had ever identified them with the author's views. As Vasyl Shchurat pointed out, Purishkevich merely "revealed his own party's connection with the witch's ideas and enabled these ideas to unexpectedly triumph among Russian chauvinists." (Shchurat 1963, 168.) The point is not a trivial one. It has a more general application to the misinterpretation of Shevchenko's poetry, which often incorporates several voices and moves quickly between them. One or another voice has sometimes been attributed to the poet by careless readers uninterested in understanding a work's structure or internal dynamic.

Shevchenko was a signatory to one of the first public protests against anti-Semitism in the Russian empire. In 1858 two Jewish publicists, M. Gorvits and I. A. Chatskin, had been libeled by an anonymous columnist in the St. Petersburg journal *Illiustratsiia* (Illustration). A letter protesting the libel and signed by 140 prominent personalities was published in *Russkii vestnik* (Russian Herald). It complained that the anonymous columnist (who was in fact the editor V. R. Zotov) had distorted the opinions of his two opponents and attacked their character by accusing them of venality. In doing so he had "insulted all society, all Russian literature." In the following issue, the leading Ukrainian writers of the day, Mykola Kostomarov, Panteleimon Kulish, Marko Vovchok, Matvii Nomys (Symonov), and Taras Shevchenko, signed a letter drafted by Kulish that protested the "shameful act" of *Illiustratsiia*:

> For many centuries the Christian nations that today make up the Russian empire have branded the Jewish race—which wanders the entire world—as criminals, traitors, deceivers, enemies of God and humanity. Indignation against the Jews has been expressed not only verbally, by societies and governments incapable of drawing them by humane methods onto the path of truth and goodness. They have been expelled, drowned, burned, and cut down like wild animals. It would have been unnatural for these victims of blind, infuriated fanatics to forget the customs for which they are despised and to assume the character of their persecutors. . . . The Jews have become, and have had to become, the sworn enemies of other faiths that pour abuse on their beliefs, on their teachers, on their places of worship, and the rituals they hold sacred. . . . However depressing we find much of what we know of Jews from reliable written and published sources, this should serve only as a way of measuring the misfortunes to which the unfortunate descendants of Israel have so long and in so many places been subjected. Contemporary practical understanding provides convincing proof that the gen-

eral enmity toward them on the part of Christian nations has not brought the Jews to anything good, and that only a free enlightenment and equality in civil rights are capable of purifying the Jewish nationality of all in it that is hostile to other peoples.

The letter expresses the need for the best-known Ukrainian writers to be visible in this protest against the defamation in *Illiustratsiia* which recalls Ivan IV's attitude toward Jews. Their voices have a particular importance: "they express the opinion concerning the Jews of a people that has suffered more than Great Russians and Poles from Jews, and has expressed its hatred of Jews in past ages, leaving thousands of bloody victims. This people could not enter into the reasons for the evil, which was not the fault of the Jews but of the religious-civil order in Poland. It took revenge on the Jews with such a simple-minded understanding of justified bloodshed that it even put these terrible deeds into truly poetic songs. Regardless of this, the contemporary literary representatives of this people, who breathe a different spirit, who hold different aspirations, add their voice to the protest of the *Russkii vestnik* against the article in *Illiustratsiia*." (Kulish 1858, 245–47.)

The same letter also contains several revealing sentences that present a criticism of Jewish ways. It argues that persecution has driven Jews "from the path of truth and made them deaf to the words of the Gospels." This, as one might expect, is offered in the context of the long-term goal of assimilating non-Christians to Christianity. Jews are described as having been driven inward: they are a corporate union; persecution and legal restrictions have encouraged the use of "guile and trickery," hostility toward other faiths, and the approval in their religious teachings of "every harm that could be inflicted upon Christians with impunity." (Ibid., 246.) The letter therefore represents an attitude that combines sympathy for the present plight of Jews with a refusal to ignore past and present grievances against them. This was, in fact, the mainstream attitude among the empire's liberal intellectuals. For example, in 1859 the liberal Russian-language newspaper *Kievskii telegraf* (Kyiv Telegraph) in its very first issue began a serialized article entitled "Preduprezhdenie protiv evreev" (Prejudice Against the Jews). The author signed only as P-v, but it was probably written by Platon Pavlov, a liberal professor of history at Kyiv's St. Vladimir University. The article condemned prejudices against the Jews, pointed out their good qualities—including sobriety, thriftiness, commercial acumen, and academic ability—but also listed resistance to assimilation and spiritual demoralization as shortcomings. Jews were encouraged to reform their religion, reject the Talmud as a spiritual guide, and stop awaiting a Messiah who would lead them to Palestine. They were urged instead to affirm their allegiance to Russia. (Serbyn 1988, 86.) Such views were also widespread among Jews who supported the Haskala. The protests against *Illiustratsiia* may not have illuminated complexities in the issues raised, but they were nonetheless important gestures of support for the Jews. In fact, the letter that Kulish, Kostomarov, and Shevchenko signed represented the first public demonstration of sympathy for Jewry by Ukrainian intellectuals in the empire.

It is worth pointing out that on at least one occasion Shevchenko expressed personal sympathy for Jewish misfortune. One eyewitness has described how in 1846 the poet helped a Jew in Pryluky to put out a house fire. After working with others to remove various things from the home, he "spoke passionate words of condemnation to those present for their indifference, arguing that a person in need and misfortune, of whatever nation, of whatever faith, becomes our closest brother." (Chuzhbinskii 1861, 95.) This, however, should be set against the recollections of Varfolomei Shevchenko, a close friend of the poet, who has described how Shevchenko and his friends, after drinking "more than they should have," witnessed a Jewish tavernkeeper berating a peasant. The poet, we are told, cried out: "What are you waiting for, lads? Stretch the Jew out and whip him!" The Jew was beaten with switches until the poet ordered an end. A complaint was laid by the tavernkeeper but the incident was apparently hushed up after Shevchenko's brothers paid off the police. (Drahomanov 1970, 2:79.)

Shevchenko's great early poem *Haidamaky* (The Haidamakas, 1841) deals with the bloody rebellion of 1768 known as the Koliivshchyna. The main conflict is between the Ukrainian rebels or outlaws known as haidamakas on one side, and the Poles and Jews on the other, and the chief interest lies in the issue of violence. The blessing of the knives—symbols of power, strength and commitment—occurs on the eve of the rebellion. The ceremony sanctifies the impending political struggle. It coincides with the eve of the Maccabees, the day on which the Church remembers the five brothers who in the second century B.C. led the successful Jewish uprising against Greek rule. On this occasion, the Jews took back rule of their country and retained independence for almost a century. Shevchenko's readers are asked to consider whether violence is justifiable in a revolutionary cause. Many would have answered positively. *Haidamaky* became a part of radical culture within the Russian empire and had a large influence on Soviet culture, particularly in the decade following 1917. It was also embraced as a revolutionary poem by leftist Jews, like Parvus (Izrael Gelfand), who affirmed that the poem thrilled him as a high-school student and taught him class struggle. (Hrytsak 2004b, 84.)

The narrator's voice at times blends with that of the revolutionaries, capturing their viewpoint. When it does so, it relates a national epic, the tale of an enormous explosion of popular hatred directed against serfdom and national oppression. The rebellion is seen as an attempt to overthrow a regime, and not simply as an outburst of senseless violence, which is the way it has generally been described in imperial accounts. In Shevchenko's poem, plunder is not the primary goal; the rebels are motivated by an anger that the poet's contemporary, the scholar Mykhailo Maksymovych, described as accumulating for more than a century after 1596, the date of the Union of Brest, when most of the Orthodox hierarchy accepted papal authority and after which the polonization of the Ukrainian gentry accelerated. (Dziuba 2004, 72.)

The political background is deftly sketched. Catherine the Great has lent support and sent arms to the revolt as an attempt to undermine Poland:

In the grove stood
Wagons with steel blades:
A generous gift from the lady. (Shevchenko 1983, 80.)

These lines refer to the support that was at first provided by the empress. However, as soon as the frightening scale of the rebellion became apparent, her imperial troops crushed it. The rebels, whose aims were social and national liberation, could have threatened the empire's stability, and were put down with great cruelty in order to prevent the spread of violence to the Left Bank. Political censorship allowed only this muted reference to the Russian intervention, and the poem was probably only published because the censor interpreted it as an anti-Polish diatribe. However, it should be recalled that Shevchenko had personally witnessed the suppression of the Polish revolt of 1830 and that during his student days in the St. Petersburg Academy of Arts he had many Polish friends. Dziuba has suggested that the poem may actually have been written under the influence of these friends, who expressed admiration for the revolutionary potential of the Ukrainian people. The drive for freedom is depicted as blindly savage, but irrepressible. Fear of the rebellion's volcanic energy spurred tsarist authorities to hinder the work's dissemination and to attempt banning it completely in 1893. It became particularly popular during the Ukrainian national revolution of 1917–20, with five separate editions appearing in 1918 alone. (Dziuba 2004, 85.)

Dziuba has also discussed the work's reception, reminding readers that during the revolutionary period (1917–20) it was interpreted as a glorification of popular revolts; both nationalists and Bolsheviks laid claim to it. In 1912, Anatolii Lunacharsky, who was soon to become the Bolshevik commissar of enlightenment, wrote of the terrible scale of popular vengeance it describes, but cautioned that any true revolutionary must see that the desire for vengeance issues from "the ocean of tears and injustice that has gathered over centuries." The "revolutionary is ruthless precisely because he is humane." This, suggests Dziuba, was probably the beginning of Shevchenko's "Bolshevization"—the attempt to present him as the voice of justified revolutionary violence. A similar line of argument has occasionally been taken by nationalist critics. Leonid Biletsky summarized the poem's message as the call of a nation: "Kill within yourself all that is most precious, leave your father, mother, family, sacrifice even your children and follow Me, if you wish to be My faithful son." (Bilets'kyi 1941; quoted in Dziuba 2004, 85–86.) This, however, is a tendentious and misleading reading, best explained by the fact that Biletsky's interpretation of the poem was published in occupied Prague in the heavily charged atmosphere of 1941, just as a German offensive was being launched against the Soviet Union.

How is the reader to interpret the depiction of violence? The portrayals of Yarema and the Jewish tavernkeeper Leiba are of particular interest in answering this question. The young Yarema is caught between the two implacable forces of rebellion and reaction. He is thrown into the maelstrom of violent hatreds and succumbs to the demon of revenge. In the course of this drama he gains greater social and national awareness, but in the end emerges as a moral cripple. As Dziuba's article notes, two great contrapuntal themes—love and revenge—run through all Shevchenko's work. When Yarema meets his Oksana, it is already too late, because he has been drawn into the rebellion that will be initiated in Chyhyryn at midnight with the blessing of the knives. His fundamentally gentle nature has been seduced by violence and the promise of social improvement. Leiba is initially portrayed as a demanding taskmaster, who makes Yarema's drudgery unbearable. He cries: "Yarema, do you hear, you son of a boor!" Like a stereotypical miser, he counts his money at night. But Leiba is also a victim. The Poles might oppress Ukrainians, and the Jews might exploit them, but it is the Polish confederates (followers of the nobles who had formed the rebel Confederacy of Bar) who rob and whip Leiba. In this scene of humiliation the reader's sympathy suddenly shifts to the tavernkeeper.

There is a strong parallelism between Ukrainian and Jewish fates. In order to save his own money and daughter, Leiba leads the confederates to the sacristan's money and daughter. As a result, the sacristan is tortured and murdered, and his daughter Oksana abducted. As soon as Yarema learns of this, he is consumed by the desire to find his beloved and avenge her fate. Leiba's daughter also captures the reader's sympathy. Like Yarema, she is isolated and lonely, and like Oksana she is defenseless. Shevchenko confers sensuality and beauty upon her, but this is done more to represent her extreme vulnerability than to make her an object of erotic fascination. Leiba would do anything to save her, just as Yarema would do anything to save Oksana. Their common motivation is a passionate desire to protect young womanhood.

The final, terrifyingly violent section depicts the revolt's leader Gonta in Uman. He kills his sons to remain faithful to his vow to kill all Catholics, made during the consecration of knives, and only grieves over their bodies later in private, far from the community's gaze. The episode exposes the human capacity for hatred and violence, suggesting that it can be connected to and driven by great love. The final section demonstrates that the poem is, in Dziuba's words, "not an apology for revolutionary bloodshed, as the Soviet school taught us in essential Bolshevik style (which, naturally, elicits an ethical protest), but a tragedy in the Shakespearean manner of clearly giving a name to human madness." (Ibid., 77.) The sack of Troy, Bartholomew's Night, and other acts of violence that have captured the imagination of writers are recalled in order to suggest a universal message. The poem is therefore both a call to remember the struggle for freedom and a cry of anguish at the cruelty unleashed by all such revolts. The quiet, subdued voice of the narrator, which is heard at the beginning and end, frames the action, and indicates that the poem is a meditation on the eternal, tragic recurrence of violence in human conflicts.

Like all Shevchenko's work, the poem can be read as a dialogue between the contradictory urges of vengeance and forgiveness. The poet's archetypal characters (the raped girl, the abandoned mother, the orphan, the bastard, the outlaw, the revolutionary) collectively produce a powerful image of Ukraine as an abused and abandoned nation. This imagery raises the moral problem of how to respond to evil, cruelty, and humiliation: by punishing the guilty party, or by turning the other cheek? The first response is for many readers the instinctive one; the second is linked to a recognition of a shared humanity and of a capacity for love and friendship in all people:

Why
For what do people die?
They have the same father, they are the same children,
They should live and fraternize.
No, they couldn't, they wouldn't,
Disunity was inevitable!
Blood, fraternal blood was required,
Because what a brother had
In his pantry and in his yard,

And the happiness in his home were coveted!
"Let's kill our brother! Burn his house!"
They said, and did.
And that was the end of it, it seemed; no, as punishment,
The orphans remained. (Shevchenko 1983, 95–96.)

This passage not only recalls similar patterns of violence and revenge in biblical stories, but pointedly suggests that violence's inevitable legacy is orphanhood—a record of loss and trauma that will be passed on to future generations.

The narrator is deeply troubled by the dilemma of how to respond to evil. Thoughts of vengeance are followed by moments of prayer in which he accepts God's will. Scenes of cruelty, rape, and desecration alternate with love scenes and memories of happiness. The narrator enters into the drunken, orgiastic mood of the revolutionaries who have been summoned up by his imagination, and then stands back in stunned horror at the bloodshed. In this way *Haidamaky* shows that revenge and bloodletting is the choice of the revolutionaries, but compels the reader to consider hard whether it is a solution. Gonta is in the end punished by becoming a vampire. He wanders the battlefield crying: "Give me blood, gentry blood, because I need to drink!" (Ibid., 112.) His hatred has become depersonalized and indiscriminate: all Poles, all Jews, all Catholics are to be massacred. The victims of violence are no longer even seen as people: Gonta kills his sons as "Catholics" or "Poles." Depersonalization and desensitization are, no doubt, necessary to carry out killing, but they inevitably rebound on and devour the perpetrator. In the final scene, Gonta, Yarema, and the haidamakas are shown to be caught up in a cruelty that has no end and no purpose. Such a portrayal is not a defense but a critique of violence. It shows Ukraine as a country in a state of arrested development, unable to create a mature, stable, productive society, and capable only of glorifying revolt. If there is an initial Miltonic sympathy for Satan, for the challenge issued to God by the archrebel, in the final scene this sympathy has dissipated. In its place remains an understanding that revenge and pride are dead ends. The hero is left to continue his life as an isolated, tortured, and self-hating individual.

The historical Gonta never killed his sons, but this is hardly important. What matters is the vision of self-destruction in an apocalyptic hell. The writer and critic Oksana Zabuzhko has argued that a beast-like male rage drives Gonta to this subhuman state. The revolutionaries begin, as have many revolutionaries, from a position of moral principle: they oppose social evil, take up a holy war to purify the world by punishing the victimizers and rescuing women. However, by committing murder, they become agents of evil. Having entered the cycle of violence, their capacity for doing good is paralyzed. The initial impulse to free one's lover or sister sinks in a sea of blood. As a result, the romance of Yarema and Oksana cannot end happily. Their marriage remains unconsummated; their night together never occurs. (Zabuzhko 2001b, 123.) After their wedding, we learn:

> So as not to offend the chief
> He left Oksana:
> He is finishing off the Poles; celebrating
> A wedding with Zalizniak
> In Uman, on charred ruins. (Shevchenko 1983, 108.)

During the final banquet scene the kobzar sings songs not of heroism, but of flirtation, and some lines suggest vulgar sexual references: "Drive the hen into the barrel." The lowered tone is another reminder that the revolution has degenerated into the satisfaction of animal appetites. The killing of children is only the final atrocity, one that signifies a severing of all ties to humanity. Gonta and Yarema can have no children and no future; they are cursed.

The poem is important for its treatment of Jews. As suggested above, the initial presentation of Leiba, who is associated with tavernkeeping and the lord's unsavory business, is part of the negative stereotype disseminated by *Istoriia Rusov*. However, at the end of the poem it is Leiba who travels with Yarema to Lebedyn in order to rescue Oksana, while Zalizniak and the haidamakas turn away from him with the words "You will find another!" They are focused only on killing:

> While the boys danced,
> Yarema and Leiba crept stealthily
> Into the building, the very vault;
> Yarema stole the half-dead Oksana
> From the vault and made off to Lebedyn. (Shevchenko 1983, 105.)

The identity of Leiba has by this point become bewildering. When he appears in Zalizniak's camp, apparently in disguise, claiming to be a messenger from Gonta, he carries the kopek coins that haidamakas used as tokens by which to identify one another. Yarema immediately recognizes the tavernkeeper and demands his help in rescuing Oksana. It remains unclear whether Leiba is a spy, has become a haidamaka, or is maneuvering between the two sides. Has his treatment at the hands of the Poles changed him? Does he feel guilt over the fate of the sacristan and Oksana? Has he courageously taken up the remarkably dangerous task of infiltrating the rebel camp? Whatever the truth, it is evident that

Yarema's relationship with Leiba is far more complex and intimate than the reader has suspected and critics have often assumed. Not only is his cooperation with his former employer in rescuing Oksana successful, but the earlier return to the smoldering ruins of the tavern and barn produce mixed feelings, including a dose of nostalgia:

> Here, here, the day before yesterday
> He bent before the Jew,
> But today . . . he felt regret,
> For the passing of bad times. (Ibid., 97.)

The initial rage directed at Leiba's role in aiding the Polish oppressor, now, with the passage of time and perhaps with an awareness of the scale of destruction around him, has brought regret for a shared common space and a former life.

It is significant that power and traumatic violence are associated with masculinity, while both powerlessness and the possibility of healing are associated with femininity. The haidamakas call upon Yarema to repress all emotions other than anger, to avoid a relationship that involves caring, and to cultivate a callous disregard for the humanity of others. As is typical in Shevchenko's poetry, the reader is made to recoil from this stance: the feminine is not rejected but embraced.

Over the course of his life Shevchenko's views evolved. Later in life he became concerned that *Haidamaky* and his poetry as a whole might be seen as directed against all Jews. He did not wish his depiction of the 1768 conflict to be interpreted in racist terms. Leiba is, after all, also a victim of the Polish confederates, and his tragedy is powerfully portrayed. In later poetry Shevchenko refrained from attacks against "Poles" and "Jews," but considered instead the issue of establishing understanding between people.

One of his most controversial poems, *Maria,* is a retelling of the Gospel story, but Shevchenko's version deviates significantly from the New Testament. In fact, it can be read as a rewriting of the Christian narrative using secular characters. There is no virgin birth, only the tale of an unwed mother. The story resembles other New Testament infancy narratives that have been examined by Jane Schaberg. She indicates that although the claim that Jesus was illegitimately conceived has been erased in Christian narratives, it has survived in Jewish writings. In her opinion, the reasons for this erasure have to do with biblical sexual politics and the promotion of a patriarchal ideology. The virgin birth was, perhaps, the projection of a male fantasy for "a tame and 'pure' woman who is asexual or does not exercise her sexuality; for a woman especially untroubling to the celibate male psyche; for a mother who has no partner." (Schaberg 1987, 193.)

The Church did not use the cult of Mary, which was very popular among exploited groups, to promote the liberation of women or their equality, but instead honored her "for the nonuse of her sexuality." In this interpretation, the Mary myth reduces woman to "something less than a whole human being." (Ibid., 121, 13.) Shevchenko's retelling of the story is similar to feminist readings in that it hypothesizes a female reader-listener who understands the story according to a different, woman-identified set of codes and inflections. Like Luke, who has been called "the strongest 'feminist' among the evangelists, the one who most reflected the open attitude of Jesus toward women," Shevchenko vindicates women in his stories and shows them to be more faithful and effective disciples than men. (Ibid., 142.) In this way, he challenges patriarchal and authoritarian ideology. The poet's retelling of the New Testament narrative has God siding with the outcast, the endangered woman, and her child. Schaberg has argued that this is also how Matthew handed down the tradition of the illegitimate conception and of Joseph's acceptance of the messianic child and his mother: God acts "outside the patriarchal norm but within the natural event of a human conception." (Ibid., 74.)

In Shevchenko's *Maria* the miraculous is deemphasized and the ethical heightened. The message of salvation emerges from the experience of love within the family unit, and especially from the powerful bond between a parent and child. Neither priests nor politicians can offer the world a way forward. Instead it is Mary who grasps the message of her prophet-son: love will save humanity. She is the exemplary disciple, who rallies the apostles after her son's crucifixion and carries this message into the world. The poem can be read as an answer to the revenge theme in *Haidamaky*. But it is also interesting because to a great degree it "secularizes" the Gospel story, blurring the Christian and non-Christian perspectives. Joseph hears a prophecy that a Jewish sect will renew the law of Abraham and Moses, and that a Messiah will come to spread this word. (Shevchenko 1983, 512.) Mary is a Jewish girl, drawn to a charismatic prophet by a searing sexual attraction. She has a child by him. Because of these elements, some have considered the poem blasphemous. In fact, in 1882 it was republished in Geneva by Mykhailo Drahomanov who interpreted its message as a call to oppose the rule of "priests, lords, and tsars." (Hrytsak 2006, 262–63.) Others, however, have seen it as simply an unorthodox recreation of the Annunciation story and praised it for its universal message that peace will come from the kindness and generosity of ordinary people, who will find a way to carry the message of love into the world. In Shevchenko's late works, this message of forgiveness, love, and understanding progressively stifles the urge to vengeance.

Shevchenko was steeped in the Bible. The Old Testament, and especially the psalms, influenced him deeply. Early in his career, in 1845, he translated ten psalms of David and began translating more psalms at the end of his life. These poems are requests for God's intervention on the nation's behalf and they show the author wrestling with the urge for revenge. A similar tension is evident in other poems that appear to be modeled on psalms. For example, his "Zapovit" (Testament) recalls psalm 136, "By the Waters of Babylon." In the translated psalms, the Egyptian and Babylonian captivities have, of course, been taken by most readers to be an allegory for Ukraine's subjection—a motif that has since been widely used in Ukrainian writing, most famously by Franko and Lesia Ukrainka, but also by Panteleimon Kulish, Stepan Rudansky, Yakiv Shchoholiv, and Olena Pchilka. It links the concept of the poet to the biblical prophet: both can foresee the eventual destruction of the oppressor and both nurture the people's faith in their ultimate liberation.

Another key concept in Shevchenko, glory (*slava*), can also be traced back to the Bible. It represents the history of the people, their good name, the consecration and idealization of a just and honorable past. This is an Old Testament view of history. Glory is associated with the Ukrainian nation's past, especially its Cossack history, but also with the people's honorable name which gives it a right to exist. Sometimes this emphasis on past glory clashes with the New Testament's stress on the future coming of the Kingdom of God, but in the end Shevchenko's vision embraces both testaments. In fact, his thinking often moves, as in the psalms, from contemplating past greatness and contemporary oppression, through a kind of revelation, to the promise of rebirth. This movement occurs, for example, in his reworking of psalms 132 and 133, and in his "Zapovit." The poet's meditation on biblical texts and Jewish history therefore deeply influenced not only his portrayal of Jewish character, but his entire oeuvre.

The Romantic Nationalists: Mykola Kostomarov and Panteleimon Kulish

As we have seen, Kostomarov and Kulish were signatories to the letter of protest against *Illiustratsiia*. Their writings, however, reveal a much less nuanced attitude toward Jews than can be found in Shevchenko. In fact, they are largely responsible for introducing into literature the stereotype of the exploitative, pro-Polish, and anti-Orthodox Jewish orendar. Kostomarov's dramatic works, particularly his *Sava Chalyi* (Sava Chaly, 1839) and *Pereiaslavs'ka nich: Trahediia*

(Pereiaslav Night: A Tragedy, 1841) give a literary embodiment to the historical account in *Istoriia Rusov*. The author was not particularly careful with his sources. The action of *Sava Chalyi* was transferred to the early seventeenth century, whereas the historical Chaly lived in the eighteenth century. In the first act the Jews are described by Chaly as "multiplying insects" (*komashnia, rozplodyla-sia*) (Kostomarov 1967, 147). The Catholics are described as "plundering the churches, giving the sacred to the Jews as a way of ridiculing, abusing the Ortho-dox people, defiling the women and children." (Ibid., 160.) Chaly himself, even though he goes over to the Poles, cannot stomach the Uniate or Catholic faith and eventually tries to return to the Cossacks, but it is too late and he is punished for his apostasy. In *Pereiaslavs'ka nich*, which is set in 1649, the "keys to the church" theme from *Istoriia Rusov* becomes the master plot. The refusal to un-lock the church is the event that initiates the action. Kostomarov has it occur during Easter week; services are prevented, because, one character says, "the cursed Jews did not allow us into God's church; they put the sacred up for rent. Unless we collect enough to pay, we will not have the holy day." (Ibid., 209.) When the church is opened, it is because Father Anastasii has begged permission of the Jews to hold the service and has spent a whole day collecting money to pay the orendar Ovram. Additional outrages against Orthodoxy are elaborated: a Uniate bishop is described as being carried by twelve Rus men, with a Jew as driver; it is forbidden to bake paska and a woman who tries to do so is dragged off by her hair and thrown into prison. Even after paying the required money and receiving the keys, the priest is prevented from taking the *plashchanytsia* (repre-sentation of Jesus in the grave) from the altar and walking with it in procession, because Ovram demands extra money for this privilege. An unseemly scuffle over the *plashchanytsia* occurs and Ovram runs from the church to the castle chief to complain.

Kostomarov also promoted the "keys to the church" theme in his influential histories. He even expresses surprise that the fiercest critic of the Jews, Galia-tovsky, had failed to mention this issue in his *Mesia pravdyvyi* of 1680. Ilia Galant pointed out that Galiatovsky had an excellent opportunity to make the charge because at one point in his work he has a Jew challenge a Christian with the words: "Why do you Christians destroy our synagogues, when we do nothing bad to your churches?" The Christian makes no response. Rather than complain of Galiatovsky's forgetfulness, Kostomarov should, according to Galant, have seen in this omission "evidence of the falseness of the dark legend." (Galant 1909, 10.)

Charges of Jewish perfidy that have been formulated by the Christian religion, in particular the rejection of Christ and Christ's teaching, are important for the devout Kostomarov. However, in his literary works he ultimately embraces the New Testament message of peace. In *Pereiaslavs'ka nich* Father Anastasii describes Christ's behavior "when the Jews came to Him" as nonresistance to evil. Eventually this message prevails even with the most bloodthirsty character in the book and the hardest of heart, Lysenko, who is fixated on massacring Poles and Jews in order to drive them out. He says:

> In the morning we will all be Christians,
> But tonight we will be beasts. (Kostomarov 1967, 230.)

Lysenko seems aware that he is cutting himself off from humanity:

> I am already dead, dead to peace
> And to myself. I am no longer a man. (Ibid., 231.)

When he whips up the crowd to violence, his only opposition is Father Anastasii, who issues a warning that Lysenko will lose his soul:

> Save us from this, O Lord! A great crime
> It is to repay crime with crime
> For we need not revenge but freedom. (Ibid., 229.)

Before the revolt, Maryna, Lysenko's sister repeats the main charges against the Poles to her lover, who is the town's governor and a Pole:

> the Jews in Pereiaslav
> Rent out the holy churches,
> Catholic priests ride to their churches on the backs of people,
> And every day dozens of innocents
> Die of torture or hunger. (Ibid., 250.)

However, this is set against the equally appalling behavior of the enraged mob, which is described by Father Anastasii:

> The people have turned savage as beasts,
> Destroying everything, killing and burning . . . Poor children
> Are smashed against stone! (256.)

In the end, shortly before he dies, Lysenko heeds the priest's advice: he orders an end to the killing and frees all the captured Poles.

Kostomarov's ideology negotiates between justified social and political anger on the one hand, and Christian forgiveness on the other. The writer, who was the child of a liaison between a landowner and a serf woman, was particularly sensitive to the burning social question of serfdom. He craved unity between landlord and peasant, and with typical romantic enthusiasm anticipated the fusion of both classes into a national entity. But his romantic populist ideology also drew on the traditionally negative portrayal of Jews in the Christian churches. In one of his translated poems from Byron's "Jewish Melodies" (1841), "Pohybel' Ierusalyma" (The Fall of Jerusalem), the city's loss and the suffering of the Jews are blamed on the rejection of Christ by the people of Israel. Nonetheless, the writer was committed to the New Testament message of forgiveness. Accordingly, in *Pereiaslavs'ka nich* the revolt of 1648, which is explained in terms of social and religious oppression, is eventually halted by the virtuous priest, who brings Christ's message of peace.

The image of Ukraine as a suffering Christ was used by Kostomarov in *Knyhy bytiia ukrains'koho narodu* (Books of the Genesis of the Ukrainian People), a manifesto of the secret Cyrillo-Methodian Brotherhood, which was formed between December 1845 and January 1846 and which Shevchenko joined shortly afterward. Kostomarov wrote the *Knyhy bytiia* in imitation of the style of the first five books of the Bible. In his text the Ukrainians become the chosen people with a special mission: to save European nations by arising and showing all Slavs the way to a virtuous democratic existence. This appears to be both an identification of his nation with the Jews of the Old Testament, and a suggestion that in recent history his own nation has suffered the most—partly as a result of Jewish oppression.

Although Shevchenko came out of the same romantic nationalist milieu as Kostomarov and Kulish, there were important differences in their views. Shevchenko universalizes his plots, sacrificing Church dogma in order to speak to all races and religions. Kostomarov's ideological attitude is more rigid and spills over into a religious fanaticism that denies sympathy for other religions, especially Catholics, Uniates, and Jews. In *Pereiaslavs'ka nich* forgiveness and peace come late in the proceedings, long after the guilt of the oppressor has been demonstrated and punishment administered.

An important discussion took place in the journal *Osnova* in 1861–62 during a brief period of liberalization that allowed for the appearance of Ukrainian and Jewish-Russian publications. Kostomarov and Kulish wrote several articles for the journal and conducted a polemic with Jewish writers. The initial discussion focused on the word *zhyd*, which, it was pointed out, had always been the standard Ukrainian word for "Jew" (as it is in most Slavic languages, although derogatory in Russian). The discussion soon moved on to other topics. Kostomarov's article "Iudeiam" (To the Jews) summarizes his attitude toward Jews.

He complains of their lack of sympathy for Ukrainian aspirations, and argues that they have done little to try and understand Ukrainians, often acting against the latter's interests.

In dealing with the social role of Jews, the argument is couched in terms of class: whereas in the West the middle class resisted the arbitrary rule of barons, in Ukraine the largely Jewish middle class sided with the magnates: "When the Judeans settled in Poland and Little Russia, they occupied the place of the middle class, becoming willing servants and agents of the mighty nobility; they clung to the stronger side, and they fared well until the people rose against the lords and also subjected to their judgment those who aided the latter. The Judeans, caring only about their own benefits and those of their tribe, began to extract these [benefits] from the relationship that had developed between the nobles and the serfs. In this way, the Judean became the factotum of the lord, entrusted by the lord with his own income, taverns, mills, factories, property, and serfs, and sometimes even the faith of the latter, when it, in the eyes of his fanaticism, ceased to have any sacredness." (Kostomarov 1862, 43–44.)

After establishing the crucial historical reference point and the link to the emotive issue of profiting from the Orthodox church services, the author provides vivid details of how the people were victimized. Then the description of past social exploitation fuses with images of present injustices: Jews do not sympathize with a Ukrainian's wounds when he is "whipped by the steward," or when his daughter is taken away for seduction, or when his son is sent to the army, or when there is a failed harvest, or a fire.

The charge of selfishness or callousness is reiterated. Although the behavior of Jews is highly moral when dealing with their own people, they are accused by Kostomarov of taking advantage of the moral failings in others. In Ukraine, Jews pander to the indolence of both "the powerful lord" and "the backward muzhyk." They loan money for alcohol and then lead the debtor to ruin; they incite theft, they facilitate debauchery and the seduction of women. (Ibid., 48.) As with the first accusation of class exploitation, this one is immediately generalized: the reader is led to think that one is dealing with all Jews in all places and in all times. In this way, Kostomarov essentializes the Jews, even invoking Shakespeare's portrayal of Shylock in *The Merchant of Venice* and nineteenth-century portrayals of the Eternal Jew as the "image of the European banker" to support his case. (Ibid., 46.) The tone is one of strong moral condemnation.

Another charge focuses on defective religious education. Although their achievements have been great in giving "almost the whole educated world a reli-

gious order" and laying "the foundations of the human race's moral development, of civilization," Jews are still wedded to "old forms," and in a radically
changing world live "in the past, without regard for the future." (Ibid., 45–46.)
This line of argumentation suggests the traditional Christian view that the New
Covenant has superseded the Old. Because of their attachment to "old forms,"
Jews act with a "coldness and indifference toward the world beyond Judaism's
boundaries." (Ibid., 48.) In spite of what Jewish patriots have to say about universal values, the "spirit of Judaism," Kostomarov argues, carries a message of
isolation from and superiority to other races. (Ibid., 43.)

The Jewish newspaper *Sion* (which published in Russian) challenged *Osnova*
(whose articles were sometimes published in Russian and sometimes in Ukrainian). *Sion* was prepared to concede that Ukrainians need not avoid the word
zhyd if it carried no pejorative meaning. However, it bristled at the suggestion
that Jews should unite the interests of their nationality with that of the state or
broader humanity. It countered that Ukrainians were themselves pursuing "exclusively national" goals. *Osnova* was accused of indifference to "the common fatherland—Russia." The very idea of creating a Ukrainian literature was seen by
Sion as an attempt to separate peoples who by their "tribal origin" or common
political and economic interests formed one whole. (Osnova i vopros o natsional'nostiakh 1861, 159–61.) This accusation of seditious, separatist practices
undermined efforts by *Osnova* to convince authorities of its political loyalty, and
was interpreted as a public denunciation, an attempt to end the discussion by
calling in the state. The Jewish press appeared to be lining up with reactionaries
against the Ukrainian movement's right to exist. Some Russian newspapers did
in fact side with *Sion*. Mikhail Katkov took this opportunity to ridicule the
Ukrainian movement and its claims that a Ukrainian language and nationality
existed; he praised Jews for sacrificing their own nationality "in the interest of
the common fatherland." (Serbyn 1988, 95.) However, other Russian periodicals, like the *Severnaia pchela* (Northern Bee) came to *Osnova*'s defense, arguing
for the existence of the Ukrainian language and nationality. Roman Serbyn has
shown how, after *Sion* appealed to public opinion, the *Osnova-Sion* polemic became a broad debate involving a number of Russian periodicals. Serbyn's verdict
is that both journals "were more interested in scoring points before the reading
public and the tsarist authorities than in establishing historical truths, in acquir-
ing a better understanding of the issues involved and in arriving at some com-
promised agreement." (Ibid., 104.) Within a year, Katkov was demanding the
suppression of the Ukrainian language and all Ukrainian activities. In ensuing

decades he became both a leading Ukrainian-baiter and anti-Semite. In 1863 the Valuev edict was issued; it banned the publishing in Ukrainian of any school or religious texts, including translations of the Bible.

Both Ukrainians and Jews, as Serbyn's article points out, were victims of discrimination and national oppression within the empire. However, each community suffered in different ways. Foremost on the minds of Jews were restrictions on movements and civil rights, in particular equal access to education and employment. On the other hand, Ukrainian demands, at this time focused on the banning of their language, literature, and schools. The Jewish intelligentsia, as represented by *Sion*, aimed to overcome Jewish linguistic, cultural, and territorial isolation through integration into the whole Russian empire. It had no time for Ukrainian particularism, which it considered regressive and a threat to its own integrationist aspirations. The rise of the national movement in Ukraine presented it with a dilemma: a choice between emancipatory movements and even between identities. The Ukrainian intelligentsia, on the other hand, could see that assimilated Jews in Ukraine were gravitating toward the Russian language and culture, and were siding with opponents of their own drive for national emancipation. In this way, Jews were playing the role of russifiers in Ukraine. In one of its last articles on the issue, *Sion* wrote:

> Where, in what schools, by what textbooks, with the help of which dictionaries could we learn the proper use of the Little Russian language? And in fact, do such rules exist; that is, has the language become established in lexicon and grammar? Is it distinguished from related languages and dialects? Is the language of Kulish himself correct? . . . Where are your great poets, besides Shevchenko? Where are your prose writers, besides Kvitka; where are your scholars? Weren't they obliged to follow the example of the great Gogol and, after perhaps some unsuccessful attempts in the Little Russian language, to adhere to the general Russian literature, in which we also, who have only recently joined the circle of Russian education, sincerely take part, and have even made some contribution. Weren't they obliged to adopt Russian in order to find in it the breath of their thought, their feeling, and their fantasy, and in order, finally, to assimilate and transmit pan-European scholarship to others. (Serbyn 1988, 102.)

The main thrust of Kostomarov's argumentation was that Jews were not supporting Ukrainians in their emancipatory struggle. In making this case, he linked past social grievances with the contemporary struggle for national-cultural rights, and with generalizations about Jewish "psychology" and cultural attitudes. One should emphasize, however, that he rejected any idea of expelling Jews, discriminating against them, or making them assimilate. Religious persecution was for him a blind hatred, fanatical and barbaric. During the 1880s the ageing Kostomarov successfully opposed a project for the Khmelnytsky monument in Kyiv that would have depicting a Jewish corpse under the horse's hooves. (Kohut 2000, 352.) He firmly defended equal rights for Jews. But in the same breath he demanded an end to monopolistic practices that hindered a Ukrainian middle class from competing on equal terms. Behind this argument lay the fear that Jews were "offering their nationality in service to the Russian" and letting it be known that they were "ready to transform themselves into Great Russians while refusing to be Little Russians." (Ibid., 57.) This fear of a russifying Jewish role was shared by Poles, who at this time idealized the Polish patriotism of Jews, devoting great attention to the example of Michal Landy, a young Jew who fell in battle at the side of his Polish comrades while fighting the Russians and before his death was baptized.

Seeing Jews as equal citizens, Kostomarov no doubt felt that this gave him the moral right to criticize them. Yet his disapproving view of the Jewish role in history predisposed him to look for negative images, expressions of what he saw as an unchanging Jewish essence. A late story written in Russian, "Zhidotrepannia v nachale XVIII veka" (Jew-Beating in the Early Eighteenth Century, 1883) describes the murder of a Ukrainian student called Mykola Sokhno by a Jewish tavernkeeper in 1703, in the reign of Hetman Mazepa. It is based on an actual event that Kostomarov had come across in his archival research. The murder is sanctioned by the Hasidic community's tzaddik, who is incensed by the student's criticisms of Judaism. Sokhno has learned Hebrew and knows Jewish texts, especially the Talmud, from which he is able to quote during a violent verbal exchange with the tzaddik and thirty gathered elders. The most important accusation is the blood libel. Sokhno, a fanatical anti-Semite, maintains that the evidence presented at various trials shows that this accusation has some basis in reality. The tavernkeeper admits to murdering the student and is then tortured into stating that he distributed the victim's blood for ritual purposes. A widespread pogrom breaks out in the Chernihiv region, resulting in the loss of numerous Jewish lives and the destruction of much property. The Hetman orders an end to the violence. He does not believe the libel and asks that the two arrested Jews be transported to his capital, Baturyn, for questioning, but they are murdered en route by an enraged mob. Although the story exposes as ridiculous the charge that Sokhno's body or blood was used for ritual purposes, it also portrays the student's murder as sanctioned by the Jewish community and motivated by religious fanaticism, and a great deal of time is devoted to the "evidence" that the student has discovered while reading about earlier trials for ritual murder. Most disturbing is the narrator's suggestion that in some cases there may be truth to the accusations. Although Sokhno can find no evidence in Jewish writings, he has read everything written by Christians on the subject and is convinced that such murders occur. The narrator informs that "nothing infuriates a Jew more than to be reminded of this secret, terrible question, which in spite of many historical facts, remains to this day unresolved." (Kostomarov 2005, 160.) Since the story appeared shortly after the 1881–82 pogroms, it indicates a lack of sympathy for the suffering of Jews and can even be read as an apologia for the pogromists.

Very similar attitudes were expressed by Kulish. During the *Osnova-Sion* debate he contributed several intemperate articles describing mutual antagonism between Jews and Ukrainians, among them "Drugoi chelovek" (Another Person, 1861), "Peredovyie zhidy" (Leading Jews, 1861), and "Deshcho pro zhydiv" (About the Jews, 1862). Initially an ardent supporter of a Ukrainian-Jewish dialogue, he had praised the Ukrainian verse of Kesar Bilylovsky for that writer's attempt to adapt his Jewish identity to a Ukrainian one. But soon afterward Kulish was claiming that a Jew cannot become a Ukrainian any more than a camel can pass through the eye of a needle, a change of heart that filled Bilylovsky with bitterness and caused him to complain privately about Kulish's bigotry. (Petrovsky-Shtern 2005, 198.) Bilylovsky tried to translate notions and motifs of the ethical Jewish tradition into Ukrainian. In poems like "Zhyteis'ka mudrist'" (Life's Wisdom), "Zhyteis'kyi dosvid" (Life's Experience), "Chervonyi shliub" (Red Wedding), "Daite-bo zhyt!" (Let Live!), and "Elehiia" (Elegy) published in *Ukrains'kyi deklamator* (Ukrainian Declaimer), the writer, according to Petrovsky-Shtern, gave a universal meaning to Judaic ethics while circumventing Christian connotations. (Ibid., 208.) This kind of verse might not have resonated well for a romantic nationalist like Kulish, whose early writings glamorized popular rebellions during the Cossack era. The mock-dumas that Kulish wrote early in his career embellish the stories of atrocities committed against the Orthodox faith. Polish priests are described as traveling from village to village not on horseback but on the backs of people; "all" the Orthodox churches are leased to the Jews; the Jews take the keys from the churches and the ropes from the bells to the taverns and allow the Christians to celebrate mass "for a large fee"; Jews sell hard liquor in the churches and themselves bake the bread that will be consecrated. (Kulish 1908, 62, 66.) This is a further materialization of the "keys to the church" theme, imagined in still greater detail and vividness than earlier accounts: the fee has become "large," "all" churches are affected, hard liquor is now sold in the place of worship. Moreover, Kulish differs from Shevchenko and Kostomarov in his insensitivity to the moral implications of human violence, and in his almost complete indifference to Jewish suffering. His plays *Kolii: Ukrains'ka drama z ostann'oho pol'sk'oho panuvannia na Vkrainii* (The Kolii: A Ukrainian Drama from the Last Polish Rule in Ukraine, 1860) and *Irodova moroka: Narodnia vertepna dyvovyzhka* (Herod's Troubles: A Folk *Vertep* Spectacle, 1869) imitate in the first case the duma's epic impassivity, and in the second the humorous treatment of Jewish stereotypes characteristic of late eighteenth-century Vertep puppet drama.

Hanna Barvinok, Kulish's wife, also wrote stories in the spirit of romantic populism. Even the subtitle she gave to several tales, *z narodnykh ust* (from the mouth of the people), gives the impression that she is recording ethnographic evidence and not composing original literary works. Her "Zhydivs'kyi kripak: Uryvok iz podorozhzhia" (The Jew's Serf: A Fragment from a Journey, 1861) was written in 1847 on her honeymoon, although it was only published in *Osnova* in 1861. In it she describes a journey through Volhynia. The anti-Semitic coachman is ready to "hang all the Jews on one branch," a comment that leads the narrator to recall "Khmelnytsky's time before the bloodbath that has been immortalized by *lira* and *bandura* players [wandering minstrels whose songs were accompanied by play on the two folk instruments]." She and her husband stay at a cold, forlorn inn with broken windows. The Jewish innkeeper is an odious creature who fleeces "the lord and the muzhyk," but whose appearance is "as ragged as that of his animals." (Barvinok 2001, 25.) The poor servant in a threadbare coat is the most wretched of all. Perhaps the most revealing aspect of the narrative is Barvinok's reading of past history into contemporary reality. She sees visions of the past in every detail of life around her. The ragged servant becomes for her an eighteenth-century haidamaka. He has a "haidamaka face," and might have just only yesterday been with Gonta: "Everything that I had read about the haidamakas appeared to me in that Jewish servant in this house." This poor creature earns no money, because even his tips are taken from him by the Jew. Christians are prevented from eating nonkosher food on the inn's tableware and are given the worst fare, while the Jew and his wife eat well. During the night, which is a Sabbath, the Jews praise their lord with "a wild wailing like wolves. 'Give, give, give! And only to us, and destroy all the foreign dens'. . . . This is what we seemed to hear in the sad prayers of the Jews." (Ibid., 28–29.) The poor servant suffers abuse in silence while mentally cursing his employers. His only possession is a fine knife, which, the narrator suggests, would be his only way of "competing with the Jews," in the same way as people in his position had done during the haidamaka uprisings. The narrator repeatedly hears the "delayed echo of a haidamaka roar." At the river ferry, Jews monopolize the job of baggage carrier. They cheat peasants by buying goods at low cost. "Who," exclaims the narrator, "rules Volhynia now that the Princes Ostrozky and Vyshnevetsky have given ancient Rus to the Poles, and the Poles have given it to their sycophants the Jews?" Jewish domination, it is affirmed, prevents the townspeople and peasants from flourishing. (Ibid., 31.) Barvinok's observations are obviously filtered through Kulish's interpretations of history. She presents a relentlessly negative picture of exploitation and abuse, and even uses the contemptuous term *zhydiuha* to describe Jews.

However, by the 1880s, Barvinok's views, like those of Kulish, had evolved away from a naïve populism that glorified the Cossack and the peasant. Accordingly, her story "Pianytsia" (The Drunkard, 1887) shifts the blame for social misfortune firmly onto the shoulders of the alcoholic, wife-beating muzhyk who spends all his time in the tavern, where he attempts to pawn everything the family owns. The Jewish tavernkeeper's wife sympathizes with the muzhyk's wife, and tries to help her by refusing to accept, or by returning, certain goods. The story demonstrates the solidarity and mutual sympathy between these two women. It transpires that the Jewess is also deeply unhappy, because her husband is having an affair with a Ukrainian woman, who, according to the muzhyk's wife, has worked a spell on him. The muzhyk's wife also subscribes to a superstition that Jews and Ukrainians should not mix too closely, although her own conduct contradicts this idea. The story shows the grim face of peasant life (alcoholism, family violence, superstition)—one determined by a range of circumstances for which the Jews cannot be held responsible. In fact, the behavior of the Jewess represents a generous attempt to help.

The populist writers grouped around *Osnova* exhibited different attitudes. The rather conservative Oleksa Storozhenko mentions the "keys to the church" theme twice in his *Marko Prokliatyi* (Marko the Cursed), but on both occasions uses it to denounce the Poles, and appears to be entirely uninterested in Jews. He portrays Bohdan Khmelnytsky's lieutenant Kryvonis as a sadistic and cruel fanatic. In his retelling of history, the 1648 revolution takes on anarchic and senselessly destructive forms. However, the ending to the story was added by an anonymous author after Storozhenko's death. It shows Kryvonis first sleeping with a beautiful Jewish woman, then murdering her. The final pages describe Marko searching the world for the Wandering Jew, whom he hopes to convince that Jews should not practice tavernkeeping and "all kinds of deception" but take up honest trades. We have no way of knowing how Storozhenko himself might have ended this tale, but given his military background and long, loyal service to tsarism, his attitude to Marko could not have been one of unreserved sympathy.

The writer disliked the anarchic destructiveness of mass rebellions, even though he admired the courage of serf-rebels. In Storozhenko's interpretation, the figure of Marko represents another version of the Ukrainian curse: he is a man who was born and raised in revolt, and can never expiate his original sin—the murder of his own people. This sense of unexpiated guilt, a romantic convention dating back to gothic tales of evil, in particular to Gogol, may have been used by the writer to hint at the killing of innocent people, including Jews, during popular revolts. It is unlikely that Storozhenko would have provided the kind of ending that was added later. In any case, the Marko Prokliaty story captured the imagination of many readers, and, as will be seen, was later reworked by a number of writers.

The Realists: Ivan Nechui-Levytsky and Panas Myrny

Literary realism, the dominant style of the 1870s and 1880s, was allied to positivism, and to liberal and socialist ideals. Some anti-Semitic attitudes were undermined by this new sensibility, which focused on socio-economic conditions as the primary source of evil and exhibited a strongly moralistic tone. At this time, individual Jews were participating in the Ukrainian national movement, even in its earliest organizational stages. Vsevolod Rubinshtein and Viliam Berenshtam, for example, were active in the Ukrainophile Kyiv Hromada in the 1860s. From 1900, Jews were involved in the Revolutionary Ukrainian Party, the Ukrainian Social Democratic Labor Party, and the Ukrainian Social Democratic Union or Spilka. Nonetheless, overall the depiction of Jews in literary realism remained negative. They were often linked to capitalist exploitation, or seen as hostages of a backward religious culture.

Such a negative portrayal was part of a xenophobia that was often based on fear of the money economy. Karl Marx in his "On the Jewish Question" (1843) linked the emancipation of Jews to the growth of capitalism. In his view, money had become all-powerful and "the Jew has emancipated himself in a Jewish manner." He "has become the practical spirit of the Christian people. The Jews have emancipated themselves in so far as the Christians have become Jews." (Marx 1990, 59). In Russia, the negative portrayals also reflected contemporary political paranoias. For example, Dostoevsky in his March 1877 entries in his *Dnevnik pisatelia* (Diary of a Writer) speaks about his hopes for the empire's victory in the Turkish war, and for the capture of Constantinople. He thinks that Russia's expansion ("finally to leave that locked room in which it has grown to the ceiling") is prevented by her enemies: the Turks, and also the British, who are linked to the

Jews in the person of Disraeli. He fears and hates Jews, along with all others who oppose Russian expansion. In "The Jewish Question" he describes Jewish hostility and condescension to poor Russians and suggests the prevalence of the following Jewish attitude: "Go forth from the other nations, form thine own entity and know that henceforth thou art *the only one before God;* destroy the others, or enslave them or exploit them. Have faith in thy victory over the whole world; have faith that all will submit to thee. Shun everyone resolutely, and have no communion with any in thy daily life. And even when thou art deprived of thy land, thy political individuality, even when thou art scattered over the face of the earth and among all the other peoples—pay no heed; have faith in all these things that have been promised unto thee; believe, once and for all, that all this will come to pass; and meanwhile thou must live, shun, cling together, exploit, and—wait, wait. . . ." (Dostoevsky 1994, 910.) The writer holds that Jews are responsible for their own predicament: they have taken up the idea of hating and destroying all others. The Russians, on the other hand, are depicted, to use Safran's words, as "innocent victims in a nation-eat-nation world, where all the players, especially but not only the Jews, are driven to oppress and conquer one another." The Russian nation is a united and unchanging entity. It is the Jews who must change their behavior in order to facilitate a "brotherhood" or limited rapprochement. (Safran 2000, 140–41.)

This attitude, which is close to Kostomarov's, influenced Ukrainian realist writers of the 1870s, who were turning literature's focus away from national history and popular rebellions to contemporary socio-economic conditions. A new interest in individual psychology emerged, one that gradually fragmented the earlier view of national types and general characteristics. These developments can be seen in one of the best works of realism, Ivan Nechui-Levytsky's *Mykola Dzheria* (1876). It begins with the powerful paradigm created by Shevchenko and the romantic nationalists. the contrast between a lost peasant paradise and an intrusive, exploitative, and cruel order that has been imposed by outsiders. In the first scene, a young and handsome Mykola daydreams in a beautiful village setting. He hears the singing of a girl drawing water from a well:

> The song seemed to him a marvel. It was as though he was not sleeping but looking up into the branches. The green leaves on the pear tree were made of glass. Through the leaves he could see the blue sky; he could see how the rays of the sun pierced each and every leaf, how the quiet breeze swayed the leaves. Each leaf touched another and rang. He seemed to hear the voice and the song pouring on him from above, from the leaves. Every leaf seemed to be singing, even expressing words, and those words, that voice were quietly falling on his face, his arms, his breast, and his very heart. He examined the strange leaves and noticed at the

very top of the pear tree a strange bird with golden and silver feathers. The bird spread its wide wings, its sumptuous tail, like that of a peacock, singing all the time and moving lower on the branches. Flaming sparks fell from the golden wings onto the crystal leaves, making them ring and sing in consort even better. The bird came still lower and lower. The idea came to Mykola to catch it. . . . He reached out his hand and the sparkling bird flew up higher to the very top, and only sparks fell on the grass, his hands, his cheeks, and burned him. (Nechui-Levyts'kyi 2001, 8.)

This passage prefigures the action of the novel. The beautiful village paradise will prove to be illusory and the young man's aspirations for happiness will be denied. Throughout the novel the reader's attention is continually directed to the perverse workings of a socio-economic system that is the root of all misery, in particular to serfdom, which breaks people both physically and mentally. Inhuman exploitation by the lord, Bzhozovsky, who forces peasants to provide him with four days or more of unpaid labor each week, makes hundreds of peasants into runaways, tramps, and outlaws. When these runaways find work in a sugar-refining factory, they have to deal not with the factory owner, but his factotum, the local executor of the absentee lord's will, a Jewish leaseholder called Moisei Brodovsky. It is significant that the two names are so similar. They represent the dual face of exploitation in Ukraine: the landowner, whose name betrays his Polish background, and the Jewish businessman and leaseholder. Brodovsky and his wife are of poor origins and lack refinement, but dress like *pany* (gentlefolk), even ostentatiously. He wears gold chains and rings with expensive stones, although his shirt and collar are not clean. This depiction has been called the "first note of sentimental sympathy for the Jewish pauper" in Ukrainian literature. (Skurativs'kyi 1998, 51.) It would be more accurately described as an unflattering depiction of the contemporary nouveau riche. While the leaseholder and his wife insist on being recognized and treated as *pany,* the tramps who inquire about the possibility of obtaining employment behave toward them in an insolent manner, using the familiar second person singular ("ty"). This infuriates Brodovsky:

"I am in charge here. Didn't you know that?"

"No, of course not! Who knows what you are?" said Mykola rather gruffly, in the way peasants speak.

"Why are you shouting! We didn't tend swine together! If you want to work for me, drop the "ty" because I'm the *pan* here," said Brodovsky, this time angrily. Mykola almost began cursing Brodovsky, but managed with difficulty to hold his tongue. Nonetheless, he continually avoided the wretched "vy" form. He still saw before him a Jew, although a rich one. (Nechui-Levyts'kyi 2001, 54.)

The passage is revealing. The leaseholder demands the respect that accrues to his new position, but the peasant finds it painful to bow to Brodovsky, because he knows that the latter, who speaks perfectly idiomatic Ukrainian, is a recent arrival from his own social sphere. Once the word "vy" (an indicator of social status) is avoided, the behavior of both, however strained, remains correct.

There is another revealing detail—the association of Brodovsky with sordid factory conditions and a particular smell: "The tramps recognized this smell under the expensive clothing in the same way that wolves recognize the smell of wolves in wolf skin." (Ibid., 53.) There is a long history of associating Jews with a particular smell, the *foetor Judaicus.* Here the issue is not so much uncleanliness or attachment to a particular cuisine, or even that Jews are, perhaps, to be associated with the unhealthy and contaminating aspects of industry. Nechui-Levytsky seems to suggest that there exists an ineradicable sign of Jewish difference, a boundary between Jews and gentiles that cannot be dissolved after other marks of distinction have been removed.

A tavern has been set up in order to extract the monthly wages back from the workers. Brodovsky has made an investment in the factory after borrowing heavily from a rich Jewish merchant, Shmul Kaplun. To make his payments, he not only withholds the wages of workers, but also provides them with extremely poor food. Eventually, this leads to an epidemic and deaths. Brodovsky has to pay a large sum to cover up the scandal. Workers begin complaining that "the Jews have sent a plague on the people" and break his windows. A government inspection orders that the workers' barracks be cleaned but finds that nobody is at fault. There is a final verbal confrontation with Brodovsky, after which the workers begin to run away to the distant steppes of Kherson in search of better employment.

Here they are employed by a Ukrainian fisherman. Once again, they spend their wages in the tavern. The Jewish tavernkeeper behaves with calm and dignity, although he serves a lower-quality wine for a high price, or waters down the drinks. However, the intoxicated, vulgar, and raucous tramps who drink away all their money are portrayed in a highly negative light. After the emancipation of the serfs in 1861, Mykola returns to his own village and leads a movement to get better land for the peasant farmers, rather than have the lord present them with the worst. He is successful in this, as he is in gaining local control of the tavern. The narrator informs readers: "From then until the end of his life Dzheria went against the lords and the Jews. They had caused him so much harm, offended him and ruined his life." (Ibid, 116.) Mykola even organizes a letter asking that the Jews be removed from the village. He is in conflict with all middle- and upper-class authority. Bitter, short-tempered and given to bouts of violence, he avoids any meeting with the lord, and even refuses to sell his products to the latter at the market. After the priest demands large payments for services, he stops attending church. Proud and solitary to the end, he finds some comfort in his return to a natural paradise, where he tends bees and recounts fairy tales to his grandchildren.

The Jewish characters are recognizable human beings, whose language and behavior is individualized and whose motivation is understandable. Nonetheless, they are identified with the oppressive social system that is grinding down the population. Relations between Mykola and the leaseholder are so strained that there is a continual suggestion of suppressed violence. On the strength of this one story, a reader would only see Jews as tavernkeepers, leaseholders, and businessmen. It is, however, a different approach from Kostomarov's. Nechui-Levytsky is concerned with the exploitative system in which Jews play a role, not with national essences. His later writings tend to reproduce a dualistic picture of Jewish character, contrasting the ugly rich with the noble poor. The story "Ievreis'kyi sknera" (The Jewish Miser, 1914) introduces the reader both to the rich Kharaob, a stingy owner of an inn, and the poor but honest Moshko. Kharaob borrows money from the narrator, who lodges at the inn for an extended period of time, and does not return it until the very last moment in order to obtain the maximum interest from the sum, which he has secretly banked.

The other major realist of the seventies was Panas Myrny. His novel *Lykhi liudy* (Bad Folk, 1875) paints a broad canvas of feudal-like exploitation and authoritarian rule. A Jew is mentioned as part of the oppressive system: when the hero asks whose fields he is looking at, he is told that Hrap "the German" is in charge of administration, while "the Jew" handles the money. Both are doing well. The German occupies the mansion, while the Jew owns the refinery. This exchange conjures up a picture of social relations in which non-Ukrainians control the economy. Skurativsky writes: "in spite of the radical-democratic orientation [of this literature], the idea that the Jewish 'middleman' was completely dependent on landowner capital came to it with great difficulty, as did the possibility of an alliance between Ukrainophiles (the legal synonym of Ukrainian populists) who were steadily growing stronger with emancipated Jewish intellectuals and with the impoverished townspeople." (Skurativs'kyi 1998, 50.)

In the years 1877–79, Myrny wrote the story "Za vodoiu" (Over the Waters). A version entirely reworked by Ivan Bilyk was published in *Literaturno-naukovyi zbirnyk* (Literary-Scientific Miscellany) in 1918. It could not appear under tsarist rule due to its portrayal of a heartless landowner, who floods the homes of his peasants every spring in order to maintain a watermill he has built. When the lord finds that he is unable to prevent the annual flooding, maintain sanitary conditions (dead cats and dogs are found in the millpond), or make a profit, he leases the mill to Leiba, who already runs the local tavern. Myrny's original story contains a more nuanced presentation of the social conflict than one might expect. Under Leiba's management things become easier for the villagers. He lowers the water to prevent flooding and allows for community use of the millpond. There is one anti-Semitic dissenter, who criticizes the community for agreeing to the new arrangements, but he is ignored by the villagers because he is a drunkard and a wastrel who spends his nights in the tavern. Leiba charges the community for animals that come to the pool to drink and confiscates those that have been caught and remain unclaimed. However, in the end, the lord, Leiba, and the villagers all benefit from the new arrangements, which are a vast improvement on the old. Leiba allows the ancient pagan festival of Ivan Kupala (Midsummer Night) to be celebrated—something that could not happen earlier because the lord forbade access to the river. When the festival is renewed, Leiba allows his boat to be used for the rituals, which his family comes to observe. The mysterious folk beliefs associated with the festival intrigue and amaze Surka, Leiba's wife, who questions the peasants about them. Kupala is successfully celebrated as a result of the leaseholder's support.

An unfinished story from 1868–70 is entitled "Zhydivka" (The Jewess). In it Petro Petrovych Mukha describes his first, tragic love affair with a beautiful Jewish girl named Liia. Instantly smitten when he notices her among the many Jewish girls in town, he seeks her out at a Jewish wedding celebration to which all are invited. The two fall in love and begin to arrange secret trysts under the willows by Liia's home. The barriers to a marriage appear insuperable: neither is prepared to break with family, religion, or traditions. However, an interesting discussion takes place concerning religious differences, the possibility of conversion to Christianity, and the gulf between the two communities. Liia asks: "Why are your customs different from ours? Why do you and we refuse to know one another, refuse to live together, why do you despise us?" (Myrnyi 1968, 4:44.) She receives the answer that Jews are a bad people (*pohanyi narod*), who are inhuman (*u vas nema nichoho liuds'koho*), and who would sell their souls for money. When Petro explains Christ's teachings, Liia listens with interest, particularly to the message of goodness and forgiveness, but refuses to leave her people (it would be "a knife in their hearts") or to change her faith. In considering the Christian faith, she asks: "Is it as good as our faith?" and "Will I then have the right to accept the eternal glory that our parents await, that our ancestors awaited?" (Ibid.,

45.) In the denouement Liia drowns herself, unable to contemplate the marriage her parents have arranged for her. When the body is recovered, a small cross, a present from Petro, is found around her neck. Soon afterwards, her distraught father also dies. This early Ukrainian narrative of tragic union, like later ones, suggests insuperable divisions between the two faiths, but at the same time also shows the possibility not only of cultural interaction (Liia speaks Ukrainian well, and the streets, marketplaces, and wedding celebrations are zones of social contact), but also of personal attraction. During their conversations Liia comments: "Wouldn't it be fine if we were equals with you, if you visited us, and we visited you. . . . How I would love you then!" (Ibid., 45.) This unfulfilled desire points a way out of the impasse in which the couple finds itself.

Petro, the narrator, shows a strong degree of self-criticism. He gives the following account of his thought process at the time of his infatuation: "Poor, pathetic people! Your whole glory lies in money, your whole life in profit! You cannot see the fire that blazes in the eyes of your Jewish women, the wellspring of life that beats in their high breasts. . . . You do not live the life of humans. Money is your life, your thoughts, your dreams, joys and sorrows, love, will—everything! A small coin elicits an envious fire in your eyes, while a gold coin captures your whole heart, your whole soul with a hellish, heavy yearning and draws you into the depths, in the same way as our people are seduced by the bright eyes of a woman." (Ibid., 41.) The narrator attributes such thoughts to himself at the time when he was desperately in love and violently resented his inability to see Liia. The implication is that his anti-Semitism is linked to personal frustration and unhappiness.

The overall import of these realist portrayals is to identify Jews as part of a socio-economic system that exploits the peasantry. Yakiv Shchoholiv also wrote of the socially privileged Jewish population, and Stepan Rudansky's most famous work, *Spivomovky* (Song-Rhymes, 1880), which is a collection of poems, proverbs, and stories that mimic popular humor, contains a section on Jews alongside others devoted to peasants, Cossacks, priests, Poles, lords, Russians, bureaucrats, Germans, and gypsies. The comic in these simple anecdotes stems from seeing the pompous or affected brought down to earth. Among those ridiculed are the rabbi who retreats into twenty-seven years of silence and study, or who does not work himself but has someone do things for him, or the Jew who attaches a sword to his belt and acts the Cossack. This last image of the Jew as fearful, incapable of military action, and deferential to the strong Cossack is part of the eighteenth-century stereotype that makes its appearance in the Vertep drama. Also traditional is the delight in fooling the Jew, or avoiding being fooled by him. The strange, incomprehensible logic of Hasidic stories is also mocked. However, there are also stories that celebrate Jewish quick-wittedness and ability to verbally outmaneuver an opponent.

The attitude of writers in Western Ukraine was not substantially different. Because of the ban on Ukrainian publishing within the Russian empire, many of the above-mentioned works actually appeared in Galicia and were then smuggled back across the border. It was not until after the pogroms of 1881–82, which profoundly shocked a younger generation of writers, that a philo-Semitic current began to challenge anti-Jewish stereotypes and became part of a new sensibility.

CHAPTER 2

Meeting at the Crossroads, 1881–1914

The situation of Jews on the territories that are today Ukraine in this period has often been portrayed as oppressive, but it was not the same everywhere. It may have been best in Austrian-ruled Bukovyna. Although Aharon Appelfeld's novel *Katerina* (1989, English translation 1992) paints a gloomy picture of local anti-Semitism, there appears to have been some cooperation between Ukrainians and Jews. Bukovynian Jews have been described as "the most accepted and least persecuted Jewish community in Eastern Europe." In this period they enjoyed full citizenship, elected Jewish mayors to the capital Chernivtsi (Czernowitz), and rectors to the university. The rabbis had close, friendly relations with Orthodox Christian archbishops (they even laid the first stone of a new synagogue together in 1873). Rabbis and Orthodox or Protestant clergy might pray together on occasions. Ukrainians "would bring their New Year celebrations to Jewish houses . . . and Jews would send a delegation to welcome any bishop who visited the town. And when the Russians invaded in 1914, Archbishop Repta of the Orthodox Church safeguarded the Torah and other holy texts from the main Czarnowitz synagogue." (Stambrook n.d., 12.) Chernivtsi was the home of the first Jewish secular community center in Eastern Europe, and of prominent Jewish figures such as the Yiddish writer Josif Burg and the German-language author Paul Celan (Paul Antschel/Ancel). Yiddish culture continued to maintain strong institutional forms in Bukovyna well into the Soviet period: the Yiddish theater was only shut down in 1950.

The Ukrainian and Jewish intelligentsias in Eastern Galicia also sometimes lived cooperatively. The patriotism of the leading Ukrainian feminist and member of the Polish parliament, Milena Rudnytska, for example, had no conflict with her Jewish origins. She organized civil activism among Ukrainians while supporting other cognate movements. In 1888 her father had married Ida Spiegel, the daughter of Orthodox Jews, against the wish of both sets of parents. Ida became a Christian, taking the name Olha, and "made the jump from the Jewish ghetto to the world of the Galician intelligentsia." Rudnytska affirms that she never witnessed any overt expressions of anti-Semitism toward her mother. Her father "was supportive toward the Jews, with no shadow of anti-Semitism. Did he do this out of loyalty to Mama? He lived in good relationships not only with Mama's family, near and far (Maks, Tynka, Poloniecki), but in general had no prejudices against Jews. Dr. Ravich, when still a law student, worked in Daddy's office; my instructors were Jews." (Rudnyts'ka 1998, 48, 54.) Rudnytska affirms that the situation deteriorated in the decades between the world wars when "mutual resentments" erected walls between the two communities. (Rudnyts'ka 1957.)

The situation was worst in the Russian empire, where Jewish memory has often pictured the prerevolutionary years as a time of poverty, persecution, and violence. However, even here some have recalled life in the shtetl not only as "relentlessly dark and dreadful," but also as a reflection of a "splendid, holistic community where, before it was leveled, Jews were happily free to be themselves." (Zipperstein 1999, 6.) Although the overall story is not a simple one, the dominant account is clearly one of intense official anti-Semitism, discriminatory policies, and outbursts of a fierce hostility. Government anti-Semitism intensified after the assassination of Alexander II in 1881 and pogroms spread. The result was a mass emigration. 1,889,000 Jews left for the United States and other countries in the years 1881–1912. Part of the intelligentsia embraced Marxism or joined revolutionary groups. The Bund (General League of Jewish Workingmen in Russia and Poland) was formed in 1897 and soon adopted the idea of "national-cultural autonomy," which envisaged each nationality as having the right to conduct its own cultural affairs in a democratic state. By 1898 Jews made up 24.8 percent of all political prisoners, at a time when they made up 4 percent of the empire's population. (Khiterer 1999, 79.)

Although revolutionaries were a small proportion of the community, Jews were often collectively accused of fomenting revolution. The minister of internal affairs, Nikolai Ignatiev, at the time of the violence blamed them for the pogroms, which he saw as an understandable reaction to exploitation. Regulations drawn up in May, 1882 (the so-called May Laws), banished Jews from the villages of the Pale and prevented them from buying more land. In 1887 a quota system was created which limited them to 10 percent of schoolchildren, and to only 3 percent in Moscow and St. Petersburg.

Some Russian intellectuals, like Ivan Aksakov and Gleb Uspensky, agreed with authorities that the pogroms were a legitimate expression of popular anger against tavernkeepers, shopkeepers, and moneylenders. Although the new tsar Alexander III did not condone the pogroms, he suggested that the Jewish role in the economy had led to the attacks. Kostomarov and Drahomanov were the most prominent among Ukrainians who failed to distance themselves from such attitudes. Drahomanov's articles in *Vol'noe slovo* (Free Word), a Russian paper published in Geneva in the years 1881–83, reveal strong anti-Semitic views. The majority of Jews were for him part of the capitalist system that exploited the masses. He wrote that "the Jewish nation (*natsiia*) is not only largely composed of one estate (*soslovie*) but this estate is parasitic." (Galai 1974, 48.) Even so, both men supported equal rights for Jews. Drahomanov considered Jews a distinct nation and was the first to propose that they be given not only equal civil rights with Ukrainians, but also national-cultural self-government, protected by appropriate constitutional guarantees.

Solzhenitsyn exonerates the tsarist government and the Russian intelligentsia, reasoning that "although the pogroms originated in the main from the Ukrainian population, they [the Russian administration] were not forgiven and they were forever linked to the Russian name." (Solzhenitsyn 2001–2, 1:207.) He quotes approvingly the statement of a Jewish author that "among the broad masses of the people anti-Semitism hardly existed, and even the very problem of relations with Jewry did not arise." It only existed "in a few parts of the so-called Pale of Settlement, in particular in Ukraine, where from the time of the Polish state, as a result of particular circumstances . . . anti-Semitic feelings were widespread among the peasantry." (Ibid., 319.) However, Solzhenitsyn is silent on the obvious facts: that the imperial administration created the Pale, instituted harshly discriminatory policies, and created the poisonous climate in which xenophobia grew. It did little to prevent the spread of anti-Semitic propaganda in the printed media. In a country without press freedom, this implied support for public incitement. Klier has stated that "Russian bureaucrats borrowed from Western Europe the belief that it was not circumstances that directed the Jews into unproductive, parasitical, and exploitative commercial activities, but the teachings of Judaism itself, especially as conveyed by the Talmud." (Klier and Lambroza 1992, 7.)

Under Nicholas II, who ruled from 1894 until 1917, pogroms were incited by ultranationalist Russian organizations, collectively known as the "Black Hundreds." The tsar accepted honorary membership for himself and his son in one of these organizations, the "Union of the Russian People," assured its delegations of his support, and wore its insignia. Although Solzhenitsyn dismisses this organization as insignificant, it had hundreds of branches across the country and received government subsidies. (Pipes 2002, 28.) There is circumstantial evidence that the second major wave of pogroms that took place during the revolution of 1905 was stimulated and abetted by circles close to government for political reasons. (Khiterer 1992, 37; Lambroza 1992, 224, 232–33; Weinberg 1992, 268–72.)

Many intellectuals of different backgrounds protested the pogroms and united in the struggle for civil rights. A number of Russian-language writers—particularly Vladimir Korolenko and Nikolai Leskov, both of whom came from Ukraine—contributed to a more sympathetic view of Jews and Judaism. On the request of a group of St. Petersburg Jews, Leskov produced a study, *Evrei v Rossii: Neskol'ko zamechanii po evreiskomu voprosu* (The Jews in Russia: Some Notes on the Jewish Question, 1884), which defended Jewish rights and called for an end to residence restrictions. A growing awareness developed that relations had to be improved and positive attitudes encouraged. Volodymyr Doroshenko, a member of the Revolutionary Ukrainian Party in the first years of the twentieth century, has written: "The struggle for national self-expression (*samovyiavlennia*) and political freedom united the Jewish and Ukrainian youth into groups in the gymnasiums, the university, and beyond the lecture rooms. This was the case in Poltava, Lubny, Pryluky, Nizhyn, and Kiev, which I know from personal experience. This relationship was sometimes so strong that individual comrades from the Jewish revolutionary youth joined the RUP." (Boshyk 1986, 176.)

Vladimir Jabotinsky was one of the first to realize that "the aims of the Ukrainian national movement—democratization of public life, recognition of national equality, and broad cultural and national autonomy—were analogous to the goals of the Zionist movement within the Russian Empire." (Kleiner 2000, 25.) He called upon Jews to take account of Ukrainian national aspirations and to resist the role of russifiers in the empire's non-Russian territories. In his article "Na lozhnom puti" (On the Wrong Path, 1912), he spoke of the russifying role played by contemporary Jews in towns that were almost completely Jewish and Ukrainian, describing the comical situation at celebrations of Pushkin or Komissarzhevskaia, during which Jews, the only speakers, used terms like "we Russians" and "our Russian literature" in front of an entirely non-Russian audience. (Zhabotinskii 1922, 84–85.) In a series of far-sighted articles he warned the Jewish community and Russian readers that the Ukrainian national move-

ment was not only powerful and unstoppable, but progressive. Kleiner states
that these collected articles, anthologized under the title *Felietony* (Feuilletons,
1913), could be found in thousands of Jewish homes and became a popular present at festive occasions. (Kleiner 2000, 64.)

Just as the Polish author Eliza Orzeszkowa had complained that Jews were
more sympathetic to Russians than to Poles, a fact that in her mind threatened
Polish-Jewish solidarity, Jabotinsky complained that the drift toward Russian
culture endangered solidarity with Ukrainians, maintaining that deep roots in
Ukraine and close proximity to Ukrainians would in the long run serve Jews well
if they supported the national movement's aspirations. Like Orzeszkowa, he was
offended by the fact that many Jews considered Russian culture "universal" and
more likely to help them gain political rights, a line of thought that he condemned as unprincipled and misguided. He felt that contemporary Ukrainian
literature did not show endemic hostility to Jews, while Russian literature un-
consciously drew support from government violence. As indicators of hostile attitudes in Russian literature he cited such portrayals as the usurer in Pushkin's
Skupoi rytsar' (Covetous Knight, 1830), the prostitute in Turgenev's "Zhid"
(The Yid, 1847), and Chekhov's "Tina" (1886), the nouveau riche in Nekrasov's
Sovremenniki (Contemporaries, 1875), and Dostoevsky's journalism. Only, he
argued, when serious national liberation movements arose within the empire
would Russian attitudes change. (Zhabotinskii 1922, 126–30.) There was some
justification for Jabotinsky's views. Writing in 1918 Simon Dubnow (Dubnov)
also drew attention to the "backyards" of Russian literature where widely read
novels like Taddei Bulgarin's *Ivan Vyzhigin* (1829) portrayed Jews as the embodiment of all the mortal sins and "instilled Jew-hatred into the minds of the Russian people." (Dubnow 1946, 139.) In an afterword to a recent anthology of Russian literature dealing with Jews, another scholar has argued that, when it came
to the Jews, in the century preceding the 1917 revolution the classics of Russian
literature "drew one and the same portrait, extremely infrequently departing
from a quite primitive pattern that had been formed at the very beginning of the
nineteenth century. The same weak character, unfit for physical work, sickly, ef-
feminate, sometimes touching, but more often repulsive and speaking with a
bizarre accent, migrated from work to work. Practically no one deviated from
this pattern." (Edelshtein 2005, 390–91.)

Gogol and other authors from Ukraine had played a crucial role in creating
the Jew of Russian historical fiction. These early depictions, along with portraits
of the Jewish miser in Pushkin, Lermontov, and others, have been dismissed by
Edelshtein as cardboard characters who lack any internal dynamic, "classicist al-

legories of evil that found themselves by accident in a romantic text." (Ibid., 385.) Gogol's *Taras Bul'ba* is, according to this critic, dictated by the rules of the epic genre, which require supermen and supervillains. Two seminal works on the subject have taken a different approach. Joshua Kunitz in his *Russian Literature and the Jew* (1929) suggested that because they were more familiar with Jews, the work of Ukrainians has a different tonality. For example, he argued that Gogol presented features of the "living Jew" that were based on real experience. The writer "does not hate the Jew; he is used to him. The relationship here is too subtle and too complex for Gogol to fling him 'some shekels and curse the old Jew' [a reference to Pushkin's "The Black Shawl"]." (Kunitz 1929, 36.) Vasilii Lvov-Rogachevsky's *History of Russian Jewish Literature* (1922) charted the appearance from the 1880s of Jewish authors like Lev Levanda, Semen An-sky, Osip Rabinovich, and Semen Frug, who were able to present the inner life of Jews to a broad public. A large number of such writers, including the last two, came from Ukraine and were associated with Ukrainian centers of Jewish cultural life. Jabotinsky dismissed this writing as insignificant, in much the same way as he dismissed the philo-Semitic writing of Russian authors like Maksim Gorky, Vladimir Korolenko, and Aleksandr Kuprin. His views were a reaction to the appearance of a spate of Russian fictional works exhibiting a virulent anti-Semitism and depicting a world controlled by an international Jewish conspiracy. Among the more lurid are Vsevolod Krestovsky's *T'ma egipetskaia* (Egyptian Darkness, 1881–88), the first volume of his trilogy entitled *Zhid idet* (The Yid is Coming, 1888–92), Kot-Murlyka's (N. P. Wagner's) *Temnyi put'* (Dark Road, 1890), V. I. Kryzhanovskaia's *Mertvaia petlia* (The Loop, 1907), and E. A. Shabelskaia's *Satanisty XX veka* (Twentieth-Century Satanists, 1912). Scholars have suggested that the roots of modern Russian anti-Semitism lie in this fiction, which portrayed Russia as the last bulwark of Christendom in conflict with a world controlled by Jews: it has been described as the "midwife" and "wet-nurse" of Russian anti-Semitism. (Dudakov 1993, 134.) In the years of reaction that followed the suppression of the 1905 revolution, numerous anti-Semitic books and pamphlets appeared. Around 1902 the forgery known as the *Protocols of the Elders of Zion* was created and propagated with the encouragement of individuals in the tsarist secret police. Russian radical rightists at this time developed intensely antiseparatist, antisocialist, and anti-Semitic views, which they disseminated widely—sometimes in the guise of apocalyptic scenarios in which the Jews were associated with the Antichrist. Many of these reactionary monarchists moved to Ukraine after the Bolsheviks took power in 1917, and then, when the German-supported government of Hetman Skoropadsky collapsed at the end of

1918, emigrated to Berlin, bringing anti-Semitic literature with them, along with warnings of a monstrous Jewish-Bolshevik world conspiracy. Hitler quoted frequently from the *Protocols,* which went through thirty-three editions by the time he came to power in 1933. (Kellogg 2005, 76.)

Ukrainian, Russian, and Jewish colleagues in the liberal-democratic movement expressed sympathy for the Jewish people's emancipatory struggles. Hrushevsky's *Ukrainskii vestnik* (Ukrainian Herald), which came out in St. Petersburg from 1906, and the journal *Ukrainskaia zhizn'* (Ukrainian Life) which appeared in Moscow from 1912 as a result of Symon Petliura's efforts, are examples. During the 1905 revolution Hrushevsky wrote that Jews were victimized by foreign domination as much as Ukrainians, and welcomed the submission to the Duma of a bill to abolish the Pale. The linking of Jewish and Ukrainian interests was not merely rhetorical. Arnold Margolin, a leading Jewish defense lawyer in prewar Kyiv who later became a diplomat in the government of the Ukrainian National Republic, had widespread Ukrainian support for his election to the first State Duma, and his memoirs provide evidence of cooperation between Ukrainian and Jewish political leaders in electoral campaigns during 1905–17. (Margolin 1977, 18–24, 45.) At the same time, Ukrainians and Jews in Eastern Galicia forged a political coalition that elected candidates who promoted minority rights.

In 1913 the liberal-democrats rejoiced in the acquittal of Mendel Beilis, who was accused of the ritual murder of a Christian boy. Many prominent figures of all nationalities protested the trial. Despite a broad propaganda campaign against the Jews and attempts by the judge to sway the jury, the government was stunned to learn that twelve peasants (all intelligentsia had been removed by a motion of the prosecuting attorney) declared a verdict of "not guilty" in the trial. The outcome was welcomed by liberal opinion throughout the Russian empire as a great victory.

The Great Tradition: Biblical Narratives and Popular Dramas

Ukrainian literature of the late nineteenth century reflects a sympathy for Jewish cultural self-assertion and identifies strongly with Jewish oppression. Representations of Jews can be categorized according to three settings: the biblical and ancient, the modern, and the contemporary.

The use of Jewish biblical and ancient history became particularly popular in the years 1881–1905, when it served Ukrainian writers as a metaphor for a people struggling to assert its identity in the face of overwhelming hostility. Olena Pchilka's poems "Iudyta" (Judith), "Debora" (Deborah, 1887), and "Prorok" (The Prophet, 1886) are typical early examples. The stress is on national enslavement, and the need for clear-sighted, courageous leaders. The biblical situation serves as an allegory of contemporary Ukraine. In Galicia, Ivan Franko's *Moisei* (Moses, 1905) is the most celebrated example of this kind of writing. The theme came to Franko in Vienna after a conversation in February 1893 with Theodor Herzl. Vasyl Shchurat, who was a student at the University of Vienna and shared lodgings with Franko at the time, witnessed this conversation and described it in the August 5, 1937 issue of *Chwila* (Time). Franko was interested in Herzl's ideas of a Jewish state and the importance of great leaders who are thrown up by circumstances. He later wrote a review of Herzl's *Der Judenstaat* (1896) for the *Kurjer Lwowski* (Lviv Courier) edition of March 9, 1896, where he expressed an interest in the cultural-national aspirations of the Jews. *Moisei* aligns the images of ancient Israel and contemporary Ukraine as subjugated nations. When described within the framework of biblical narratives—the realm of the sacred—the portrayal of Jews is always positive, and their strong sense of national identity and purpose are greatly admired.

Like Pchilka and Franko, Lesia Ukrainka put biblical themes to allegorical use. In the early "Samson (Na bibleis'ku temu)" (Samson: On a Biblical Theme, 1888) the captive and humiliated Samson brings down the palace and, by implication, the state. Egyptian or Babylonian captivity, glossed by readers as Ukrainian captivity in the Russian empire, is described in "Ievreis'ka melodiia" (Jewish Melody, 1896) and "Ievreis'ki melodii" (Jewish Melodies, 1899). The prophet Jeremiah appeals for the preservation of national identity, while the picture of a destroyed state and temple reminds readers of their own political and cultural dispossession. Ukrainka's dramatic poems, *Vavilons'kyi polon: Dramatychna poema* (The Babylonian Captivity: A Dramatic Poem, 1903) and *Na ruinakh: Dramatychna poema* (Among the Ruins: A Dramatic Poem, 1904) also deal with Jewish captivity and lament the fate of Jerusalem. Their aim is to awaken national consciousness and stimulate a struggle for freedom. Like Franko, Ukrainka studied the enormous distance between the national leadership and the common people. In her poem "Prorok" (The Prophet, 1906) she complains that the poet must be a prophet who drags along a reluctant and disillusioned nation. Sometimes she herself assumes the prophet's voice, as in "I ty kolys' borolas', mov Izrail'" (You too once struggled like Israel, 1904), where she asks God whether He is punishing the people for their sins and for how long they must continue to wander in search of their land.

"Iohanna, zhinka Khusova: Dramatychna poema" (Yohanna, Wife of Khusa: A Dramatic Poem, 1909) which is set in Galilee in the years following Christ's death, paints a more complex picture of the contest between Roman, Jewish, and Christian religion. The new Christians have renounced personal property, share everything in common, and have rejected patriarchal family customs, but Melokha, Khusa's mother, refuses to change her Jewish customs or to adapt to Roman hegemony. For her, the Romans will always be foreigners. The presentation of the Jewish situation is considerably nuanced. Jews are portrayed as having three choices: uncompromising resistance (Melokha's position), accommodation to power with a renunciation of one's traditions and values (Khusa's position), and adoption of Christianity (Yohanna's position). Ukrainka does not suggest that Khusa's position would be an improvement for contemporary Jews. According to one critic, the author's purpose was to indicate "two souls" in the Jewish people, the assimilationist and the defiant. Although sympathizing with the latter, the poet does not portray Khusa's assimilationism as simply a capitulation to authoritarianism or the product of power hunger. His actions are conditioned partly by personal weakness—especially the love of material possessions, comforts, and power—and partly by the pressure of political circumstances. (Laslo-Kutsiuk 1987, 228.) It is significant that Ukrainka explores the connection between the two faiths and sees the origins of Christianity in Judaism. Her use of biblical themes often produces a seamless fusion of Ukrainian and Jewish issues, so much so that in her plays *Oderzhyma* (Possessed), *Vavilon-s'kyi polon*, and *Na ruinakh*, it becomes impossible to separate the two. She admitted that she "liked Jewish themes, because there is always much of the turbulent, passionate element in them." (Ukrainka 1979, 55.) They also offered the possibility of an anti-imperial voice.

A number of lesser writers exploited biblical themes in a similar fashion. Mykola Cherniavsky, for example, also turned to the prophet Jeremiah. In his poems "Koly, iak vil, Izrail' spynu hnuv" (When, Like an Ox, Israel Bent Its Back, 1889) and "Iak iudeievi v zemli obitovanii" (Like a Jew in the Promised Land, 1908) he draws parallels between the Babylonian captivity and Ukraine's contemporary situation. Nonetheless, Ukrainka was unique in her passionate messianism, her focus on the need for a savior, and on the redemptive power of language. These features of her work owe much to her reading of the Old Testament. They would find their strongest resonance a century later in the poetry of Moisei Fishbein.

At a deeper level, her plays communicate troubling messages. Her brilliant *Lisova pisnia* (Forest Song, 1911) depicts a peasant community that is focused on practical tasks, hostile to art, and uncaring toward its own intelligentsia. It is, in the words of one critic, "incapable of valuing its prophets and poets." (Aheieva 1999, 8.) In this regard, her work can be seen as a polemic with Franko's "stone-mason" image of the writer: the stonemason's fingers, calloused with hard work, are unable to produce harmonious sounds on the cittern, just as the practical-minded Lukash in *Lisova pisnia* forgets how to play on the flute. Ukrainka was one of the first to reject the paradigm—dominant since Shevchenko—of the writer standing guard over the poor peasant hearth. (Ibid.) In *Lisova pisnia* she raises some uncomfortable truths, emphasizing, society's guilt, heartlessness, and cravenness in the face of oppression. This deeper message, which also draws on biblical images of the outcast and the oppressed, was often unpalatable to, or went unrecognized by populist-minded readers.

The second category of writings, depictions of Jews in modern history, was taken up by dramatists. In 1881 the Russian government had granted Ukrainians permission to create traveling theaters. It was almost the only form of cultural expression allowed them within the empire. Since the very presence of the Ukrainian language and culture was considered threatening by tsarist authorities, these theaters were banned from performing in the city of Kyiv and a number of regions, although, ironically, they could perform in St. Petersburg and Moscow. They were restricted in the topics they could depict: satires, histories, plays of middle-class life, and romantic verse plays were not allowed. They were instructed that middle- and upper-class characters were to speak Russian, and that a Ukrainian play could only be staged if a Russian one of the same length had preceded it on the same night. (Makaryk 2004, 10.) The theater was to depict Ukrainian as a folk culture, to include some burlesque element and a few folk songs. In spite of these restrictions, the Ukrainian "theatre of the *coryphaei*" (theatre of the star actors) became a very important cultural medium and an expression of the community's values. Characters and scenes from village and small-town life allowed audiences to recognize themselves and reflect upon their lives. Among the *coryphaei* were the playwrights Mykhailo Starytsky and Marko Kropyvnytsky; the actress Maria Zankovetska; and the three Tobilevych brothers, who went by their stage names: Ivan Karpenko-Kary, Mykola Sadovsky, and Panas Saksahansky. The theater historian Dmytro Antonovych has written: "In the eighties and nineties the number of amateur Ukrainian groups grew incredibly. In almost every county town, of whatever size, there were groups of amateur actors, and [they could be found] even in small towns, large villages, sugar beet factories, and other industrial plants, in railway junctions and so on. . . . In the sad reactionary times of the eighties and nineties, the Ukrainian stage was almost the only way to gather the Ukrainian community and to give its activities an external expression." (Antonovych 1925, 170.) In Kyiv, there were underground theatre groups that performed in people's homes. The draconian restrictions that had been imposed by the Ems Ukase of 1876 were finally lifted in 1905 and Mykola Sadovsky established the first permanent Ukrainian theater in Kyiv in 1907.

The theater troupes developed a melodramatic style known as "ethnographic realism," with a focus on strong contrasts and social injustice. The features of melodrama have been described by Makaryk: "Its dependence for action upon external pressures and adversaries (an evil-doer, a social group, a hostile ideology, an accident) necessitates its resort to extremity of incident, consequences, and solution. Tending toward the moralistic, it publicly acknowledges virtue and punishes (or converts) villainy. Of necessity entailing the conflict between clearly opposing sides usually represented by "whole" characters incapable of development (though conversion is possible), melodrama at its best reaches toward the archetypal. Intent not on ambiguity, ambivalence, plurality, or polysemy, it depends upon boldly stated oppositions between light and darkness, good and evil." (Makaryk 2004, 15.)

Within the possibilities of this genre, the plays are an exercise in autoethnography: they provide a description of Ukrainian life that engages with the way it is imagined by the audience. This is evident in, among other things, the evolving portrayal of Jewish characters. Starytsky's plays gradually move away from stock figures like the tavernkeeper or the orendar. An early play, *Ne sudylos' (Panske boloto)* (It was Not Fated: The Lord's Mire, 1883), which is set in the 1860s, contains a typically negative picture of an orendar who is in league with the landowner and favors employing ruthless tactics toward the peasantry. However, the later play *Iurko Dovbysh* (Yurko Dovbush, 1888, 1910), which depicts the legendary outlaw, already portrays a Jewish tavernkeeping family with great sympathy. Not only does much of the action take place in the tavern, but the old Jew himself, his son Yudko, and his daughter Rakhil are friends and allies of this Ukrainian Robin Hood. Yudko joins the outlaws in order to avenge his sister, who has been captured and abused by a local landlord. Starytsky is here deliberately drawing on the Ukrainian and Hasidic folklore that links Dovbush and the Baal Shem Tov, the founder of Hasidism, in a friendly relationship.

In his Russian-language novel about the haidamaka uprising of 1768, *Poslednie orly* (Last Eagles, 1901; translated into Ukrainian as *Ostanni orly*, 1968) Starytsky portrays an orendar offering a defense of his unhappy situation. He complains that he is forced by the lords to squeeze the peasants and thereby bring hatred and violence upon himself. The Polish lords, who have risen up against their king and formed the Confederacy of Bar, "are going back to their old ways, doing the dirty work with our hands: they give us—nay force on us—the leasing of peasant roads, bridges . . . immediately fleece us of ducats, . . . gold, and insist that we fleece the naked peasant. If we fail to give the lord his due, he immediately reaches for his sword and rope; if we fleece the peasant, the haidamaka goes for his knife and lance." (Staryts'kyi 1968, 127.)

There are significant nuances in the presentation of villains. In Karpenko-Kary's play *Bondarivna* (1886), which is set in the seventeenth century, the orendar Mordokhai is a negative character who serves the lord and the gentry, but he despises them and acts unwillingly. It is worth noting, that, although captured and exposed, he is not punished. It is clear to the spectator that he is not the real culprit, nor even a willing accomplice. The subject of the seventeenth- and eighteenth-century Cossack-Jewish conflicts and their bloody outcomes, an obstacle to any rapprochement, is largely avoided in writings of this period. If alluded to, it is viewed as a tragedy that has produced a barrier between two nations who share much common history.

In late nineteenth-century Ukrainian literature this attempt to characterize Jews with sympathy and to move beyond ingrained images of mutual antagonism was not an uncommon feature. It is, for example, the subject of Pavlo Hrabovsky's "Narodu ievreis'komu" (To the Jewish People, 1894):

> O nation ever divided against me
> In shameful human hostility!
> The lost traveler stands between us as a barrier;
> The signs of savagery have still not been erased.
>
> So the Cossack hung "the Jew" without sympathy,
> And "the Jew" wished no good to the Cossack . . .
> Those days come to mind with disgust;
> Let's forget that bitter past!
>
> I will remain foreign to you in blood;
> [But] constantly will carry in my heart
> A sacred feeling of great love,
> Which no one will again extinguish. (Hrabovs'kyi 1964, 41)

The third category of writings, the depiction of contemporary relations, was taken up by many writers. Starytsky's later plays, for example, are usually set in the present and often include Jewish characters in minor roles, like the old Jewess in *Rozbyte sertse* (Broken Heart, 1891) who lends money and rents rooms, Moshka Shpihel the tavernkeeper and his wife Ryvka in *U temriavi* (In the Dark,

1893), and Avram Yurkovych, the ingratiating young newspaper reporter in *Talan* (Destiny, 1894). These portrayals are far more nuanced than earlier ones and allow for greater depth in the presentation of character. Although not always admirable in their behavior, Jewish characters are shown to be sensitive to and dependent on community politics and public opinion. *Talan* was also the only drama depicting the life of the intelligentsia allowed by the censors.

The 1890s witnessed a drive to fashion a high culture out of national forms. Major operatic works like *Taras Bul'ba* were produced by Mykola Lysenko, Starytsky's cousin and brother-in-law. Drama developed greater complexity in plot structure and characterization, and found ways of raising issues of national importance. These initiatives could often not be presented to the public because all Ukrainian publications, schools, and political parties were forbidden until 1905. The governor general of Kyiv, Podillia, and Volhynia, General Alexander Drenteln, who had been the tsar's chief of political police in the years 1883–88, retained the ban on any Ukrainian professional theater in these provinces, even though Ukrainian companies were welcomed in the two imperial capitals as charming ethnographic curiosities. When asked why Ukrainian theater was allowed in the imperial capitals and forbidden in Kyiv, he replied: "Because there it is only theater and here it is politics." (Antonovych 1925, 171.) In developing their panoramas of Ukrainian life, dramatists were sensitive to the Jewish presence. Some of the most popular plays, like Starytsky's *Iurko Dovbysh* and Ivan Tohobochny's [also Tohobichny, pseudonym of Ivan Shchoholiv] *Zhydivka-vykhrestka* (The Jewess-Convert, 1896, published 1909) successfully integrate Ukrainian and Jewish histories and viewpoints. They were probably designed to play simultaneously to Ukrainian and Jewish audiences. Some troupes of actors toured educational institutions, including Jewish yeshivas (higher religious schools) and needed plays that reached out to this public. And on a personal level, the victimization of Jews during pogroms weighed heavily on writers, who felt the need to respond. Karpenko-Kary in 1878 tried to change the law preventing poor Jewish children from attending schools for artisans, and during the 1881 pogrom in Elizavetgrad (today's Kirovohrad) he gave shelter to several Jewish families.

When, in the wake of the 1905 revolution, many of the censorship laws and restrictions were lifted, the opening of the first permanent Ukrainian theater in Kyiv in 1907 became "an event as significant to the history of Ukrainian culture and theater as Yeats's and Lady Gregory's creation of the Abbey Theater for the Irish or Stanislavsky's of the Moscow Art Theater for the Russian." (Makaryk 2004, 14.) Significantly, the theater immediately included in its repertoire plays by Jewish playwrights like Avraam Goldfaden, Sholem Asch, and Jacob Gordin. The latter's *Mirele Efros* and *Syritka Khasia* (Khasia the Orphan) were enormously successful. Another hit, Tohobochny's *Zhydivka-vykhrestka*, was performed numerous times both in Ukraine and abroad, including at least twenty-four times in Canada between 1913 and 1923.

This last play owed its success in part to the topical issue of converting and assimilating Jews, and in part to the sympathetic treatment of Jewish characters. Sara falls in love with Stepan, becomes a Christian, and marries him, breaking her father's heart by doing so. Both she and her father Leibe are much liked by the villagers. The depth of the father's suffering, which leads to his disowning her and losing his mind, is deeply tragic. Sara has, however, married a philanderer, who quickly returns to one of his previous loves. She changes back into the Jewish clothing in which she eloped, takes her baby, and returns to her father. After observing the unfaithful Stepan with his lover, she hangs herself. Her behavior toward others has been exemplary; she is loved and admired by all. The viewer is asked to consider Stepan's cruelty toward her and his destructive infatuation, which even, at one point, turns his mind to the idea of murdering his wife and baby. The story ridicules anti-Semitic gossip among village women, some of whom swear that during Sara's christening they saw with their own eyes steam rising from her "as though from a chimney" and accuse her of using charms to overcome Stepan. Sara, now christened Maria, complains: "An animal has more respect from people than I . . . an animal is pitied by its master, cared for, while I . . . (sighs). Why? What have I done to them? Did I cross them, did I ruin their fate? When I walk through the village, they laugh at me, avoid me as though I am cursed, despise me . . . for what? . . . Do I not have a soul, a heart like theirs? Even small children are taught to ridicule me! A sorceress they call me . . . What kind of sorceress am I?" (Tohobochnii 1922, 37.)

In spite of the fact that Sara is now a Christian, she is still identified as a Jewess and ostracized. Her fear is that her son will also fail to find acceptance. Although her mother-in-law and neighbors love her and are appalled by the behavior of Stepan and his lover Priska, they are unable to save her. The message appears to be directed both at those who hold prejudices, like the village women, and those who manipulate these prejudices to further their own immoral actions, like Stepan and Priska. Sara's conversion and death is a tragic loss to both the Ukrainian and Jewish communities.

Ukrainian writers in this period do not express concern with Jews becoming Christians. Converts are always motivated by personal love and can expect no material reward. On the contrary, conversion requires great courage and its failure is seen as tragic. The stress is on the self-sacrificing and honorable behavior of the convert, which only makes prejudices appear more ridiculous. Moreover, it is not the religious conversion that is the focus, but the move into a Ukrainian community. The "false conversion" theme of European tradition also occurred in Russian writing at this time. In Aleksei Pisemsky's play *Baal* (1873) a Jew converts to Orthodoxy in order to marry a Russian woman and accepts a fifty-ruble government payoff. In Mikhail Saltykov-Shchedrin's *Sovremennaia idillia* (A Contemporary Idyll, 1883) a Jew plans to convert so as to obtain a residence permit. It was government policy that Jewish converts receive thirty rubles, a practice that was referred to as "the law of the thirty pieces of silver." This law in fact created a scenario that cast the Jewish convert as a Judas, who had been paid in silver to betray Christ. (Safran 2000b, 113.) When the *vykhrest*, or convert, theme appears in Ukrainian plays, its focus is never on fear of the assimilated, but always on the tragic personal situation of the convert. Nor is there any suggestion in these plays that Jews should be converted or that Judaism has outlived its time, which Safran describes as "a commonplace of both Christian apologetics and Romantic historiography since Hegel." (Ibid., 183.) The Ukrainian dramas played in small towns to both Ukrainian and Jewish audiences—an entirely different context from that in which Russian literature was produced. Viewers would have found foreign and unacceptable the idea of Jews or Judaism as condemned to extinction.

Starytsky's *Iurko Dovbysh* and Tohobochny's *Zhydivka-Vykhrestka* give convincing portrayals of Jewish character. The attraction to the details of Jewish culture in these dramas implies an acceptance of cultural diversity. There is no play with mispronounced words or a faulty grasp of language; the Jewish characters are fluent in Ukrainian. They live side by side with Ukrainians as full members of the community—known, respected, and accepted. No cultural foreignness is emphasized, although a cultural specificity is recognized. Jews have their own religion and rituals, their own food, interiors, clothing, and view of the world. It is precisely because Ukrainians know their Jewish neighbors well, that the tragedy of Jewish suffering and the need to avenge or alleviate it is felt so strongly by the other characters.

It was also Sadovsky's theater that staged the Russian writer Evgenii Chirikov's *Evrei* (Jews) in Ukrainian translation with the great Maria Zankovetska playing the role of Leia to universal acclaim. Sadovsky prepared the play for his opening 1907 season in Kyiv, but the police banned it because the message was directed against Russian chauvinism. It was only shown in later seasons. The staging nonetheless served an important role in Ukrainian theatrical history: it was seen as a bold civic act aimed at checking the growth of anti-Semitism and responding to the recent 1905 pogroms. It also had an important influence on the development of two future directors, Les Kurbas and Hnat Yura. The Ukrainian translation, published in 1907, contained an introduction written by the journalist Symon Petliura. Petliura's philo-Semitic views, a characteristic trait of the Ukrainian intelligentsia in this period, are well documented. Moisei Rafes, a leader of the Bund, wrote that "one of Petliura's favorite ideas was always the creation of an alliance of the Ukrainian and Jewish democracies. Placing the Jewish intelligentsia and merchant class in the service of the Ukrainian state would secure 'independence.'" (Rafes 1920, 133.) In his introduction to the play Petliura wrote: "The suffering of Nachman in Chirikov's *Evrei* will evoke profound sympathy in everyone, regardless of whether they belong to this nation whose historical destiny has been to carry the heavy cross of oppression and violence." (Petliura 1907, xvi) At this time Petliura was editor of the Kyiv weekly newspaper *Slovo* (Word) and printed an article by Yakov Munt exposing the chauvinism and anti-Semitic views of some authors in the newspapers *Rada* (Council) and *Ridnyi krai* (Native Land). (Khonigsman and Naiman 1992, 149.)

There were close organizational, personal, and artistic ties between Kyiv's Ukrainian theater and its Jewish theaters, which before 1905 were also refused permanent facilities and had restrictions placed upon them. In the Yiddish theater, Sadovsky found melodramatic plays with topical social conflicts that could help him make the transition from village to urban settings and from sentimental realism to a more intense exploration of psychology. The city's growing Jewish population was pleased to visit his theater to see its favorite classics, while Sadovsky was pleased with the packed audiences that assured financial stability. (Veselovs'ka 1998, 178.) The Jewish plays had, in some cases, already been successful in cities like Berlin, St. Petersburg, and Moscow, and were therefore a safe bet. Indeed, Sadovsky's Ukrainian productions of these plays received enthusiastic reviews. His actors were first class, and he often employed a large number of Jewish musicians, a fact that led to problems when the troupe toured and these musicians were not able to leave the Pale. Goldfaden's *Sulamif*, for example, was a major production, a recreation of the panoply of Jewish culture, with folkloric traditions, music, and dance. It played continually during the years 1910–12. Gordin and Goldfaden were themselves from small Ukrainian towns, a world that Sadovsky knew well and could evoke charmingly.

Karpenko Kary's plays also frequently depict Jews. Maiufes is the factor, or broker, in *Khaziai* (Owners, 1900); Hershko is simply identified as a Jew in

Burlaky (Vagabonds, 1895); Leiba is the tavernkeeper in *Rozumnyi i duren* (The Wise Man and the Fool, 1897); Borokh, Rukhlia, and their son Yankel have slightly larger roles as the heroine's employers in *Naimychka* (The Servant Girl, 1897); Moshko is the tavernkeeper in *Bat'kova kazka (Hrikh i pokaiannia)* (Father's Story, or Sin and Contrition, 1893). In *Sto tysiach* (A Hundred Thousand, 1891) an anonymous character (identified only as Nevidomyi: literally Unknown) is a typical Jewish *luftmensh* (a man of no definite occupation) who makes a living deceiving provincials. Before disappearing from the village, he pays the peasant Herasym Kalyta with forged banknotes, driving the latter to suicide. A number of the Jewish characters are concerned with making money, though not necessarily unscrupulously. The significant point is that in almost all cases they are portrayed as members of a tightly knit village or small-town community. When a character is portrayed entirely unsympathetically, as in the case of Nevidomyi, he represents an outsider who has briefly wandered into the local circle. More often than not, the Jewish characters are vulnerable members of one and the same Ukrainian society. The tavernkeeper, for example, is sometimes portrayed as simply a man doing his job, stoically serving alcohol to a rowdy, insolent, and rather foolish clientele. The tavernkeepers depicted in these plays are significantly different from the ones presented in the earlier works of Nechui-Levytsky, where they tend to be held responsible for the deliberate spread of alcoholism or the cynical pursuit of profit. Ukrainian plays of the late nineteenth century discredit this stereotype more often than they reproduce it.

A third playwright, Marko Kropyvnytsky, produced *Hlytai abozh Pavuk* (The Shark or the Spider, 1882) which contains a very minor role for Yudko, the inevitable tavernkeeper. Here, too, the figure is not a villain. When the play was republished in Soviet times (Kharkiv: Rukh, 1923) his name was dropped and *shynkar* (tavernkeeper) substituted. The 1937 and 1959 editions also drop the character's name and retain *shynkar*, and even in the 1961 edition the words "zhyde Yudko" (Jew Yudko) are changed to "kliatyi Yudko" (damned Yudko). The censors appear to have feared recognizing the character's Jewish identity. The cuts were only restored in later editions. In a later play, *Olesia* (1891), Kropyvnytsky introduces two visiting Jewish merchants, Shlomo and Hershko, who speak with accents—an indication that they are interlopers visiting the village to try and make a fast profit. However, the dramatist was moving away from these stock characters. The ruthless exploiter in the first play, the *hlytai*, is, in fact, a local Ukrainian; the two merchants in the second play do not make any profit, nor do they do anything dishonest. In both dramas, the Jewish characters argue their point of view convincingly and behave with considerable dignity. In this way the plays largely ignore the tradition of the Jew as unscrupulous merchant.

Western Ukraine

According to Hrytsak, a literature infused with the ideology of modern anti-Semitism first appeared in Lviv in 1879 in a Polish text (Teofil Merunowicz's *O metodzie i celach rozpraw nad kwestią żydowską*), and in Berlin in a similar German text (Wilhelm Marr, *Der Weg zum Siege des Germanenthums über das Judentum*). (Hrytsak 2006, 343.) Gradually this ideology would manifest itself in all aspects of public life, notably in the Polish National Democratic Party. Ukrainian leaders like Stepan Kachala, a leader of the populists, and Ivan Naumovych, a member of the russophile tendency, also expressed in print their fears that Jews were using unfair means to buy up Ukrainian lands or leading the local population into drunkenness. (Ibid.) But these statements have to be set against the fact that Jewish and Ukrainian parties cooperated in the election of 1873, and continued to do so as Polish nationalism developed. In 1907, Yulian Romachuk, a Ukrainian deputy in the Viennese parliament, called for the recognition of the Jews as a separate nation.

The popular theater of Western Ukraine in this period, which reached into all villages and small towns, often reflected this kind of negative image of Jews. Melodramas were generally written by lesser-known writers who tried to reflect what they thought were popular attitudes, and to respond to topical issues. The plot of I. Mydlovsky's *Kapral Tymko abo scho nas hubyt'?* (Corporal Tymko or What Causes Our Ruin? 1910) deals with the rivalry of two Ukrainian soldiers in the Austrian army for the hand of a village girl. The orendar Hershko counsels the unscrupulous and unworthy suitor Tymko to throw the suspicion of theft onto his competitor. Hershko also draws Olia's alcoholic father into his power, getting him to sell his house for money to buy alcohol. At the play's end, these machinations are exposed. Another popular play, Izydor Trembytsky's *Its'ko-Svat* (Itsko the Matchmaker, 1915), focuses on the manipulations of the village orendar Itsko's attempts to make some money by aiding two suitors to get their girl. One offers him rams, the other geese to act as a go-between and matchmaker. The melodramatic farce ends with the arrival of the girl's true love and the failure of the two suitors and their matchmaker. In both plays the Jew is a comic meddler, but here too he is an integral part of village life, an indispensable ally and go-between in various negotiations and dealings, shady or otherwise. In

Petro Fedysiv's *Selo Tyndrykivka* (The Village of Tyndrykivka, 1903), the second of three acts is set in the tavern, where a Jewish family that includes two orendars meets to discuss the community boycott from which the tavern and other businesses are suffering. The boycott has been initiated by the village priest, who is campaigning against alcoholism. During a meeting of the village council, which is also being held in the same tavern, the innkeeper gets the entire council drunk in spite of his promise to the hero not to serve liquor. It soon becomes apparent that the head of the council has been neglecting his duties, which include repairing the roads, mainly due to his fondness for alcohol. The tavern's competition is the reading club, where peasants can discuss the newspaper and other publications. It is to the reading club that the council head is brought after he nearly drowns in an enormous mud hole by an unrepaired road. Chastened by this experience, he vows to avoid liquor, fix the road, and let someone else take over the village headship.

The Jews in these portrayals have to be distinguished from earlier depictions, in which they hold the power to punish or deny church services. Here, they are not cast as the threatening other; they are neither foreign spies, nor haters of Christians, nor Christ-killers. Such characterizations do not appear in the literature, and only extremely rarely in overt propaganda. One pamphlet, translated from the Polish and entitled *Vichnyi Zhyd rodom iz Ierusalyma imenem Ahasverii* (The Eternal Jew born in Jerusalem and called Ahasuerus, 1909) went through numerous editions (six by 1909). It tells the tale of the Jew who refused Christ a resting place and has since been punished by living eternally while being driven from country to country. According to the pamphlet, he has been sighted in various European cities throughout the centuries. The second chapter lists the sins against Christ committed by each of the twelve Jewish tribes and the punishment their descendants must suffer as a consequence. It is an unsophisticated brochure aimed at a naïve, gullible audience, and appears to have been inspired by the Catholic Church. The introduction says that the translation has been made for villagers who do not read or understand Polish but who need to hear of "God's wonderful deeds." (*Vichnyi Zhyd rodom iz Ierusalyma imenem Ahasverii* 1907, 3.) Ukrainian literature demonstrates no animus against religious "superstitions" in favor of the secular ideals of progress and education. Most writings of this period accept the place of Jews in the Ukrainian world, and show an implicit understanding that the Jewish and Christian faiths and cultures coexist. However, the recurring figures of the orendar and the tavernkeeper bear witness to a tension that exists over the Jewish role in the economy.

Western Ukrainian writers from this period often supported civil rights for

Jews, and their full autonomy in cultural and educational life. Drahomanov was a key influence, notwithstanding what has been described as his inclination "to speak in much too sweeping terms about 'Jewish parasitism' despite occasional attempts to qualify his judgement." (Rudnytsky 1987, 290.) His views were applied in Western Ukraine by Ivan Franko and Natalia Kobrynska. The latter was a leader of the women's movement. She married a Greek-Catholic (Uniate) clergyman, Teofil Kobrynsky, at the age of nineteen. After his death in 1882, she traveled to Vienna, became acquainted with some leading Ukrainian intellectuals, and devoted herself to improving the economic and social status of women. In 1884 she founded a literary society for women, and in 1887 edited and published in Lviv the first anthology of women's writing, *Pershyi vinok* (First Wreath, 1887). After attending lectures in political economy in Zurich and Geneva, she adopted some Marxist ideas. Throughout the nineties she published collections of women's writings in Galicia, and lobbied the government to allow women to attend universities.

Her literary work in the years 1882–93 can be described as populist and realist, although it shows a modernist interest in individual psychology. Kobrynska portrays women of various ages and classes, who are kept within the boundaries of the home and alienated from social life. In 1884 in a speech to the literary society she founded, she called for writings that could speak to women. Unless their literary tastes were cultivated, most women would remain fixated on material concerns and rituals, and would be unable to react adequately to changes in the world around them. In her stories she indicates the disadvantages of limiting one's intellectual horizons and shows the path to a richer interior life. But she did not conceive of feminism as an international sisterhood in which all subjects are the same. On the contrary, her prose recognizes the coexistence of different worlds.

Kobrynska knew Yiddish, and Jewish characters often appear in her stories, which are set in the small Western Ukrainian towns where Jews predominated. No obvious ideological messages are attached to the depictions; they have a calm, understated, matter-of-fact quality. In the story "Ianova" (Yanova, 1885) Jews make up most of the throng of people at a railway station, and one Jewish woman advises the main character on how best to obtain a ticket for the train. In "Vyborets'" (The Voter, 1889) during parliamentary elections some Jews attempt to influence voters by offering free sausage, bread, and head cheese while praising their candidate. A different candidate supports a teetotaling campaign which is in large part aimed against Jewish tavernkeepers. When the man promoted by the Jews fails to get elected, they quickly switch their support to the successful candidate. In "Iadzia i Katrusia" (Yadzia and Katrusia, 1890, rewritten 1893) a doctor visits the sick wife of the Jewish orendar Mendel. This is an occasion to exchange information about various business dealings and a mutual acquaintance. Jewish wagon drivers who transport people and goods between the villages and towns also figure in the story. They carry seasonal workers from outlying areas to the tobacco fields, and the ride provides occasion for some banter. But all ethnic-national descriptions are neutral: the difference in appearance and behavior of Bukovynian and Galician villagers is just as interesting and notable as are the manners of Jewish travelers. A Jewish foreman and a Jewish orendar who lends out seed grain at a high interest rate are mentioned, but this is done in a tone that accepts tension in any business or employer-labor interaction. Kobrynska's Jews either speak fluent Ukrainian, or the reader is notified that they speak Yiddish. There is no dialogue marked by accent.

The story "Zhydivs'ka dytyna" (The Jewish Child, 1890; also sometimes "Kupets'ka dytyna" (The Dealer's Child)) recounts the life of a poor Jewish girl who becomes fixated on saving money, buying cheaply, and living frugally. It is notable for being set almost entirely in a Jewish milieu and contains a couple of Yiddish songs, which not only reveal popular attitudes toward gentiles, who, according to the song, drink "because they are goys," but also toward those in their own community who are focused on gathering every scrap as possible material for trade or barter. The story shows the debilitating effects of poverty, and particularly the way in which it can kill an appreciation of beauty and a taste for life. The main figure, Hinda, finally succeeds in raising money to purchase an attractive hat. However, in doing so she behaves in an ungenerous manner toward her own mother, and her niggardliness causes her to lose respect in her own community. In the end she sells the hat, sacrificing personal grace and beauty of appearance for a meager financial profit. The final sentence "It was a good deal" is meant to be read ironically. Hinda's fixation on thrift and practicality leads to an atrophy of other qualities, especially human sympathy and generosity. Kobrynska's work shows an understanding of the impoverished social conditions in which many Jews lived, but she is also critical of individual behavior.

Ivan Franko

Franko is a key figure in any discussion of how Jews have been constructed in Ukrainian literature, both because of his stature as a writer and thinker, and because of the range of characters he presents. He did not idealize Ukrainian-Jewish relations, but continually cited ownership of land and industry, control of commerce, usury, and sale of alcohol as areas of conflict. Educated by the European socialist movement, he reflected its view of Jews. Marx, as has been seen, reduced Jewish culture to self-interest and expressed the fear that capitalism would somehow make non-Jews into "Jews." Eugen Dühring in his influential *Der Judenfrage* (The Jewish Question, 1881) considered the Jewish "race" immoral and a danger to European nations. The general view among liberals and socialists was that Jews embodied the spirit of capitalism, and the fear was that the "Jewish" economy would turn everyone into victims and victimizers, prostitutes and pimps, a perception only reinforced by the fact that many Jews maintained brothels and worked in them. (Safran 2000, 150, 152.) These views colored the anti-Semitism of otherwise "progressive" Russian writers like Nikolai Nekrasov and Mikhail Saltykov-Shchedrin, who produced negative portraits of the rich and exploitative Jew, although it should be noted that in 1882 the latter was stirred to respond to the pogrom wave with a moving article. The leading socialist thinkers were also biased against all small nations and their resistance to assimilation. Even the young Theodor Herzl as a student in Vienna saw the desire of small nationalities for self-assertion as reactionary, and considered it the duty of every liberal to combat it.

Franko's views have to be seen within this context. Yaroslav Hrytsak has written that his anti-Semitism was aimed at two groups: "Firstly, against rich and privileged Jews, who lived well at the expense of the misfortunes and backwardness of ordinary people, both Ukrainians and non-Ukrainians. Secondly, against those educated Jews who left their ghetto and willingly assimilated into the dominant German or Polish culture, and did not want to show solidarity with the thousands of their own poor, causing equal harm to the poor of other peoples. This kind of 'narrowly focused anti-Semitism' was expressed by Karl Marx, Victor Adler, the young Theodor Herzl, Sigmund Freud, and Ludwig Wittgenstein." (Hrytsak 2004b, 158–59.)

Ukrainian socialists and liberals differed from the European mainstream in one regard. Franko, like Drahomanov, saw that the assimilationist model would not work in Eastern Europe and that the concept of cultural autonomy should be embraced instead. The Ukrainian movement adopted this idea, and considered any intervention into internal Jewish affairs unacceptable. Political parties in Western Ukraine, like the Ukrainian Social Democratic Party (USDP) and the National Democratic Party (NDP), recognized the Jews as a nation and formed electoral alliances with them. By the turn of the century the view of Jews as a nation was strongly rooted in Western Ukraine—a departure from the views of Western or Russian socialists and liberals. However, like their Western and Rus-

sian counterparts, Ukrainian activists expected the Jewish community to gradually embrace reforms and undergo an internal transformation. In 1895, the
Ukrainian Radical Party, of which Franko was a leader, drew a distinction between upper- and lower-class Jews, condemning the former in the same terms as
it condemned Christian exploiters. This dualistic, class-based attitude marked
all Franko's works.

The Boryslav stories are evidence that Franko's portrayal of Jews changed as
his political views evolved. The Boryslav oil boom first figured in his work in
the years 1876–82, when he was active in the Galician socialist movement. By
the century's end, the town was the fourth biggest center of oil production in the
world. Its rapid growth appeared to follow the "classical" Marxist pattern, a fact
that Franko used in debates with ideological rivals among Galician socialists who
insisted that socialist theories were inapplicable to a poor, agrarian land like Galicia. (Hrytsak 2004a, 176.) For Franko, however, Boryslav proved that Galicia was
following the same evolution as the rest of Europe. He was so intent on making
reality fit theory, particularly Marx's ideas concerning the primitive accumulation of capital, that he described an organized labor movement that did not yet
exist and, in *Boryslav smiiet'sia* (Boryslav is Laughing, 1881–82), a worker's
strike that never occurred. In 1881, when Franko moved to the Boryslav area to
organize Polish, Jewish, and Ukrainian workers, he still believed in the subordination of national issues to a common working-class cause. *Boryslav smiiet'sia*
and the second edition of *Boa konstriktor* (Boa Constrictor, 1884), which is the
one usually translated, reflect this ideology. Herman Goldkremer in the latter
book is an archetypal early capitalist. But with the appearance of the third edition (1907), Goldkremer becomes a skilful entrepreneur who shows appropriate
concern for his workers. They, in turn, call him "our father and protector." The
explanation for this transformation, Hrytsak plausibly suggests, lies in Franko's
new ideology of the 1890s: his renunciation of his earlier socialism, and his em-
bracing of liberal nationalism and the idea of Ukrainian state independence.
Now the nation, not the working class was seen as the central agent of history.
(Ibid., 187.)

Such a perception of Franko's evolution is only partially correct. In some
ways his adherence to a "class line" became even more rigid. The 1881–82
pogroms in the Russian empire and his disappointments with Polish socialists,
who, in his opinion, placed their own national concerns ahead of the fair treatment of Ukrainians, forced him to recognize the strength of racial and religious
prejudices, and the power of nationalism. As a result, his views on eliminating
the root cause of evil—economic exploitation—hardened. He took a strong line

against exploiters of all nationalities, complaining among other things of the "demoralizing advantage of Jewish capital and exploitation." His suspicion of commercial interests even led him to suggest in an article in the Lviv newspaper *Dilo* entitled "Pytanie zhydovske" (The Jewish Question, 1883) that some Jewish businesses had provoked pogroms for profit because they were being well compensated for material losses by local governments and international relief organizations, and in 1884 he published the poem "Shvyndelesa Parkhenblyta vandrivka z sela Derykhlopy do Ameryky i nazad" (Shvyndeles Parkhenblyt's Journey from the Village of Derykhlop to America and Back, 1884), the story of a Jewish tavernkeeper who uses various tricks to keep his profits in a village that has sworn off alcohol.

In accord with this "class line," his literary works lay blame on all exploiters, such as the rapacious Goldkremer in the second edition of *Boa Constrictor*. And yet, this protagonist is also shown to be deeply unhappy, a victim of a feverish moneymaking obsession. He himself is being squeezed by the boa constrictor of capitalism as much as the exploited workers. The writer makes it clear that socioeconomic conditions are to blame for bringing out the worst in people. Much of the story is devoted to Goldkremer's deprived upbringing in a sordid slum in order to show how his grasping nature has been formed. Nonetheless, the reader also glimpses the protagonist's secret desire to change his life, and witnesses his inability to act upon this desire. In line with the tenets of naturalism, the grim, depressing reality of human and social degeneration is presented with "scientific" rigor, but the author also strains to show a way forward. The positive character is Itsyk, the good Jew who raises Herman and tries to educate him. Herman spends his happiest years living with Itsyk in the healthier surroundings of the countryside. This memory of a natural paradise continually draws him toward goodness. Although these features might not redeem the ideologically driven narrative for some readers, they do complicate the characterization of Herman and they shift the main burden of blame for social evil onto the capitalist system. In this Franko differs from some other writers who described conditions in Boryslav, such as the Poles Janusz Rogosz and Arthur Gruszacki and the Ukrainian Stefan Kovaliv, for whom Jewish capital was the main culprit. It is also worth mentioning Franko's resistance to the message that individuals are unchangeable. Although social and economic conditions determine the way in which most people live, protagonists still have individual choices to make. They carry responsibility for their actions. Goldkremer has chosen to disregard the voice of conscience, to assimilate into mainstream society, and to become part of the established machinery of exploitation. By contrast, another story set in Boryslav,

"Iats' Zelepuha" (Yats Zelepuha, 1887), introduces the reader to Yudko Lybak, a Jew whose behavior is both honorable and generous. Having done well in his own land speculation and oil exploration, he selflessly gives some of his profits to Zelepuha in the latter's time of need. Zelepuha, however, has been driven half-insane by the desire to strike it rich and, although he does make a fortune, soon loses it, along with his own life. The goal of enrichment completely devours both the grasping and scheming Zelepuha and Mendel, but not Yudko, for whom it is not an end in itself. Even though Franko became more sensitive to national issues in the nineties, he maintained the line between exploiter and exploited.

Jewish capital was present in Boryslav. In 1873 during the first oil rush, when ten to fifteen thousand wells were drilled, 779 small Jewish entrepreneurs were present and the largest paraffin works was a Jewish one, Gartenberg and Gold-hammer. However, when in the 1880s large-scale foreign capital entered the industry almost all these small enterprises were squeezed out. By 1890 there were fifty-nine large firms and thirty small ones. (Hrytsak 2006, 279, 282–83.) In 1884 an incident occurred in Boryslav in which Jewish property was destroyed and then, in retaliation for what was seen as an act of anti-Semitism, Christian residences were smashed by angry mobs. What triggered the violence remains a matter of dispute. The Polish newspapers initially reported it as a clash between a large French company and small local Jewish entrepreneurs. Since the French company was owned by Jewish capitalists, subsequent reports presented it as a clash inspired on both sides by competing bourgeois interests. (Ibid., 292–93.)

During his incarceration in 1889, Franko heard various stories from Jewish fellow prisoners, which he then reworked into the poetic cycle *Zhydivs'ki melodii* (Jewish Melodies, 1890) and the collection *Z vershyn i nyzyn* (From Highlands and Lowlands, 1893). Some poems portray Jewish hard-heartedness. For example, "Surka" tells the story of a poor, plain Jewish girl who works long hours by day and night in a tavern. She is made pregnant by the Jewish tavernkeeper Yudko, and loses her job. Initially he finds her a place at his grandmother's home, but she is soon homeless again with a child to care for. She leaves the infant as a foundling, but then, in an attack of guilt, changes her mind and returns to the house where she abandoned the infant. Here she is given shelter and nursed back to health by a kindly peasant woman, who chides her: "Why didn't you knock? We are not dogs, like that Yudko, but people." Another poem, "Po-liuds'ky" (Decently) depicts a Christianized Jew explaining how he used to serve the local duke in expectation of a reward. Seeing that the duke enjoyed beating peasants and watching their suffering, he made sure that they were all beaten every week. Seeing that the duke liked money, he invented new taxes. Understanding that the duke liked young women, he procured them. His judgment is that "our tribe" has lived for centuries in this land "sucking its blood . . . Like a leech without its own blood, we suck that of another." (Franko 1976–86, 1:244.) However, four of the eight poems in this cycle were not republished in Soviet times. Along with many other works on Jewish themes, they were even left out of the massive fifty-volume edition of Franko's works produced in the years 1976–86. The four poems omitted from this cycle are "Sambation" (which draws on the legend of David the tsar-liberator who comes to the help of the Jews, and which asserts the indestructibility of the Jewish spirit), "Pirrie" (Feathers) (which describes the destruction caused by the pogroms), "Asymiliatoram" (To the Assimilators), and "Zapovit Iakova" (Jacob's Testament). Each retells a song or tale heard from prisoners, reveals sympathy for Jewish suffering, and allows a Jewish voice to speak in its own words. At this time the writer produced stories like "Do svitla" (To the Light, 1889) that show compassion for Jewish suffering, and ones like "Hershko Goldmakher" (1891) that contain Jewish villains.

As Franko focused more on national consciousness, he had to align this new perspective with the complexities of socio-economic life. The Goldkremer of the second edition of *Boa Constrictor* still represents the acculturated Jewish businessman who is cut off from his own community and acts alone. Individual virtuous Jews who are victims of the exploitative system also act alone. But how were Jews and Ukrainians to get along as organized communities or nations? At the beginning of the twentieth century Franko's fiction begins to include Jewish protagonists who struggle to reconcile their community's development with that of the Ukrainian movement. These figures face the dilemmas of national identity. The literature of the Haskala had encouraged Jews to master secular knowledge and change their way of life. An acculturated Jew had already appeared in Polish literature as early as the 1850s, and had received sympathetic treatment in Boleslaw Prus's social novel *Lalka* (The Doll, 1890). However, unlike the situation in Germany, the Haskala movement on Ukrainian territory did not lead to mass assimilation or to mass conversions. In fact, some have argued, it ultimately led to a strengthening of Jewish national awareness and distinctiveness, because even those adherents of the Haskala who took an active part in the Ukrainian revolutionary movement, with few exceptions, did not cut ties with their own people. (Khonigsman and Naiman 1992, 65.) Jews, in other words, remained Jews and continued to work within their own communities. The issue was how to influence the Jewish Galician community as a whole in its attitude toward Ukrainians. What tensions were created when a pro-Ukrainian Jew appeared, one who was also a Westernizer and modernizer? This issue is explored by

Franko in ground-breaking works. Vahman in *Na perekhresnykh stezhkakh* (At the Crossroads, 1900) is particularly interesting because in many respects he represents a summation of the writer's ideas concerning the way forward for Jewish-Ukrainian relations. Some commentators have argued that Vahman's transformation from a usurer into a philanthropist is unconvincing and a failure of artistic taste, but others have maintained that in the context of Hasidism his generous attitude is credible. (Feller 2001, 47.) Vahman does not favor Jewish assimilation, nor does he turn a blind eye to the suffering and poverty of the Ukrainian people among whom he lives. His ideology is best presented in a discussion with an assimilationist Jewish mayor. Here Vahman argues that Jews, while remaining Jews, must become good citizens, which in Eastern Galicia means being sensitive to the needs of the majority Ukrainian population. As we have seen, this is a view that closely resembles the position argued at this time by Jabotinsky. Vahman, however, is subjected to a *herem*, a public ostracism, for defying the community's religious and social norms. The story ends with his departure from the shtetl, as required by the *herem*. In the end, the two communities remain alienated and distant. The required middleman, the enlightened Jewish reformer, has been removed.

Some time before publishing this novel, Franko wrote a polemical article on the Jewish question in Galicia, "Semityzm i antysemityzm w Galicji" (Semitism and Anti-Semitism in Galicia, 1887). In it he put forward his ideas concerning the future of the Jewish community. It is, for him, a distinct nationality with the right to an autonomous existence and religious freedom. However, the large Jewish population in Eastern Galicia displays a distorted social structure. Whereas in England merchants make up 5 or 6 percent of the population, in Galicia they make up 15 percent, of whom 90 percent are Jews. Sixty percent of industry and 90 percent of commerce are in their hands. Franko wants to see them become equal citizens with equal rights and duties, but this equal citizenship will be achieved only when they show "a feeling of solidarity" with the ideals of the Ukrainian people and "work for the realization of those ideals." He is for the full opening of society to the Jews, but he reminds them that "in many ways they hold a privileged position with respect to the great mass of the non-Jewish population." (Franko 1887, 442–43.) The influence of the kahals, the power to punish whoever they wish with a *herem*, their avoidance of certain regulations such as the recording of births, he sees as inimical to developing the required sense of common citizenship. The writer wishes to see equality and mutual understanding based on the same rules for all, and wants the Jewish community in Galicia to sympathize with the struggle of the Ukrainians. His frustration with the impasse between the two peoples leads him to suggest three possibilities for the Jews: voluntary assimilation, emigration to a country where they can "live and develop fully as a monolithic, self-determining people," and remaining in Galicia "with the rights of foreigners." (Ibid., 434.) This view was influenced by the mass emigration of Jews that began after 1880 and also by the growth of the Zionist movement. In fact, it has been pointed out that these views are simply a repetition of those advanced by Alfred Nossig, a Polish Jew who moved from assimilationism to Zionism and wrote a series of articles in 1886–87 that were widely discussed. (Hrytsak 2006, 354–59.) Franko's position is also in many ways a mirror image of the views expressed by the Polish writer Eliza Orzeszkowa. Like her, he is disturbed by the fact that when Jews do choose cultural assimilation, it is to the dominant power, and they become indifferent to the struggles of the dominated.

Nonetheless, in spite of the views expressed in this article, Franko's literary works make it clear that for him the solution was neither assimilation nor flight, but a recognition of Ukrainian aspirations. Some forces that resist Vahman's pro-Ukrainian stance are to be found in the traditional Jewish community. They are criticized not for their refusal to acculturate or assimilate, but for their refusal to reach out to another group. The issue is blindness to the socio-political demands of the surrounding population. Traditionalist fanaticism, something that contributes to the Jewish community's cohesiveness and strength, prevents it from seeing the Ukrainian national movement. Vahman's personal attempt to reach out to non-Jewish communities and then to explain this gesture to Jewish traditionalists is misunderstood and rejected. Franko displays the same ambivalence toward the Jewish tradition that was typical of much Haskala literature, which admired the tradition's spiritual and moral strength but criticized the harmful effects of its conservatism, showed sympathy for Hasidic piety but feared obscurantism crushing the individual.

A similar message is carried by *Petrii i Dovbushchuky* (Petrii and the Dovbushchuks, first version 1875, second version 1912). In the second version Isak Bliaiberg witnesses the growth of a dull hatred toward Jews in the mass of the population and tries to work toward reconciliation and cooperation between the two communities. He himself used to be a young orendar, but a poor one, and was attacked by criminals who were convinced that he was hiding a fortune. Rescued by Kyrylo Petrii, he is now on close terms with the latter. Bliaiberg has given up being an orendar and is thinking about how to improve Jewish-Ukrainian relations. In a conversation with Kyrylo, he says that he has tried to follow a path that no other Jew has traveled "in our country," where there are far more

Jews than in other lands: "I went to other countries deliberately to learn their life and attitudes toward Christians. You know, Kyrylo, things are different there in many ways. There a Jew is a citizen, like everyone else, but here he is a leech, who sucks the whole people! . . . Usury, drunkenness, deception, these are the sores that they bring and that weaken the people. And, besides that, how contemptuously they look upon the goys!" (Franko 1976–86, 22:398.)

Both companions reach the conclusion that spiritual change and economic reforms are required to overcome racial and class prejudices. Isak travels the country propounding a closer union between Jews and the local people, along the lines of what he has witnessed in Germany. He objects to the idea that there should be no morality in economic and commercial life (suggested by the phrase "business is business!") Instead he calls for introducing "fairness and good works" into practical life. (Ibid., 461.) A group of Jewish fanatics, however, drag him out of a meeting and publicly reprimand him. Bound, he is driven off in a cart and plays no further role in the story.

Bliaiberg's fate appears to be another pessimistic commentary on the impossibility of pro-Ukrainian advocates appearing within the Jewish community. Nonetheless, the idea of Jewish-Ukrainian cooperation has been recorded in the legends of Oleksa Dovbush's contacts with the Baal Shem Tov. The reader discovers that Kyrylo Petrii is Dovbush's descendant and knows where the famous outlaw's treasure is buried. He wishes to use this wealth for the education and social improvement of his people. His cousins, however, claim the treasure is their birthright and are prepared to go to any lengths, including torturing Kyrylo, to discover its hiding place. Kyrylo therefore finds himself in a similar situation to that of the former orendar: he is hated and envied because people think he owns wealth that they covet or think is rightfully theirs. When his efforts at reaching a mutual understanding are rejected, both he and his son are attacked with the same brutal violence that earlier had been unleashed on Bliaiberg. This identity confusion is quite explicit in the first version of the story, where it is revealed that Bliaiberg is also the son of Dovbush. His mother died in a tavern while escaping with her child from pursuers, and the tavernkeeper, whose name was Bliaiberg, then raised the child. (Franko 1976–86, 14:175.) Kyrylo Petrii and Bliaiberg are therefore brothers, and suffer similar fates: both try to spread enlightenment and agitate for social progress, and both meet with violent opposition from their communities.

Franko's message was a call to end exploitation, deceit, and violence. He admired the moral strictness of Jewish law, and the appeals in both Judaism and Christianity to the values of compassion, kindness, and fairness. It is precisely the neglect of these values among Jews and Christians that he admonishes against, particularly the elevation of profit-making over public spiritedness and community solidarity. Although a quixotic hope is held out for future understanding between Jews and Ukrainians, his fiction invariably illustrates the difficulties barring the way to this hope's realization. On the one hand, a significant portion of the Jewish community finds itself in an exploitative relationship with Ukrainians, while, on the other hand, many Ukrainians are ruled by prejudice, ignorance, and violence. These problems bar the way to harmony and social improvement.

In the final analysis, Franko's works produce a dualistic image of Jews, who are assigned the virtues of dignity, pride, and endurance, but are also condemned as disorganizers of the Ukrainian community. Individual Jews can be friends and political allies, thus furthering the dream of national and social emancipation, or they can align themselves with the class of exploiters. Late in life, Franko produced a cycle of nine poems entitled "Iz knyhy Kaaf" (From the Book of Kaaf), which was published in his collection *Semper Tiro* (1906). Here he drew on his admiration for the strength of Jewish faith. The original *Book of Kaaf* was written in the fourteenth or fifteenth century probably on the territory of today's Ukraine. Two versions have been found in Western Ukraine and two in northern Russia. (Mnykh 2000, 114.) Composed of seventy questions and answers, the text interprets the first five books of the Old Testament. It is generally seen as a polemic with the Jews and a reflection of the debate with the *zhydovstvuiuchi* (Judaizers), who were a force in the intellectual life of Kyivan Rus and were challenged by Christian writers, and it is considered one of the best examples of the attitude toward Jews held by Rus polemicists: combative, but not as dismissive as the stance toward the Catholics. Franko discovered the *Book of Kaaf* and published it. Although conceding that it might have been written by a Greek who had learned Church Slavic, he though it more probable that it was one of the earliest expressions of the Ukrainian-Jewish discourse. (Franko 1976–86, 38:24–25.) He took the book's title for his own cycle of poems, because at the time of writing it he was struggling with the issue of religious faith and national identity. Franko describes the debate he is holding with himself at the end of his life. He struggles with the issue of faith, both in the religious sense and in the sense of belief in the nation's future. As in *Moisei* (Moses), written shortly after this cycle, he meditates on the importance of belief for a poet and leader. The first poem informs the reader, somewhat evasively, that Kaaf is the name of a plant that can drive away doubt and restore courage and confidence. The writer then offers instructions to poets: to search for truth in their own souls, to be humane in dealing with others, not to expect understanding and mercy from the crowd, to search for love wherever it can be found, to listen to one's heart. The last and longest poem is entitled "Strashnyi sud" (Last Judgment). In it the writer imagines his conversation with God at the gates of heaven. He presents himself as he is, with all his "criticism and skepticism." The Lord accepts him, over the protests of priests and bishops. After listening to these church elders, the narrator expresses a desire to take his place alongside the freedom-loving philosophers, heretics, revolutionaries, and haidamakas in hell. God intervenes to assure him that his work on earth was done in accordance with His divine will. The narrator suddenly understands that all along he has worked to accomplish God's plan. It appears therefore that both the Rus scribe and Franko were inspired by the strength of Jewish faith, and appropriated this strength for their own convictions. In the case of the scribe, this conviction was focused on showing that the New Testament had superseded the Old. In Franko's case, it was a question of defending political convictions that had guided his entire life.

Some readers have accused Franko of anti-Semitism (or praised him for it), drawing particular attention to the poem "Shvyndeles Parkhenblyt," or to the articles "Pytanie zhydovske" and "Semityzm i antysemityzm." A fuller examination of Franko's career reveals a number of complexities and a definitive analysis of his writings on the Jews is still to be written. Some intriguing questions remain to be answered. Do, for example, the endings of *Na perekhresnykh stezhkakh* or of *Petrii y Dovbushchuky* suggest that the time is not ripe for a Jewish-Ukrainian rapprochement, or rather that it is an altogether quixotic project? Is the writer criticizing only the most fanatical opposition to change, or the most traditional ways? Among contemporaries, insightful answers to these questions, based on a thoughtful reading of his works, were in short supply. The texts themselves indicate that their author was conflicted; he partly supported the idea of the Jewish hero's acculturation to gentile society as demanded by reason, science, and justice, but partly resisted cultural assimilation on principle. In the end, he was left with the idea of two self-sustaining and mutually supportive communities that were traveling together along the road to self-determination. Given the weak political preconditions in his day for the realization of such a vision, it is not surprising that he had trouble articulating it with any degree of optimism. Vahman and Bliaiberg are whisked away by a conservative and xenophobic community that reaffirms its claims to its native sons. The new type of liberated, modernizing, and pro-Ukrainian Jew can only appear in the future; he will share with Ukrainians a fellowship based on intellectual equality, freedom of expression, and nonexploitative relations. Jews should not give up their religion or identity, but they should play a different economic and political role. Through Franko's works this new dream of intercommunity dynamics entered Ukrainian literature.

The First Jewish Voice: Hryts Kernerenko

At this juncture a Jewish voice emerged within Ukrainian literature. Hryts Kernerenko (Grigorii, Hryhorii, or Hirsch Kerner) was one of the first Jewish authors to write in Ukrainian and perhaps best represents the generation of Jewish intellectuals who in the 1880s met their Ukrainian counterparts "at the crossroads"—to use the title of Franko's novel—and opened a dialogue with them. This was a pioneering group that assumed a Ukrainian identity, and forged the rapprochement that eventually, in 1917, resulted in the declaration of Jewish autonomy by the Ukrainian National Republic.

Born in 1863 into an affluent family in Huliai-Pole, Kernerenko completed his university studies in Munich, traveled throughout Italy and Austria in 1883, and then returned to help manage the family estate, which included an agricultural machinery factory, a liquor plant, a large store, and five hundred hectares of land leased to German colonists. A Ukrainophile with a large library, he began publishing in the 1880s and authored four books of poetry: *Nevelychkyi zbirnyk tvoriv Hryts'ka Kernerenka* (A Small Collection of Works by Hrytsko Kernerenko, 1890), *Shchetynnyk* (The Fleece Buyer 1891), *V dosuzhyi chas* (In Leisure Time, 1896), and *Menty nadkhnennia* (Moments of Inspiration, 1910). He also wrote one story *Pravdyva kazka* (True Story, 1886 and 1890), and a play entitled "Khto pravdy vkryvaie—toho Boh karaie, abo Liubov syloiu ne viz'mesh" (God Punishes Whoever Conceals the Truth, or Love Cannot Be Forced), which deals with conscription in the reign of Nicholas I. This last work was banned by the censor because of its depiction of corrupt administrators and appalling prison conditions, particularly for women inmates. (Petrovsky-Shtern 2005, 212.) Kernerenko's lyrics appeared in all the leading anthologies of his day: Ivan Franko's *Akordy* (Chords, 1903), Oleksa Kovalenko's *Ukrains'kyi deklamator* (The Ukrainian Declaimer, 1905 and 1908) and *Ukrains'ka muza* (Ukrainian Muse, 1908), and Bohdan Lepky's *Struny* (Strings, 1922). He also published translations of Heine, Sholom Aleichem, and Semen Nadson. From 1900, he corresponded with Franko, who published his verse in *Literaturno-naukovyi vistnyk* (Literary and Scientific Herald), the most important periodical of the day, which began appearing in Lviv in 1898.

Kernerenko's lyrics often deal with love and loneliness. Pavlo Hrabovsky, under the mistaken impression that Kernerenko subscribed to the ideal of "art for art's sake" and avoided social issues, attacked him in an essay entitled "Deshcho pro tvorchist' poetychnu" (On Poetic Creativity, 1896). However, Kernerenko did write civic poetry. In his "I znov na Vkraini" (Once More in Ukraine, 1900) he describes the country as a promised land overflowing with milk and honey, a "holy" and "sacred" realm. Through his translations of poems by Semen Frug (who wrote in Russian and Yiddish), he developed explicitly Jewish themes and began to express Zionist sentiments. Kernerenko admired Frug, who also came from southern Ukraine and who pioneered a Jewish voice in Russian poetry, in the same way as Kernerenko tried to pioneer a Jewish voice in Ukrainian poetry. Frug's Zionist enthusiasm was translated into Ukrainian ways that enabled the Jewish content to pass unnoticed. The critic Yohanan Petrovsky-Shtern has pointed out that the translations modify references to Judaic terms and imagery by adapting them to a Christian context. "Novyi rik" (New Year, 1908), a translation from Frug, contains the image of a harp hung on a tree—a reference to the psalm "By the Waters of Babylon," which laments the loss of Zion and reminds Jews to remain focused on their liberation from bondage. As we have seen, this kind of biblical imagery was widely used in Ukrainian poetry at the time and could be read allegorically as an expression of sorrow over Ukrainian oppression. The ambiguity allowed for the expression of Jewish sentiment in an accepted form. (Petrovsky-Shtern 2005, 222–23.)

Kernerenko was the first writer in Ukrainian literature to clearly raise the issue of a Jewish Ukrainian identity. In "Ne ridnyi syn" (Not a Native Son, 1908), he portrays himself as an orphan, who has been adopted by his stepmother, Ukraine. His life has been one of suffering because of the mockery he has endured. Although he loves his stepmother, he feels that he has to leave her. It is not clear whether she has been unwilling, or is simply unable to shield this child of a different faith from insults:

> Farewell, my Ukraine,
> I must leave you,
> Although for you I would give
> My life, and freedom, and soul.
>
> But I am only your stepson,
> Unfortunately, I know this well.
> And among your children
> I do not live, but suffer.
>
> I can no longer bear
> The excessive mockery

That I have a different faith
From your other sons.

You, my Ukraine
I will always love:
Because although a stepmother,
You are, nonetheless, my mother. (Kernerenko 2005, 241)

Published in 1908, the poem presents in a memorable way the situation of Jews who wish to see their Ukrainianness accepted, but who feel that the obstacles to creating a Jewish Ukrainian identity are perhaps insurmountable.

Another poem by Kernerenko on a civic theme, "Monopoliia" (Monopoly, 1902), was placed by Franko on the first page of *Literaturno-naukovyi vistnyk*. It deals with the prohibition against Jews selling alcohol. They had received this right in past centuries from Polish kings, but it was taken from them in the wake of the 1881–82 pogroms by Count Nikolai Ignatiev, the minister of the interior, who introduced a state monopoly on alcohol production. The poet makes the point that the stereotype of the innkeeper can no longer be applied to Jews. The prohibition, in other words, has succeeded in drawing Ukrainians and Jews closer together by removing an obstacle that divided them. The poem expresses sympathy for both sides and provides a perspective that transcends the divide:

And so it was decided to take tavernkeeping away from Jews
And give it to the lords, let them manage it!

Are they managing it, or just drinking there,
That's not our business, time will tell.
However, Jews no longer sell liquor,
And now no one calls a Jew "tavernkeeper"!

In his day Kernerenko's exploration of a hybrid or hyphenated identity was treated with sympathy by Mykyta Shapoval and Khrystia Alchevska. Recently, his identity has received a new but entirely fanciful interpretation in David Markish's Russian-language novel *Poliushko-pole* (Field, 1991) which portrays Kernerenko as a supporter of Nestor Makhno's anarchist movement. Makhno is portrayed not as a criminal or anti-Semite, but as a man of egalitarian ideals who tries, with the assistance of Jews like Liova Zadov, his chief of counterintelligence, to unite Ukrainians and Jews. Kernerenko supports the revolution financially and writes songs in its praise. However, there is no historical evidence to support such a portrayal.

Petrovsky-Shtern has emphasized the fact that the conscious choice of Ukrainian as a literary medium was a strong statement—anticolonial and vi-

sionary. In spite of the language's marginal status within the empire, the poet selected it to fashion a Jewish Ukrainian identity. It was a decision that flew in the
face of all received imperial opinion. The poet saw Ukrainian as a medium of
great sophistication, and one that was open to other nations such as the Jews because of its saturation in the discourse of national self-determination. This sentiment aligned him with the views of Jabotinsky and other Jewish intellectuals
who were supporters of the Ukrainian national movement. Kernerenko was
among the first "to discover that the Ukrainian language suits Jewish political,
social, and cultural concerns," and the first to choose a Jewish-Ukrainian literary identity. In doing so, he "underscored similarities between the national agen-
das of the Jews and Ukrainians" and made the language into a medium for the
expression of national concerns of non-Ukrainians. His verse successfully negotiated the obstacles of community animosities and created a language of cultural
rapprochement. (Petrovsky-Shtern 2005, 236–37.)

The Modernists: Khotkevych, Krymsky, Vynnychenko, and Pachovsky

The generation of modernists who appeared at the turn of the century often expressed unqualified sympathy for Jewish suffering and oppression. In fact, at
this time such an attitude became the literary norm. This was in part a reaction
to the waves of pogrom violence, and in part because the Ukrainian and Jewish
struggles were viewed as analogous. Hnat Khotkevych's "Serdechna opika"
(Heartfelt Protection, 1902) is the story of a Jewish boy who dies of fever after
being denied entry to the gymnasium (high school). The narrator is a university
student who is hired as a tutor by a poor Jewish family. The parents, Yasl and
Sara, have a small grocery store, while the eldest son, Abram, works in a factory.
The twelve-year-old Khaim is preparing to take entrance examinations for the
gymnasium, into which he has been denied entry for two years due to the 5 percent quota for Jews. The Jewish home is clean but poor. Quickly realizing that he
cannot teach Khaim anything more than the boy already knows, the tutor goes to
Yasl and asks to be released from his post, explaining that the boy is already well
prepared and tutoring would be a waste of money. Asked to stay on, he refuses
payment but visits often and himself learns a great deal from the family, which
reads widely and has lively discussions. He compares them to pioneer families
that work hard all day, then read books by the light of the fire. A new minister of
education is appointed who promises "heartfelt" protection and reform, but in
fact the quotas are lowered and some schools even refuse to accept any Jews. The

whole family is distraught. Yasl becomes a despot, who drives Khaim to study harder. Although the boy gets top marks in all subjects, he is rejected. Yasl beats him and the boy dies of brain fever. The tutor goes through a "revolutionary baptism"—his eyes are opened to the falsehood and loathsomeness of official Russian life.

Khotkevych also responded to the 1905 revolution with a play called *Lykholittia* (Bad Times, 1906). It portrays a family in which the father is a reactionary and anti-Semite, but the son is a revolutionary who is engaged to a Jewish girl. Memorable for its portrayal of the psychology and organizational methods of the Black Hundreds, it ends with the hero's death on the barricades. The play holds out a strong sense of hope for future change: witnessing the enormous crowd at the funeral convinces the father to support the liberal-socialist opposition, and the Jewish and Ukrainian youth are allies in the common cause of winning democratic rights and social equality. Although translated into Russian, German, and Polish, the text never actually appeared in print in these languages, and even the Ukrainian original could not be published in the Russian empire, but appeared in Lviv, where it won an award as the year's best play. However, the Austrian government did not permit its staging until 1909, when only a single performance to a select audience was allowed.

Powerful expressions of compassion for Jewish suffering can be found in Oleksandr Oles's "Nad trupamy" (Over the Corpses, 1906), which concerns the killing of a Jewish doctor and his son during a pogrom. The poem's first half is a lament over the death of the father:

> You killed the husband . . . he lies in blood . . .
> I do not know the mystery of why you killed . . .
> Why a black nail in the head . . .
> . . . He was a doctor, a good one . . . You liked him . . .
> I do not know the mystery of why you killed . . .
> Khaim! Did you, perhaps, do them wrong? . . .
> Tell me, dear friend, why they killed you?
> All your life you fought for the freedom of slaves,
> You feared neither suffering, nor the grave, on their behalf . . .
> . . . Silent he is . . . And his face
> Says nothing of the sin . . . (Oles 1990, 1:107–8)

His famous "Narode-stradnyku, navchy i nas v vyhnanni Liubyty svii Ierusalym . . ." (Suffering People, Teach Us in Exile to Also Love Our Jerusalem, 1919) draws the familiar analogy between the sad fates of the Jews and the Ukrainians, but does so quite explicitly, even pointedly. (Ibid., 279.) Perhaps the leading lyrical poet of his generation, Oles emigrated to Czechoslovakia after the revolution, and his writings were banned in the Soviet Union for several decades.

Ahatanhel Krymsky was both an innovative writer and an eminent Orientalist. He wrote several very sympathetic portrayals of downtrodden Jews. "Zhyd-pohonych" (The Jewish Cab Driver, 1890) is a frequently cited example. This is the story of an impoverished cab driver, who has to put up with anti-Semitic comments and mistreatment. The story puts many stereotypical criticisms of Jews into the mouths of the cab riders and allows the reader to see how humiliating and unjust they are. Mykhailo Kotsiubynsky's famous story "Vin ide" (He Comes, 1903) portrays the senseless violence of a pogrom, as does Leonid Pakharevsky's "Bat'ko" (Father, 1906). In this last story, the father of a Jewish family, who has always counseled against violence, finally takes up a gun and drives off the attackers by shooting them. The message is that a better world will come only if the community is prepared to fight for it. This is one of the first stories to suggest the need for ruthless self-defense in the prevention of violence. The reader is encouraged to see the old man's renunciation of his Job-like philosophy and behavior as justified.

Modernists implicitly endorsed religious tolerance and equality before the law for Christians and Jews. They produced depictions of the quiet, modest Jew, who lives side by side with Ukrainian neighbors, sharing the same fate under the same oppressive system. The Jew in these writings is, in fact, a metaphor for ordinary, suffering humanity. The overarching framework is a morality that teaches a sense of justice tempered by mercy and moderation, an argument for democracy and pluralism, and a rejection of vengeful behavior. The modernists argue implicitly that a healthy modern society has to be guided by a sense of moral decency, and this involves eradicating divisive hatreds. Such a tone and shift in the representation of Jews was one of the contributions to literature of this generation.

Among Western Ukrainian prose writers of this time one should mention Tymofii Borduliak (also Tymotei Boduliak), a Greek Catholic priest, who at the end of the century wrote short stories in a sentimental vein, depicting the life of the contemporary Galician peasantry and their interaction with Jews. His collection *Blyzhni: Obrazky i opovidannia* (Neighbors: Sketches and Stories, 1899) was republished in Kyiv as *Opovidannia z halyts'koho zhyttia* (Stories of Galician Life, 1903). The author treats the fate of impoverished Jews with sympathy and understanding. The story "Bidnyi zhydok Ratytsia" (The Poor Jew Ratytsia, 1895), for example, describes a modern-day Job, a simple, good-natured Jew who follows in his father's footsteps as a fish merchant, buying from the villagers and selling in the town. Like his father, he is respected and loved by the village fishermen, although one would hardly guess this from the rancorous bartering over the price of fish. The fish, however, become scarcer. As other Jewish merchants move in from the town, he is squeezed out of the business. The villagers themselves suffer from an economic crisis and Ratytsia is reduced to begging. The richer town Jews despise him as a "peasant" and a "Ukrainian Jew." Ratytsia becomes a laborer who surprises local people when he joins them to work in the forest as a woodcutter. He collects alms from the town Jews until one day he freezes to death while walking back to the village with a sack of provisions. The town Jews provide his widow with financial help and in the following spring she moves with her children to the town. The narrator is unsure of their further fate. Perhaps, he suggests, they did well, as their father hoped they would. Unfortunately, this family has now disappeared from the village community, where its existence became economically unviable: "When the fish disappeared, Ratytsia disappeared." (Borduliak 1958, 124.) Ratytsia is deeply rooted in village life, an accepted part of society, and a victim of new economic processes, just as are the rest of the villagers. All Borduliak's stories present Jewish figures in an entirely positive light. For example, the tavernkeepers in "Halileivs'kyi viit (Kartyna z halileivs'koi istorii)" (The Village Head from Halileia: A Scene from Halileia History, 1896) are just as concerned with the alcoholism of the village chief as the rest of his acquaintances and try to usher him out of the tavern. No stigma is attached to their profession; it is the village chief who behaves shamefully.

Much of this writing reflects what Joshua Kunitz in his study of Russian literature between 1887 and 1917 described as a "reign of pity" for Jews. The "old stencil of the Jewish upstart," as he puts it, "is discarded, and a new stencil of the little Jew is adopted." (Kunitz 1929, 107.) The picture in Gorky, Korolenko, or Artsybashev is often flat, or nauseatingly sentimental—the result, Kunitz feels, of an intellectual admiration masking a deep-seated aversion: "Sweetly lachrymose stories about the 'poor' little, 'good' little, 'honest' little—but 'funny' little—Jew. Verily, the liberal Russian writers of the last three decades have shed more tears over the Jew than the Jew has managed to shed over himself. And that is saying considerable! How many didactic, sermonizing stories have been written about the pale, anemic Jew!" (Ibid., 133.) There is a good deal of this sapless writing in the more sentimentally inclined Ukrainian authors like Krymsky, Borduliak, Stepan Vasylchenko, and Modest Levytsky. But there is also powerful feeling and convincing characterization, particularly among younger modernists. A strong interest in the psychology and pathology of anti-Semitism characterizes Osyp Shpytko's work. His first book was a collection of poems,

Novomodnyi spivanyk: Perespivy Hrytsia Shchypavky (New-style Songbook: Paraphrased Songs of Hryts Shchypavka, 1901). It was confiscated by the censorship and later appeared in the satirical journal *Komar* (Mosquito), but without ten proscribed poems, which the author described as "paraphrases of a few dozen popular Galician songs with a strong political, antigentry, and anti-Semitic coloring." *Vyrid* (Monster), his best work, gives the fullest portrayal of an anti-Semitic Galician. It was serialized in *Literaturno-naukovyi vistnyk* in 1901, but was only published as a book in 2000. The narrator lashes out at all Ukrainian reality. Lords, priests, Jews, Poles, and Russians are denounced as victimizers of the common people. The narrator describes himself as knowing the Bible well: "I loved Christ, and hated the Jews, who destroyed Him for the truth. I saw this hatred for the Jews everywhere: on pictures dealing with biblical history I poked the eyes out of all the Jews, I beat them on the street, threw stones after them, broke windows in houses and synagogues, and once, having met a Jew on the banks of the river kicking a Christian student in the head, I took him by surprise and put a cloak over his head, threw him into the river, and that was the last time he was seen alive." (Shpytko 2000, 18.) He steals chickens from Jews, and deceives them when buying tobacco. This character is the monstrous product of abject circumstances. We learn that as a youth he was publicly humiliated and disowned by his own father. Some Jewish merchants took pity on him and made an unsuccessful attempt to placate the father. After this, the hero gravitated toward the company of the tailor Gross, a Christianized Jew, and took to visiting a tavern owned by three Jewish sisters, whom he describes as respectful, polite, and given to complaining less than others in bad times. (Ibid., 27.) He recounts how he fell in love with the youngest sister, Esther, who loved music and spoke "better Ukrainian than many a priest's wife." She pitied a local drunk, whom she regularly provided with a glass of beer and bread when her sisters were not looking. The narrator describes how he and Esther learned musical pieces, including Bortniansky's setting of the psalm "Sviatyi Bozhe" (Sacred Lord). She would stand outside the church on Sunday listening delightedly to the singing. Even though he tried to convince himself that a Christian should not love a Jewess, their mutual attraction was overpowering. Esther decided to become a Christian and the couple were to marry. Her honesty and good character made him a better, nobler person. However, shortly after this she disappeared, kidnapped by Jews who had uncovered her plan. The novel provides a rich and complex presentation of the narrator's anti-Semitism, which is a love-hate relationship and exposes the intimate details of Ukrainian-Jewish interaction in a provocative, uncompromising manner.

Shpytko's works probably reflect the acculturation to Ukrainian ways of Galician Jews. In the 1900 census in Eastern Galicia 5 percent of Jews (40,475 individuals) gave Ukrainian as their main spoken language (Yiddish was not on the census). Many Ukrainian texts were produced in Jewish publishing houses in Stryi, Brody, Zolochiv, Lviv, and Kolomyia. Yakiv Orenshtein's Kolomyia publishing house, for example, put out 120 Ukrainian books in the years 1903–15. Orenshtein was acquainted with many of the leading writers in Western Ukraine. After 1917 he would work with the new Ukrainian government in Kyiv to create a large bookstore, and in 1918 he traveled to Germany and Switzerland to print and import Ukrainian scholarly, educational, and creative literature. In the 1890s a Jewish amateur theatrical group in the Kolomyia even put on a play called *Brandles—Kozak iz Kolomyia* (Brandles—The Cossack from Kolomyia). (Monolatii 1998, 148.)

The Jewish theme was prominent in the prerevolutionary writings of Volodymyr Vynnychenko, a widely read author who became a leading figure in the Ukrainian National Republic in 1917–19. His short story *Talisman* (1913) portrays the transformation of a meek and timid Jewish youth after he is jokingly elected by a group of prisoners as their "elder." He takes his position seriously and gradually wins their respect. In the final scene, in order to help the others escape, he does a brave and self-sacrificing deed that costs him his life. The play *Dysharmoniia* (Disharmony, 1907) is a more significant work. It deals with the events leading up to the Kyiv pogrom that followed the tsar's manifesto of October 17, 1905, and is remarkable for the analysis of the mentality of the common pogromists, and of how they were manipulated, provoked, and sometimes paid to use violence. A revolutionary committee contains not only Ukrainians but also a Jewish girl called Liia. Although she has always considered herself Ukrainian, at the end of the play, after witnessing the brutal attacks, she suddenly redefines herself as Jewish. The political naiveté of the revolutionaries is brought out, along with their different characters and ideals. Events drive two individuals, the dreamer Hrytsko and Liia, to quit the revolutionary party; they also put an end to Liia's relationship with Mazun, and Olia's with Martyn. Vynnychenko suggests that superficial political loyalties will be tested and only deeper ones will prevail. The revolutionaries, with their innocent faith in universal brotherhood and democratic liberties have underestimated not only the importance of the national question, but also the ugly reality of racial, social, and political prejudices. The leading protagonists in the play go through a sudden maturation, and gain the understanding that they have a responsibility to transform intolerable circumstances. However, this must be done through a "long" revolution—years of work on behalf of the collective to which they are bound. Commitment to this collective is the key, psychologically transforming moment.

Grabowicz has pointed out that Khotkevych's *Lykholittia* and Vynnychenko's *Dysharmoniia,* which were both published in 1906, were programmatic statements on the Jewish question: "For both writers it is manifestly clear that volens nolens the Jew and the Ukrainian intelligentsia, the progressive forces, are allied; indeed, in the eyes of the Black Hundred all of the Left, all the intelligentsia, all the students are by definition 'Jews.'" (Grabowicz 1988, 340.) But whereas Khotkevych's play anticipates the arrival of a new order with confidence, Vynnychenko's appraisal of the future is more pessimistic. He fears the collapse of a Jewish-Ukrainian identity, and a loss of faith in political change. Nonetheless, despite this hard-headed pessimism, he refuses to envisage a renewal of enmity between the two people—in Grabowicz's phrase, "to turn the clock back on history." (Ibid., 341.)

Vasyl Pachovsky was another influential modernist, and a product of Western Ukrainian society, unlike, for example, Khotkevych, who had been forced to move to Lviv from Kharkiv because of political persecution. His works are particularly interesting in their continual reworking of the Marko Prokliaty theme, first introduced by Storozhenko in the 1860s, and their attitude to the curse of violence. In *Sfinks Evropy: Drama v 3-okh diiakh* (Sphinx of Europe: A Drama in Three Acts, 1914), which was published on the eve of the First World War, the writer presents a prophetic account of ensuing events. Ukrainian leaders are split between those who give primacy either to the national or to the social questions, between those who lean toward Moscow and those who rely on the West. But the key figure is Marko Prokliaty, who represents the fierce, powerful, but unsophisticated masses. Kochubei, a descendant of the historical figure who betrayed Mazepa in 1708, instigates Marko against the Jews, Poles, and Germans, and claims that the Ukrainian nationalists want to give the country to these foreigners: they have "sold the faith, nation, and tsar to the Jews!" (Pachovs'kyi 1914, 31.) The gullible Marko is easily whipped up and kills Sviatopolk, who represents the dream of statehood. At the end of the play the ghost of Mazepa curses Marko. Here Pachovsky's use of the Marko Prokliaty theme differs significantly from its use in his later *Zoloti vorota: Mistychnyi epos v 3-okh chastiakh* (Golden Gates: A Mystical Epos in Three Parts, 1937, 1984), a fact that underscores the philo-Semitic character of the prerevolutionary years.

The most outspoken anti-Semitic voice of this period was probably that of Olena Pchilka, who edited the popular weekly *Ridnyi krai* (Native Land) from 1907 to 1914. After she published a series of articles critical of the Jewish presence in Ukraine, her journal was strongly denounced by other leading publications like *Rada* and *Literaturno-naukovyi vistnyk*, and she was strongly criticized by most of the Ukrainian intelligentsia. Drawing heavily on the argument that Jews had persecuted Ukrainians during Polish rule, she held that Jews had consistently acted against Ukraine's national interests. She claimed that archival sources gave evidence of contractual arrangements with Jewish orendars that proved the existence of church leasings, and insisted that the dumas and folksongs, which she took to be historically accurate, proved the widespread nature of this practice. However, the statement of hers that drew the most attention was published after the acquittal of Beilis. Pchilka was upset that some Ukrainian journalists in their own words "bowed" to Beilis, a gesture that she judged to be demeaning and undignified: "Well, Beilis is innocent in the murder of a Christian boy, but does this oblige us to bow before him? Why do we not tell everyone who has been imprisoned and then exonerated 'I bow before you!'" (Pchilka 2006, 229.) Moreover, she objected to what was in her view the construction of an excessively positive literary image of Jews, singling out for ridicule Ivan Tohobichny's *Zhydivka-Vykhrestka*, as well as works by Modest Levytsky, Dmytro Markovych, and Stepan Vasylchenko. Pchilka challenged this picture of kindly and altruistic Jews, insisting in response to a story by Modest Levytsky that in her own experience Jews were more likely to rob than to help a train passenger, and that she had never come across such gentleness and kindness among Jewish fellow travelers. She was particularly offended by Vasylchenko's *Zilia Korolevych* (1913) because the play shows a Ukrainian schoolteacher's attraction to the son of a Jewish merchant. Her comment: "Why could not a capable, intelligent, young villager or Cossack be favored with the young lady's attention?" (Ibid., 225.) But her discomfort was clearly caused by more than a lack of verisimilitude: a positive image of Jews went against her understanding of literary decorum because she considered the "Jewish national type" as a priori "hostile to the Ukrainian nature." (Ibid., 232.) Hence her resistance to any ennobling of the Jewish image or any blurring of demarcation lines between the two "types" or "natures." It should be said, however, that within the corpus of Pchilka's work the Jewish theme is a relatively minor one. Her primary focus was the struggle for civil and national rights.

The majority of works from this period present sympathetic, individualized images of the Jewish population, and the years 1900–1914 in particular demonstrate humane attitudes and an intolerance of anti-Semitism. Moreover, by identifying with Jewish history and the fate of individual Jews, Ukrainian authors were able to present an alienated view of themselves and a critique of their own obsessions; the modernist writings of this period reveal a strongly self-critical introspection and an interest in psychology. Overall, the large number of Jewish characters that appear in the prerevolutionary literature provides a picture of rich interaction between Ukrainians and Jews, and a discourse on mutual relations in which the Jewish protagonist is not the ugly foreigner, but in most cases a member of the village or town community, someone who can exhibit divided loyalties, but who understands and identifies with this community. The major exception here is Franko, whose works investigate the conflict between the two communities as national entities. His focus is on the difficulties of integrating these two distinct organisms. A significant public was reached by the populist-realist writers—particularly through their plays which were able to tour the countryside and towns—and by the modernists. Unfortunately, the ban on Ukrainian publications within the empire throughout most of this period and the limitations set on the production and publication of plays prevented a wider dissemination of this literature's influence. Nonetheless, Ukrainian literature in this period developed what Yurii Sherekh has described as its mainstream, "normal" spirituality: idealic and lyrical, the expression of democratic and humanistic values. (Sherekh 1948, 15–16.) This tradition was to be fiercely challenged in the thirties, particularly by the writers grouped around Dmytro Dontsov's *Vistnyk* (Herald, 1933–39). It is worth recalling, however, that at the end of the nineteenth and beginning of the twentieth century the Jewish theme played an important role in shaping this mainstream current.

CHAPTER 3

A Dream of Rapprochement, 1914–1929

Jewish and Ukrainian leaders drew closer in the twentieth century's second decade. Henry Abramson has written that "one of the major coups of the nascent Ukrainian movement was its early success in winning the support of Jewish political activists from their Russotropism." (Abramson 1999, xviii.) After the fall of tsarism in February 1917, first the Central Rada (the Ukrainian parliament formed in March 1917 after the fall of the tsarist state) and then the Ukrainian National Republic (UNR) proclaimed and built national-cultural autonomy for Jews. The government allocated 30 percent of its parliamentary seats and positions in the General Secretariat, the supreme administrative organ, to members of national minorities. The Law of National-Personal Autonomy gave the Jewish population freedom in matters of culture, education, and self-government. A Minister of Jewish Affairs was created and apportioned 10 percent of state funds. (Ibid., 68–69.) Yiddish became an official language of the state, and Yiddish wording appeared even on Ukrainian banknotes.

The new state proclaimed independence in its Fourth Universal of January 22, 1918, and tried to develop an educational policy that would counterbalance the influence of Russian culture and garner it support. Encouragement for Jewish education and culture was one aspect of this policy. Networks of Jewish secular schools were created with Yiddish and Hebrew as languages of instruction. Jewish research sections were formed within Ukrainian academic institutions, and organizations like the Kultur-Lige appeared. Private, religious Jewish organizations, such as the heders (basic Hebrew schools), Talmud-Torah schools, and yeshivas, were not subordinated to the Ministry of Jewish Affairs. It is worth recalling that in 1917 most elected Jewish representatives supported the Ukrainian government and the right of Ukrainians to determine their political destiny. They were delighted that parliament showed willingness to grant more concessions to Jews than had any other constituent assembly in history. In 1917 Joseph Schechtman, one of Jabotinsky's closest allies, published *Ievrei ta ukraintsi* (Jews and Ukrainians) in which he wrote: "Who if not we, children of an oppressed people, can grasp the feelings and sufferings of a neighbor who along with us has endured the cruelty and abuse of the old regime! We have been united by common aspirations and common goals. The moment has arrived when these aspirations are close to realization. Our common path is still a long one, but we believe that a free Ukrainian people will support us on this path!" (Kleiner 2000, 47.)

An important reason for this alliance lay in the fact that Ukrainians formed a minority of the urban population. Aware that neither the Polish nor the Russian minorities were well disposed toward it, the new government nonetheless felt that it could win over the Jewish minority. Observers have described the pervasive, optimistic faith in the fruitfulness of the Ukrainian-Jewish accord. (Vynnychenko 1920, 297–98; Goldelman 1967, 21.) In fact, the Ukrainian leadership saw the parallel development of Jewish cultural autonomy and Ukrainian national-territorial autonomy as a linchpin of its political strategy. The head of the Central Rada, Mykhailo Hrushevsky, offered the national minorities all the rights that Ukrainians had fought for before the revolution, short of territorial autonomy, and pledged to fight manifestations of chauvinism and intolerance. In return he asked that the minorities support Ukraine in its bid for self-determination. Loyalty to the territory and its people, not to Ukrainian nationality or ancestry, was proclaimed as the new government's principal requirement of citizens. With the declaration of that principle, "Hrushevsky was laying the cornerstone of Ukraine's proposed relations with its national minorities." (Plokhy 2005, 77.) However, events leading up to the defeat of the UNR, and in particular the appalling pogroms of 1919, in which demoralized units loyal to the UNR participated, badly damaged this rapprochement.

Prominent Jewish figures served in the UNR government, among them Solomon Goldelman, Arnold Margolin, Moisei Zilberfarb, and Mark Vishnitzer. Jews were also part of the press and secretarial sections of government missions to France, the Netherlands, and other countries. Margolin tendered his resignation as deputy minister of foreign affairs on March 11, 1919, stating that although the government was doing all it could to stop the pogroms, as a Jew he could not retain an official position while his people were being killed. He accepted the proposal to stay on and work in London as a diplomat for the UNR.

The worst pogrom wave broke out in January 1919 as the UNR troops were forced to evacuate Kyiv. Only when the front stabilized in June 1919 and the UNR government settled in Kamianets was the anarchy brought under control. The appearance of the disciplined Ukrainian Galician Army, which was retreating from the west in the face of stronger Polish forces, restored order and peace on UNR-controlled territory, and the Ministry of Jewish Affairs helped to establish a state inspection in UNR forces to prevent any arbitrary or illegal acts against the civilian population. In the ensuing months, relations with Jewish groups and political parties were reestablished. Individuals from the Folkspartei, Poale Zion, and the United Bund were employed in the government's ministries.

The position of the Western Ukrainian National Republic (WUNR) was analogous to that of the UNR. Support was declared for Jewish cultural autonomy and there was Jewish representation in parliament. Armed conflict between Poles and Ukrainians broke out on November 1, 1918, when Poles began to take control of Lviv. As in Eastern Ukraine, Ukrainians hoped that Jews would support them in the struggle for independence. Jews comprised as much as 60 percent of the urban population of Western Ukraine, while Ukrainians only accounted for 15 percent. Jewish aid was therefore of crucial importance in overcoming Polish rule in the towns. However, on November 1, 1918, when representatives of Jewish parties gathered in Lviv, they declared a policy of neutrality in the conflict.

When the Polish army gained control of Lviv on November 22, 1918, a three-day pogrom began that shocked the Jewish population and strengthened its sympathy for the Ukrainian revolutionary forces, who had armed the Jewish militia when they recognized that they could not guarantee safety in the Jewish quarter. Although there was no mass Jewish support for the Ukrainian forces, some Jews were mobilized in Zbarazh, Zboriv, Mykulyntsi, and Ozirnia, and in Ternopil twelve hundred Jews volunteered to serve in the Ukrainian Galician Army, enabling the First Jewish Kurin (Company) to be created from university and high-school students under Solomon Liainberg's command in December, 1918. The unit served with distinction throughout the war. However, the lack of greater Jewish support caused resentment. In April 1919, Goldelman, who at the time found himself in Stanislaviv (today's Ivano-Frankivsk), noted: "The negative effects of the declaration of neutrality can be felt almost everywhere. They are detectable in all walks of life, in all relations between Jews and Ukrainians." (Goldelman 1921, 28.) The WUNR fought anti-Semitism, punishing robberies with executions. President Yevhen Petrushevych forbade the mobilization of Jews against their will or forced contributions to the military.

In the early months of 1919, as anarchy spread in the wake of the retreat from Kyiv, an estimated fifty to sixty thousand people were killed, many at the hands of Ukrainian troops. (Abramson 1999, 110.) The violence during the crucial months, from January to April, has been blamed on the reluctance of Symon Petliura, the head of the army, to take decisive action for fear of desertions. Vynnychenko wrote: "My departure from the position of head of the Directory finally freed Petliura, who tried by indulging and condoning anti-Semitic incidents to win personal popularity among the warlords. From that time the pogroms began to take on a more and more threatening and open form." (Vynnychenko 1998, 157.) This may have been a self-serving view, since it has been suggested that Vynnychenko himself was reluctant to shoot soldiers taking part in pogroms. When a Jewish delegation approached him in January 1919, he "promised to do whatever he could, then remarked on the Jewish support for the Bolsheviks, adding, 'don't you embroil me with the army.'" (Margolin 1977, 232.) It is on this perception of Petliura's passivity and reluctance to alienate army commanders, who are assumed to have been anti-Semitic, that accusations of complicity are based. (Kenez 1992, 295–96, 303.) The most authoritative account is Abramson's. He notes that the government condemnations and the actions taken against the perpetrators were insufficient to trammel the warlords. Using the most reliable estimates, he attributes about 40 percent of the pogroms to Ukrainian forces. (Abramson 1999, 80.) The reality was that in many cases Petliura had little control over his partisans, and there may have been individuals in the government who countermanded his orders or refused to act with resolve. It should be noted that pogroms were also the work of the White Army, the Poles, the Red Army, and various marauding bands. Adhering to the same ideological premises as the Black Hundreds, the White Army (Russian Volunteer Army) made almost no attempt to combat anti-Jewish violence. On the contrary, it spread pogromist leaflets and used anti-Semitism to recruit support. Peter Kenez has written: "The Volunteer Army succeeded in murdering as many Jews as all other armies put together, because its pogroms were the most modern: they were the best organized, carried out like military operations, and the most ideologically motivated." (Kenez 1992, 302.) He continues: "The leaders and officers of the Volunteer Army were obsessed with anti-Semitism. Secret reports, obviously not meant as propaganda, make it clear that this anti-Semitism, full of paranoid delusions, bordered on the pathological. In the thousands of documents in the White army archives there is not a single denunciation of pogroms. On the contrary, the intelligence agents simply assumed that Jews were responsible for all miseries—whether Bolshevism, inflation, or defeat in battle." (Ibid., 304.)

On March 4, 1919, Oleksandr Bezpalka, who at the time was minister of labor and gave many speeches condemning pogroms, wrote the following in *Robitnycha hazeta* (Workers' Gazette), the organ of the UNR government:

One is amazed at where our patriot-haidamakas have uncovered the most determined enemies of Ukraine: not on the boulevards of Ukrainian cities, not in downtown offices, but in the poor side streets and byways of small Ukrainian towns.

The very appearance of those homes in the byways is pitiful: crooked, thatched roofs reaching to the ground, walls held up with boards, windows hanging low out of their frames and barely held together with patches. Within the houses are poor, dirty dens, and in each one there are several smudgy-faced children living like mice. Walking past such houses one wonders how people could live there, and one feels a desire to take out of those burrows whoever the people in there might be, lead them to the sun, and show them how a creature of the sun should live.

And one day, on a Saturday afternoon at three o'clock in the town of Proskuriv, strong young men, members of the civilized Ukrainian people, force their way into those Jewish side streets, smashing the doors and windows with a blow, rushing into the dens not to bring sunshine into the houses, but destruction and death.

And the terrible enemies of Ukraine and the Ukrainian people cry out like frightened animals. The enemies whom the Ukrainian heroes, the Cossack-haidamakas, challenge with their swords, are old women and men, little girls and boys, five-year-olds, six-month-old and ten-day-old infants. All are driven out. It is terrible, terrible; there are no words that can express one's indignation, one's sense of offended human dignity. No people in any age, anywhere in the pages of history, has seen similar scenes.

Who were those enjoying themselves on the Proskuriv marketplace? People? These creatures do not deserve the name of any animal, because it would be an insult to the animal. . . . These Proskuriv pogromists cannot even be described as brave, because in Proskuriv the lucky Jews were the ones who lived in strong stone houses with firm oaken doors. Not a single haidamaka entered them, because taking oaken doors off is hard work and there might have been strong resistance behind them. But the poor homes were broken into with a heel; courage and force sufficed for that. Therefore, our friends—the Jewish bankers and rich of the town of Proskuriv—survived, while our accursed enemies—the bakers, furriers, factory workers, coachmen, and stallkeepers—were all killed. Around fifteen hundred people were put to the sword by haidamakas. . . .

The Jews who are left walk about with frightened eyes and complain to their old friends among the townsmen and village women: well, now our turn has come, last year you were the ones lined up in the villages and told to look into the hot sun, beaten, whipped, and killed, and now it is we who have been killed. We have learned not to take pleasure from someone else's grief, and so you must not take pleasure from our unhappiness. Both the Jew and the local man weep. I spoke to more than one old man, more than one woman; they all had tears in their eyes when they spoke about the killing and described how mothers were stabbed with children in their arms.

Our national conscience and honor could be heard speaking through these old men and women, condemning this brutality, for which there can be no forgiveness, but only a curse and the voice of indignation. (Bezpalka 1928, 84–85.)

A similar assessment of the killings is that of Osyp Nazaruk:

On the Left Bank of the Dnipro the Ukrainian troops were commanded by otaman Bolbochan, an elegant gentleman of old views, who loved perfumes and gallant company. This is why he accepted into his command officers of the old regime who considered every meeting of the peasants or workers an expression of "Bolshevism" and beat them continually. This obviously only spread Bolshevism. . . . The government was powerless and Vynnychenko was very disturbed by the brutality that was appearing everywhere. In Vinnytsia I gathered a council of representatives of the Jewish parties and of the city community to discuss how to prevent this misfortune. I was actively involved in this issue until the very end. I wrote proclamations and articles, gave speeches. The most effective argument was that the pogroms destroyed all trade in Ukraine and by this fact made provisioning of the Ukrainian army and the further construction of the Ukrainian state impossible. They answered that the Jews were organizing Bolshevism, that they often attacked Ukrainian troops from the rear. I replied that among Bolshevik insurgents everywhere there are ten times more Ukrainians than Jews, and, in any case, the organizers of Bolshevism are not Jewish children and old women who are also being killed. (Nazaruk 1920, 117, 143–44.)

The pogroms took place against a background of anarchy produced by three years of revolution and four years of world war. There was no effective government; armies and warlords roamed the land; relations between town and countryside had been severed; disease and hunger were everywhere; waves of killing and plundering by partisans and marauders swept the country. Over 1.5 million people died in the seven-year period and the devastation was far greater than Western European countries experienced during the Second World War.

Some Ukrainian literature on the violence deserves to be better known. Kedrovsky's "Borot'ba z pohromamy v Ukraine" (The Struggle with Pogroms in Ukraine) was first serialized in the U.S.-published daily *Svoboda* (Freedom) in

1930. The Central Rada had assigned him the task of ending the pogroms. He describes the background of anarchy, characterizes the pogromists, and provides documentation on attempts by the UNR government to influence events. In his estimation, the devastation caused by years of war and the decades of anti-Jewish agitation were responsible for turning criminal elements into mass killers. Realizing that its reputation had been gravely damaged by the pogroms, the UNR provided its minister of Jewish affairs with funds to help those who had suffered. Kedrovsky had under his authority two hundred inspectors, who frequently executed perpetrators. Unfortunately, by June of 1919, when the government regained some control of the situation, it was already too late for many areas. Although he asserts that some acts were provoked by the Bolsheviks to discredit the UNR, the pogromist element and ideology are squarely blamed. He concludes that no mercy should be shown to pogromists, who have to be fought "resolutely and ceaselessly." (Kedrovs'kyi 1994, 70.)

Writing in 1922, Pavlo Khrystiuk, who served in the UNR government in 1918, argued that the government had protested against pogroms, assigned funds in aid of the victims, listened carefully to the endless accounts, complaints, and petitions, and organized special investigatory commissions composed of members of the socialist parties in order to uncover and punish the guilty. "But none of these efforts had the slightest impact." (Khrystiuk 1969, 26.) Why was this the case? Khrystiuk sees the reason in the staffing of the UNR with reactionary officers who had served alongside Russian monarchists and still retained the same xenophobic and brutal attitudes. (Ibid., 25–26.) Another argument is that a great distance separated the elite from the masses. Abramson has argued that this gulf was in fact a fundamental reason for the failure of the entire rapprochement between Jews and Ukrainians; it did not have widespread support in all strata of society: "The Ukrainian socialist parties could not communicate their liberal program to the peasantry, and the Jewish activists were too far removed from the ordinary Jew to mobilize grassroots support for the Ministry of Jewish Affairs." (Abramson 1999, xv.)

The moment of rapprochement was altogether too brief to take firm root because the fragile new state had only a matter of weeks to establish itself before it was at war. The Jewish working masses were not supportive of the UNR, while the Ukrainian masses were often quick to blame "the Jews" for many of their political and economic difficulties. It should be recalled that the first pogrom by UNR troops already occurred in March of 1918, when several units returned to Kyiv after the Bolsheviks had been driven out by the Germans. Political relations were already strained at that point because many Ukrainian leaders were angered by the refusal of Jewish parties to vote for the Fourth Universal (the declaration of independence) on January 22 of the same year.

Another minister in the UNR, Goldelman, who after the war became a professor in the Ukrainian Academy of Economics in Czechoslovakia before emigrating to Palestine in 1939, has written that in the years 1917–20 Jewish autonomy and the Ukrainian national revolution were indivisibly linked. He has reminded readers that in spite of the stain left by the pogroms, it is indisputable that the Ukrainian revolution consistently struggled to build autonomy for the Jewish population in Ukraine. (Goldelman 1967, 135.) Moreover, although the Bolsheviks, upon coming to power, immediately began an antireligious campaign, closing down synagogues and attacking Judaism, many of the UNR's policies and institution-building efforts with regard to Jews continued to bear fruit in the 1920s under Soviet rule.

Ukrainian society went through a profound change during the revolution. Observers have attested to the immense and rapid growth of national awareness in these years. Yaroslav Hrytsak has written that "there is no doubt that if the Ukrainian state had survived, most individuals would have been loyal to it." (Hrytsak 2004b, 76.) The strength of national feeling explains the introduction by the Soviet regime of a policy of Ukrainianization or indigenization in the years 1923–28. It was accompanied by a great surge of interest in Ukrainian culture. Ten thousand people gave "poet" as their occupation in a census in Kyiv; in 1927 *Kultura i pobut* (Culture and Life) claimed there were six thousand dramatic groups in Ukraine serving twelve million spectators. In the following year *Nove mystetstvo* (New Art) stated that seventy thousand people were involved in amateur theatricals and over five thousand laid claim to being dramatists. (Makaryk 2004, 143.) The indigenization policy also allowed the continued development of Jewish secular institutions and structures. In the early twenties, the urban Jewish population was still the second largest after the Russian. The Soviet Ukrainian government's policy of support for Jewish institutions and cultural life, like the UNR's, was conceived as a continued bridge-building with the Jewish community. Jewish newspapers, libraries, clubs, and theaters were created. Although religious schools were banned, national schools for Jews, including a network of Jewish secondary institutions (technicums, professional-technical schools) were maintained. Ironically, Kyiv, which had traditionally been seen by Jews as a gentile city hostile to them, became a leading center of Jewish life. In the years 1917–23 it boasted 39.9 percent of all Yiddish titles published on the territory of what is today Russia, Ukraine, and Belarus, as compared to Odesa's 15.3 percent, Petrograd's 13.5 percent, and Moscow's 13 percent. (Estraikh 2005, 37.) Before 1903 Jews had practically been forbidden permanent residence in the city but by 1910 there were 50,792 (10.84 percent of the population). In 1919 the number rose to 117,041 (21.04 percent of the population), and in 1923 to 128,041 (31.95 percent). In 1926 Jews constituted 26 percent of the city's inhabitants. (Khiterer 1999, 143–44.) The real figures were probably higher because the statistics were based on self-identification. During the revolution and its aftermath other populations fled the city for the villages, or emigrated. The number of Ukrainians plummeted in the years 1919–20 from 136,775 to 52,443.

The indigenization policy made Ukrainians and Jews allies in cultural construction. Parallel institutions were created and analogous tasks undertaken. A flowering of Ukrainian and Yiddish literatures took place. Skurativsky has described the two literatures as "pointedly loyal in their mutual relations." (Skurativs'kyi 1998, 54.) Some important friendships were forged, among them that of Pavlo Tychyna and Leib Kvitko. Tychyna learned Yiddish and translated Kvitko's verse into Ukrainian, contributing to the latter's phenomenal popularity. Kvitko, in turn, translated Tychyna into Yiddish. By the Second World War, Kvitko had published a hundred books in Yiddish, thirty in Russian, and thirty in Ukrainian, and had been translated into twenty-two languages of the USSR. His works appeared in over 6.4 million copies. Almost all were removed from the shelves and destroyed when he was arrested and killed in 1952. He was also a member of the organization VAPLITE (the Free Academy of Proletarian Literature) formed by Mykola Khvylovy in 1925, and his spirited criticism in 1929 of the Communist Party's control of literature was, like Khvylovy's, treated as subversive. Les Kurbas's friendship with Solomon Mikhoels was also fruitful. In 1933, after being dismissed from the innovative Berezil theatre in Ukraine, Kurbas, who spoke Yiddish and maintained close contacts with Jewish theatres, was invited by Mikhoels to work in Moscow in the GOSET (State Jewish Theater). Both enjoyed this collaboration, which produced a stunningly innovative *King Lear,* one of the great Shakespeare productions of the 1930s. Although Kurbas was arrested on December 26, 1933 on his way to rehearsals and shot in a labor camp in 1937, the production that premiered on February 10, 1935, with Mikhoels in a starring role, bore the Ukrainian director's fingerprints in conception and outline. (Makaryk 2004, 191–95.) Yurii Smolych was a close friend of the Yiddish writer Der Nister (Pinkhus Kahanovych). He had grown up in Western Ukraine and his parents knew many Jewish families, some of whom they hid during the 1905 pogrom. Smolych and Der Nister regularly attended Yiddish theaters and discussed performances. Later, when Smolych wrote his memoirs, he was compelled to weave a careful path between supporting non-Russian cultures and denouncing an attachment to them as "nationalistic." Even these "politically correct" pages written in 1968 were censored. One editor insisted that before they could appear the author had to drop his call for a revival of Jewish theater in Ukraine, his reports of Der Nister's negative attitude toward the creation of a Jewish autonomous region of Birobidzhan, and complaints about Soviet anti-Semitism. (Soloviova 1990, 175.)

Smolych has argued that many Jews in the 1920s were "native speakers" of Ukrainian. They came from Ukrainian villages and towns, lived and grew up among Ukrainians, and were born of parents who knew only Yiddish and Ukrainian. If they knew Russian, they did so badly. It was only the later, post-Stalin generation of Jews that grew up without speaking Ukrainian and was prejudiced against it. "Along the way," he writes, "we lost a good colleague in our cultural process." (Smolych 1990, 161.) Jews participated strongly in the creation of a modern Ukrainian culture and identity, making major contributions to literature, art, cinema, and scholarship, creating "a home" for themselves in the culture and simultaneously helping to define that culture as diverse and complex. Olena Kurylo, for example, was a leading linguist who explored Ukrainian dialects and folklore. Osyp Hermaize was a prominent historian. Abram Leites, Samiilo Shchupak, Volodymyr Koriak, and Yarema Aizenshtok were leading critics. The last worked on the complete edition of Shevchenko's diary, and produced studies of Ukrainian folklore and of many classical writers, among them Shevchenko, Kvitka, Koliarevsky, Kotsiubynsky, and Franko. Accused of Ukrainian nationalism, he was forced to move to Leningrad. (Revuts'kyi 1985, 164–65.) Writers of Jewish origin made names for themselves in Ukrainian literature, among them Leonid Pervomaisky (Illia Hurevych), Sava Holovanivsky, Ivan (Izrail) Kulyk, Aron Kopshtein, and Raisa Troianker. Natan Rybak and Abram Katsnelson debuted in the thirties, and Naum Tykhy (Shtilerman) in the forties. Many Jewish writers contributed heavily to postrevolutionary literary journals, in particular *Molodniak* (Youth), the organ of the Komsomol or Communist youth organization, and *Hart* (Tempering), which defined itself as the organ of the proletarian writers.

Many talented individuals of Jewish origin participated in the Ukrainian film industry. By the middle of the decade Ukrainian film production, headed by the All-Ukrainian Photo-Cinema Management (VUFKU) was enjoying rapid growth. In the years 1925–30 it produced the internationally famous films of Alexander Dovzhenko and Dziga Vertov, and laid the foundation of a national industry. The Odesa and Kyiv studios expected by the end of the decade to be releasing a hundred films each year. A push was made to create products that would be appreciated by the large Jewish minority of 1.5 million, and that would portray Jewish life for the Ukrainian public. A range of films were produced. In 1930, however, the production of films on Jewish themes was stopped and VUFKU's autonomous status was revoked; it became a branch of Soiuzkino and all decisions about production, distribution, and exhibition were made in Moscow.

The Kultur-Lige, the largest Jewish organization that ever existed in Ukraine, was conceived as a practical demonstration of Jewish cultural autonomy. Head-quartered in Kyiv, in the years 1918–25 it actively promoted Jewish cultural life through publishing, the organization of musical and theatrical performances, art exhibitions, an art school, a school of music, libraries, museums, university courses, and kindergartens. Created in Kyiv in January 1918, by the end of the year it had a 120 branches throughout Ukraine. More branches were later created in Russia, Lithuania, Romania, and Poland. Kyiv's role in the Eastern European Jewish world was particularly important in view of the decline during the First World War of cultural activity in such traditional centers of Yiddish culture as Warsaw and Vilnius. At the time Kyiv attracted some of the most active figures in Jewish culture and politics who had escaped from Petrograd and Moscow in the wake of the Bolshevik revolution. They contributed to the flourishing growth of Kyiv's Yiddish culture in education, theater, book publishing, and art. The main organizers and literary figures in the Kyiv Kultur-Lige were David Bergelson, David Hofshtein (Gofshtein), Moshe Litvakov, Yekhezkel Dobrushin, Der Nister, and Nakhman Maizil. The scale and intensity of this Yiddish literary life was remarkable, especially in Kyiv, which served as the incubatory center in which scores of writers developed their careers. (Estraikh 2005, ix.) Since it grouped together leading individuals from a number of political organizations, the Kultur-Lige also acted as a kind of interparty association. It was an independent organization under the UNR, but after the arrival of Soviet rule its central committee was dismissed and replaced with Communists. The organization was committed to preserving and furthering the autonomous life of Jews as a diasporic people by developing a contemporary Jewish culture in Yiddish, the vernacular language at the time of most Eastern European and American Jews. Particularly in the early years, the Kultur-Lige saw Yiddish not simply as a means of communication but as a unified cultural phenomenon, the product of a collective national creativity. The aim was to develop a modern Yiddish culture that would be a synthesis of the old and the new, the national and the universal, a culture of the whole Jewish diaspora "from Moscow to New York and from London to Johannesburg." This vision, which has been characterized as a hybrid of nationalist tradition and proletarian internationalism, was analogous to the one that motivated the Ukrainianization movement in the twenties. (Estraikh 2005, 113,)

The artistic section of the Kultur-Lige was particularly successful. It promoted a "Jewish style" that fused leanings toward abstraction with the devices of folk art. The section included Borys (Barukh) Aronson, Mark (Moisei) Epshtein, Issakhar-Ber Rybak, Oleksandr (Aleksandr) Tyshler, Yosyf Elman, Isaak Rabichev, Solomon Nykrytin, Nisson Shifrin, and Sara Shor. They were soon joined by El (Lazar) Lissitzky, Yosyf (Josif) Chaikov, Polina Khentova, and Mark Sheikhel, who arrived from Petrograd and Moscow. Abram Manevych came early in 1919. In spite of all the difficulties posed by the political situation, the period 1918–21 was the most productive. Artists discussed the nature of national art in the Jewish Literary-Artistic Club. Chaikov and Rabinovich taught drawing and sculpture in the Kyiv Jewish High School of the Kultur-Lige. In 1919, a Jewish art and theater studio was opened in Kyiv which continued to exist as a part of the Kultur-Lige until 1924, when it became the Jewish Art-Industrial School, with Mark Epshtein as director. It was one of three Jewish art institutes in the world, alongside the Bezalel Arts Academy in Jerusalem, and the Educational Alliance Art School in New York. Children's books were published in the Kultur-Lige's own printing house. The illustrations by El Lissitzky, Issakhar-Ber Rybak, Sara Shor, and Mark Chagall are considered some of the best Jewish book art of the twentieth century. Exhibitions by the artistic section took place in Kyiv in 1920 and 1922. Influenced by Alexandra Ekster, whose studio many had attended in the years 1916–20, these artists were attracted to her version of cubo-futurism with its geometrical, flattened forms, arresting colors, and kinetic energy.

Like their Ukrainian colleagues, Jewish artists often searched for national forms. To this end, they explored ethnography and folk art. Nathan Altman had in 1913 copied ancient gravestones in the Jewish cemetery in Shepetivka. El Lissitzky and Issakhar-Ber Rybak had in 1915 surveyed and copied the designs in about two hundred wooden synagogues in small towns along the banks of the Dnipro. Solomon Yudovyn had participated in ethnographic expeditions in which he painted tombstones and ritual objects. Elman and Chaikov had studied the designs on Jewish silverware. This work allowed the artists to discover the shtetl as a distinctive topos in art. (Kazovskii 2003, 73,) Jewish primitive art and children's art were topics of special investigation. Even gingerbread figures, toys, and stencils were examined in the quest for national archetypes.

The influence of this Kyiv milieu was felt abroad. Aronson, the son of Kyiv's chief rabbi, who had studied set design in Ekster's studio in 1917–18, subsequently worked in over a hundred productions in the United States. Shifrin and Tyshler, also Ekster's students, moved to Moscow in the twenties, where they became well-known theatrical designers. Issakhar-Ber Rybak moved to Berlin and then Paris in the twenties, where he found fame after publishing albums of lithographs depicting the shtetl and Jewish types in Ukraine. A number of artists also studied in Mykhailo Boichuk's studio of monumental art, including Nisson Shifrin, Emanuil Shekhtman, and Teofil Fraierman. This powerful artistic flowering made Kyiv in 1919–21 a leading center of Jewish and Ukrainian avant-garde art.

The Kultur-Lige's leadership was split between those who wanted to promote cultural and national values and those who gave pride of place to political-ideological issues. When the conflict flared up, many left. Many in the artistic section moved to Moscow; Leib Kvitko and Perets Markish left for Germany; Hofshtein went to Palestine. Disillusioned by the situation abroad, most of the writers returned to Ukraine, where they were to share the fate of all the Ukrainian intelligentsia: some were killed in the thirties, while others, who survived the purges—like Leib Kvitko and thirteen other members of the Jewish Anti-Fascist Committee—were murdered by Stalin's secret police in 1952.

Although the Soviet government made attempts in the 1920s and 1930s to deal with anti-Semitism, its antireligious agitation, which targeted Judaism and Zionism, exacerbated the problem. It forcibly closed synagogues, confiscating all gold and silver objects in them. In 1919 the Bolsheviks banned the teaching of Hebrew, liquidated Zionist organizations, and all Jewish party, political, professional, and cultural organizations created under the UNR. However, Zionist parties mushroomed. Show trials against the "Jewish counterrevolution" began in 1922 and over a thousand individuals were sentenced to prison terms or to Siberian exile. An antireligious campaign, which often identified Judaism with Zionism, was spearheaded in 1921–22 by the Jewish sections of the Communist Party. The strong reaction against these measures made the sections retreat temporarily, but they went on the offensive again in the late twenties and early thirties. Severe limitations on expressions of religious life were made law in 1929, and the last synagogue in Kyiv was closed in 1936. The network of Jewish secondary institutions was shut down in the second half of the thirties. Khiterer reports that newsreels of many of these closings have been preserved in Ukrainian archives. (Khiterer 2002, 10.)

Terry Martin has shown how the indigenization movement was conceived as an attempt to disarm and depoliticize nationalism by granting national territories and by providing support for languages. The movement slowed and was gradually reversed during the "Socialist offensive" of 1928–32. (Martin 2001, 117–22,) The Soviet policy refused the idea of extraterritorial national-cultural autonomy, which would have meant the election of representatives from a given nationality to bodies that would have jurisdiction over cultural policy as it affected that nationality. This was the UNR policy. Instead the Soviet state opted for the territorialization of ethnicity, creating not only republics and autonomous oblasts, but hundreds of small national territories, even the size of villages. The proliferation of these small territorial units proved a failure. From Moscow's viewpoint, it was unsuccessful in defusing nationalism, and from the point of view of minorities, it did not provide the cultural support they required. When, in 1933, Ukrainian nationalism (and not Russian great power chauvinism, as had previously been the case) was declared the "greatest danger" this became the signal to dismantle Ukrainian and Jewish cultural institutions.

Nonetheless, Jewish institutions could claim some important achievements. In 1918 (under the UNR) the newly created Ukrainian Academy of Sciences formed two research centers for the collection and study of Jewish materials: the Jewish Historical-Archaeographical Commission (1919–29) headed by Ilia Galant, and the Jewish section at Kyiv's National Library of Ukraine. Later, in 1928–29, when two Leningrad institutions were closed down—namely the Society for the Spreading of Enlightenment among Jews in Russia (Obshchestvo dlia rasprostranenia prosveshcheniia mezhdu evreiami v Rossii: OPE, 1863–1929) and the Jewish Historical-Ethnographic Society (Evreiskoe istoriko-etnograficheskoe obshchestvo: EIEO, 1908–30)—their collections, which included part of A. Harkavy's and S. An-sky (Shloyme Rapoport's) libraries and manuscripts, were sent to the National Library in Kyiv.

The Institute of Jewish Proletarian Culture (1929–36) became the main research center for Jewish history and culture in the USSR. In 1930 its library obtained part of the OPE and EIEO collections. In 1936 this library was told to transfer its holdings to Kyiv's National Library. Evacuated to Ufa during the Second World War, it was returned to Kyiv but not made available to readers. Until 1990 its materials (which included the collection of folk music and recordings made by An-sky during his famous ethnographic expeditions of 1911–13) were kept in reserve vaults, where they survived almost entirely intact thanks to the staff.

Although preconditions for a Ukrainian-Jewish dialogue existed in the post-revolutionary decade, political circumstances worked against its development and eventually cut short the rapprochement. By the late twenties, Jews were no longer drawn into the work of Ukrainianization, Jewish education and scholarship in Ukraine were curtailed, and the development of Jewish literature and culture was undermined.

CHAPTER 4

Constructing Jewish Identity in Ukrainian Literature, 1914–1929

The philo-Semitic stance characteristic of prerevolutionary Ukrainian writing was carried over into the immediate postrevolutionary years. Stepan Vasylchenko, Modest Levytsky, and Klym Polishchuk are good examples of this kind of fiction. The first two owed much to the earlier sentimental approach (Kunitz's "reign of pity"), but their works were published and republished during the revolution and the twenties. These minor writers not only captured a substantial readership but could claim to represent widely held attitudes.

Vasylchenko made a name for himself in prerevolutionary years with his portraits of the downtrodden who yearn for a better future—the "gentle, helpless, dreaming soul" that Kunitz has identified dismissively as the main interest of late nineteenth-century Russian authors. (Kunitz 1929, 120.) A schoolteacher, Vasylchenko was arrested by the tsarist regime and spent a year and a half in prison. His first collection of stories was confiscated by the censorship in 1914 and its publishers taken to court. He was drafted into the tsarist army and served until 1917. Always sensitive to social injustice and inequality, he noted the appalling treatment of Jews by the army in a letter from April 18, 1915 from Przemyśl: "It is the Jews who have a difficult time surviving these times. They all walk around sad, frightened. There is a rumor among them that they will be sent away from here to Russia. In the last days they have been driven out to work: clearing the dung and all kinds of rubbish that the Austrian garrison left behind in the streets and courtyards of the town. The picture was worthy if not of an artist's brush, then at least of a good photographer. There are many of them scattered around the carts full of loathsome rubbish, old and young, with side curls, in long coats—they move through the streets perspiring and dirty, while their women look out of the windows and doors crying." (Vasyl'chenko 1959–60, 4:355.) Western Ukraine was taken by the Russian army in the early years of the First World War. Much of the Jewish population was robbed, its institutions were closed, and its rights curtailed. Jews were again forbidden to live in villages or practice agriculture, and were restricted in their movement. The army looked upon Jews as enemies, informers, and spies: they were sometimes given twenty-four hours to clear an area near the front and move east. As half a million were uprooted and moved to the interior, the Pale of Settlement ceased to exist.

During the revolution, Vasylchenko wrote stories that portrayed the Jews with sympathy and understanding, reportedly in response to Symon Petliura's request for short popular prose that would counteract the wave of pogroms. One such story, "Pro zhydka Marchyka bidnoho kravchyka" (About the Poor Jew Marchyk the Tailor), was first published in the newspaper *Ukraina* (Ukraine, 1919) and simultaneously as a separate publication. It depicts a poor Jew, who, along with his fellow townspeople, welcomes the February 1917 revolution, but perishes a year later. The revolution's early days are a time of great elation, when people come together and call one another comrades. In this world that promises so much freedom, Avrum and his wife Liia conceive a child. However, when the baby is born, the country has already experienced invasion and the spread of anarchy. To avoid the approaching violence, Avrum and his family take refuge in a cellar, but the quarter is surrounded and burned down. Those who try to escape are bayoneted. Avrum and his family perish; his story, the one he began telling in a state of euphoria at a meeting in the revolution's early days, remains unfinished. Vasylchenko's story is meant to reflect the tragic fate of the Jewish population, but also to suggest that the moment of coming together was within reach before being suddenly lost. The dream of a happy birth and a future in freedom perishes in violence and destruction. The author's earlier stories had documented the growth in mutual understanding of the two communities; here he documents the violent end to that process.

The stories that describe the interaction between Ukrainians and Jews in small towns show a strong interest in issues of identity. "Za muramy" (Behind the Walls, 1913) portrays an unhappy marriage between Duvid Volynsky and his wife Sonia, who has begun to rebel against Jewish customs under the influence of her reading. Their home contains not only "Jewish pictures," but also portraits of Tolstoy, Gorky, and Shevchenko—all three represent rebellious freethinking. The Christian narrator lodges with the family and immediately feels the presence of ancient traditions, of "another God" and the passionate promise to remain faithful to Him in the words of Psalm 137: "If I forget you, O Jerusalem, let my right arm wither." Sonia's intellectual abilities are obvious; she studies, passes her exams, and is accepted into midwifery courses in the city. Her illiterate husband is convinced that he will lose her if she travels, and opposes her desire to move. Violent arguments follow, until Sonia decides to convert to Christianity and leave her husband. The Jewish community gathers to pray and lament the loss of one of their own. Both Khrystyna, a young Ukrainian woman who works as a housekeeper for the family, and the narrator are deeply moved by the singing and praying: "In this storm of a foreign yearning the tears of more than one human being could be felt. One sensed the powerful, elemental cry of an entire nation that was dying, that was being abandoned and wronged." The story is told in jail, where some of the narrator's fellow prisoners are Jews. They all experience the same yearning in captivity for a better life. The ending holds out hope: news arrives that in his home village people have begun "beating the tocsin, awaking from age-long slumber a country that captivity has lulled to sleep." (Ibid., 2:122–23.) Vasylchenko accepts that a new and better society must be built on the ruins of the old, but he nonetheless understands the links to tradition in any reinvented identity. He maps the internal borders that separate a culture from its own traditional past and from another culture with which it coexists. But his manner of doing so is tentative. The narrator-protagonist's vantage point is removed from events. In the first part of the story he can only reconstruct a picture of the neighboring culture from overheard conversations and glimpses of unfamiliar rituals, and in the second part he can only surmise from letters what the clash with tradition entails. It is a diffident, groping construction of how the new affects another culture.

One work by Vasylchenko devoted to Ukrainian-Jewish relations, as we have seen, incurred the wrath of Olena Pchilka. In the play *Zilia Korolevych* (1913) Tania, a young, lonely village schoolteacher, meets her Prince Charming (Korolevych means prince) during the Christmas holiday. Zilia Haievsky, a student of Jewish origin and the object of her affection, shows himself to be more concerned with the issue of what will occur when the sun loses its energy. Left alone at the end of the play, both Tania and Zilia realize that they have nowhere to go and they come together: As is common in Vasylchenko, lost souls in modest surroundings find comfort and love. There is, no doubt, something timid and "sapless" (to use Kunitz's phrase) in this writing, but it presents Jewish protagonists with sympathy and recreates the aura of small-town life.

Modest Levytsky contributed stories to the prerevolutionary newspaper *Rada* that were marked by the same gentle humor as Vasylchenko's. His world is also that of sleepy small towns and byways in Right Bank Ukraine, with their many Jewish characters. The description of interiors is an indication of his intimacy with Jewish life. In one story a Ukrainian and his Jewish acquaintance have their pockets picked on a train by a con-man; in another the narrator mistakes the intentions of a decent Jewish innkeeper for something nefarious; in a third members of both communities share a panic over the rumor of an epidemic. Denouements usually reveal the common humanity of ordinary people and demystifies some fear or prejudice. Levytsky worked as a physician and had many Jewish patients with whom he spoke Yiddish and among whom he was a popular figure. While living in Okna in southern Podillia, he produced a play. The priest and the rabbi turned out to be great fans of the theater, but because of their social position and age could not participate as actors. The priest took the job of prompter, while the rabbi worked backstage, where he helped enthusiastically. (Levyts'kyi and Doroshenko 1967, 11.) This kind of easy cultural interaction occurs often in Levytsky's prose. During the revolution the writer worked for the UNR Ukrainianizing teachers. In 1919 he headed the government's diplomatic mission to Greece, in 1922 directed a sanatorium for Ukrainian veterans in Zakopane, Poland, and then lectured in the Ukrainian Academy of Economics in Poděbrady, Czechoslovakia. Several collections of his stories appeared between 1919 and 1928.

Klym Polishchuk's stories deal with the revolution in central Ukraine, but were published in Lviv, where he spent the years 1921–25. After returning to Soviet Ukraine he stopped writing about the revolution. His protagonists are unavoidably caught up in events, find themselves first in one army then another, fight not out of conviction but in order to survive, and show little enthusiasm for ideology. The story "Manivtsiamy (Iz zapysnoi knyzhky nevidomoho)" (Side Roads: From the Notebook of an Unknown, 1921) presents the diary of a Red Army soldier, a former nationalist supporter, who has been killed in battle. It records his horror at witnessing the violence on both sides, particularly at finding Ida Golberg, a celebrated actress, murdered during a pogrom. Ironically, the commanders of both nationalist and communist armies know one another intimately, having grown up together. Both claim to be fighting for an independent Ukraine. But the two sides do not encompass all of Ukraine: as the diary's author records burying his beloved actress, he comments poignantly that two Ukraines are fighting one another, while a third lies buried in the grave before him.

In Polishchuk's wartime stories, idealism and honor often play an insignificant role in human conduct. When authorities are challenged over atrocities, the response is always a complacent recourse to ideology—the rightness of the cause. In "Revoliutsiinym shliakhom" (The Revolutionary Way, 1921), the narrator admits his loss of faith in everyone he "considered devoted to the struggle for the rights of the oppressed and who appeared to be summoned by the revolution itself." (Polishchuk 1922a, 45.) His slogan becomes a Kantian one: "The starry sky is above me and the moral law is within me." He tries to prevent innocent individuals from being executed by nationalist forces as spies, but cannot stop the maelstrom of events. In "Za vsikh—odyn (Iz zapysnoi knyzhky)" (One For All: From a Notebook, 1921) an old Jew, Avrum Shtutsman, whose mind has been unhinged, approaches him with the idea that he should suffer on behalf of all: "Let them shoot me, one old man, and let the young people go." (Ibid., 61.) As the troops retreat, a cavalryman shoots the old man, because the "procurator" said he was a spy and should be killed. Naturally, the "procurator" has already fled the town. The narrator comments: "One thought disturbs me to this day. I would not like those who are following in our footsteps to think that they are 'better' than we are." (Ibid., 64.) This ambiguous phrase can be read as directed at both the Red Army that is entering the town, and at future readers of the story.

"Kazka, iakykh bahato (Iz 'mandrivnykh' zapysok)" (A Story Like Many: From 'Wandering' Notes, 1923) describes a conversation between the narrator and an old man who is the caretaker in a Jewish cemetery. The gravestones appear to be ghosts, and the atmosphere breathes a majestic calm. The old man tells the narrator that the earth, which feels and senses every word and action, will not tolerate all things: the stones and those who are beneath them "are silent and think their own thoughts, which they will utter one day when the limit of all endurance has been reached!" (Polishchuk 1923, 157–58.) Like the old man, the narrator has faith that those who have willingly gone against the people will be punished. The righteous have found their peaceful resting place, while on the other side of the road the black cross of a Ukrainian who served foreigners remains a reminder of evil and treason.

Polishchuk is especially interesting for the way he presents the ideology of the Greens (independent, anarchist revolutionaries), and of warlords who controlled small local territories. In "Na voli (Iz zapysnoi knyzhky)" (In Freedom: From a Notebook, 1919) a local thug interprets liberty as his personal license to satisfy his own passions. He attempts to rape a Jewish woman. When she resists, he stabs her. He has served all sides in the past, "the light blue, the red, and the black." Guilt-ridden, confused and degenerate, he is described as a "disgusting figure" who is "incapable of any intelligent struggle." It turns out that he is the son of a cantor. The young gentleman has, in the words of one old woman, become "worse than an animal." (Polishchuk 1921a, 48.) In "Mizh svoimy (Iz zapysnoi knyzhky)" (Among One's Own: From a Notebook) the narrator is captured by a band and taken to the village commander Bronevyk, who confesses that he needs to kill another ten Jews to make his "Jewish century": "Today, when I told the chief (otaman) that I had to complete my Jewish century, he almost jumped in the air with fury. He roared that I was ruining his whole cause. . . . To tell the truth, I am not the one to blame: he is the one that is ruining the cause. . . . He has hooked up with some teacher, who tells him day and night: 'Don't beat the Jews; they are people too!' . . . May she drop dead, along with her Jews!" His comrades agree that "if the chief isn't a womanizer, he must be a real Jew." (Ibid., 87–88.) When confronted, Bronevyk offers no answer to the question of why he hates Jews. These dialogues expose confused political thinking and prejudices, and the degeneration of ordinary people into unreflective, unfeeling murderers. Two images in particular capture the senselessness and indiscriminate nature of the killing: a black crow that pecks out the eyes of corpses, oblivious of which army the victims fought for, and a plaster Christ on the cross that prompts the narrator to wonder "whom he died for."

In "Chervoni riadna (Iz zapysnoi knyzhky)" (Red Linen: From a Notebook, 1919) the Bolsheviks have displayed their red banners throughout a recently taken town. On the night before they move out they conduct a pogrom, leaving behind ruined houses and corpses on the main boulevard. The narrator writes: "The black birds of human anger fought in the air and evildoing roared with laughter like a savage hurricane. . . . My native, quiet, placid little town went mad with savage instincts from its lower depths." (Ibid., 133.) In the morning the narrator's friend Aron is found crucified on the pedestal of a statue of Pushkin. This image can be read as a metaphor for the desecration of prerevolutionary Russian culture, or, if the choice of statue is presumed to be deliberate, for the culture's conscious rejection of a Jewish presence. It is to Polishchuk's credit that in stories like this he looked into the abyss of violence and attempted at least in part to chronicle and understand it.

The author also produced a favorable depiction of a peasant army. In the novel *Otaman Zelenyi* (The Warlord Zeleny, 1922) the hero is a conscious patriot who supports the government of the UNR and acts ruthlessly to prevent any abuse of the Jewish population. His psychological evolution is presented as typical of the insurgents in the Dnipro valley. Zeleny (the name translates as "Green") comes from a poor village in which the people are aware of their social and national oppression: they take pride in their long tradition of struggles against landlords and foreign rulers. Zeleny has been educated through reading Ukrainian literature, in particular Shevchenko's verse, and through discussions with patriotic social revolutionaries. The peasant rebellions, however tragic in outcome, are seen as glorious pages in history, evidence of the indomitable spirit of the Ukrainian steppe. The approaching revolution is therefore greeted with sympathy as a mass liberation movement. Although one local schoolteacher blames the Jews for "inventing" the revolution in order to rebel, this view is dismissed by the hero, who affirms that it is a movement for equality.

The novel presents the national revolution's interpretation of events. The collapse of tsarism is greeted with universal enthusiasm, but the toppling of the UNR government in Kyiv by its rival in Kharkiv is the work of Russian Bolsheviks. These are the same Russians, the hero argues, who invaded with Andrei Bogoliubsky and Peter the Great, and who were resisted by the same population of the Black Earth lands that rose up with Khmelnytsky and during the Koliivshchyna revolt of 1768. When the Germans take over the country in 1918, Zeleny returns to the village, bides his time, and organizes his fighters. At the year's end, when the Germans and their protégé Hetman Skoropadsky depart, he joins the popular uprising that restores Ukrainian power. However, the Russian Bolsheviks again organize a counter-government and move against Kyiv. Confused rumors spread among people about their policies and intentions. Zeleny calls an assembly, and the people begin to organize themselves into an independent insurrectionary body. They demand that all councils (soviets) and commissars be elected, and that Ukrainian culture be allowed to develop freely. Zeleny is elected the leader of this body. He forges alliances and eventually controls a large territory on both banks of the Dnipro from Cherkassy almost as far as Chornobyl. Invading Bolshevik troops can do nothing against these forces, which are able to melt into the villages and then reemerge at a moment's notice. When the Ukrainian government regroups in Kamianets, Zeleny recognizes its authority. His successes are so great that the Bolsheviks regret their refusal to recognize peasant councils, elected commissars, and the Ukrainian language.

The national revolution has no place for national nihilists or anti-Semites, and Zeleny vigorously attacks both. When instances of anti-Semitism or cruelty to Jews occur, they are dealt with swiftly. A Jewess is captured by a group of drunken insurgents, who claim that she is with the Reds. The attempted rape is stopped by Zeleny, who cuts down one of the men assaulting her. She is the widow of a lawyer, whose hands, one character asserts, "were kissed by commissars." When asked who owns the land in the area, she answers "it is all mine." The reader learns that her son is indeed a commissar. Nonetheless, she is released, and the following day a trial is set for the men who were involved in the attempted rape, although one grizzly soldier comments that the culprits will all be gone from the camp by morning. (Polishchuk 1922b, 106–7.) Eventually Zeleny is killed in action. His dying words are an encouragement to continue fighting for a free and independent Ukraine in which social justice prevails.

The most important element of this story is perhaps the myth of the freedom-loving steppe people who have always struggled courageously for liberty and dignity. The opening paragraphs make clear that we are dealing with an elemental force: "The fertile soil of the Black Earth moves and breathes in alarm, feeling within itself the still unborn powers of its faithful children, who only need to raise themselves onto their elbows for their heads to move the azure of the skies. . . . When one of them did arise, the world marveled at his invincible powers, his beauty and unblemished purity. . . . In the settlements and villages they will long remember the famous insurgent Otaman Zeleny, who was summoned by his muzhyk fate to be the leader of the oppressed and to bear the sword of punishment and justice, and whose victory brought joy to those who were without light." (Ibid., 5.)

Polishchuk depicts Ukrainian-Jewish relations as a complex issue, suggesting the possibility of mutual understanding and coexistence without underestimating their difficulty. In "Hanebna sprava (Opovidannia)" (Shameful Business: A Story, 1918) the February revolution is greeted with a religious service held jointly by an Orthodox priest, a Catholic priest, and a rabbi, who each speak of their community's aspirations. They are followed by revolutionary orators, who emphasize liberty and human solidarity. The revolution, however, has stimulated people's greed. Some want to take away land and possessions from others. Khaika, the beautiful young daughter of the orendar Berko, has fallen in love with the teacher. No one sees anything strange in this, even though everyone knows that she is Jewish. The Orthodox priest's daughters gossip about the relationship, but this is ignored because everyone knows "that they were getting to be old maids and so it was understood why they disapproved of Khaika's friendship with Vakulenko." When Khaika, a reader of socialist literature, runs off with the teacher, who is a fiery revolutionary orator, eight wagons full of armed Jews set out in pursuit. Vakulenko is caught and beaten. The villagers do not defend him, but allow him to be imprisoned for two days. He thinks: "Those Talmudist fanatics, and that God-fearing and evil Christian herd! . . . What do they want from me? . . . I tried to teach them about the free life that every human being should live! . . . It seems that all this is wasted on them. They are still divided among themselves; 'the goy' and 'the Jew' will exist among them for a long time yet, without giving way to 'the people.'" (Polishchuk 1921a, 143.)

When Vakulenko and Khaika catch the first train out of town, Red Army soldiers, who recognize him as a fellow revolutionary, protect them, beating off the pursuing Jews. Khaika marries Vakulenko and becomes a teacher in Polissia. Eventually her father writes her a letter, saying that he will forgive her. The reader's sympathy is distributed among the participants, and the resolution is clearly a compromise between opposing camps and traditions.

Polishchuk also records hearing the legend of the Eternal or Wandering Jew. In his retelling of this tale, Ukraine is portrayed as a country cursed by a tragic political fate. From the time of Hetman Doroshenko's rule (1665–76), it has been divided between foreign powers, who have meddled in its internal politics and set up their own protégés. The town of Kamianets has witnessed the banquets and harems of Sultan Mehmet IV, who supported Doroshenko and built Turkish forts and bridges. The Eternal Jew, Ahasuerus, has lived through many somber times after Christ prophesied that he would "travel all over the wide world and wherever he went grief and trouble would accompany his footsteps . . . until the Day of Judgment." Ahasuerus has witnessed the suffering of the Jews throughout the centuries, and has now returned to Ukraine. Fascinated by the tale, the narrator comments skeptically, "life is life and a story is a story," but promises to record the legend. Shortly after this he meets an old Jew, a tzaddik from Uman whose family has perished and who wanders the earth bereft. The narrator comments: "I traveled on thinking of what could be the difference between real life and the mystical legend. Is not this Jew the same Ahasuerus, who in his limitless grief adds to our own misfortune?" (Polishchuk 1921b, 7, 11.) Here, as in the previous examples, the author's focus is on the suffering of Jews and their connection to Ukraine's tragic fate.

Volodymyr Vynnychenko played a major role in shaping attitudes toward Jews, both as a political leader and a writer. The plays *Mizh dvokh syl* (Between Two Forces, 1919) and *Pisnia Izrailia (Kol-Nidre)* (Song of Israel: Kol-Nidre, 1922, 1930), like his prewar *Dysharmoniia*, present youthful enthusiasms coming up against hard realities. Set in 1918, *Mizh dvokh syl* describes the Bolshevik camp in which all Ukrainians are viewed as real or potential counterrevolutionaries: they are expected to speak Russian and to reject national sympathies. Even Grinberg, a Jewish Bolshevik leader who is more sympathetic toward Ukrainians, dismisses their political and cultural aspirations. Sophia and her brother Tykhon have helped the Bolsheviks, naïvely expecting communism to guarantee national, as well as social and personal rights. Her father and her other two brothers, on the other hand, have joined the national movement. Sophia and Tykhon are cruelly disappointed in the Bolsheviks, who treat them with suspicion and contempt because of their nationality, and, of course, the national movement now considers them traitors. When her father and one of her anti-Bolshevik brothers are about to be executed as nationalists, Sophia pleads with Grinberg for their release. In return for sexual favors, he allows the father to be released, but, despite his promise to Sophia, orders her brother's execution. This manipulative and dishonorable behavior is linked to his growing aversion toward all things Ukrainian: he gradually stops speaking the language and drops all sympathy for national aspirations. Grinberg is not portrayed as a sexual predator. He has long been attracted to Sophia and his initial use of Ukrainian is an attempt to please her. The play focuses more on the way power over individuals and nations changes people, breeding contempt for the vulnerable.

Pisnia Izrailia demonstrates the prejudices in prerevolutionary Ukrainian society toward an assimilated Jew. It recalls earlier portrayals of tragic liaisons and, like them, shows sympathy for the Jewish party. Completed in 1922, the play was allowed publication in the Soviet Union in 1930 even though Vynnychenko lived abroad after 1919. The action occurs during 1905. Nata Konchynska, the daughter of a prominent Ukrainian marshal of the nobility (the chair of the district assembly of the nobility), marries Aron Bliumkes, the son of a tailor, who is a musician and composer. The courageous and politically liberal Nata falls in love with Aron and insists on the union, against her parents' wishes. Aron also breaks with his family and community by accepting Christianity. The rupture in both cases is painful: Nata endures a hunger strike to get her way, while Aron is disowned by his grandfather Moisei and his father Leizer. The snobbish and anti-Semitic upper-class Ukrainian environment is portrayed in the figure of Mitiakhin, a lawyer and member of the State Duma, and Pamfilov, a student. But much of the parental opposition stems from pressures to observe social proprieties. Nata's father fears being ridiculed in the administration's eyes: "A fine marshal of the nobility it is, who is family with some Jewish tailor! Naturally, they will not only fail to reelect me, but . . . will not allow me into any decent home! You are gambling away your entire life, our peace, health, our social standing, our honor, for what?" (Vynnychenko 1930, 58.) The idealistic Nata and her brother Kolia appear to have no prejudices, nor does Professor Sukhonin who appreciates Aron's talent and calls the Jews "a people of genius." But it is partly headstrong radicalism that attracts her to the idea of marriage with Aron because it represents a slap in the face of conservative society. She is determined to prove her family's fears misplaced. Aron takes the name Mykola Bliumsky, becomes an acclaimed performer, and appears to have fully assimilated. Nata claims triumphantly that her husband is now "Mykola" and exclaims: "There are only human beings! And artists! There are no Jews, no Christians, no Ukrainians [rus'kykh]!" Even her father is finally convinced that his son-in-law is no longer a Jew but a "European." However, Aron's assimilation has taken place at the cost of self-denial. Nata has extracted a promise from her husband that he will never return to his Jewish roots, and forbids him from playing the Song of Israel. Moreover, she appears suspiciously concerned with the fact that there is "nothing Jewish" in her son's appearance. Just as Bliumsky celebrates his greatest success, a pogrom begins. Mitiakhin has spread rumors of ritual murders, which he claims are a "scientific fact," and has pointed the finger at Leizer Bliumkes, who is arrested. In response, Mykola announces that he has once more become Aron:

> *Aron.* All these two years the greatest scandal and torture for you was everything Jewish in me. Yes, yes. Like the traces of some disgusting, shameful sickness, you have been uprooting everything in me and our child that was reminiscent of Jewishness.
> *Nata.* Yes I am uprooting it! I did not deceive you. Because I did not marry a Jew. You yourself said that you are not a Jew, but simply a human being and an artist.
> *Aron.* "Simply a human being!" With people who are simply human beings I really am simply a human being, but with haters of my people I am a Jew. (Ibid., 78.)

Aron refuses her offers of conciliation with Mitiakhin and her father, who is also convinced that ritual killings are a reality. Nonetheless, he is about to capitulate to his wife's request to compromise, when his sister arrives with news suggesting that his family has been killed and that the growing fire on the street outside, which can be seen from the window, indicates the spreading violence. Aron takes up his violin and once more plays the Song of Israel.

The message is a complex one. For one thing, the burden for the failed liaison lies heavily on the anti-Semitism in the Ukrainian intelligentsia. But the picture is also one of government-generated hatred and of resistance to it. Like other works on Jewish-Ukrainian relations, the play captures both the potential for cooperation and the distance that still separates the two nations. It represents a critique not only of reactionaries who poison the social atmosphere, but also of the liberal youth who show a limited self-awareness and a refusal to contemplate any alternative to assimilation. In both plays a sense of social or intellectual superiority makes some characters blind and unfeeling toward others. The plays suggest the existence of a firm moral law that must guide people in both their personal and political behavior. Those who act dishonorably in their private lives inevitably so do in politics. Moral obtuseness and dishonesty, especially when it is deemed socially acceptable, produces similar tragedies in both personal and political life, and eventually corrupts all society. Vynnychenko, like other Ukrainian authors of his generation, was not hostile to Judaism or Christianity, or at least not more hostile to one than the other. His interest is in presenting situations in which individuals are called upon to make moral choices under duress, and he is especially convincing in his analysis of hypocritical behavior.

Failed liaisons are also the subject of two melodramas by A. Kozych-Umanska (pseudonym of the Russian playwright Isaak Khanish) that were published in Ukrainian by émigrés in New York. *Pimsta zhydivky* (The Revenge of a Jewess, 1919) is the story of the beautiful nineteen-year-old Rakhyl, who is kidnapped from her father's tavern by the haidamaka Korshun. She admits to loving him, even when she rejects him: "They say you are not a knight, but a haidamaka. I find it terrible to think that the hand that touches mine has been dipped in human blood. My soul grieves, Cossack, when I think of you. God gave you intelligence, a fine figure, and beauty. Look at yourself—an eagle, not a Cossack. But your heart is fiercer than that of a wild animal!" (Kozych-Umans'ka 1919a, 11.) Her father Abrum plans to poison Korshun in order to protect his daughter, but dies when he is made to drink the poisoned wine. Forced to join the haidamaka band, Rakhyl has a passionate affair with the handsome Korshun. However, her first instincts were correct: he turns out to be nothing more than a criminal. When he grows tired of his lover, he tries to drown her.

Another outlaw, Bulat, who has long been secretly in love with Rakhyl, rescues her. He had earlier remained silent when Korshun poisoned Rakhyl's father, saying: "My poor dove, what will happen to you? Who will help you in your hour of need? Why cannot I tear apart all the haidamakas together with Korshun?! I am powerless, I can do nothing to protect you!" (Ibid., 15.) After rescuing her from drowning, he confesses his love and asks for her hand in marriage. Bulat must still serve with the outlaws and Rakhyl asks for time in making a decision. She disfigures her face, plays the madwoman, and becomes known in town as the "mad Hanna." There she exposes Korshun when he tries to marry the unsuspecting daughter of a rich family. Korshun is tracked down by a posse, imprisoned, and beheaded. In the last act, Rakhyl-Hanna, who still loves him even though she now views him as a cruel man, refuses to free him from prison when she has the opportunity. In the final scene, like a contemporary Salome she picks up the head of the executed outlaw and runs off stage crying, "Now you are mine, mine, and I will not give you to anyone." Rakhyl is the star. The viewer is able to identify with her tragedy of spurned love, and to see the baseness of the "Cossack" and "haidamaka." It is difficult not to read into the play a sense of shame and atonement for the mistreatment of Jews at the hands of criminals masquerading as noble outlaws—a message that is not only in the plot and characterization, but also in the play's foreboding atmosphere, which is shrouded in a nightmarish sense of horror, madness, and violence.

Vykhrest (V chadu kokhania) (The Convert: In the Power of Love, 1919) deals with the fatal passion of the wealthy young Jewish storekeeper Leizer for the Christian Vassa. He leaves his wife Khaia and their two children, and becomes a Christian in the hope of marrying her. However, Vassa and her mother are primarily interested in his wealth. When Vassa discovers that he has been disowned by his father and will not receive his half of the family fortune, she marries her village lover. The action is evenly divided between Jewish and Ukrainian homes. All the characters are treated with sympathy. If there are villains, they are Vassa and her mother, whose social ambitions and materialism cause them to lead Leizer astray. The rest of the village tries to help Khaia recover from the marital disaster and after the repentant Leizer dies, she remarries in the Jewish tradition.

In both plays the efforts by Jewish characters to assimilate into a Ukrainian milieu are thwarted by the Ukrainian partner, with traumatic and destructive effects. The converts still feel outsiders; they are mistreated, rejected by their lovers, and driven to madness or death. Like Vynnychenko's dramas, these plays can be viewed as examinations of Jewish self-transformation. Kozych-Umanska's plays focus on abusive relationships in which the Jewish partner is the victim, and perhaps suggest that the conditions set for Jewish assimilation are too high. Publication of these plays in Ukrainian, like the publication of Chirikov's *Evrei* in Ukrainian translation in 1907, was probably part of an attempt to address the trauma caused by political violence, and to repair damaged Ukrainian-Jewish relations.

The traditional role of the orendar, and more often of the tavernkeeper, still recur in the twenties, particularly in the popular dramas of Western Ukraine, which found itself under Polish rule after 1921. In these plays the Jew's strategic position as a go-between might allow him to pick up information and use it to further the villain's plans and his own material gain. An orendar who is ready and willing to take advantage of sinfulness in the village community plays a role in *Peshchena dytyna* (Spoiled Child, 1923) by Roman Surmach (pen name of Yeronym Lutsyk). The play deals with a good-for-nothing son who has been spoiled by his affluent family and ends up by selling everything to Mortko, a clever and unscrupulous orendar. Another play, *V kikhtiakh rozpusty abo Nad bezodneiu propasty* (In the Claws of Debauchery or On the Brink of the Abyss, 1921), is set in 1910–12, and describes the hard life of a family that has moved from the village to the town. The husband is an alcoholic and the women have to make money by ironing for a Jewish business. The Jew is both an orendar and keeper of a tavern frequented by whores and thieves. It is in his interests, and those of the criminals, that alcoholics be drawn into their nets, with predictably lamentable results. However, by no means all depictions of innkeepers are negative. A. L. Sukhodolsky's *Khmara* (Cloud, 1919), which was also published in emigration, uses a Jewish inn as a structuring device. All of the third act takes place there. The innkeeper must deal with the villain Semen, in whose name he leases the inn. He maintains some degree of peace between mortal enemies and protects the beautiful heroine, whom the villain has intentions of seducing. All the characters arrive at different times to rest or spend the night. The innkeeper's behavior remains dignified and diplomatic, despite the intense hatreds swirling around him. It is perhaps significant that this play was published by supporters of the Ukrainian Sharpshooters Regiment (Sichovi Striltsi), the professional core of the UNR's army which was initially recruited from Western Ukrainians who had served in the Austro-Hungarian military. Their attitude toward Jews was often sympathetic, in part because they valued Jewish support. A significant number of plays produced in the early twenties include a role for the Jew as the crafty entrepreneur who tries to make a deal of some kind. In most cases he is not presented as a villain, but as an indispensable part of the social scene, particularly in its financial and commercial dimension. If his plans involve self-enrichment, they are invariably unsuccessful.

Some of the above-mentioned works (in particular those of Vasylchenko and Vynnychenko) were published in Soviet Ukraine, but most appeared in Western Ukraine, which in the years 1921–39 was part of Poland, or in North America. Soviet writers had to be cautious in treating any sensitive social question, including the Jewish question. When Jewish-Ukrainian relations were raised in Soviet Ukrainian literature, this was frequently done in an oblique and muted manner.

Maik Yohansen's *Podorozh liudyny pid kepom (Ievreis'ki kolonii)* (Journey of a Person in a Cap: Jewish Colonies, 1929) provides another insight into the representation of Jews in Soviet Ukraine. The book describes Jewish agricultural communes in the Kherson area, which were part of the attempt in the twenties to develop a Jewish farming class. The economic condition of most Jews was difficult, since the Soviet state had banned private commerce in the period of so-called War Communism (1918–21), and nationalized not only industries but many artisanal workshops. Although private commerce was again allowed in the period of the New Economic Policy (1921–29), artisans and merchants were often viewed as "unproductive elements," taxed at high rates, and treated harshly. One solution to the threat of unemployment was to draw Jews into the industrial and agrarian workforce. Another was to settle them on land in southern Ukraine. This policy, initiated in the mid-twenties, had by 1927 attracted 107,000 Jews (7 percent of the republic's Jewish population) to agricultural colonies. (Orlian- s'kyi 2000, 77.) Despite economic conflicts, local hostility, and disorganization, the colonies were viable. By the end of the decade they counted over two hun- dred thousand settlers. Maik Yohansen in his travelogue argues that despite the pioneer-like conditions, the colonists are doing well and living in good relations with other farmers. More recent arrivals, according to Yohansen, particularly those who are not used to working the land, complain and return. Life for the older emigrants (those who came in 1925) remains hard. Some still live in earthen huts. The best settlers, as a Jewish agronomist points out to the author, are those from Poltava or Chernihiv. The worst are those from Volhynia and Podillia, because they have usually come from small towns and are unfamiliar with farming. The writer describes the arrival of neighboring farmers with the customary music and drinks to invite the newcomers to Christmas celebrations, although he also comments that some neighbors take a hostile attitude because they see Jewish settlers receiving support from the government and the Ameri- can Agro-Joint, an organization funded by the Jewish American Joint Distribu- tion Committee to assist Jewish land colonization efforts in the USSR.

The author also describes a steady process of Ukrainianization. The wall- newspaper is in two languages: Yiddish and Ukrainian. The local theater staged six plays over the winter: two in Yiddish and four in Ukrainian. Children are taught in both languages. The older generation speaks Yiddish and the younger Ukrainian. There is intermarriage between Jews and Ukrainians. Moreover, he argues that the stereotypical images of Jews who are unable to ride horses, drink wine, fire revolvers, fight with swords, or be good soldiers has to be discarded. Yohansen describes Jewish girls who race about the steppe on horseback, boys who plow the land, footballers who play for the Ukrainian national team, and one massive, physically intimidating agronomist. Like the drawings of the colonists made by Mark Epstein in these years, Yohansen's portraits underscore the fact that the old colonies already differ little from neighboring German and Ukrai- nian ones. At one point he recounts listening to a long conversation between four men on a train. The talk is of horses, taxes, and prices. In the end, he realizes that two are Jews and two Ukrainians. The message is that the two communities have so much in common that they are sometimes indistinguishable; both form an in- tegral part of the new country.

The background to this work was the discussion of Jewish agrarian settle-ments in the contemporary press. Soviet Jewish periodicals like *Rul* (Steering Wheel) and *Shtern* (Star) were making damning criticisms of the farms. They described conflicts between the Jewish colonists and local Ukrainian farmers, and the difficult lives of settlers who often began with no equipment or living space. The press reported robberies by requisitioners, violent resistance to collectivization, and the desertion of collectivized farms. Some commentators questioned the rationale behind creating Jewish agrarian colonies, calling it utopian. These doubts were then aired in newspapers and publications in Berlin, Prague, New York, and Chicago. The Jewish colonists were, for exam-ple, described as martyrs of postrevolutionary social and economic develop-ments. (Estraikh 2005, 88.) Yohansen's report was no doubt commissioned by the authorities to present a more positive version, and to put the best face on difficulties.

Jewish characters occur in the writings of several Soviet authors: Mykola Khvylovy, Borys Antonenko-Davydovych, Yaroslav Hrymailo, Yurii Smolych, Mykola Bazhan, and Myroslav Irchan. Smolych and Bazhan in particular were well known for their close contacts with Jewish colleagues. The former left mem-oirs detailing these relations—some professional and some personal. Both au-thors expressed sympathy for the Jewish community. In the increasingly fanati-cal atmosphere of the late twenties, however, they could only offer limited resistance to the requirement that all religious fervor be denounced as obscuran-tist. Bazhan's poem "Getto v Umani" (The Ghetto in Uman, 1929) can serve as an example. A blazing fire in the ghetto reminds the author of the many previous persecutions of Jews in Spain, Germany, and Ukraine. The old, moss-covered synagogue situated on the hill witnesses the frenzied praying of aged Hasids. The poem can be read as a negative depiction of irrational and hysterical reli-gious practices that are dying in the flames—lines like "The crowd of a hundred mouths and eyes / Cries like one epileptic mouth" are calculated to elicit a neg-ative reaction toward prayer—but it also testifies to the undeniable power of faith. The author comments that Zion must burn, but the future of this "tor-tured, despised people" will be born on new fields. He builds ambiguity into the poem, so as to maintain the ideological stance required by the regime while si-multaneously rescuing some respect for Judaism and the Jewish people. This ef-fort has since been viewed as an embarrassing and unfortunate tribute exacted by the time, an anathematization of all that was considered conservative in Jewish culture, especially Judaism, but others feel that the poem is "a tragic Ukrainian epitaph" to the Jewish past. (Skurativs'kyi 1998, 55.)

This was a time when Soviet authorities demanded ferocious antireligious propaganda and intransigent class hatred of all writers. In the same year as Bazhan's poem appeared, Irchan wrote his "Bat'ko (Z imperiialistychnoi viiny)" (Father: From the Imperialist War, 1929). This is a harrowing picture of an attack on the home of Yankel, a poor, devoutly religious Jewish farmer by some pro-tsarist troops from the Kuban. Irchan had earlier made a name for himself by un-flinchingly portraying scenes of brutality during the wars that followed the 1917 revolution. Here he describes the rape of Yankel's two daughters and their sub-sequent death. The traumatic events, however, lead to an unexpected conclu-sion: Yankel renounces God and his Jewish religion. The story is an ideologically conformist response to the Stalinist propaganda campaign then under way. However, the breaking down of the door to Yankel's house by Russian-speaking troops who have come from afar, and their brutal ransacking of his home, might have reminded readers not only of the period 1914–18, but also of later Soviet grain requisitioning campaigns and the punishment of farmers who resisted the contemporary collectivization of agriculture. The story may well have been writ-ten in order to exploit this ambiguity, and in this way to draw a parallel between the suffering of Jews and Ukrainians, while on the surface producing a narrative acceptable to the censorship.

The Jewish voice in the twenties found remarkable expression in Raisa Troianker's verse, which combined nostalgia for a Jewish childhood with an as-sertive eroticism. At the age of thirteen she ran away from her Jewish family in Uman to live with an Italian tiger tamer from a visiting circus. Later she fell in love with Volodymyr Sosiura after hearing him read his poetry, and followed him to Kharkiv, where she became part of the leading literary circles of Pluh, Hart, and Avanhard, and published two collections: *Povin'* (Flood, 1928) and *Horyzont* (Horizon, 1930). Yurii Smolych's memoirs *Intymni spohady* (Intimate Confes-sions, 1945) focus on her sexual adventures and her image as a femme fatale, but her poetry also deserves attention, both for its Jewish themes and for the persona it constructs of a passionate, vulnerable lover:

Father drove me out and cursed me,
Because I have a "goy's" child.
He wanted the earth to fall
Beneath you and me, Olenka.

Father is as old
As the yellowed leaves of the Talmud.
He weeps: "For my daughter's sin
I will be a laughing-stock among people!"

Oh, cursed, cursed child,
You couldn't find a Jew!
And there are tears in his eyes,
And silvery hoarfrost in his beard.

Mother cries: "She has an Olenka,
Not a Debora, a Liia or a Nekham . . ."
I know, I know, for my gray mother
This is a very great drama . . .

My own aging momma
With hands covered in fish scales,
For she has to cook
To earn a little bread.

Olenka has blue in her eyes
And fair, blond hair.
What will my girl say
To the pointed question "nation"?!

And father cannot forgive
That I have a child from a "goy".
But momma said: "You . . .
You might visit some time . . . with "her." (Tsymbal 2004, 14.)

The poem reveals a woman struggling to reconcile two identities, while dealing with the possibility of rejection by both the communities they stand for. It could serve as a coda to the representation of Jews in this period, one that saw them participating far more intensively in Ukrainian cultural life than before, and struggling to define themselves as Soviet citizens, Ukrainians, and Jews.

CHAPTER 5

A Jewish Voice: Leonid Pervomaisky

Jews contributed to Ukrainian literature over several generations and provided a Jewish voice—one that expressed Jewish concerns and articulated the problems of a Jewish Ukrainian identity. The development of this voice can be traced in the work of three writers. It received early expression in the poetry of Hrytsko Kernerenko, was then in early Soviet times given articulation by Leonid Pervomaisky, and in the late twentieth century has been represented by Moisei Fishbein. Pervomaisky is, in many ways, the most complex case, since his writings reflect almost the entire Soviet experience, show a significant evolution, and raise many issues concerning the Jewish-Ukrainian identity. He is also the most enigmatic of these writers.

The Ukrainianization policy brought many Jews to Ukrainian culture, some of whom have been mentioned in chapter 3. Pervomaisky was the greatest talent in the cohort of Jewish writers who entered literature in the twenties and worked alongside Ukrainian colleagues. He shared with them the Soviet experience, with its many dark periods, and his writings reflect the political requirements of each decade. Many aspects of his career are still shrouded in mystery and await a fuller assessment that will become possible when his unpublished works and personal papers are made available. Many readers do not have access to his early published works in their original form, but only to later, substantially reedited versions. His earliest works are close in spirit to the sentimental current of the century's first decades. "Parasol'ka Pinkhusa-Moti" (Pinkhus-Moti's Umbrella, 1926) can serve as an example. It describes a poor and aged Jewish carpenter who lives according to the stoical belief that everything is for the best: "A simple mixture of fatalism and optimism kept the old man on the earth." (Pervomais'kyi

1985, 3:219.) When the Red Army evacuates the town, he remains behind and is beheaded by some White Guards. The focus is on the simplicity and defenselessness of the victim and, as in Klym Polishchuk's stories, on the senselessness of the killing. The old man's explanation of faith in God is unorthodox. He says: "There are many Gods: I have one, you have another. . . . Do not pray either to yours or mine, but to God! Dream one up and pray. . . . If your God betrays you, drive him out of your heart and search for another!" (Ibid., 3:222.) Religious faith, however, provides him with the courage and dignity required to face danger and evil. This passage indirectly suggests that all ideologies can and should be examined if they prove to be harmful or mistaken—a message that can also be turned against revolutionary fanaticisms. The original 1926 text describes the killing of the old man in a much more brutal, graphic, and disturbing manner than later editions. Some specifically Jewish references disappeared in the 1958 and subsequent republications: the all-powerful Hebrew God became "nature," religion became philosophy, the Reb became a generalized good man. The impact of these changes here and in other works was to downplay the importance of the Jewish context for an understanding of the main protagonist's identity. This was unfortunate, because the struggle to define this identity was the most interesting aspect of Pervomaisky's writings in the twenties.

An autobiographical story called "U paliturni" (In the Bookbindery, 1928) describes the transformation of the young Faivel, who works as a bookbinder—a traditional Jewish trade—into a Bolshevik. Jews and Ukrainians work together in the enterprise and are radicalized each in a different way. Faivel joins a Bolshevik cell and has to leave town. The Ukrainian Panko discovers Shevchenko's verse, which he then carries with him everywhere. Mobilized by the tsarist army, he is eventually shot for spreading revolutionary agitation, which includes reading "Shevchenko and other books to soldiers." (Ibid., 3:247.) Events are viewed through the eyes of the young narrator who works in the bindery. He loves to read, and develops a friendship with Panko. However, when the latter is drafted, his replacements are the supervisor Andrii and the ruffian Manka, a bully and boor, who when drunk can be violent. Manka makes the boy's life a misery and prevents him from reading at night. Panko and Manka represent a spectrum of Jewish-Ukrainian relations. Panko is a friend, and a runaway from a poor village, much as the narrator is a runaway from a hateful schoolmistress. Manka is a narrow-minded, insensitive villain, who has assimilated the authoritarian behavior around him. Treated badly by his supervisor Andrii, a distant relative, he in turn mistreats his own underlings. Although news of the revolution seems to change

everyone's mood for the better, holding out the promise of a new social solidarity, the continued presence of drunkenness, indiscipline, and violence in society
suggests that the revolution will be a mixed blessing. Since the story appears to
be autobiographical, most readers probably assume that the young narrator is
Jewish. Indeed, the original version of the text (Pervomais'kyi 1928) makes this
autobiographical element explicit: it reveals the narrator's Jewish background
and connection to book culture.

One of the most important articulations of Pervomaisky's Jewish identity is
his novella *Zemlia obitovana* (Promised Land, 1927). The point of view is again
that of an adolescent. This perspective produces an "estrangement" from events
and makes any cruelty or fanaticism appear grotesque. Yerukhym escapes from
the stifling atmosphere of the shtetl and his alcoholic, abusive Jewish father, and
takes up with young thieves in the city. Eventually he returns, but only to leave
again, striking out on his own. He begins to understand "that his escape was a
kind of protest," against the synagogue, "the traditional, conservative spirit,"
and "the implacable Jehovah—a vengeful, degenerate old man." (Pervomais'kyi
1927, 98.) And yet, in the final pages, when all other Jews have turned their backs
on him, an old man who has read the kaddish over his father's grave (something
Yerukhym has refused to do), turns to the boy in a gentle and friendly way, and,
placing his hand on his shoulder, says: "You are stubborn. That is very good. It is
very good to be stubborn. You will reach your goal." Yerukhym warmly shakes
the hand of the old man, who accompanies him to the cemetery gates and wishes
him good luck. The narrative makes the required gesture toward antireligious
agitation, but also indicates that for the new generation of urbanized and assimilated Jews the break with their former identity is not an easy one. The surface
message is that the promised land of Israel is being supplanted in the minds of
young people by the "promised land" of socialism on the territory of contemporary Ukraine, but a deeper message is that the replacement of one goal by another will be a long, difficult process. Yerukhym's evolution ends with his joining
the Komsomol. However, the significant thing here is not his political alignment,
but his move from the village or small town to a new urban environment. He is
torn between worlds, struggles to break with the past, and must deal with the imprint upon him of the old world. As a result, this early work is tinged with ambiguity and a subtle, tragic irony, qualities that are also evident in his play *Kom-
mol'tsi* (Komsomol Youth, 1930).

At the end of the decade, a ruthless spirit made itself felt in literature. Pervomaisky's communist heroes and heroines now begin to make brave, uncompro-

mising, politically correct speeches, as in the verse play *Nevidomi saldaty: Tra-hema* (Unknown Soldiers: Tragic Drama, 1930). This is the most controversial period of the writer's career and it has often been avoided in surveys of his achievement. Like most Soviet authors of the time, he moved away from examining the possibility of human understanding. His "Trypil's'ka trahediia" (Trypillian Tragedy, 1929) is an elegy to a Komsomol detachment from Kyiv that was destroyed in an engagement with Zeleny's army in July, 1919. Zeleny's forces are referred to as "the Greens," or peasant anarchists drawn from the countryside, but in reality they were supporters of the UNR and in Soviet propaganda were identified as such. The list of names makes it clear that most of the Komsomol youth (one could be a member of the organization until around the age of twenty) are of Jewish background: Liuba Aronova, Betia Palei, Olena Birk, Orlykova, Zaverukha, Burshtein, Polonsky, Sheinin, Dymyrets, Mykhailo Ratmansky. The last was a well-known troop commander. This singling out of Jews for special honors as revolutionary fighters disappeared from the writer's later work, but in 1929, such a gesture, coming as it did at a time when the Stalinist hard line was being increasingly asserted, was bound to rekindle Ukrainian-Jewish antagonisms. The poem is a Bolshevik call to arms. It recognizes the presence of lawlessness and gratuitous violence within revolutionary ranks, but ascribes these to recently recruited Ukrainian peasants and former nationalists, men who are described as undisciplined, drunken, and "hardened through thieving and rape." (Pervomais'kyi 1947, 72.) Moreover, the entire countryside is characterized as anti-Bolshevik:

> The duped village loudly cried "glory" . . .
> Duped village, you went with the Greens,
> And only the blood was red, left by the day. (Ibid., 77)

This particular poem was frequently anthologized until 1949. Criticized in that year for its hostile attitude toward the countryside, it was rarely republished afterwards.

Pervomaisky was drawn into the atmosphere of the thirties, a period when literature was called upon to glorify violence and to stimulate hatred against enemies of the state. In a poem like "Iamby" (Iambs, 1933), the writer's former gentle persona disappears. A conscious break is made with the past; the narrator cuts his ties not only with the village, but with all tradition, including, by implication, his Jewish roots:

> I hate the old in me
> From ancient days of shame in captivity
> That has to die and will die. (Ibid., 205)

In 1934, when Pervomaisky published his collection *Zbroia* (Weaponry), his metamorphosis into a militant Stalinist appeared to be complete. In the poem "Lyst z Kyiva" (Letter from Kyiv, 1933), he identifies himself as a member of the Osnaz (from the Russian term *chast' osobogo naznacheniia*—special military sections created to combat "counterrevolutionary forces")—and describes how he laughed along with other Chekists when the "sour mug" of the "autocephalous savior" was smashed. This is a reference to the banned Ukrainian Orthodox Church, which established itself as autocephalous (self-governing) in the years 1917-20 and was strongly supportive of Ukrainian independence. He continues:

I am not afraid of complex, urgent life.
I am not afraid of the tedious frog-like wailing.
I have one road. There is no turning back
I know firmly what I want, and in action, act purposefully. (Ibid., 223)

These uncompromising words were written during the worst years of the requisitioning and famine. Pervomaisky turns to his enemies and detractors:

And why do you look at me from your Petliurite dens?
We will travel our road in spite of all treachery.
I know your nature—in feeble, farmstead nights
You have been fashioned by Stolypinites with their cozy, rich peasant women.

And later you grew up and returned to your dark corners,
Having completed commercial and agro-veterinary institutes.

And then near Trypillia you used to kill my brothers . . .
But we filled your guts full of devils anyway! . . .
We know. What we want. We are an Osnaz detachment.
I am a soldier of poetry in it. A rank-and-file soldier. (Ibid., 223–24)

The poem is dated March 1933, not long after Molotov and Kaganovich traveled to Kharkiv in late 1932 to issue instructions to party activists and Molotov told them "to fight with the Petliurites and semi-Petliurites." On the same day two Central Committee decrees referred to the need to "liquidate kulak and Petliurite dens." (Martin 2001, 304.) The phrases from these pronouncements are used in Pervomaisky's poem, which appears to show his complete support for the campaigns then under way, and to tolerate no resistance. Another poem in the same cycle, "Syn partii" (Son of the Party, 1933), describes the role of the Communist apparatus:

Turn over the virgin lands and plow across the boundaries
And destroy savage sentiments—
The thirst for possessions, the thirst for accumulation,
The thirst: Give! Me! Mine! Don't dare!—

> The thirst to live at another's expense,
> On the backs of others!—to live in the morass
> Of eternal rural idiocy,
> Divided by the thirst for riches. (Ibid., 228)

Here the individual farmer is portrayed as backward, driven by selfish greed, with no claims on human sympathy. This kind of dehumanizing description allowed collectivization (and the violent requisitioning and destruction that accompanied it) to be more easily justified as a progressive act. The world is simplistically divided into two camps: "two worlds, two classes, two elements—water and fire! . . . in the deadly struggle for life, for bread, for the world." (Ibid.) The village represents "the savage and the numbskull desire for ownership, which has eaten its way deeply into the peasant's eternal nature, like a sharp piece of shrapnel into a wound that cannot be healed." (Ibid., 229.) In "Stolytsia" (Capital City, 1934), another poem in this collection, the poet once more insists that those who died in the revolution have sealed the fate of the republic: "There is no return from the grave!" (Ibid., 235.) Although Pervomaisky was born in 1908, making him nine years old when the revolution broke out, and only published his first poem in 1924, nevertheless he identifies with revolutionary combat:

> I fought for you with songs, fire, and bayonet,
> In Bolshevik platoons—ranks filled with stubbornness! (Ibid., 235)

The early parts of Pervomaisky's *Molodist' brata: Roman u virshakh* (Youth of Brother: A Novel in Verse, 1933), which deals with the revolutionary wars, also contains scenes in which village resistance is brutally suppressed. The violence is justified by providing an unsavory picture of the *kurkuli* or rich peasants. Here, as in his other works from the thirties, the Cheka leaders are eulogized. One of them is admiringly described as a merciless local Marat, while the nationalists who fight the communists are demonized. The last section of the poem, written decades later, depicts the hero as a Soviet army commander advancing on Berlin in 1945 in order to take revenge for Babyn Yar, Maidanek, and Auschwitz. The effect here is to homogenize all enemies of the Soviet Union, whatever period of time is being discussed, into one fascist camp.

Much poetry of the thirties reflects what Hellebust has called "flesh-to-metal" imagery. (See Hellebust 2001.) It constructs the individual as a machine, part of an enormous collective that feels and thinks as one, that is disciplined and absolutely ruthless in action. Readers understood the aggressive attitude toward the peasantry and non-Russian national movements manifest in this kind of pro-

Cheka literature as support for Stalin's brutal campaigns. The Bolshevik cult of violent action is associated with youthful virility. In her study of rhetoric and ideology in Italy in the 1920s, Barbara Spackman has linked this rhetoric of virility to the cults of youth, duty, sacrifice, heroic virtue, stamina, obedience, authority, physical strength, and sexual potency. All these "characterize fascism" and "are all inflections of that master term, virility." (Spackman 1996, xii.) They also characterize the virtues promoted by the literature of militant Bolshevism in the late twenties and early thirties. One master trope of the Italian pro-fascist writings is "the creation of a scenario in which the virile leader 'rapes' the feminized masses." (Ibid.) Such a scenario is also the underlying trope in much of the pro-Cheka writing. The "turning over" of virgin lands, the "plowing across boundaries," and the war on the peasantry can be seen as typical deployments of the trope. Spackman's description of Italian writings could be applied to many Soviet works: "The positing of nonverbal violence gives meaning to the rhetoric, while the rhetoric gives new meaning, as performative threat, to violence already committed." (Ibid., xv.)

Petrovsky-Shtern has suggested that Pervomaisky's writings from the thirties, like much literature of this period, also reveals the influence of Rudyard Kipling, or at least the Soviet version of the English writer that was then in vogue. Kipling provided a useful all-conquering, "imperial" framework and the requisite optimism and unbending faith in a global cause. (Petrovsky-Shtern forthcoming, 26–27.) The English writer's influence allowed for a milder version of militant Bolshevism, one that focused more on the individual virtues of courage and steadfastness. This version was represented by a number of writers, among them Oleksa Vlyzko and Leonid Chernov (Maloshyichenko), whose works describe strong characters and daring personalities (who were often women), and continue the romance with aircraft, motorcycles, automobiles, electricity, and technology that had characterized some futurists, constructivists, and other avant-garde writers of the early twenties. One critic has described this writing as a recognition that the age of technology had arrived, and that Ukraine needed either to embrace it or remain a tragic, dreamy, and ridiculous Little Russia. (Hordyns'kyi 1942.)

Pervomaisky soon moved away from this flesh-to-metal imagery in ways that underline his Ukrainian patriotism. In the late thirties and early forties, Ukrainians were participating in the shaping of a revised brand of "Soviet patriotism"—one that allowed them to express, in a limited degree, love for their own country. Pervomaisky's war stories, which were published in the collection *Ataka na Vorskli: Opovidannia ta narysy* (Attack on the Vorskla: Short Stories and Sketches,

1946) contribute to the cautious elevation of Ukrainian traditions. He finds analogies to current acts of sacrifice and heroism in the glorious national past. The opening story, "Zhyttia" (Life) contains the following description of the wind in the steppes: "Perhaps it is searching for a place to sleep for the night, like a tired Cossack returning from a campaign? Perhaps it is flying like a messenger from a Cossack girl, looking in the dark for her friend, to embrace him, to whisper in his ear a barely audible word, the echo of a dear name, to awaken a sad memory, and to then fly onward tirelessly, silently, tracelessly, and more swiftly than a fast horse in pursuit?" (Pervomais'kyi 1946.) The poeticization of time and space as national history and topography runs through these stories. "Virna krov" (Faithful Blood) contains the following passage describing an ancient *kurhan* (burial mound) in the steppe:

> The years sailed over its crest like herds of sheep, like flocks of cranes. Cossack sentries built their fires here to alert distant settlements of approaching danger. A Tatar horseman on his pony brandished and cracked a whip, raced up the steep slope, and fell into the grass pierced by a hot Cossack bullet. The steppe eagles pecked out the eyes of the corpses. Grey wolves tore the yellow flesh with their sharp fangs; the bones of unbidden guests were washed by rains and dried out by the sun; the wind whistled a menacing song in the empty bones as though on resonant pipes. . . . Under the *kurhan* lay the remains of faithful Cossacks, who defended the steppe from unexpected enemies, who took the first blow and stood firm in uneven combat with the enemy, until regiments arrived from deep in the native land. (Ibid., 25)

Another passage, this time the opening of "Ohnenna dusha" (Fiery Soul), was considered too nationalistic and dropped from the later republications: "In our people there lies a powerful force that reawakens whenever danger threatens their existence. This force, hidden in the breasts of millions, can be called heroism, although it is not only heroism. It can be called love of the source of human happiness, of the native land, but it is not only love. All the best that has been born, that has matured in the human spirit over centuries of labor and struggle is fused in this force, the name of which is the greatness of the national spirit." (Ibid., 63)

Like Babel's *Konarmiia* (Red Cavalry), the book follows an advance by the Red Army from east to west. The narrator describes incidents near the Don, then in the Carpathian mountains, and finally in Hungary and Austria. Throughout, he aligns himself not only with the Soviet soldier, but with the Ukrainian patriotism of the war years. Portraits of devastated Jewish communities occur in the last story "Z uhors'koho shchodennyka" (From a Hungarian Diary). The narrator describes two destroyed synagogues with the possessions

of slaughtered Jews piled to the ceiling and meets Holocaust survivors. (Ibid.,
184–85, 194.)

In 1946 Pervomaisky was awarded the Stalin Prize for his books *Den' narodzhennia* (Birthday) and *Zemlia* (Earth). In a couple of years, however, suddenly
and dramatically, as it seemed to many, a campaign against "rootless cosmopolitanism"—directed principally against Jews—was launched by the Soviet authorities. Solomon Mikhoels, the chairman of the Jewish Anti-Fascist Committee, was killed in January of that year. Stalin had required the committee, as the
unofficial voice of the Jewish community, to serve as a propaganda tool in turning the state of Israel (created in May 1948) against the United States and Great
Britain, and was angered when Israel took a pro-American stance. On November
20 the Politburo called the committee "a centre of anti-Soviet propaganda that
regularly gives anti-Soviet information to organs of foreign secret services."
(Shapoval 2001, 218.) It was disbanded and its publishing organ *Einikait* (Unity)
was shut down. All publications on Jewish themes, with the exception of anti-
Semitic ones, were forbidden. Many Jews in high positions were dismissed and
leading cultural activists were arrested. On August 12, 1952 the best of the Yiddish writers were shot, among them David Bergelson, Perets Markish, David
Hofshtein, Leib Kvitko, and Itsik Fefer.

Pervomaisky was directly affected by this campaign. A case was mounted
against him in the press and in 1953 he was driven to attempt suicide. The writer
found himself attacked both as a Jew (for "cosmopolitanism" and lack of patriotism) and as a Ukrainian (for excessive nationalism). In the postwar years the
campaigns against Jewish and Ukrainian "nationalisms" alternated or were
conducted simultaneously. The anti-Semitic campaign reached its peak in the
months before Stalin's death. Every week there would be an article in the press,
the investigation of some individual case, or a lecture by a party leader in which
Jews were accused of Zionism and lack of Soviet patriotism. Finally, in January
1953, *Pravda* announced that a plot by Jewish doctors to kill Soviet leaders had
been uncovered. This became the signal for many Jews to be thrown out of work.
Press reports of "dissatisfaction with the Jewish people" and demands that Jews
be deported to "distant parts of the Soviet Union" fueled rumors that the entire
Jewish population was to be deported to the eastern regions of the USSR. Mass
campaigns of persecution and killing were always prepared in the Soviet Union
by the spreading of hatred for the targeted group, class, or nation. In this case
too, disgust for the victim group was consciously stimulated. Fortunately, Stalin's death put an end to the "doctors' plot" and the arrested physicians were
freed.

In the post-Stalin period, Pervomaisky began writing again in the humane, generous, and optimistic spirit that had characterized much of his early work. He produced a collection of short stories with masterful psychological portraits, *Materyn solodkyi khlib* (Mother's Sweet Bread, 1960), and one of the best novels of the Soviet period, *Dykyi med* (Wild Honey, 1963), which will be discussed as part of postwar literature. In the late sixties and early seventies he wrote his best lyric poetry and published excellent translations of Heine and other writers. Fishbein has written that some of Pervomaisky's friends could not forgive him for his public statements and his "Osnaz attitude" of the 1930s. They even tried to convince Fishbein that almost from childhood Pervomaisky was hostile to Ukraine, its history, and any expression of Ukrainian national awareness. (Fishbein 1996, 224.) When, at Bazhan's insistence, Fishbein met Pervomaisky in 1972, he was charmed by the older poet's erudition and his sensitivity to poetry and art. Fishbein feels that at the end of his life Pervomaisky "began to understand and see much (or maybe he understood and saw much earlier, but raised in the damp vault of the 1930s, 1940s, 1950s, did not allow himself to open his eyes widely so as not to lose his eyesight). His last, wise and pellucid books, *Uroky poezii, Drevo piznannia*, and the posthumous collection *Vchora i zavtra* (Yesterday and Tomorrow), testify to this. They are markedly different from his early, 'Osnaz' works and from his boring poems of the 1940s." (Ibid., 225.)

Uroky poezii (Lessons of Poetry, 1968) and *Drevo piznannia* (Tree of Knowledge, 1971) contain moments of revelation, caused by the mixing of memory and desire. Lucid imagery, measured rhythms, and a wise economy of expression provide the reader with a powerful aesthetic experience. It is the poetry of a wise old age that has experienced and understood much, but is still full of passionate feeling. The poet's great consolation and love is poetry itself; it is for him the only way of reaching self-understanding. He looks back upon life from a philosophical distance and attempts to speak simply of the essential, human experiences (youth, love, old age, approaching death), and of the great twentieth-century tragedies (war, Babyn Yar, Maidanek, idol worship, and lack of self-knowledge):

> It could exist without humanity,
> This boundless universe, for billions of years,
> And could die as the tail of a meteor
> Dies headlong in the spaces of time,
> And could again come out onto forgotten paths
> In new cosmic transformations,
> But it could not understand itself
> In its hidden essence without the human being.

Humans have long existed in the world
Without joy, without pain and striving,
And millions of years were lived
In the constant changing of generations.
Humans learned to hunt the beast,
Invented everything: the wheel and oar,
But long could not understand themselves:
They lacked poetry. (Pervomais'kyi 1976, 59)

He has a quiet, optimistic faith in the life force animating all things. The phenomena of the natural world (spring, rebirth, storms) provide subject matter for many of these poems, but they are ultimately about the earth's powerful cyclical forces and the mystery of human life:

There are forces of death and forces of creation,
The moist earth and the heaven's warm vault,
The root is reborn in the young offshoot,
And in the early blossom senses the late fruit.

Forget that ripening resembles death,
That it already contains the fusion with nonexistence,
Stay calm: nothing will overcome
The new embryonic life in the flower. (Ibid., 61)

Pervomaisky also writes poignantly of the mistakes his generation committed. This has been taken by most readers as a reference to the grim period of Stalinism, when many young people had been fanatical supporters of the repressive regime and when writers had often played a deplorable role in justifying, however indirectly, murderous policies. In another poem "Mynuloho ne pereboresh" (The Past You Will Not Overcome) he strikes a tone of both forgiveness and repentance:

The past cannot be overcome.
Recently or long gone—
Not behind you and not alongside you,
But always inside you it lives.

All your days—far, and near—
You remember the false step,
As though it was only last week
That ancient lesson occurred.

If only, if only you could today
With one sweep of the hand,
As though from a school blackboard, clean
Your failures and mistakes—

All sufferings and old pains
Still crowd into your dreams,
And with your will or without it
Hang onto your hunched back.

You honestly strive with sensitive heart
For that initial purity,
But have to travel into the future
Carrying all your past.

And the late judgment of your conscience
Will not justify or release
You from dark tremblings
In the last inevitable moment. (Ibid., 70)

Pervomaisky's oeuvre captures the complexities and contradictions of the Jewish writer's entanglement with Soviet reality throughout six decades, and is one of the best sources for understanding how the twentieth-century Jewish identity had to be negotiated in Ukrainian literature. His development can be contrasted with that of Natan Rybak, another prominent Jewish Ukrainian writer, who throughout his life became an increasingly conformist Soviet writer and steadily eliminated almost all references to Jewishness. Pervomaisky moved in the opposite direction: he began as a communist neophyte but gradually eliminated almost everything "Soviet" in himself. At the end of his life he appeared to most readers as simply a Ukrainian writer, whose literary persona encompassed his Jewishness without emphasizing it. His later poetry was addressed to humanity, and, as the last poems indicate, it was often concerned primarily with his own conscience and with the Creator's judgment.

CHAPTER 6

The Rising Tide of Resentment, 1929–1939

The collectivization, violence, famine, and terror of the thirties were accompanied by the crushing of the indigenization policy. Those who had conducted Ukrainianization were accused of being nationalists, Petliurites, and fascists, and an entire stratum of leading cultural and political figures was executed, imprisoned, or cowed. Ironically, one complaint against them was that they had also introduced compulsory Jewish education for Jewish children, a tactical move, it was claimed, to "create a bloc with Jewish nationalists." (Halii and Novyts'kyi 1934, 63.) Jews who had played a role in Ukrainianization were also repressed. They included scholars like Yarema Aizenshtok, Olena Kurylo, Abram Leites, and Samiilo Shchupak. In spite of this, the catastrophes of the thirties sparked a virulent form of anti-Semitism in the population. Lazar Kaganovich had been highly visible in suppressing the "nationalist deviation" in 1925–28. He now played a prominent role in the grain requisitioning that led to the great hunger of 1932–33, in which perhaps five million people died. He and Mikoyan "led expeditions into the countryside with brigades of OGPU troopers and armoured cars like warlords," while 180,000 party workers sent from cities "used the gun, the lynch mob and the Gulag camp system to break the villages." (Montefiore 2003, 46, 57.) In the popular mind, Kaganovich's status as Stalin's executioner in Ukraine became firmly linked to his Jewish origins.

Serhii Yefremov's *Shchodennyk, 1923–1929* (Diary, 1923–1929, 1997), an uncensored account of the twenties that could only be published seventy years later, records popular attitudes in Kyiv. It is particularly interesting in the way it reflects attitudes toward Jews. The population, Yefremov writes, felt that communism was being policed by Jews, who appeared to have been given the task of monitoring participation in the communist festivals that had often been designed to compete with national or religious commemorations. On January 22, 1924 (the anniversary of the 1918 declaration of independence) he writes: "I woke up early; Nastia had rushed in. "Quick, hang out the flag, the Jewish women are walking through the street looking for places without a flag." (Iefremov 1997, 59.)

However, Yefremov also records anecdotes, apparently true, that show the solidarity of Jews and Christians in the face of antireligious propaganda. Under June 21, 1925, he notes that in the town of Ovdiopol Communists were no longer permitted to organize religious debates. An Orthodox priest, a rabbi, and a Roman Catholic priest had joined forces to debate some unsophisticated local Bolsheviks:

> After the priest's speech about the existence of God, the rabbi said: "I agree with my comrade the priest in everything." "How can you be in agreement," the Communist provoked him, "when he says that Christ was God?" "Well, that is an issue we will solve between ourselves, but I am in agreement with my comrade the priest when he says that God exists." "But he will probably tell you that the Jews killed Christ. Do you agree with that too?" "What do you mean, they killed Christ? What Jews? Maybe Jews like you killed him, but why would all Jews want to kill him?" "Well, in any case, we here in Ovdiopol think that there is no God." "The entire world (with a solemn gesture to the heavens) believes and accepts God, and only Ovdiopol (a contemptuous gesture to the ground) does not accept him!" (Ibid., 247.)

Some popular jokes appear to be omens of bad times, like the tale of the "responsible Jew," recorded on January 28, 1924: "A passenger enters a train compartment in which someone is lying on each bench, even though it is not a sleeping car. He says to one person: 'make room, I need to sit down,' and receives the reply: 'I am a responsible worker, who has traveled to conduct agitation. I am tired and need to rest.' He asks a second and gets the same response: 'a responsible worker.' A third also tells him he is 'responsible.' Finally, he sees an ordinary Jew with side locks: 'Make room, so that I can sit down.' 'I am responsible too!' 'How?' 'I am a Jew who will have to take responsibility for them,' he says, pointing at the Communists, 'when they take to their heels. So I have to at least get some sleep now.'" (Ibid., 64.)

Yefremov records that Jewish-Ukrainian relations reached a low point during the trial of Samuel (Shalom, Sholem) Schwartzbard, who assassinated Petliura in Paris on May 25, 1926 and was acquitted when proceedings turned into an indictment of the Ukrainian leader as the man responsible for the 1919 pogroms. It has been suggested that the assassination was Soviet-inspired. (Shapoval 1994, 73.) Whatever the real facts behind the killing, it is clear that the assassin's Jewish background was used to discredit the national movement and intensify Ukrainian-Jewish antagonisms. The Soviet Union worked to represent the assassinated leader and the entire independence movement as anti-Semitic and fascist. Security forces instructed their operatives to deny that the UNR forces represented a broad national consensus, and to stress instead their criminal nature. During the trial Petliura and the national movement were labeled "adventurist"—an epithet that would be routinely employed by Soviet authorities for decades. Joseph Schechtman, an editor of the Jewish newspaper in Paris, *Rassvet* (Dawn), urged readers not to confuse pogromists with the cause of Ukraine's freedom, and Lev Chykalenko, writing in *Tryzub* (Trident), the UNR organ, also published in Paris, argued in a similar vein that the assassination should be seen not as a Jewish but as a Bolshevik act directed against Ukrainian democracy and statehood. However, these statements had little effect on the popular mood. The demonization of Petliura was supported by the Jewish and much of the non-Jewish press. Schwartzbard's trial became a watershed event, with what Kleiner has described as "fatal significance" for Jewish-Ukrainian relations. (Kleiner 2000, 133.)

Among unnecessary and counterproductive measures Yefremov records censorship of the word *zhyd*. Deemed offensive to Jews, it was expunged from all publications, including all academic works and literary classics, where it was replaced with the word "ievrei." The works of the nineteenth-century humorist Stepan Rudansky were purged not only of this term and its derivatives, but also of the words "Cossack" and "Pole," ostensibly to prevent any offense against nations or religions. This linguistic-political prudishness was, of course, not only foolish but completely hypocritical. As Yefremov indicates, there were posters in the streets around April 25, 1929, proclaiming that the Christian and Jewish Paska [the same word is used for Easter and Passover] were "feasts of the exploiters." (Ibid., 758.) Such crude censorship and antireligious propaganda infuriated both ordinary Ukrainians and Jews, for whom it represented a concerted attack on their beliefs and cultures.

Relations between the two communities were further strained by a show trial intended to discredit the national liberation movement that was held from April 19 to September 19, 1930, in the Kharkiv opera house. It was accompanied by a mass propaganda campaign and widespread arrests of the Ukrainian intelligentsia. Forty-five people were accused, and Yefremov was treated as the ringleader of the counterrevolutionary SVU (League for the Liberation of Ukraine).

The organization was a fabrication of the GPU, and the charges were trumped up. Jews were prominent dramatis personae during the staged and widely publicized event. Valerii Gorozhanin and Borys Kozelsky, who acted as the principal conductors of this trial and many later cases, were both Jews who rose to the highest ranks after the trial. The prosecution's plan was to "expose Ukrainian patriots to further charges of anti-Semitism" by linking Yefremov to Petliura and the pogroms of 1919. (Snyder 2005, 52.)

The Image of the Jew as Commissar and Chekist

Most Jews, like most Ukrainians, had welcomed the overthrow of tsarism in February 1917 and few had joined the Bolshevik Party. The overwhelming majority threw their weight behind Zionist parties, in the same way as the vast majority of Ukrainians threw their weight behind Ukrainian socialist and social-democratic parties. Individual Jews had, however, been prominent in the leadership of revolutionary parties. Jews appear to have begun joining the Bolsheviks in larger numbers after September 1918. A leader of the Jewish Bund, Moisei Rafes, in a book completed late in 1919, described Jewish parties as staunchly loyal to the Ukrainian government in the revolution's first year. The Poale Zion party even held negotiations with the Ukrainian social-democrats with a view to fusing with them. When Jews joined the Bolsheviks, they were initially treated with suspicion and refused leadership positions, but, argues Rafes, when it became evident that they could produce strong support for Soviet rule "the task of drawing Jewish workers into the Red Army attracted the attention of military-political authorities." (Rafes 1920, 164.)

In Ukraine Jewish participation in the Cheka was heavy. Schapiro has written that after the revolution "Jews abounded at the lower levels of the party machinery—especially in the Cheka, and its successors the GPU, the OGPU and the NKVD." (Schapiro 1988, 286.) They were soon also prominent in leading positions within this machinery. Some work has now been done on the biographies of Cheka members and an incomplete list of the organization's leadership in Ukraine from 1919 to 1937 is available. (Shapoval and Zolotarov 2002, 363–445; Bilokin 1999, 346–59.) Although researchers still have difficulty in gaining access to the relevant files, and full disclosure of all the evidence lies in the future, it is clear, nonetheless, that the participation of Jews in the Ukrainian Cheka-GPU-NKVD was greatly disproportionate to their weight in the population. Even at the all-Union level, in the years 1934–37 Jews appear to have been the largest single nationality group among the leading cadres. (Slezkine

2004, 221, 254–55.) By 1939, however, most had been arrested in the purges or removed from the top leadership. (Rayfield 2005, 305.)

In the thirties, the proportion of Jews in the all-Union party began to fall and by 1937 they constituted only around 5.7 percent of its membership. However, in Ukraine during the revolution's early years, their percentage was high: they made up about a third of the Communist Party (Bolshevik) of Ukraine—the CP(B)U—and were the second largest group after the Russians. In 1921 Ukrainians constituted only 19 percent of the CP(B)U, and even as late as 1923 were still only the third largest group. It was therefore easy enough in Ukraine to form the impression that Communists and Jews were the same thing. As Schapiro puts it, in the early years of the revolution the identification of Communist with Jew was likely to appeal to ordinary people: "For the most prominent and colourful figure after Lenin was Trotsky, in Petrograd the dominant and hated figure was Zinoviev, while anyone who had the misfortune to fall into the hands of the Cheka stood a very good chance of finding himself confronted with and possibly shot by a Jewish investigator." (Schapiro 1988, 286.) By the late twenties, following the recruitment of Ukrainians to all levels of administration, the situation had changed significantly. However, reality and popular perceptions could be at odds, and the perceptions that had been formed in the early years of the revolution were reinforced when the rhetoric of militant Bolshevism was redeployed in 1928–33 and the Chekist or commissar (who was often identified as Jewish) became a prominent literary figure.

This figure's literary life in the early twenties had been ambiguous and less visible, but toward the end of the decade he was glorified as a fierce combatant. The trend was set in Russian literature by Aleksandr Fadeev's protagonist Levinson from *Razgrom* (The Rout, 1926), who became a prototype of the Jewish Bolshevik as unflinching fighter. Eduard Bagritsky, who came from Odesa and wrote in Russian, described Ukrainian realities. In his "TVS" (1929) he fanatically embraces communist doctrine and ritual. Felix Dzerzhinsky, the first head of the Cheka, visits him and says: "But if it [the century] should say 'Lie,' then lie. And if it should say 'Kill,' then kill." His "Razgovor s synom" (Conversation with My Son, 1931) describes a pogrom, then speaks of steeling the will for battle and of marching under the Red flag to liberate the planet. These poems harmonize with the time's unforgiving, ruthless mood, and no doubt confirmed many readers in the belief that the image of the fanatical Jewish commissar was justified. Toward the end of his life Bagritsky appears to have reassessed his pro-Soviet fanaticism. Maxim Shrayer has argued that "his idealism crashed against the ferroconcrete dams of the emerging Stalinist state, when he witnessed the death of an idyll, the impossibility of a poet's harmonious existence in a world of cultural and political violence." (Shrayer 2000, 18.) In the last two years of his life, the poet turned his attention to the formative experience of the First World War and the February revolution. "Posledniaia noch" (The Last Night, 1932) describes how the experience of the war transformed his generation. "We assimilated the habits of warriors," he writes, indicating that the ideal of the warrior-Jew as a figure representing strength, self-sufficiency, and public admiration was absorbed by young Jews who suddenly sensed themselves masters of a sixth of the earth's surface. In "Fevral" (February, 1934, published 1936) he depicts the heady atmosphere that reigned in the months following the collapse of tsarism. The narrator recalls his appointment as deputy district commissar of the militia, a law enforcement agency that policed Odesa against gangsters: "My Jewish pride sang, / Like a string stretched to its limit." The poem was roundly condemned by most Soviet authors (and was later pounced upon by anti-Semitic critics during the "anticosmopolitan campaign" of 1949–53) because its ending describes what has been seen by most readers as the rape of a Russian prostitute. Critics have remarked upon this as a prime example of russophobia and extreme hatred. Bagritsky's detractors were particularly concerned with the idea of cultural miscegenation. A key point is that the poem deals with a pre-Bolshevik reality. As Shrayer has persuasively argued, the poet's paean to freedom and a new identity is a tribute to the first weeks of the February revolution. (Shrayer 2000, 67.) Shrayer's interpretation of the ending is much less convincing. He does not see it as a rape: "Sexual intercourse with his former Russian beloved is the modicum of the protagonist's revenge upon and liberation from the prerevolutionary world of legal Jewish inequality and popular anti-Semitic prejudice." (Ibid., 90.) Most readers would probably disagree. The whole point of the final scene lies precisely in the protagonist's ability to dominate the woman, just as she dominated him. He punishes her for earlier rejecting him, and, as he says, to avenge upon her the bashful and timid nature he has inherited from his ancestors. The act of rape makes a great deal of sense in psychological terms as an attempt to compensate for former powerlessness.

One of the most famous portrayals of a Jewish commissar occurs in Bagritsky's "Duma pro Opanasa" (A Duma about Opanas, 1926). It describes a tragic conflict between a Ukrainian peasant who is drawn against his will into the revolution, and the fanatical Jewish commissar Yosif Kogan. The poet shows an understanding of the dilemmas faced by both protagonists. Kogan is a ruthless expropriator of grain; he shoots anyone who protests, until the black earth turns "to mud / From the blood and sweat." Opanas is conscripted into Makhno's army. When Kogan is captured, Opanas is prepared to let him escape, even though he has been ordered by Makhno to execute the commissar. He proposes that Kogan take to his heels, promising to shoot in the air. Kogan refuses, seeing it as below a Communist's dignity to flee: "It is unseemly for a Communist / To run, like a greyhound!" The poem captures the sense of an almost predestined, inescapable conflict between the two people. Yet, it is a complex relationship that is rarely given a careful, nuanced reading. Opanas has usually been dismissed as simply a pogromist; his intimacy with Kogan is seldom mentioned. They are, after all, close acquaintances. Kogan even suggests to "Panko" that he should take the rest of his clothes after the shooting. This detail, by the way, suggests the method of execution practiced by Chekists, among others. Witnesses have recalled that victims were shot in their underclothes; the rest of their clothing and valuables went to the Chekists, who were seen carrying these home in sacks after a "night's work." (Bilokin' 1999, 106.) As Opanas agonizes over whether to shoot Kogan, he recalls their common fate as soldiers during the First World War and the very earth seems to urge him not to kill. Eventually he does shoot Kogan, but the awareness of intimacy between the adversaries changes one's reading of the poem, in the same way as an awareness of the intimacy between the prostitute and the narrator changes one's reading of "Fevral," and, it might be added, in the way that an awareness of intimacy between Yarema and Leiba changes the interpretation of Shevchenko's *Haidamaky*. This last poem was, in fact, one of Bagritsky's literary models. The meter, rhythms, and phrasing are Shevchenko's, and a quatrain from *Haidamaky* is used as the epigraph. As in Shevchenko's poem, the focus is not on anti-Semitism, but on the moral choices people must make in times of violence, and on the tragedy of a divided land.

How portrayals of the figure of the Jewish commissar might have resonated with the reading public in Ukraine can be grasped by examining eyewitness accounts. In 1923, Vynnychenko described the typical Chekist of the revolutionary period as a jumped-up officer who had come from a small town, who had likely attended the yeshiva, and who spoke faulty Russian. Many Jews found their way into the Red Army or the communist administration because they had remained in the towns and joined the Bolsheviks to obtain jobs and avoid dying of hunger: "The former doctors, lawyers, students of pharmacy, journalists of the banned bourgeois press, shopkeepers, foremen, various commercial middlemen, commissioners, and so on quickly began representing 'the workers and peasants' of Ukraine." (Vynnychenko 1998, 159.) Soon almost all the executive power in Ukraine ended up "in the hands of the Jewish petty bourgeoisie and intelligentsia," who did the bidding of the Moscow Politburo, which included requisitioning grain in the villages. Only when the killing of Jewish commissars took on a mass character did the Politburo give the instruction for them to "avoid work in the villages." By then the damage had been done: the rural population concluded that Jews and Communists were synonymous. (Ibid., 161.)

Vynnychenko's views are supported by eyewitness accounts. Lazar Bilynkis provides a harrowing picture of revolution in a town near Uman. He describes how the Ukrainian population suddenly saw Jews "on all levels of the Soviet administration, even in the highest state posts; the institutions most hated by the population, such as the Cheka, the organs of provisioning, and those of requisitioning, were all chock full of Jews, who brought with them many negative features of the Jewish ghetto." (Bilynkis 1998, 235.) He writes:

> The large number of Jews in these and in all other institutions can be explained by the fact that in the first years of the revolution Ukrainian youth—all Petliura supporters and enemies of Soviet rule—did not want to serve in them, and sabotaged them, because of the instability of this rule in Ukraine, because they feared to compromise themselves in the eyes of the partisans, and also because they were already settled in other, nonpolitical institutions (schools, cooperatives, various peasant banks, mills) and had little need to serve. The Jews, on the other hand, who had an enormous number of unemployed youth before the revolution as a result of their lack of rights, had been driven out of villages and small towns into large towns by the pogroms during the revolution and civil war. The destruction of private trade, the ending of extramural studies and private tutoring, the cutbacks in educational institutions, and the curtailing to a minimum of artisanal work hugely enlarged this army of the unemployed. It is not surprising, therefore, that they threw themselves into their only salvation from death by starvation—Soviet service. They were uncultured, poorly educated, unprincipled, infuriated, and confounded by the horrors of the pogroms in defenseless, obscure small and large towns, where they saw their relatives and parents die before their eyes in terrible agony, their homes destroyed, their property—collected over generations—stolen. Morally crippled, they entered Soviet service to eat their fill and reward themselves for their losses, but they also expressed an entirely natural sense of anger and an insatiable jealousy and thirst for revenge, even against those of their co-religionists who had not yet suffered. If in the army, thanks to Trotsky's energy, order was achieved through ruthless punishment for robbery and violence, in the civil administration, which grew to enormous proportions (in Moscow and Piter [Petrograd] a third of the entire population worked in the Soviet civil service) no punishments or even executions could halt the plundering, bribe-taking, and mercenary behavior. It should therefore be understandable what fury this administration called forth in the Ukrainian people, which hated it for its sins, and the Jews for participating in it. They turned their fury upon the defenseless and innocent Jews in terrible, brutal

pogroms, in which all Jews to a person were killed: children, women, the aged. (Ibid., 236.)

Bilynkis presents the horrors of the pogrom that occurred in his town of Talniv, but he also describes the events that preceded it in the six months of Bolshevik rule. The head of the *revkom* (revolutionary committee) was a certain Popov:

> . . . drunken, with almost unlimited power, he led a dissolute life, surrounded by women and a whole flock of dissolute youth, to whom he handed the administration of the Cheka, the court, and the school. Only the economy and health care were in capable hands. The first was run by a former officer Kapliuchenko; the second by a young, energetic, and honest doctor Mylovanov, a former political émigré. These two commissars were able to do much good for the population. The other commissars of the *revkom* were incapable of creating anything and only spread destruction, particularly the commissars of education, of whom there were four in six month. The first was a twenty-year-old salesman, a Jew called Bliakher, who had two years of secondary education. He signed a decree forbidding the teaching of religion in local schools. One can imagine the impression that the announcement of this law made on the local fanatical and anti-Semitic Christian population, and what a rich theme it became for pogrom agitation. . . . He was followed by an eighteen-year-old half-educated merchant, also a Jew, from Shpolia. Although he was in the job for only two weeks, he succeeded in destroying our only, quite valuable, community library, which I had put together with great effort over twenty-five years, and which had greatly increased in the revolutionary period (I had donated a thousand volumes from my own library, and many others had given generously). . . . One of the saddest figures in the revolutionary committee was an apprentice shoemaker Kaminsky, who was the commissar for contributions and, I think, for justice. A tactless, brutal, uncultured, excitable nineteen-year-old with a strong Jewish accent and a typical, rather good-looking appearance, he had the most unpleasant employment. He was sent, or maybe himself volunteered, whenever there was a need to abuse and insult someone. Along with another similar disreputable type, the factory worker Hertlein (later executed by Tiutiunnyk), he was assigned the job of collecting contributions. Of what cruelty, scorn, and abuse of human individuals, especially Jews, they were capable! They threw all the arrested who were even a little better off into a cold, narrow place which lacked even a layer of straw on the floor, and at night led them into the woods in groups to terrorize them by shooting into the air. (Ibid., 236–37.)

Bilynkis writes that the entire revolutionary committee of this town and of neighboring Uman appeared to be composed of Jews. The parade of May 1, 1919 also consisted mainly of Jews and all the speeches were given by Jews. Victor Serge, a Belgian-Russian who became an anarchist in France and then witnessed the events in Petrograd, has left a similarly sardonic characterization of Chek-ists:

> The only temperaments that devoted themselves willingly and tenaciously to this task of "internal defence" were those characterized by suspicion, embitter-ment, harshness, and sadism. Long-standing social inferiority-complexes and memories of humiliations and suffering in the Tsar's jails rendered them in-tractable, and since professional degeneration has rapid effects, the Chekas in-evitably consisted of perverted men tending to see conspiracy everywhere and to live in the midst of perpetual conspiracy themselves. (Serge 1967, 80–81.)

The cult of torture had from the first been a hallmark of the Chekists, who were selected for their ability to do the revolution's dirty work. Various stomach-turning atrocities have been documented and described. (Ibid., 99–102, 104; Rayfield 2005, 82–84, 306.) The brutality was deliberate: the Chekists were out to terrorize the population into submission, to inflict cruelty and violence on an unprecedented scale. It should not, however, be forgotten that even in the early years there were also prominent Ukrainian figures in the Cheka. Mykola Khvylovy was one, according to Mykhailo Derehus. (Derehus 2004, 97.) The poet Dmytro Levchuk, who wrote under the pseudonym Falkivsky, was another, and has described his service in the Cheka from 1918 to 1920 in a number of works. Some of Falkivsky's poems show a blind fanaticism. In one, the narrator admits that he "dug in the refuse of October" and that he "used to shoot hun-dreds in succession." (Fal'kivs'kyi 1989, 47.) There is little reason to doubt the factual basis of these experiences, which are presented with a degree of pride. In their literary works Falkivsky and Khvylovy tried to work through their memo-ries. The lives of both writers were cut short: Khvylovy committed suicide in 1933, and Falkivsky was executed in the following year. It should also be stressed that although Jewish cadres had been highly visible among the Chekists, com-missars, and requisitionists during the revolutionary and postrevolutionary years, this was less true, as literature and eyewitness reports suggest, in the vio-lence that led to the famine of 1933, or in the terror of the thirties.

The militant Bolshevik writing of 1928–33 that has been mentioned above and in connection with Pervomaisky's work constitutes an entire poetic style. The focus is always on a crisis, an immediate threat that demands action and the suspension of careful reasoning. The appeal is to raw emotions: the diction be-longs to the realm of military brutality, and the imagery is associated with wrenching disruption. War is the dominant metaphor; it is heroic and vital, while peace and compassion are associated with weakness. The village, which is naturally bountiful but set in its wrongheaded, traditionalist ways, must be

forced into submission. It becomes the body to be raped. Symbolic violation—
of the peasantry, the countryside, or the bourgeoisie—is a dominant trope.

An important aspect of this writing is its attempt to condition readers to the
overstepping of moral norms, to what was viewed as a Leninist contempt for
sentimentality. The continual exacerbation of conflict and striving to extend civil
war, the calls for the maximum number of executions—all in the expectation of
an imminent new world order—were, according to the historian Dmitri Volkogonov, characteristic of Lenin's atrophied sense of morality. According to one
observer, in early 1918 at practically every session of the Council of People's
Commissars, Lenin insisted that socialism could be realized in Russia in six
months. (Volkogonov 1999, xix.) The frenzied atmosphere and bloodthirsty
rhetoric in the literature of the early thirties appear to have been an attempt to
rekindle this "Leninist" mood of 1918. The most notorious examples of this
kind of writing in Ukrainian literature are probably to be found in Pavlo Tychyna's poetry of 1929–33, in particular his "Partiia vede" (The Party Leads),
which appeared in *Pravda* on November 21, 1933: "let them . . . go insane, let
them die, . . . throw all the *pany* [gentlemen] into one hole, we will kill one lot of
bourgeois after another, we will!" (Tychyna 1976, 1:121.) The regime was aware
that victims debased through abuse in this way could find little sympathy.

The image of the Chekist plays a central role in this writing. Shapoval reports that Izi Kharik's poem in Yiddish called "GPU" was written on December
29, 1929, the day before the official holiday in honor of the Chekists. It is an ode
to the secret police that lauds severity and the joy of revenge. (Shapoval 2001,
208–9.) The writer was arrested and killed in 1937. The same militarized, anti-
sentimental style was employed by the seventeen-year-old Aron Kopshtein in
the following poem from 1932:

> Let my song be counted in the general stock
> Of Red Army weapons.
> Maximum speed
> And accuracy of fire,
> A preselected target. (Kopshtein 1941, 20.)

The death of Hryhorii Chuprynka, a modernist poet famous for his play with as-
sonances, is denied any tragic associations because he fought on the side of the
national movement:

> End the recollections of Chuprynka.
> Believe me—
>   His blinding tinkles and clinkles
> Are bloody, treacherous lines,

That decorated the sword
And are woven into the saddle leather.
Some slobber:
    "A fine lyricist has died . . ."
Drop this thinking—
    Can a criminal be a poet?!
With the blood of Mykhailovych and Aronova
I will feed my hatred,
I will feed my lyrics
With the blood of Mykhailovych and Aronova. (Ibid., 30–31.)

The author adds his own footnote to this poem, explaining that Mykhailovych and Aronova were both Komsomol members who died in battle.

The overall effect of this writing is a kind of psychic numbing that might be compared to the role of Basic Training, which strips the recruit of his civilian identity and makes him unthinkingly accept military authority and discipline. This verse spread the conviction in the public mind that its authors were spiritual descendants of the Cheka, unflinching and unfeeling Bolsheviks. Understandably, the general reader's attitude was hostile, especially since the literary Chekist recalled the very real Chekist who was then raping the countryside. The fact that Jewish authors were contributing to this poetry reinforced for many readers the association between Jews, Communists, Chekists, and terror. Contemporary newspapers reported trials against anti-Semites and large runs of books on the subject were printed, among them: A. Khvylia, *Antysemityzm* (Anti-Semitism, 1928); D. Ortenberh, *Iak borotysia z antysemityzmom* (How to Fight Anti-Semitism, 1928); M. Gorev's *Protiv antisemitov* (Against Anti-Semites; 1928); Yu. Larin's *Evrei i antisemitizm v SSSR* (Jews and Anti-Semitism in the USSR, 1928); and L. Radishchev's *Iad—ob antisemitizme nashikh dnei* (Poison—On Anti-Semitism in Our Time, 1930). Schools began to make compulsory the reading of stories sympathetic to Jews by well-known authors like Sholem Aleichem and Korolenko. The regime's message was, however, contradictory. By liquidating Jewish communities, banning the use of Hebrew, and persecuting Judaism, it was itself practicing and legitimizing forms of anti-Semitism.

The dynamic between this militant literature and the harsh realities of forced collectivization, requisitioning, famine, and terror has not been investigated. In 1927 the OGPU had taken control of the concentration camps and by 1935 the number of prisoners was almost a million. Maksim Gorky visited the Solovetsky camp in 1929 and characterized the slave labor as successfully transforming criminals into useful citizens. He used language calculated to depersonalize the prisoners, describing the kulaks (an almost meaningless term whose function was purely abusive) as "half-animals." As for the peasants, he had the following to say about them in *Pravda* on November 15, 1930: "If the enemy does not surrender, he must be exterminated." (Montefiore 2003, 84.) Stalin referred to them as "enemies of the people," "vermin," "pollution," "filth," and "weeds." (Applebaum 2003, 112.)

In the thirties a host of Ukrainian writers competed with one another in sycophancy, penning dithyrambs to Stalin and to Bolshevik leaders in Ukraine, among them Vsevolod Balytsky, the head of the Ukrainian NKVD in the years 1934–37. The propaganda campaign of which this kind of literature formed an integral part boosted the image and prestige of the Chekists. Black leather (the Chekist uniform ever since Dzerzhynsky appropriated a consignment of leather coats sent from Western Europe for Russia's air force pilots in the First World War) became fashionable. Ann Applebaum states that Gorky's daughter-in-law, who accompanied him on his trip to the Solovetsky camp, wore a "leather jacket, leather jodhpurs, high boots and a leather cap," presenting herself in what she no doubt thought was "the costume of an authentic 'chekistka.'" (Applebaum 2003, 59.) It was a style that harmonized with the literary vogue for violence and macho brutality—the accompaniments to terror and perhaps essentials for making the violence psychologically palatable to perpetrators and observers alike. The building of the White Sea—Baltic Canal became a dominant literary theme. In plays produced in Moscow theaters in 1934–35, 22 percent of the characters were builders of the canal. This literature eulogized the Gulag and the heroic Chekist (Estraikh 2005, 159). It did not escape public notice that in fact, all the leadership positions in the canal project were held by Jews: Genrikh Yagoda was in charge; Semen Firin was head of the labor camp; Lazar Kogan was head of construction; Matvei Berman was head of the Gulag; Naftaly Frenkel was head of the work organization.

The famine of 1932–33 was preceded by government theft of all agricultural products, food of any kind, and farming and food-making implements. This was generally accomplished by recruiting local people. When eyewitnesses were asked in an oral history project "Who conducted the requisitioning and collectivizing?" the answer was most often "our people, locals," even though outsiders were sometimes present and, of course, the policies were initiated in Moscow. Many interviewees could name those who conducted the procurement or dispossession because they were fellow villagers. (Noll 1999, 123, 170–75.) Not only individual farms were collectivized. Club premises attached to collectives were often constructed out of confiscated priests' homes, churches, and synagogues. Jewish farming colonies were also collectivized, and there is evidence that they also starved in 1932–33. They were subjected to the same high taxes and government theft, which led in many cases to the requisitioning of almost every grain. (Naiman 1995, 218–19.) Malnourishment and hunger in the Jewish population is mentioned in some newspapers and party circulars from the famine years. (Ibid., 220–22.) In the spring of 1933 people were dying of hunger in Berdychiv, Zhytomyr, Uman, Bila Tserkva, Fastov, and Proskuriv, where there were large Jewish populations. According to official data, in February of that year 918 corpses of Jews who had died of hunger were picked up off the streets of Kyiv. The fact that in 1936–37 almost all the activists of KOMZET (the Committee for Rural Placement of Jewish Laborers) were repressed, and that Jewish collective farms dropped by 30 percent, while the number of Jewish farmers fell by 60 percent, is indirect evidence of the devastation and resistance. (Ibid., 221.)

At this time Soviet propaganda attempted to channel the fervor for a new homeland aroused by Zionism into the realization of this dream within Soviet borders and within the context of collectivized agriculture. Agitation to settle Jews on land in the Crimea continued throughout the thirties. Jewish sections of the Communist Party and OZET (Society for Settlement of Working Jews on the Land) helped to colonize these lands. Four Jewish national districts and 127 national village Soviets were created in southern Ukraine and the Crimea by 1931. These were abolished in 1937–38 as emphasis shifted to full assimilation. In 1934, Birobidzhan, in the Soviet Far East, was declared a Jewish autonomous region within the Russian Republic, but few people moved there, because resettlement policies were by that time viewed as punitive mass deportations.

The xenophobia that accompanied militant Bolshevik writing was easily transferred to any group. Poles and German Mennonites in Ukraine were forcibly resettled in 1929–30 and the removal of many other national groups followed. (Martin 2001, 311–43; Brown 2004, 118–52, 180.) In fact, it has been calculated that about one-third of political victims and executions were the result of "national operations" in the Great Terror. (Martin 2001, 338, 341.) By the thirties many in the population were conditioned to accept a national or ethnic dimension to mass arrests and social engineering.

Western Ukraine: Nationalism and Popular Dramas

Petliura's assassination led to a deterioration of Ukrainian-Jewish relations in Western Ukraine. A number of observers have described relations between Ukrainians and Jews as friendly with considerable interaction until the thirties. After

1933, when the Nazis came to power in Germany, the Polish government and many leaders in the Ukrainian community became increasingly anti-Semitic. Many young Ukrainians began to place their hopes for change in the new, powerful Germany. Although some scholars worked to counter these views and the accompanying growth of anti-Semitism, an increasingly hostile attitude began to seep into literature.

Western Ukraine officially became part of the new Polish state in 1920. A Polish-Jewish accord was struck in 1925 in the Sejm, according to which Jews supported Polish interests in return for some concessions. This naturally caused anger among Ukrainians. In 1930, the Polish government conducted the infamous "pacification campaign" in which the army carried out beatings and repressions against the Ukrainian population. The increasingly authoritarian behavior pushed Ukrainians to more radical positions and Dmytro Dontsov's brand of nationalism began to put down roots. At the time of the Schwartzbard trial, he impugned Jews for hostility to Ukrainian political demands, writing: "From the end of the last century, from the first attempts at organizing the Ukrainian masses under national slogans, who if not the Russians and Jews threw stumbling blocks under our feet at every step—in both legal and illegal work? Who if not they prevented us from making out of human dust an obedient nation aware of its national goals?" (Dontsov 1948a, 11.) In this article he already creates the image of a common enemy by merging Russians, Jews, and Bolshevism into one undifferentiated entity, speaking, for example, of the "Muscovite-Jewish union" and the "Russian-Jewish press." He suggests that this enemy is treating Ukraine as a "conquered country" to be colonized, and is demanding that Ukraine renounce its dream of independence, along with the historical figures who symbolize this dream—Khmelnytsky, Mazepa, and Petliura. The article ends by issuing a warning: when Bolshevism falls, those who today solidarize with Schwartzbard or the regime will be blacklisted and denied state jobs. (Ibid., 16.)

The OUN (Organization of Ukrainian Nationalists), which was created in 1929 in Poland and rapidly developed mass support in Western Ukraine, saw the use of violence as inevitable in the struggle for independence. The writings of its leading ideologists often ignored the Jews, as in the case of Mykola Stsiborsky's *Natsiokratiia* (Nationocracy, 1935), a call for national solidarity and state corporatism that went through three editions, or his *Stalinizm* (Stalinism, 2d ed., 1942). In 1930, Stsiborsky agreed that Ukrainians were generally hostile toward Jews, seeing this as the outcome of a long history. However, it would be a mistake, he argued, to think that all Jews supported Bolshevism. Most of the Jewish intelligentsia were neutral or opposed to communism. The pogroms of 1918–19, which had poisoned Jewish attitudes toward the UNR, were the work of "ignorant and adventurist elements" and not of the broad masses, and their victims were peaceful Jews who had no relationship to the revolution or Bolshevism. OUN's task was to convince Jews that a Ukrainian state posed no danger to them. Their activities, especially commercial skills, would benefit the future state. There should be no discussion of limiting their rights. Ukrainians needed to establish close contacts—both political and "psychological"—with Jews on the national and international levels. (Stsibors'kyi 1930, 273.)

Oleksandr Mytsiuk produced a long text entitled *Agraryzatsiia zhydivstva Ukrainy na tli zahal'noi ekonomiky* (The Agrarianization of the Jews of Ukraine and the General Economic Background, 1933), which rehearsed the idea that Jews had consistently failed to support Ukrainians in their national liberation struggle. Like Stsiborsky, he indicated 1918–19 as a disastrous turning point in Ukrainian-Jewish relations, which until then had been improving. It is worth noting that both Stsiborsky and Mytsiuk were cautious when it came to identifying Jews with contemporary Soviet policies. In fact Mytsiuk showed that requisitioning and collectivization also victimized new Jewish settlements, which put up a violent resistance. (Mytsiuk 1933, 150–59.) His text was first serialized in the Prague journal *Rozbudova natsii* (Development of the Nation) in the years 1931–33. This organ of the OUN presented issues surrounding Jewish-Ukrainian relations in a manner that recognized their complexity, even though the thrust of the articles was to show past Jewish complicity in the socio-economic and national oppression of Ukrainians.

In the late thirties, however, some OUN ideologists began to openly hint at the segregation of Jews. Volodymyr Martynets in his *Zhydivs'ka probliema v Ukraini* (The Jewish Problem in Ukraine, 1938) voices the often-repeated charges of parasitism (the selling of alcohol and the practice of usury) and hostility to Ukrainian national demands, before reaching the conclusion that Jews had to be isolated from Ukrainians—economically, politically, and culturally. This suggestion is never explained, but the author does make it clear that there must be no attempt to forcibly assimilate or convert Jews: they should enjoy all the rights enjoyed by Ukrainians. The reader is left to envisage Jews living in a parallel universe: "we want nothing from the Jews, but we also desire that they desire nothing of us." (Martynets' 1938, 15.) To some readers these statements may have implied a future Ukrainian state that would copy the intensified ethno-nationalization initiated in Poland after 1935. At this time the government repudiated the Minorities Treaty that had been accepted in 1919 as part of the Ver-

sailles Treaty and curtailed minority rights. It closed Orthodox churches and
non-Polish schools, and launched a campaign to segregate Jewish students in
universities and other institutions of higher education by making them use
"ghetto benches," while the National Democratic Party called for the "de-Ju-
daization" of the country and instigated violence against Jews in 150 towns
and villages, smashing windows and stores and beating individuals. An estimated
two thousand Jews were injured and twenty to thirty killed. (Michlic 2006, 74,
113–14.)

Although nationalist literature of the thirties showed little interest in Nazi-
inspired anti-Semitism, the fascist cult of violence and virility had a strong influence on literary works. The writings of Dmytro Dontsov had a great effect. In
the years 1933–39 he edited *Vistnyk* (Herald), which was published in Lviv.
Some of his best articles were anthologized and reissued in his *Nasha doba i literatura* (Our Era and Literature, 1936). The writer hardly mentions Jews at all,
but his cult of the heroic and vital, and especially of an amoral enthusiasm, prepared the ground for a break with normative forms of behavior. His writings
breathe the gospel of the negative sublime that Dominick LaCapra has identified
as a component of Nazi ideology. (LaCapra 2001, 135–36.) Dontsov shows a desire for ecstatic elation, which he relates to extreme transgression, and suggests
that national regeneration and redemption must come through violence. In the
collection's final essay, written in 1936, he likens his age to "the Apocalypse, the
coming of the Four Horsemen, and the great Day of Wrath." (Dontsov 1936,
170.) The validation of Dionysian excess was an aspect of Nazi ideology with
which Dontsov attempted to align his readers. It resembled the aggressive
Bolshevik aesthetic, which issued analogous calls for transgression against hu-
manitarian, "bourgeois" norms, and for a hardening of the spirit, and showed a
similar obsession with violence. Throughout Central and Eastern Europe authoritative discourses emanating from both communist and anticommunist
movements instructed readers to prepare themselves for violence in a world that
appeared to have slipped its moorings.

The interwar years in Western Ukraine saw the development of the cooperative movement, anti-alcohol and teetotaling campaigns, and the spread of
Prosvita (Enlightenment) reading clubs. The cooperatives ran into direct opposition from Jewish merchants, while the other two campaigns indirectly competed with Jewish businesses. Jews figure prominently in popular didactic plays
produced in Western Ukraine on these topics. Cooperatives are depicted as nonexploitative, community-run enterprises that serve the greater good; alcoholism
is shown as leading to indebtedness at the tavern, which then quickly results in

loss of property when the extended credit cannot be paid. These issues are examined in plays like O. Hadus's *U kozhnoho rozum ie, iak horivky vin ne p'ie* (Everyone Has Good Judgment When Not Drinking Liquor, 1929), and Arkadii Danko's *Srul' natiahailo* (Tricky Srul, 1931). In the latter play Petro encourages his countrymen to learn from the cooperative movement how to conduct exemplary businesses, and thereby to lift the cultural level in rural areas. In answer to the complaints of a Jewish merchant he responds: "The Jew will not fleece the muzhyk, nor the muzhyk the Jew if they are decent people." Ukrainians, he says, have too long looked down upon commerce, but it is "as respectable an occupation as agriculture for the mass of society." Honest enterprise is counterposed to the dishonest dealings of Les Krutii, who swindles both Jews and Ukrainians, leaving everyone unhappy. (Danko 1931, 16–17.) In I. Yaroslavych's *Pavuky* (Spiders, 1932) the hero, Andrii, tries to teach the peasants, who have become accustomed to buying exclusively from Jews and drinking in the Jewish tavern, that the cooperative's goods are just as cheap and good. The village head and Abrumko the tavernkeeper hatch a shady deal to buy up land cheaply by failing to advertise an auction ahead of time, but they are exposed. As in some nineteenth-century dramas, the villain who aims to dupe local villagers is the local Ukrainian official and he is in league with a Jewish moneyman and shark.

Toward the end of the decade a much more virulent anti-Semitism emerges in plays like Vasyl Hulyk's *Het' z lykhvoiu, pianstvom i temnotoiu* (Away with Usury, Alcoholism, and Ignorance, 1937). As the title indicates, the play is heavily didactic. The heroine delivers the following denunciation of Moshko and his fellow Jews: "You are worse than despots, you are usurers and swindlers; with your tricks you have sucked the last juices from our unfortunate people; you hang onto our feet like fetters, and do not allow us to develop our commerce and industry; with trickery you draw from our people their last, bloody coin; our people are dying from hunger and cold, and are continuously in want. You, on the other hand, drag blood-soaked earnings from us by trickery and grow wealthy, sending the rest [of the money] to Palestine. With our bloody money you build various factories and universities there. . . . Go to Palestine, to the promised land, to work and live there!" (Hulyk 1937, 11.) Moshko's business does indeed suffer and he decides to leave for Palestine. It is interesting, however, that the Ukrainian who buys the tavern from him, hoping to get rich, does not thrive.

Maksym Gon has shown how the success of the cooperative movement led in the second half of the thirties both to economic modernization and to greater conflicts with non-Ukrainians. The movement grew from 166,000 members in

1921 to 700,000 in 1939, by which time there were twenty-five hundred cooperative institutions. (Gon 2003, 94.) Jewish merchants and middlemen were often
hurt by the new businesses and complained that the slogan of the cooperative
movement, "Buy from your own!" ("Svii do svoho!") was anti-Semitic, since it
led to the shunning of non-Ukrainian businesses. Many Ukrainians avoided the
slogan in order to diminish conflicts, but the boycotting of Jewish enterprises in
some regions became a tendency. As Ukrainian storekeepers grew more numerous, tensions increased. Often Jewish and Polish merchants boycotted Ukrainian enterprises in turn. Since Jews made up a large percentage of the population in many towns, the opening of Ukrainian businesses there was often seen as
an anti-Jewish move. In the climate of economic crisis during the years 1929–33,
and then under the influence of racist views emanating from Central Europe, the
conflict was easily ideologized.

The campaign against the sale of alcohol was led by the teetotaling organization Vidrodzhennia (Renaissance). It arranged plebiscites calling for the closure
of many of the five thousand taverns in Galicia and Western Volhynia. In this way,
the problems of the Ukrainian village collided with the Jewish businessman's
struggle to survive. The slogan "A book instead of a bottle of vodka!" was aimed
at supplanting taverns with Prosvita reading halls, but the issue took on dangerous forms when some individuals called for the burning of taverns and the ex-
pulsion of their proprietors. Jews who lived in villages often faced the brunt of
this agitation, which took several forms. Moral pressure included the distribution of agitational leaflets and calls for boycotts, but violent methods were also
used. The burning of Jewish buildings became an epidemic in the Volhynia region in 1936, leaving around a hundred families homeless. Ukrainians, however,
were not pioneers in the use of violence as an instrument of economic competition: "The most militant and uncompromising struggle with Jews was led by
their old enemies, the Polish National Democrats. Their attacks were open, powerful, and indiscriminate in the choice of methods aimed at forcing Jews out of
the economy and, ideally, out of the country." (Gon 2003, 100.)

In 1933 the Ukrainian Social Democratic and the Ukrainian Socialist Radical parties held a conference with the Jewish Poale Zion Party, at which all three
agreed to work against anti-Semitic agitation in the villages, which was often
conducted by members of the OUN. Although the rise of the cooperative movement brought many benefits to the Ukrainian population, the violent methods
and the excessive politicization of the issue did nothing to improve the lives of
people. In fact, throughout this period many businesses remained in Jewish
hands and continued to serve the general public. In 1936, for example, there was

only one Ukrainian bakery in the whole of Lviv, but 28 Polish, and 142 Jewish ones. This indicates that a gradualist approach to any change was not only desirable but inevitable. (Ibid., 98.)

Spyrydon Cherkasenko and Vasyl Pachovsky

The literature of the thirties in Western Ukraine and in emigration, like the militant Bolshevik writing in Soviet Ukraine, was defined by an activist desire to shape life. Writers were particularly interested in historical fiction, which they often tried to infuse with a national mythology. Prague, the capital of democratic Czechoslovakia, was the largest émigré centre and was dominated in the interwar years by the generation that had witnessed the struggle for independence in 1917–20 and had sometimes fought for the UNR alongside Jews. Its leading writers avoided negative portrayals of Jews. However, the career of Spyrydon Cherkasenko illustrates how one member of this intelligentsia was gradually transformed in the thirties from a liberal intellectual into a violent anti-Semite. He had been a colleague and associate of Oles, Vynnychenko, and Cherniavsky, and in the years 1910–14 a regular contributor to the Kyiv newspaper *Rada,* in which he published scores of feuilletons, satirical sketches, and interviews. His dramas were regularly staged by Starytsky in the years 1910–19 and his *Pro shcho tyrsa shelestila* (Why the Feather-grass Rustled, 1916), first staged by this director on November 18, 1916, became a mainstay of the theater. He was also known for stories that described the attempts of Donbas miners to organize strikes against exploitative conditions, and in the revolutionary years he published "proletarian songs." Even though he settled in Prague in the twenties, the Soviet regime found his writings congenial and he was still being republished in Kharkiv until 1930. After this date, not only did all publications cease, but instructions were issued to remove his works from Soviet libraries and pulp them.

An early story "Na postu" (On guard, 1907) shows the abusive attitude of tsarist authorities toward Jews. A kindly old policeman is prevented from showing sympathy for a Jewish shopkeeper and her child. Brutally rebuked by his superior, the old man then verbally lashes out at the shopkeeper in the same tone. "U vahoni zhyttia" (In Life's Carriage, 1911) takes place on a train. An old kobzar is forced by a Russian-speaking conductor to give up his seat and sit next to a Jew, because a "lady" requires the seat and, presumably, refuses to sit next to either the kobzar or the Jew. These two, who are both Ukrainian speakers, strike up a conversation and get on well. The Jew asks the old man to play his instrument and sing something. When he hears a Ukrainian song, the conductor rushes in and threatens to throw the kobzar off the train. In both stories the intrusion of higher authorities poisons the social atmosphere and prevents civil interaction between people of different backgrounds.

The fact that Cherkasenko was looked upon favorably by Soviet publishers is all the more surprising since some of his poems are fiercely anti-Bolshevik. For example, his "Mozaika" (Mosaic, 1920), which is a response to Aleksandr Blok's *Dvenadtsat'* (The Twelve, 1919), paints an attack by Bolshevik commissars and Cheka brigades on a Ukrainian village that is considered counterrevolutionary for celebrating Christmas in the time-honored way—by singing carols, some of which denounce the tyranny of King Herod. After the village is burned and the people killed, the ghost of Ahasuerus appears over the destruction, suggesting that he is once more visiting a troubled land. This apparition might also be a hint at the presence of Jews in the Cheka brigades. The poem scorns Bolshevik slogans, which it says are mendacious and merely a cover for Russian nationalism. It urges the proletarians of all countries not to follow Moscow but to unite in a union of free nations. (Cherkasenko 1991, 1:311.) By the early thirties Cherkasenko had gone through a considerable evolution. The experience of emigration, the news of the famine, the rise of Stalinism and Hitlerism are all possible explanations for this. Particularly revealing is his depiction of Jews, which can serve as an indicator of his new worldview. *Tsina krovy: Drama na 5 dii z prolohom* (The Price of Blood: A Drama in 5 Acts with Prologue, 1931) follows the Gospel account, but interprets Christ's betrayal by Judas as dictated by the desire to accelerate a revolt against Roman rule. Anticipating public outrage against Christ's arrest, Judas thinks that he can channel the popular mood into an armed rebellion that will lead to Judea's independence. In order to build up Christ's authority among the people, he manipulates mass opinion. The raising of Lazarus from the dead is a hoax staged by him. So is the feeding of the masses with two fishes and five loaves of bread. Having asked the crowd, many of whom have come with provisions, to share among themselves, he then spreads the word of a miracle. The point is to contrast the fanatical Judean nationalism of Judas with the quiet Galilean spirituality that characterizes most of the apostles. This, as will be seen, was a line of argument that Dmytro Dontsov later used to draw a distinction between Judaism and Christianity.

Hanan, the former high priest, is a particularly unpleasant character who procures slaves for a Syrian slave trader, and is preparing to sell the beautiful Mary Magdalene at double the normal price. He is both an archetypal sexual predator and an archetypal miser, who trembles over the chest of gold he has accumulated through providing female slaves to brothels. Although Hanan has lost faith in the coming of a messiah who will liberate his people, he is convinced that even after their scattering, they can rule the world through their iron will and their financial acumen:

> That misfortune will sharpen our minds
> And forge a will hard as rock,
> Monolithic and with a single goal:
> Living in all countries
> For entire ages to gather
> All the gold, and then rule the world. (Cherkasenko 1991, 1:838.)

Money, he assures the current high priest, who is also his son-in-law, will buy even Caesar in Rome. He urges ruthlessness on the road to power. As a result of his machinations, the Jews call for Barabbas to be freed and for Christ to be crucified, and the cry "Let his blood be upon us and our children!" from the Gospel narrative is also mentioned. However, the character of Judas is complex. He is motivated by egoism and love for Mary Magdalen, as well as by political considerations. His ambition is to see Jesus become an earthly tsar of the Jews and to lead his people in battle against the Romans. The real conflict in the play is between those who favor violent means and those who refuse violence, between temporal and spiritual goals. These clashing views give the work depth. The author himself appears to hesitate between faith in the essential goodness of human nature and belief in the necessity of violence.

Vyhadlyvyi bursak: Komediika dlia molodi v 2-kh diiakh z chasiv Khmel'nych-chyny (The Enterprising Student: A Comedy for Youth in Two Acts from Khmelnytsky's Time, 1937) depicts a Jewish orendar, Yankel, who refuses to provide the key to the Orthodox church without a substantial payment. He is the Polish lord's agent, and a word from him to the lord results in beatings. In the previous year, the people were prevented from blessing their paskas at Easter because Yankel refused to open the church. As the uprising breaks out, the Polish lord escapes. The orendar is preparing to do the same, but is outwitted by Yerykhonsky, a student and son of a priest. He dresses as a Cossack leader to deceive the orendar into thinking that the revolutionaries have arrived. A farcical scene takes place in which Yankel hides under a chair and shows his fear of punishment. He is made to hand over the keys so that Easter can be celebrated according to tradition.

These portrayals indicate how Cherkasenko moved from a sympathetic treatment of Jews as allies in the struggle for civil rights to critiques of their immoral behavior in the pursuit of political ends, and finally to rehashing a stereotype from the early nineteenth century. Yefremov had early noted something rigid and immobile in the writer. (Syvoshapka 1940.) No doubt this desire to view the world in simplistic terms contributed to his growing hero worship of Hitler and his scapegoating of Jews. His letters in the years 1934–40 to Oleksandr Koshets, the celebrated choir director then living in Canada, demonstrate that he considered Stalin to be a tool in the hands of Jews, who, he thought, were bent on revenging themselves against Ukrainians for the Khmelnytsky revolution, the haidamaka revolts, and the pogroms of 1919. In a letter from August 22, 1939, he describes Hitler as a "saint" and "genius," and Germany's conflict with its neighbors as a war with the Jews, "the rulers of the contemporary world." The letter was written from Prague after Germany's invasion of Czechoslovakia and one day before the signing of the Hitler-Stalin pact. Hitler's invasion of Poland occurred in the following week, on September 1, 1939. Cherkasenko died less than five months later, on February 8, 1940. It is not clear how his views evolved after this letter, but it is worth quoting to give an indication of his violent feelings:

> In spite of the fact that my son is in a German concentration camp, that I am living in penury and at present see no end to this condition, I pray to the merciful Lord to help Hitler complete his sacred work—to break the neck of the Jewish golden calf and its lords. . . . What a man! How deeply he understands all their plans, how brilliantly he strikes at their every treacherous move. I say this, because the profane read in the newspapers that this is a war of democracy against dictatorship, but for me this is a war of the Jews against truth and human freedom. . . . We all here believe that God will send him victory and that from his victorious table there will fall at least a few crumbs of our statehood. . . . Until now we could hardly even hope for this, because the cursed Jews made every effort to permanently remove even Ukraine's name from the map, and set up their Jewish state on our land from Odesa to Cracow, because, as one of their brochures says, "they live there in a compact mass". . . . Let the Ukrainian God help him put a heavy German boot on the neck of that greedy scarecrow, so that it might die writhing and squirming like a snake.

A similar evolution can be seen in the work of Pachovsky. As we have seen, he began writing at the turn of the century as a member of the young modernist generation, then served in the Ukrainian Galician Army. In the late thirties, he returned to the Marko Prokliaty theme in his *Zoloti vorota: Mistychnyi epos v 3-okh chastiakh* (Golden Gates: A Mystical Epic in 3 Parts, 1937, 1985). In his early writings the figure of Marko had represented the curse of anarchism, the elemental force of the leaderless and confused masses. But in this epic poem of the late thirties Pachovsky portrays Marko as the spiritual incarnation of his people. This protagonist plays a crucial role at various points in Ukraine's history. Ukraine's leaders try to force the unreliable population to obey national requirements. Marko, who personifies the unruly masses, resists being subdued. He represents volatile, contradictory forces: the nation is composed of various "tribes" who speak Ukrainian but are often mutually hostile. (Pachovs'kyi 1984, 2:38.) In past ages, as in recent times, this rudderless, fractious people have regularly sabotaged its leadership's state-building efforts. Whereas the earlier, prerevolutionary *Sfinks Evropy* had lamented the xenophobia of the masses and the way it could be manipulated by unscrupulous politicians, here the narrator himself exhibits xenophobia, describing socialism as the dream of a "Jewish paradise." (Ibid., 39.) In commenting upon *Zoloti vorota*, the conservative thinker Viacheslav Lypynsky interpreted the character of Marko Prokliaty as representing the necessary engine of revolt that had to be quickly brought under control by "patriots" after its destructive work had been accomplished and before it could destroy Ukrainian rule. He saw Marko as a werewolf figure, a popular symbol of monstrous incongruity and incomplete development, the representation of a divided and self-destructive ethnos playing out its drama over a millennium of recorded history. (Ibid., 47, 49.)

Pachovsky's hero is in some ways the Ukrainian equivalent of the Wandering Jew. Like Ahasuerus, he appears throughout history at crucial turning points when the nation's dreams of statehood are defeated. At these moments his role is pernicious: he voices the people's desire for freedom and land, but also expresses their indiscipline, greed, and inclination to violence. Ultimately he causes chaos and brings about defeat. In the first part of the poem, published in 1937, the author portrays Marko's role in the 1917 revolution:

> Wherever the axe flashes there Marko leads—
> Dancing and trotting . . .
> The Cossack roars, and song resounds like the grove:
> > "Hey, where's the money? The Jew has it at the exchange!
> > Hey, who owns the land? The lord and rich peasant!
> > Hey, we will cut the roots of the bourgeois!" (Ibid., 102.)

The Bolshevik movement in Ukraine is led by Eugenia Bosh, a brilliant orator, described as a Judith with a Muscovite spirit. In the *Book of Judith* the heroine charms the Assyrian general with her beauty and then takes advantage of his intoxication to behead him. This encourages the Jews to rout the Assyrians. In Pachovsky's poem, Bosh is a beautiful temptress who charms the Ukrainian troops. Too late Marko realizes that under Bolshevik rule the country "has become a hell not a paradise." (Ibid., 104.) However, at this crucial turning point, when he is ready to turn against Bosh and the Bolsheviks, he meets Ahasuerus, who convinces him that the Jews have always stood for "brotherhood, equality, and freedom" and that a common front should be maintained until there are no nations and no bourgeoisie. When this idyll comes to pass, "we will create a heaven for all, for all time." (Ibid., 109.) Convinced by Ahasuerus, Marko transfers his allegiance back to Bosh. The masses follow the Bolsheviks, Ukraine is divided, and it loses the battle for independence. Bosh and Ahasuerus see their plans realized. The latter gleefully predicts that they will remove the elite and take the rabble of goys (*goiv cherniu*) in hand:

> And a sixth of the world will fall to our plate!
> We will gain not only the towns, but the fields and meadows—
> And the promise of Moses will come to pass:
> All tsars will be in our power . . .
> And the whole world will fall at our feet! (Ibid., 110.)

Both Moscow and Ahasuerus provoke and use Marko to raises the rabble against the Central Rada. In later action Ahasuerus is again linked to Moscow when he is shown conspiring to send millions to the Solovetsky labor camps, and is implicated in Schwartzbard's killing of Petliura. He also helps Moscow sow hunger and destruction in Ukraine. This entire first section entitled "Peklo Ukrainy" (Ukraine's Hell) was published in 1937.

Pachovsky died in 1942 and the poem's other two completed sections (it was planned as a four-part work) were published only in 1985. In the second part, Marko begins to understand his mistakes as the search for the holy grail of independence continues. The Antichrist calls forth the spirit of destruction and summons the Jew. Marko tries unsuccessfully to pin the latter down. A new image and myth of Ukraine is being developed by poets. Marko will once more revive, as he has always done; the only question will be: whom will his rebellious instincts serve? A great future awaits Ukraine, which will "charm the world," but before this can happen the people have to be "brought to the goal," to be "made capable of their sacred role." (Ibid., 397.) There is much that is difficult to comprehend in this ambitious mystical epic, which spans the ages and in which archetypal figures from history and legend continually reappear, but the dominant idea is the need for mastery over the politically confused and fickle masses. Ahasuerus and the Jews, who figure strongly in the first part which was published in 1937, disappear almost entirely from the later parts.

Pachovsky's evolution, like Cherkasenko's, is a good example of the intelligentsia's drift in the thirties toward right-wing and anti-Semitic positions. In 1935 Pachovsky voiced the conviction that literature had to serve the nation state. He disowned his earlier modernist belief in art for art's sake and his entire "liberal" view of the world in favor of "purposefulness" (*dotsil'nist'*). He now

saw literature's aim as transforming the world in line with national requirements, which meant organizing the people into a "state-building society." (Pachovs'kyi 1935, 4:185.) In order to best accomplish this task, literature and art
had to be "national" in character. They could not be "cosmopolitan." International movements in art exhibited "a suspect originality." He supported the
view, for example, that the "Jewish–Parisian *moderne*" (by which he means avant-
garde and modernist art) was "generally pseudo-art" and asserted the need for
national, religious, and historical subject matter. (Ibid., 5:258.) Among other
things, he called for the cultivation of national motifs and melodies in music, because otherwise pupils would grow up as "hired musicians in Jewish cafés with
the souls of werewolves, incapable of original creativity because they despise the
motifs of their own souls but [at the same time] are unable to equal those of others." (Ibid., 5:261.) Pachovsky's work from the late thirties portrays the "dark"
masses as thwarting Ukraine's interests and failing to honor the ancestral drive
for statehood. Lacking idealism, they fail to heed the wisdom of their leaders,
surrendering instead to immediate material gains.

These ideas were close to those expressed by Donstov and the journal *Vistnyk,* perhaps the most right-wing literary publication of this period and certainly
one of the most influential. After becoming its editor in 1933, Dontsov printed
numerous articles expressing similar opinions and attacking the democratic and
socialist intelligentsia of the previous generation. In the second issue he set clear
demarcation lines between the new and the old Ukraine: "A worldview instead
of party paragraphs, faith instead of knowledge, infallibility and exclusivity instead of compromise, the cult of the individual and the active minority instead of
the mass and the passive majority, proselytism instead of subordination to the
'will of the people,' rigor for oneself and others instead of humanitarianism,
idealism instead of the pursuit of mandates and the flattering of the mob, and
finally completely different forms of organization—these are the deep differences between these two types of political grouping." (Dontsov 1933, 124.)

However, not all nationalists found this attitude congenial. Ulas Samchuk's
Volyn' (Volhynia, vol. 1, 1939) is one of the most important novels of the interwar
years and devotes a substantial number of pages to Jewish life. As a boy the author had a positive view of the local Jewish population, and this largely autobiographical work describes a respectful Ukrainian interaction with Jews throughout the early decades of the century. Samchuk does not hide the existence of
other views, but they are not presented as dominant, nor do they go unchal-
lenged. The interaction of Jews with peasants who have come to the town of
Ostrih to sell their products is described, including the traditional bargaining

process. Jewish peddlers visit the villages to buy old clothes. The young hero Volodia becomes friends with Moshko and Itsko, the two sons of a neighboring Jewish farmer. Itsko, who is dumb but understands Volodia better than any other boy, becomes a close friend. The three form a band that confronts rivals in stone-throwing fights. No particular attention is paid to the fact that Volodia's two friends are Jewish. The reader learns that they are literate and able to explain certain things to the young hero, but the friendship of the three is an absolutely ordinary boyhood camaraderie in which ethnic or religious differences are far less noteworthy than childhood adventures. *Volyn'* also portrays a local Jew, Moshko Srulevych, whose opinion is viewed as more trustworthy than that of Ukrainian villagers. This kind of attitude, tolerant of difference and respectful of another culture, echoed the Ukrainian-Jewish rapprochement of prerevolutionary years.

It is worth illustrating the existence of this countertrend by examining Stanislaw Vincenz's remarkable Polish-language account of life among the Hutsuls, Ukrainian mountain shepherds in the Carpathians, entitled *Na wysokiej połoninie* (On the High Uplands, 1936–52). Descended from a French family from Provence that settled in Poland, Vincenz grew up in the Hutsul region. Having studied biology, Slavic philology, and Sanskrit, he took a doctorate at the University of Vienna. When the Second World War broke out he moved to Hungary, then in 1947 to France, and in 1949 he settled in Grenoble. The first volume of his study of the Hutsuls appeared in 1936, and the next two came out piecemeal between 1939 and 1952. As a whole, his work is valuable as both literature and ethnography.

In the first volume of *Na wysokiej połoninie*, Vincenz deals with the Pokuttia district, which had for many generations been home to a population of Hasidic and non-Hasidic Jews as well as Hutsuls. Among the Jewish figures appearing in the Ukrainian folklore of this district is the eighteenth-century founder of Hasidism, the Baal Shem Tov, who once lived and taught here. Saturated in Ukrainian folk tales and beliefs, Vincenz's narratives depict relaxed and respectful intercourse between Ukrainians and Hasids as the long-established norm. Far from urban centers, Ukrainians and Jews go about their lives as they have always done. They work side by side, eat and drink together, use the same transport (the balagula, a kind of wagon typically driven by Jews), converse, swap information and stories, deliberate over questions of faith, tradition, and theology, and examine differences in culture and customs. Vincenz even records carol singers visiting Jews in order to wish them well. (Vincenz 1955, 135–36.) Both a Hutsul and a Jewish band play at a local wedding. Catholic priests, gentlemen from various towns, Jews from the mountains, and the rabbi from Kosiv are all there. They eat

Jewish rolls and sleep on a "red, Jewish pillow." When workers gather to fell trees and send them downstream, they include Italians, southern Slavs, woodcutters from Hungary, and a tall, broad-shouldered Jew "with a fair beard and long fair side locks." (Ibid., 143.) All are united by the mountain traditions of hospitality and mutual respect. One Greek Catholic priest says: "Every faith has its own right. Respect all equally; don't annoy Christian or Jew, gentleman or gypsy, Turk, Englishman, German even though dumb, French though impious, a Lutheran though he has a stick, even a Russian with a whip, don't annoy them. That is forbidden, that is the law of God and the law of man. Whether he's white or black, red or green, poor or rich, smooth or mottled, thin or pot-bellied, shaven or shaggy, he is your brother, your neighbor, and that's enough! Don't annoy. But what if they annoy you? Then you hold on, hold yourself in, burst if necessary, but don't annoy." (Ibid., 266–67.)

The various groups consider themselves "spiritual brothers" and offer each other advice from a common pool of wisdom that includes all religions and traditions. Sometimes they bear grudges or deceive one another, as with Karabelnyk, a sorcerer and exorcist, who pretends to "purify" the Jew's tavern by casting out a devil in order to obtain a free bottle of liquor. They also support one another. The Jewish merchant Herszko acts as intermediary with the emperor in Vienna for a Bukovynian prince. One story recounts the discussion between a highlander, a Catholic priest, a Hasidic Jew, and others. It becomes clear from the conversation that the beliefs of Tanasenko, a Hutsul farmer, which are a blend of pagan legend and Christianized folklore, also resemble those of the Hasids. In fact the resemblance is so remarkable that the Jew Duwyd says: "Farmer, you're always fond of saying you're a priest's son, but I think you must have studied under our rabbis. Under Kuty and Kosow rabbis. You talk like the Chassidim—all you need are the side locks." "Possibly I did learn from the rabbis. And I'm not afraid of side locks either. What's that to do with anyone?"(Ibid., 175.) The reader is informed that Tanasenko's godfather had sworn brotherhood with the Baal Shem Tov.

Travel on a balagula, weddings, and any social gathering become opportunities to tell Hutsul and Hasidic legends, and often to compare these. "The Land of the Rachmans" provides an ideological key to the book. It becomes clear from this story that the author views Hutsul beliefs as an example of religious syncretism. The host of a wedding celebration says that the local festivals are a blend of different sources: the distant past, the Church, and local invention. This last component, local invention, is "our own weave, woven from a few foreign, precious threads, and many, often common, threads of our own, yet with our own distinctive design." (Ibid., 326.) The host describes the Rachman Easter, which comes five weeks after the Christian Easter. This ancient celebration "the finale" of the spring festivals, was once well-known in the Black Sea region but has been best preserved and perhaps developed in the Hutsul mountains. It is associated with the virtuous and friendly tribe of Rachmans (*rakhmannyi* means gentle), who. says the host, are related to the Hutsuls but have been separated from them. They maintain and renew the human world and the Hutsuls communicate with them once a year during the Rachman Easter. Having traced the word "Rachman" to the stories of India, the Bible, ancient Rus chronicles, and the Koran, the host suggests that it is a mixture of various yearnings: "the mystical exaltations of India, and her tolerance, with the Jewish cult of compassion; and if the supposition in regard to the Koran is accepted, then you have also the Mahommedan urge to the unification of the peoples. The whole forms a kind of stained-glass window against the background of the starry sky, against the somber background of mediaevalism. On these stories it has conferred a quality of remoteness, a perspective, as though these happenings occurred between heaven and earth, or somewhere in some unattainable land. But it was all blended together by Slavonic kindness, by Ruthenian [Ukrainian] sincerity, by the loving heart which is hospitable to all the world." (Ibid., 328.) This image of the local belief system and culture as a tapestry woven from many threads represents an acceptance of fraternal relations: various groups, after all, have contributed to weaving the tapestry.

Vincenz describes Dovbush meeting with the Baal Shem Tov. Other scholars who have collected folklore from the region confirm the widespread existence of this legend: in one folk story Dovbush comes across a poor Jew who is walking with a staff and allows him to pass; in another he is the protector of all people who live in the mountains, including the Jews. The legend of the noble outlaw also forms part of Jewish folklore and literature. A number of tales portray Dovbush meeting with the Baal Shem Tov in circumstances similar to those described by Vincenz. One recurring tale has the Baal Shem Tov traveling through caves in the mountains, trying to reach the Promised Land, and meeting the outlaw, who offers him help and protection. There is, therefore, a tradition in both Hutsul and Hasidic lore that links Dovbush and a Jewish sage and miracle worker in a friendship or alliance. (Fialkova 1996, 67.) In some versions, both men recognize that they are traveling parallel paths. At a time of insecurity, when some narratives stressed national exclusiveness and xenophobia, these stories of cooperation and solidarity between peoples remind readers of the existence of a countervailing mythology.

CHAPTER 7

The Second World War and Late Stalinism, 1939–1953

On August 23, 1939, Hitler and Stalin signed the pact that divided Poland. The USSR occupied and annexed Western Ukraine and the territory that is today Western Belarus. Lithuania, Latvia, Northern Bukovyna, and Bessarabia were occupied in June 1940, following the fall of France. For nearly two years the Soviet Union supplied the Nazi war machine with the food and raw materials needed to circumvent the blockade imposed by the Allies. Hitler expressed satisfaction that the purges had lessened the role of Jews in the Bolshevik party and Soviet state. In the prewar years Stalin had been forcing Jews out of the party, secret police apparatus, and state and economic organs. (Shapoval 2001, 212.) All anti-Nazi propaganda ceased as the official line became pro-German and critical of the Allies.

Western Ukraine was under Soviet occupation from the autumn of 1939 until the summer of 1941. In this time educational, cultural, and economic institutions that had been built up over the decades were dismantled. 210,271 people were sent to the Gulag. Of these, 117,800 were Poles, 64,533 were Jews, and 13,448 were Ukrainians. (Slyvka 1996, 154.) In all, an estimated 1,170,000 to 1,250,000 people (approximately 10 percent of the population) were deported. In accordance with Nazi-Soviet agreements, between twenty and thirty thousand escapees from Germany were captured and delivered into the hands of the Gestapo. (Ibid., 9.) Jewish religious communities saw their land, buildings, and possessions confiscated. Their religious holidays (including the Sabbath), bar mitzvahs, and circumcisions were banned. Their enterprises were nationalized, institutes and schools liquidated, newspapers and publishers closed, organizations and parties declared bourgeois nationalist and illegal. The muzzling of the press contributed to the population's poor understanding of Hitler's policies, especially toward the Jews.

When the Germans invaded in 1941, the NKVD was caught by surprise and did not have time to evacuate prisoners. In the first week of the war, June 22–29, it massacred thousands of prisoners in Galicia and neighboring Volhynia. The majority were Ukrainians, although a percentage were Poles and Jews. The Nazis used the discovery of the bodies to incite the local population against the Jews and large-scale pogroms occurred in Lviv, Zolochiv, and other towns, in which thousands of Jews were killed. (Hrachova 2005, 22–26.)

Many people did not have time to escape eastward. Overall, the number of Jews who died in the war in Ukraine has been estimated at 1.5 million, a figure that constitutes 60 percent of the country's Jewish population. The mass murder began as soon as the Nazis invaded. Between twenty and thirty thousand were executed in Berdychev, but skilled artisans were allowed to live in the town's ghetto until April of 1942. About ninety thousand Jews were executed in Domanivka, north of Odesa. Some 200,000 people were killed in the Yaniv concentration camp in Lviv, among them 100,000 Jews who had been sent from different parts of Ukraine. Practically all the Jews who had not escaped or left Kyiv were killed in the last days of September 1941 in Babyn Yar (Babii Yar), a ravine on the city's outskirts. 33,771 answered an order to assemble issued on September 27. They were marched to the ravine and machine-gunned. In the course of the war, approximately one hundred thousand people of different nationalities were murdered there. The population was aware of the killing. Irina Khoroshunova wrote in her diary for October 2, 1941: "Everyone is now saying that the Jews are being killed. No, not are being but already have been killed. Every single one, old men, women, children. . . . People saw trucks of warm kerchiefs and other things being driven from the cemetery. German 'precision.' They have already sorted the trophies! . . . The rumors and eyewitness accounts are growing all the time. Their monstrosity is hard to comprehend. But we are forced to believe, because the shooting of Jews is a fact. A fact that is beginning to make us lose our minds. And it is impossible to live with the awareness of this fact." (Khoroshunova 2001, 57–58.)

The victims of the Nazi extermination program were of many nationalities, but the Jews were specifically singled out for genocide. Jews and non-Jews practiced various forms of resistance, collaboration, and cooperation. On the territory of Ukraine the occupation apparatus was large and thousands of Ukrainians served in it, including the auxiliary police that guarded the execution sites and sometimes participated in the executions. Local people also exposed Jews, making the Nazi task easier, but others helped Jews to escape, or to obtain documentation that would allow them to emigrate. In all some 6.8 million people were killed on the territory of Ukraine. It should be recalled that the wartime violence came after Stalin's campaigns of terror, the famine, the killing during the years 1917–20, and the brutalities of the First World War. And the killing did not end in 1945. Grain requisitioning was again enforced in 1947 when Kaganovich reappeared in Ukraine as the secretary of the Central Committee of the CP(B)U. He and Khrushchev reported to Stalin on November 11, 1947 that every threshing machine and grain store was guarded according to Politburo decree, and that eight hundred thousand farmers would need food assistance. (Veselova 1996, 302.) Estimates of the number who starved to death range from a hundred thousand to a million. (Ibid., 13.) Mass deportations from Western Ukraine and imprisonment continued after the war. At the time of Stalin's death in 1953, the Gulag contained more prisoners than it had ever done.

This continual violence made Ukraine fertile ground for ideologies that rejected liberal and democratic values, and which turned instead to xenophobia and extremism. During the two years leading up to the Hitler–Stalin pact criticism of anti-Semitism had diminished in the USSR. In August of 1942 the Central Committee of the All-Union Communist Party circulated a memo complaining that the nationality policy had been perverted over many years in all areas of cultural life and concluded that non-Russians, usually Jews, had found their way into leadership positions in the cultural field, reducing Russians to a minority. (Shapoval 1994, 212.) Often Jewish soldiers were ignored when honors and promotions were distributed, could not regain their apartments or jobs after demobilization, or were denied entry into higher education. In the postwar years Soviet authorities avoided discussing the mass killing of Jews by the Nazis or their own discriminatory practices.

Amir Weiner has suggested that the German treatment of Jews and other minorities influenced Soviet leaders at the level of ideology. On the surface, the Soviet Union adhered to a policy of acculturation, but in fact it continually eradicated social groups that it classified as illegitimate by virtue of class or national origin. This policy hardened during the Second World War as entire populations were victimized, declared irredeemable, and deported. Political and national (or ethnic) categories became blurred. (Weiner 2001, 195.) Therefore, although the "anticosmopolitan" campaign launched in 1948 made anti-Semitism explicit government policy, the ground had been prepared by previous campaigns that had conditioned citizens to accept the demonization of entire nations and the use of violence against them.

Just before the "anticosmopolitan" campaign there had been a series of attacks against Ukrainian writers. These were a response to the emergence in the late thirties and forties of a stronger expression of the Ukrainian national identity. In the thirties, Soviet leaders had begun to see themselves as heirs to Russian imperial "achievements," including tsarist conquests. The Russian nation had progressively replaced the working class as the subject of Soviet histories. Wartime mobilizations accelerated this process. The new patriotism also allowed the voicing of national feelings by Ukrainians. However, by the war's end Stalin had become alarmed by this development and the Zhdanovshchyna campaign of 1946–48 (named after Andrei Zhdanov, the secretary of the Central Committee of the All-Union Communist Party) was launched to curtail such freedom of expression. In February 1947, just as the campaign seemed to be ending, Kaganovich was appointed as the first secretary of the Communist Party of Ukraine. He revived the search for ideological deviations and prepared a second attack on "bourgeois nationalists," similar to the one he had inspired in the twenties. Letters of protest against Ukrainian nationalism were commissioned and Jewish intellectuals were asked, or more probably required, to sign them. Shapoval reports that Yevhen Adelheim and Illia Stebun (Katsnelson) signed a letter of denunciation, dated August 22, 1947, in which they accused Rylsky and Yanovsky of "mistakes," drew attention to "faulty" ideas in the work of Petro Panch and Ivan Senchenko, and charged Andrii Malyshko, Stepan Kryzhanivsky, and others with nationalism and anti-Semitism. (Shapoval 1994, 73–79.) In a programmatic article in the November issue of *Vitchyzna* (Fatherland), Adelheim criticized Teren Masenko and especially Rylsky for considering literature to be above politics, and Malyshko for expressing his Ukrainian patriotism without couching it in pro-Soviet terms. (Adel'heim 1947, 149, 159, 170.) It appears that Kaganovich was using Jews to expose "nationalist deviations" among Ukrainians, in this way cynically fanning the flames of anti-Semitism. It was widely believed that the campaign against Ukrainian literary figures was a preparation for arrests and that the list of victims had already been prepared. However, Stalin did not carry out the repressions on this occasion and in December of 1947 recalled Kaganovich to Moscow.

Instead, the "anticosmopolitan" campaign began, and some Ukrainian writers, in what appears to have been an act of revenge, turned against Jewish colleagues, some of whom had denounced them for nationalism only a few weeks before. Liubomyr Dmyterko, the secretary of the Ukrainian Writers' Union, attacked the critic Oleksandr Borshchahivsky for his earlier denunciation of Oleksandr Korniichuk's *Bohdan Khmel'nyts'kyi*, and Yukhym Martych (Finkelshtein) for an attack on Ivan Kocherha's *Iaroslav Mudryi* (Yaroslav the Wise). Other critics came under attack for maligning the Ukrainian classical heritage, among them Abram Hozenpud, Illia Stebun, Yevhen Adelheim, Ahapii Shamrai, and Lazar Sanov (Smulson). (Yekelchyk 2004, 83–84.)

The wheel, however, kept turning and in 1951 another campaign was launched against Ukrainian writers. Attacks against the "poison of nationalism" took place in other republics and "anti-Zionist" purges occurred in 1952 and 1953. All these campaigns may have been a planned prelude to a major wave of repression against both Ukrainians and Jews. Whatever the case, Stalin spread fear, as he had always done, in order to intimidate and control people, and to divide potentially subversive groups. In his mind, both Ukrainians and Jews were to be feared because of their ability to mobilize opposition. He had learned from his revolutionary days, when he had been responsible for nationalities policy, that collaboration between these two nations presented a danger to Moscow. It is possible that Kaganovich was sent to mobilize Jews against Ukrainians, and was then removed to allow a mobilization of Ukrainians against Jews. Each group was used to expose "disloyalty" in the other. A situation of constant tension, denunciation, and insecurity suited Stalin's purpose of unnerving and preventing the coalescence of any opposition.

Soviet Narratives

As part of the war effort, the new form of patriotism tried to align Russian and Ukrainian mythologies. Writers like Mykola Bazhan, Oleksandr Korniichuk, and Pavlo Tychyna were given the task of articulating this new line in literature. The results were incoherent and contradictory, but Soviet Ukrainian writers were for the first time allowed to glorify their own historical heroes, to embrace loyalty to the national cause, to extol the people's moral character, and to lament their suffering as victims of foreign aggression. In this way nationalism was elevated as communism's partner. (Yekelchyk 2002, 55–56.) Russian writers canonized Aleksandr Nevsky, Ivan the Terrible, and Peter the Great as brilliant military leaders, while Ukrainians did the same with Prince Danylo of Halych, who defeated the Teutonic Knights in the thirteenth century, and Bohdan Khmelnytsky. (Ibid., 57.) Bazhan wrote a long patriotic poem, *Danylo Halyts'kyi* (Danylo of Halych, 1942), which showed the prince as a great warrior. Oleksandr Korniichuk wrote the play *Bohdan Khmel'nyts'kyi* (1938), which portrayed the hero as a great statesman who liberated his people from Polish oppression and created an independent state, while not even mentioning the union with Muscovy. The play ran in theaters throughout the war, and in 1941, Ihor Savchenko directed a film based on the book. The perceived need for patriotic and historical operas led to the reworking of Mykola Lysenko's opera *Taras Bul'ba* and the creation of *Bohdan Khmel'nyts'kyi* (final version 1953). Both emphasized national liberation from foreign oppression.

Toward the end of the war the Kremlin intervened to remind cultural figures that Ukraine's subordination to Russia must not be ignored. Dovzhenko's novel and film script *Ukraina v ohni* (Ukraine in Flames, 1944) was banned for emphasizing national pride; Bazhan's *Danylo Halyts'kyi* was accused of nationalist deviation for using the term "Ukraine" with reference to the thirteenth-century Galician-Volhynia princedom; Volodymyr Sosiura's poem "Liubit' Ukrainu!" (Love Ukraine! 1944) was denounced in 1951 for expressing love for "some primordial Ukraine, Ukraine in general" rather than the Soviet one. Historians, who had since 1940 been using the term "the great Ukrainian people," were prevented from doing so after 1944. Henceforth this epithet could only be attached to Russians, who had been described in this way since 1937. (Ibid., 63.)

These narratives generated by the new patriotism, in both their Russian and Ukrainian variants, marginalized Jews. They emphasized Russian or Ukrainian heroes, loyalty, moral character, suffering, and military success. Already stripped of the institutional infrastructure that the indigenization policy had provided, Jews were now denied visibility in the new imagined community. When they were portrayed, they were integrated into one or the other story of national consolidation.

In Bazhan's verse drama *Oleksa Dovbush (Narodna drama)* (Oleksa Dovbush: A National Drama, 1940–46), Jews are portrayed as allies of the Ukrainians. The writer includes a Jewish tavernkeeper and his daughter. Both are loyal friends and supporters of the outlaw. Although the action is set in the late eighteenth century, the ideological message is a contemporary one: Ukrainians and Jews in Western Ukraine must not only cooperate in the struggle for freedom against an oppressive foreign regime, but look to Soviet Ukraine for help and ultimate reunification. The Jewish girl Susanna is courageous, beautiful, and in love with Yura, one of Dovbush's young fighters. It is hard to miss the call in this work for the reestablishment of a Ukrainian-Jewish alliance.

One of the best examples of this tendency is Yakiv Kachura's *Ivan Bohun* (1940). As in Oleksandr Sokolovsky's earlier *Bohun* (1931), Khmelnytsky's colonel is portrayed as a rabble rouser and dashing hero, given to brash, independent action, although he does not go as far as disobeying Khmelnytsky. The interesting part of Kachura's book is his portrayal of a Jew called Itsyk, who joins up with the Cossacks. A former merchant from Vinnytsia, he hates the Polish lords, wholeheartedly accepts his role as a Zaporozhian warrior (a member of the famed Cossack army with its camp in the lower reaches of the Dnipro), and fights skillfully and bravely. He is distinguished by his willingness to show initiative, mental alertness, and physical courage. In this respect he resembles the charismatic Bohun. Although Itsyk takes some friendly jibes aimed at his Jewish background and the fact that some lords still owe him money from earlier transactions, he is admired as a valuable member of the fighting force. The reader is led to understand that in contrast to the treacherous Tatars, who betray Khmelnytsky at a crucial moment, and the fiercely hostile Ottoman Turks and Catholic Poles, Ukrainian Jews (and, of course, Muscovites) can be trusted as allies. When the Polish lord, Pan Rzhevuski, tries to bribe Itsyk, offering him money to betray Bohun, the thought of doing so does not even cross the Jewish Cossack's mind. In this novel the prospect of future union with Muscovy is mentioned almost as an afterthought.

The description of the Jewish Cossack may have been suggested by the historian Saul Borovoi. In his memoirs he describes how he found evidence in the archive of the Zaporozhian Sich (the name of the main stronghold below the river rapids) of Jews trading with the Zaporozhians and of converted Jews fighting on Khmelnytsky's side. (Borovoi 1993, 190, 202.) This information, according to the historian, was used as a source by a Ukrainian writer—possibly Kachura—in a novel about Jewish Zaporozhians. (Ibid., 191.) Another writer, Ivan Le in his *Nalyvaiko: Istorychnyi roman* (Nalyvaiko: A Historical Novel, 1953) made similar use of a Jew who joins Semen Nalyvaiko's revolt of 1596. Motel-Khatskel was a pitch-maker until his daughter drowned herself after being abducted by a lord. He knows several languages and becomes a scout for Nalyvaiko. This novel may also have been inspired by Borovoi's research into Jewish-Zaporozhian relations, which was published in the thirties.

The new wartime and postwar instructions to writers contained an injunction not to particularize suffering, but rather to generalize it as the shared burden of the whole Soviet people. Stalin insisted that all Soviet citizens had suffered equally and that the "dead should not be divided." Ukrainian literature was criticized for highlighting the suffering of its own people. There was even less tolerance for the portrayal of the suffering of wartime Jewry. Victims of atrocities were identified only as "citizens of the Soviet Union." Monuments to the dead carried only this information on their inscriptions, with no specific mention of Jews. Vasilii Grossman was prevented from publishing the "Black Book" detailing Nazi crimes that he, along with others, had compiled since 1943.

It appeared abroad after his death in 1964. Grossman's wartime journalism was censored. His important "The Hell Called Treblinka," which was quoted at the Nuremberg International Military Tribunal, could not, for example, mention that many of the policemen who assisted the roughly twenty-five SS men in the camp were Ukrainians. (Beevor and Vinogradova 2005, 289.) The manuscript of his masterpiece *Zhizn' i sud'ba* (Life and Fate), a novel that draws parallels between Hitlerism and Stalinism, was confiscated in 1961. Although published abroad, it only appeared in Russia as the Soviet state disintegrated.

Ukrainian writings on the war made Jewish stories part of the master narrative. Oleksandr Korniichuk's play *Partyzany v stepakh Ukrainy* (Partisans in the Ukrainian Steppe, 1941), which was produced early in the war, portrays a Jewish doctor Rozenfeld, who has volunteered to serve in a local partisan detachment. He himself has been tortured by the Germans, and has witnessed the rape and murder of his two daughters along with the killing of two hundred other residents of his town. Because he understands German, he is asked to read the diary of a captured German officer. It describes the murder of six thousand people in three days after the capture of Lviv. Although this mention of mass murder would for most readers recall the Holocaust, it is vague enough to be taken as a reference to the extermination of the population in general and not the Jews specifically. Only the burning alive of Jews in a synagogue in Rotterdam, which removes the historical memory from Ukrainian soil, makes specific mention of Jewish victims.

Some Ukrainian writers did speak of the Jewish tragedy during the war. Mykola Bazhan was one of the first Soviet poets to write about Babyn Yar in a poem of the same name written in 1945, sixteen years before Yevgeny Yevtushenko published his celebrated poem on this tragedy in 1961. Tychyna wrote "Do ievreis'koho narodu" (To the Jewish People) and "Narod ievreis'kyi" (The Jewish People) in 1942. Maksym Rylsky wrote his "Ievreis'komu narodovi" (To the Jewish People) in 1943. These poems, however, were either not allowed any prominence, or were not permitted publication at all. Rylsky's first appeared in 1988.

In 1945 and the immediate postwar years, a number of Ukrainian writers produced fictional indictments of the Nazis and their willing accomplices. Yury Smolych in his novel *Vony ne proishly!* (They Did Not Pass! 1945–46) describes the eviction of Jews from Kharkiv. Ida Slobodianyk, the only Jew left in the city, can be saved by having three "Aryans" vouch for her non-Jewish ancestry. One of the three girlfriends, Olha, comments to herself: "What a monstrous thing! To argue that you are not a Jew! Is it something shameful—to be the daughter of your own people? . . . Olha had never thought that she would be covering up for someone who denied their nationality! . . . To affirm that someone was not a Jew was almost like supporting anti-Semitism." (Smolych 1972, 96.) Olha witnesses a procession of Jews being led, she thinks, to the ghetto. Later she learns that they have in fact been shot.

Care is taken in these accounts to portray "good" characters alongside "bad," those who helped Jews as well as those who stood by while the slaughter took place. This was, no doubt, the reality, but it became an enforced literary perspective that allowed for a softened depiction of the Holocaust's worst horrors. During the "anticosmopolitan" campaign, Sava Holovanivsky was deemed to have strayed from the required proportionality in his poem "Avraam" (Abraham), in which he describes Russian and Ukrainian spectators watching a Jew being killed by Germans. He was denounced for this in 1949 by Liubomyr Dmyterko, the head of the Ukrainian Writers' Union, who considered such a portrayal a slander on the Soviet people.

In the immediate postwar years it was still possible to mention the Jewish genocide. Varvara Cherednychenko's "Ia—shchaslyva Valentyna" (I, Happy Valentyna, 1946) describes the suffering of Rakhil, who discovers that all fifteen members of her family, the Fogelmans, have been killed in Babyn Yar after secretly returning to Kyiv during the Nazi occupation. For a while the traumatized Rakhil appears to be losing her sanity. She suddenly can speak and understand only Yiddish, even though she has up to then been speaking Ukrainian after marrying into a Ukrainian family. This family helps her to begin dealing with her grief. Her mother-in-law feels guilt for not having protected the Fogelmans, even though she was unaware of their presence in Kyiv. She is concerned that Rakhil will always bear a grudge against her for not saving them. Slowly, Rakhil begins to recover. In the final scenes she is portrayed as part of a new, postwar Ukrainian family, one that is already dreaming of rebuilding its life. One character expressed the overall message: "We all suffered these years of grief and misfortune equally. . . . All honest Soviet people have become one family in the course of the war years." (Cherednychenko 1946, 121.) Significantly, the story mentions the presence of Jewish women among nurses and of Jewish boys among soldiers. In later novels, explicit references to Babyn Yar, the massacre of Jews, wounded Jewish soldiery, and Jewish participation in the war effort were deemphasized or eliminated.

On the whole, the theme of wartime Jewish suffering is markedly underrepresented. When it does occur, as in the above examples, it provides evidence of the ideological imperative to integrate Jews into a consolidatory narrative. As with other groups, they are allowed their wartime exploits and their active opposition to political evil as long as these do not intrude upon the universal war experience. Most writers were unprepared to "complicate" their national history by emphasizing a strong Jewish narrative thread. A fuller account of the Holocaust would have called for fundamentally revising the Soviet war myth and raising uncomfortable issues. Both Russian and Ukrainian war narratives therefore represent a curious attempt to portray two mutually incompatible histories and patriotisms—the Russian and the Ukrainian—while downplaying or overlooking a third—the Jewish. It has been suggested that these writings came out of a fierce battle over the commemoration of the war and the Jewish genocide, a battle that resulted in the elimination of particularistic forms of representation. Instead, Stalinist representations drove for the portrayal of an undifferentiated kinship of peoples that had been forged in war. (Weiner 2001, 11.)

Authors of Jewish background who wrote for postwar journals were rarely allowed to foreground Jewish suffering or the Holocaust even to the degree that Cherednychenko did in the above story. The pages of *Vitchyzna*, for example, published the following authors and critics: Pervomaisky, Naum Tykhy, Sava Holovanivsky, Abram Katsnelson, Natan Rybak, Yukhym Martych, and the critics Abram Hozenpud, Yakiv Gordon, Veniamin Liberman, Hryhorii Verves, Lazar Sanov, Hryhorii Levin, Illia Stebun (Katsnelson), and Mykhailo Stein. In the postwar years some Yiddish writers also became prominent as writers of Ukrainian children's literature, among them Motl Talalaevsky and Khana Levina. However, whenever writers advanced expressions of a particular Jewish experience, they were reprimanded. Itsyk [Itsik] Kipnis, a prominent Yiddish writer in Ukraine, published a story on May 19, 1947 in *Dos Naye Lebn*, a Yiddish journal in Łódź, Poland. In it he wrote: "I would like to see all the Jews, as they march with a sure, victorious step through the streets of Berlin, wear on their breasts, alongside the decorations and medals, a small, pretty Star of David. It would be our mark of shame." In this way, Kipnis suggests, each Jew would be visible and could not be ignored. The author was rebuked by a number of officials, including the leaders of the Yiddish Section of the Ukrainian Writers' Union, who informed him that Jewish soldiers had not fought for the Old Testament, but for the Soviet way of life. He was also criticized in 1947 for writing a story in which he expressed the wish that several Soviet Jews would speak to him in Yiddish. Critics asked: "And suppose they speak Russian? Are they no longer kosher, no longer Jews? And when the Ukrainian or Belarusan speaks

Russian, does he become a non-Ukrainian or a non-Belarusan?" (Choseed 1961, 157.) Kipnis was expelled for a period of time from the Yiddish Section of the Writers' Union.

Jews gradually disappeared from public representations of the war, and the Holocaust was incorporated into a general picture of epic, but undifferentiated, suffering endured by the entire population. Despite the fact that tens of thousands of Jews had been involved in combat, they were often accused of "spending the war in Tashkent," a popular expression meaning "in the safety of the rear," while others fought on the front lines. The infrequent depictions of Jewish wartime heroism may in fact have contributed to charges that they shirked the rigors of combat. Soviet authorities did little to combat these perceptions. In 1944–45 there was an outburst of pogroms in territories recaptured by Soviet troops.

Institutionalized state contempt for an internal enemy set the Soviet Union apart from other countries; ruthless exterminatory desires had become the norm. In the years 1947–49 Soviet forces again conducted ethnic cleansing campaigns that involved the deportation of hundreds of thousands of people, the depopulation of entire regions, and the killing of "nationalists."

Anti-Soviet Narratives

Peter Potichnyj has suggested that during the war the most widespread view among Ukrainians was that the Jews, although themselves persecuted, were instrumental in the persecution of Ukrainians, and he has argued that this is one important reason why under German occupation the leadership of the Ukrainian underground, while strongly anti-Nazi in its orientation, did not make public pronouncements in defense of the Jews. (Potichnyi 1985, 93–94.) It is clear, however, that pronouncements made by the OUN-B (Organization of Ukrainian Nationalists, Bandera faction—the wing of the organization that recognized the leadership of Stepan Bandera) on the eve of the war were aligned with German rhetoric. A resolution at its Second Congress in April 1941 described the Jews as the "vanguard of Muscovite imperialism in Ukraine," although it went on to add that the Soviet regime exploited "anti-Jewish sentiments of the Ukrainian masses to divert their attention from the true cause of their misfortune and to channel them in times of frustration into pogroms against Jews." (Weiner 2001, 260.) One prominent leader of OUN-B, Yaroslav Stetsko, has been described in recent scholarship as violently anti-Semitic. (Berkhoff and Carynnyk 1999, 149–84.) German propaganda was also influential, particularly at the beginning of the war, when it declared that Ukrainians were being liberated from the tyranny of Jewish-Bolshevik elements. (Lower 2005, 34, 37.) Just as German soldiers appear to have accepted the identification of Bolshevism with Jewry, so did some Ukrainian nationalist publications, especially in the late thirties and 1941. At first the Germans encouraged nationalists in the hope that an independent state might be created, and in the first months of military rule émigré nationalists were used in setting up a new administration. However, the Germans had no intention of allowing an independent Ukrainian state. They quickly imprisoned most émigrés, and conducted sweeping arrests of OUN-B members to prevent a planned uprising. At its Third Extraordinary Congress, held August 21–25, 1943, the organization adopted a moderate, social-democratic platform and dropped anti-Semitic references. The Ukrainian Insurgent Army (UPA), which was formed in October 1942 but became active in the spring of 1943, fought both the Nazis and the Red Army. There is no mention of Jews in the writings of the UPA's two main propagandists, Petro Poltava (Fedun) and Osyp Hornovy (Diakiv), whose essays were written in the period 1946–52. They condemn the racism of both Hitler and Stalin, and align UPA's struggle with anticolonial revolutions around the globe. But there is evidence that sections of the OUN or UPA murdered Jews. Weiner has stated that "throughout 1943 nationalist guerillas, wherever they gained control, continued to hunt down Jews who survived Nazi extermination." (Weiner 2001, 263.) The greatest damage had probably been done in the years 1941–42, when the tone of pronouncements coming from nationalist organizations and presses undoubtedly helped to transform some people into violent anti-Semites and cogs in the German exterminatory machine.

A glance at some Ukrainian newspapers in the early weeks of German occupation reveals a concerted effort to link Bolshevism with the Jews. *Krakivs'ki visti* (Cracow News) publishing continually from 1939 until 1944. It tried to inform readers of international developments, while also printing background articles on Ukrainian society, history, and culture. The newspaper was required to present the German point of view, which it did by reporting the speeches of German leaders. It did not mention Jews at the time of the German-Soviet pact, but after the German invasion began on June 22, 1941, it carried reports on the thousands tortured and executed in prisons abandoned by the retreating communist regime, and published lists of victims, among whom were intellectuals and public figures. Terms like "Jewish-Bolshevik Moscow" (*zhydo-bolshevyts'ka Moskva*) and "Red Army soldiers-Jews" (*chervonoarmiitsi-zhydy*) were used in some articles.

In the early weeks of the war the memoirs of Yakiv Voinarovsky-Halchevsky (Orel) were serialized. They deal with his partisan activities in 1920–21 and his encounters with Chekists, many of whom are identified as Jews. An article by Vsevolod Durbak, "Zhydivstvo v borot'bi za nadvladu u sviti" (Jews in the Struggle for World Power) from August 14, 1941, claimed that Jewish money was behind the struggle. Another article by V. Grendzha-Donsky, "Na vlasnykh sylakh" (With Your Own Forces) from August 28, 1941, wrote that Jews had gained control of economic life in the Soviet Union and had suffered very little under the regime. This writer switched to the Soviet side after the war and enjoyed a successful literary career.

Other newspapers went much further. Amir Weiner has written that on September 1, 1941, an editorial in *Volyn'* (Volhynia), which was published in Rivne during the German occupation. stated: "All elements residing in our cities, whether Jews or Poles who have been brought here, must disappear. The Jewish problem is currently on the way to being resolved and will be resolved in accordance with the general reorganization of the new Europe." (Weiner 2001, 239.) Equally menacing comments were made by *Vinnyts'ki visti,* which wrote on November 9, 1941: "The Ukrainian people have learned very well about the baseness of the Jews. All the Jews held hands with our worst enemies—Russia and Poland. Together with the Russians (moskali), they tortured our people, starved them, and deported them as far as Siberia and Solovki [the Solovetsky islands]. But the unavoidable end has caught up with them. There will be no tortures and persecutions in the new Ukraine, and the world will get rid of the Jews forever." (Weiner 2001, 245.)

Relief at the disappearance of the Soviet regime led the Greek Catholic Metropolitan Andriy Sheptytsky to greet the Germans as the country's liberators from Bolshevism. However, all his following pastoral letters, which were read in every churches, were protests against German behavior, culminating in his famous "Ne ubyi!" (Thou Shalt Not Kill!) letter of November 21, 1942. Sheptytsky also protested directly to the German administration, and informed the Vatican of what was occurring. Through his efforts and those of the Church scores of Jews were saved. Kurt Lewin, the son of a Lviv rabbi, was one of them, and has left an account of his experiences. (Lewin 1994, 11–103.)

The general attitude toward the German army was initially apprehensive. After its behavior had been witnessed, this quickly turned to fear and hostility. Sycophantic attitudes toward the Germans and support for genocidal policies were often treated with contempt. One observer has recalled the impression produced by the appearance from September 21, 1941 of the first Ukrainian news-

paper in Kyiv under the occupation, *Ukrains'ke slovo* (Ukrainian Word): "The
paper made a depressing impression. True, there was no cursing or lampooning
in it. But the fact that it praised the Germans, elevated them as 'blonde liberat-
ing warriors,' and the fact that it immediately gave its complete agreement to the
slogan 'annihilation of Bolshevism and the Jews' created the most dispiriting
mood." (Khoroshunova 2001, 47.)

Nashi dni, which was published in Lviv, generally tried to focus on culture
and avoid politics, but it also occasionally included articles like O. Hai's "Proshchannia z Kyivom" (Goodbye to Kyiv, 1942) which described the literary
scene in Kyiv in 1940 as dominated by Jewish writers who lived in the best apartments because they served the regime faithfully. An anonymous article entitled
"Oblychchia soviets'koi zhurnalistyky" (The Face of Soviet Journalism, 1942)
named Jewish editors and journalists, implying that they controlled the entire
media.

Some literary works were produced under occupation. Panas Fedenko's
Homonila Ukraina (Ukraine Roared, 1942) appeared in Prague. It is a patriotic
novel that portrays Khmelnytsky's military successes in 1648. A Jewish orendar,
Zalman, is particularly interesting, given the time and place of publication.
Chapter 8 condenses and recapitulates the literary image of the orendar and the
nefarious role of Jews as presented in the Ukrainian chronicles, in Kulish's version of the dumas, and in subsequent literary representations. It is a virtual reca-
pitulation of the stereotype from the early nineteenth century, listing every accusation made against Jews in connection with the 1648 revolution. Zelman and
his wife Rykla have moved from Cracow and have taken over management of the
lord's estate. The orendar mercilessly extracts as much profit from the estate as
possible. He manages the distillery and brewery, while the local people are prevented from making their own alcohol. They have to buy exclusively and at high
prices from his monopoly. He lends money and procures women for the lord. As
his business expands, he leases other distilleries, always placing "his co-religion-
ists" in these jobs. If a Cossack or peasant tries to make his own alcohol, the tavernkeeper arrives with the lord's *haiduky* (armed retinue) to break the vats and
destroy the stoves. Gradually dozens of towns and villages fall into Zelman's
hands. He no longer travels in an ordinary balagula but rides in an expensive carriage; peasants and Cossacks raise their hats to him. Fedenko appropriates the
language and style of the chronicles to list the new taxes on beehives, oxen,
sheep, pigs, ponds, and mills. The land and the lives of common people are of no
interest to the orendar: "In commercial dealings with non-Jews the flexible rab-
binical teaching allowed Jews all sorts of methods of profit: deception, trickery,

falsification, double-dealing, cheating. The religious Jews sincerely followed the teaching of their rabbis, thinking that only the Jew was a creation worthy of being called a 'human being,' while all other peoples had been consigned by the God of 'Abraham, Isaac, and Jacob' to be 'food for the people of Israel.'" (Fedenko 1942, 75.) Fedenko does not fail to mention the intervention of the orendar into church affairs. Previously rent for the church had been paid to the lord. Zelman introduces a system where each particular service has to be purchased, thereby increasing "profits" tenfold.

But Zelman also plays a political role. After lending money to Khmelnytsky who needs the funds to help the Zaporozhian Sich, he tries to make the Cossack leader default on his payments in order to obtain the Subbotiv estate which has been put up as collateral. The orendar learns from other Jews of Khmelnytsky's financial and political affairs, and he devises schemes to make him miss payments. For example, he sets Chaplinsky, the Polish lord, against Khmelnytsky. Eventually this leads to the killing of the latter's son. This is the last straw for Khmelnytsky, who begins to organize the uprising. Just as Zelman contemplates the prophecy that the true Messiah will come to "call all Jews from all ends of the earth to Palestine" and to "give them power over all people," outside his window he hears the duma about the orendars being sung. When Zelman's brother-in-law demands payment for the Christmas service in church, the villagers murder him and the young men run off to join the Zaporozhian Sich and the planned uprising. Zelman's portrait is a construction of the evil orendar primarily from nineteenth-century sources. However, although the book mentions the flight of the Polish gentry and the families of orendars after Khmelnytsky's victory at Korsun, it does not describe the killing of Jews. The only time that Fedenko focuses on atrocities occurs in connection with Yarema Vyshnevetsky's torture of captured Cossacks. The picture of the orendar listening to the duma being sung outside his window is a revealing example of a literary myth's recreation in a later period. The duma, which, as we have seen, was likely composed much later, appears in Fedenko's novel as contemporaneous with the historical events.

Rostyslav Yendyk's collection *V kaidanakh rasy* (In the Chains of Race, 1940) was published in Cracow under Nazi occupation. These stories deal with racial relations and focus on the supposed weaknesses of the "eastern" and "southern" races, who in classic Orientalist fashion are presented as passive and fatalistic. As the title indicates, the author believes that all races have immutable features. He also contributed an article entitled "Biodynamichni chynnyky v buval'shchyni Ukrainy" (Biodynamic Factors in the Experience of Ukraine) to the Lviv *Nashi dni* (Our Days) in 1942. The article describes different racial types:

the Armenoid agricultural type that is linked to matriarchal civilization, and the Nordic warrior type that is linked to patriarchal civilization. Ukrainians are described as belonging to the Dynaric type, which combine characteristics of the above two. Shevelov described Yendyk sarcastically and unflatteringly as "an anthropologist and a certain kind of nationalist, the author of apotheoses to Hitler in the prewar years." (Sherekh 1998, 2:307.) In a later story "Rozpovid' odnoho zhyda" (The Story of One Jew, 1957) Yendyk's narrator finds himself in postwar Germany where he meets an old Jewish acquaintance from Ukraine and hears his story of survival. Everything he hears only reaffirms the stereotype he has of the Jew as an inveterate wheeler and dealer, and a coward in the face of danger. Yendyk was an admirer of Dontsov, who drew a firm line between the European spirit (to which Ukraine belonged) and the Asian, Semitic, and American spirits. According to this scheme, Dontsov mapped a series of oppositions and contrasts, juxtaposing, for example, Christianity and Judaism. He insisted on their absolute separation, even going so far as to assert that Christ was Galilean and not Jewish. The "works of the Jewish national genius," he wrote, "are foreign to us in the same way as the works of the Ukrainian national genius are foreign to Jews." (Dontsov 1967, 281.) He mentions the sensualism of André Gide and the destruction of form in Marc Chagall as Jewish characteristics without elaborating what he might mean by this. There is, however, a profound contradiction in Dontsov's juxtaposition of Ukrainian and Jewish essentialisms. Ukrainian literature has always been deeply influenced by Judeo-Christian values. The Jewish and Christian faiths share not only the same sacred text, the Bible, but also respect for the sanctity and dignity of each human life, for compassion and tolerance. Dontsov's aversion to these values, which he associates with submissive weakness, compels him to reject almost all leading Ukrainian writers as "infected" by them. The ones he does praise—Shevchenko, Ukrainka, Khvylovy—are interpreted in a tendentious manner that usually misrepresents their writings and views. His view of Christianity is a crusader's: he sees it as a tool for mobilizing the nation in a great war against a corrupt civilization. The enemy is not only communism, but also Western materialism and hedonism, as his brochure *Khrest proty Diavola* (The Cross Against the Devil, 1948), a transcript of a speech he gave in Toronto's Massey Hall in 1948, makes clear.

On the other hand, theater productions, one of the few forms of artistic expression allowed in German-occupied Ukraine, often appear to have been expressions of political nonconformism that undermined fascist ideas. A number of groups staged Cherkasenko's verse drama *Kazka staroho mlyna: Drama* (The Old Mill's Tale: A Drama, 1913) in an experimental style. This is a symbolist play with strong neoromantic overtones, in which the idyllic innocence of the traditional Ukrainian village is shattered by the intrusion of the modern world. The villain is an engineer and colonist of German background, Gustav Wagner, who is both charmed by rural Ukraine and contemptuous of its backwardness. His ruthless, duplicitous behavior destroys a charming old mill and a local nymph-like girl, whom he seduces and then abandons. A contemporary relevance could also be read into the production of Starytsky's *Aza the Gypsy,* which romanticized the gypsies, who like the Jews were being hunted down and killed at the time, as a freedom-loving and talented people. These two plays, which were widely performed across occupied Ukraine, were veiled forms of protest. (Haidabura 2004, 195.) Under German occupation the Ukrainian Theater of the City of Lviv (later renamed the Lviv Opera Theater) staged twenty-eight plays, eighteen operas, and several ballets. It not only protected Jewish performers and musicians, who worked there under assumed names, but produced ideologically subversive plays, such as a dramatization of Bohdan Lepky's *Baturyn,* which shows the razing of Ivan Mazepa's capital by Peter the Great's troops in 1709. The idea of Ukraine's resistance to foreign invasion was immediately interpreted as a commentary on the contemporary German occupation. In spite of its success with the public, the German authorities demanded its removal from the repertoire after twelve performances. (Maksymenko 2006, 132.)

Arkadii Liubchenko

Arkadii Liubchenko was one of the clearest anti-Semitic voices among major Ukrainian writers. His wartime diary, which had appeared in fragments earlier, was only published in full in 1999. The author avoided being evacuated along with other Soviet writers to Ufa in the east, choosing to remain behind German lines. The diary details his experience through four years of Nazi occupation. It begins by recording the appearance of an enormous yellow-and-blue flag in the center of Kharkiv, and two signs in a government building, one reading "Glory to the Great German people" next to another reading "Glory to Free Ukraine." On the opposite wall another sign reads "Glory and Thanks to the German Führer Adolf Hitler who liberated the Ukrainian people from Jewish-Russian Oppression." (Liubchenko 1999, 15.) The toleration of Ukrainian national symbols in the war's early weeks seduced some, including Liubchenko, into believing that the formation of a Ukrainian government was being considered. His disillusionment was gradual but almost total. By the time of his death at the end of the war, he was very critical of German policies. However, his attitude toward Jews remained hostile and vengeful to the end.

Liubchenko's animus against them dates back to the revolution when in 1919 he was apparently denounced as a nationalist to the Cheka by a local Jewish tailor. He also recalls "Chekists and Jews with German shepherds on chains" herding a group of two hundred villagers, including some women, through the steppe. (Ibid., 16.) We are also informed that he resents the fact that there are many Jews in the official Writers' Union. According to his calculations twenty-four of the sixty writers in the prestigious Rolit building in Kyiv, where the literary elite lived, were of Jewish origin. This might be considered an example of their successful integration into Ukrainian literature, but Liubchenko sees it in negative terms. He castigates several Jewish writers as unprincipled, selfish, and aggressive, and dreams of strangling his nemesis, Natan Rybak, who, he feels, controls Oleksandr Korniichuk, the head of the Union and now in Ufa. Criticism of Jewish influence was also being raised by figures in territories under Soviet rule. Kate Brown reports that in 1943 members of the Union objected to the fact that their president was a Jew, Natan Rybak: "At the Union meeting, held well behind Soviet lines, the celebrated film director Alexander Dovzhenko made a speech in which he stated that 'Jews have poisoned Ukrainian culture. They have hated us, they hate us now and will always hate us. They try to crawl in everywhere and take over everything.'" (Brown 2004, 218–19.) It is unclear what triggered this incident, but apparently Dovzhenko was not reprimanded by his colleagues, and his speech was followed by a discussion of whether Rybak should be dismissed.

In Liubchenko's diary the negative image is quickly generalized: "the Jews" have "become insolent" and are attempting "to take everything into their own hands." (Liubchenko 1999, 65.) Countervailing facts are not recorded. Liubchenko mistrusts all Jews. When he is diagnosed with an ulcer he immediately suspects that his former doctor, a Jew, may have hidden the real diagnosis from him for the last five years. When he fears that someone might be a Bolshevik agent, he also feels they might be Jewish.

Sofia Levitina, a censor, also of Jewish background, is described as rushing about frantically during the evacuation. He takes a vindictive pleasure in her panic:

> It serves you right! How much difficulty and pain you alone, Sofia Levitina, in your time caused us while you were the censor in the Holovlit, how you poisoned Khvylovy's blood! Now you shake and whimper. It serves you right. If I could, I

would send a bullet through your narrow but cunning, malicious forehead. Wait, wait and see what is coming to you. The reckoning is only beginning. . . . And I, instead of taking part in this reckoning—on my own behalf and on behalf of my friends, and on behalf of my executed uncle Petro, and my uncle Yulko sent to exile, and on behalf of our destroyed nest in Zhyvotiv, and of all Ukraine—instead of making a reckoning for everything, taking vengeance (yes, yes, taking vengeance pitilessly and without scruples!), I have to travel somewhere to the distant Urals, to foreign, unfamiliar Ufa. (Ibid., 46–47.)

Liubchenko is somewhat disingenuous about Khvylovy, who appears not to have been anti-Semitic, but the passage is symptomatic of the manner in which he constructs a reality in which Jews are to blame both for his personal hardships and for the persecution of all Ukrainians.

Jews are for him a racial category. He has a horror of the *metis,* or mixed natures, and sees the pollution of the pure and noble Ukrainian essence by other races as a source of evil. His view of the nation is very clearly biologically constructed, and the Jew is a foreign body within this organism, preventing its proper functioning and leading to pathological deformations. His prejudices are so strong that after reading the *Protocols of the Elders of Zion,* his only comment is "If this is a forgery, then it is a very successful one. It makes an impression." (Ibid., 57.) Evidently, as a reader he was emotionally fully engaged. It appears that he would have liked to believe an account that intellectually he knew he must reject.

Although there is no mention of mass murder, it is clear from one passage that the writer was aware of what was occurring and that he denied any sympathy to the victims. On June 21, 1944, as the German army is retreating, Liubchenko finds himself on a train passing through Hungary. He writes:

On the road to the village of Mushyn I first saw an enormously long train with Jews, who were being driven somewhere out of Hungary. These were freight cars with barbed wire over the windows full of various heads and mouths eagerly catching air. Sometimes the door was partly open (although locked), and in the gap one could see a crowd of people. In other carriages, on the other hand, there were only a few people, and washed children's clothing was hanging. Grey, hooknosed, with side locks—I had no pity for them; they tortured my people for so many ages and so mercilessly. Young, angry eyes shone from the half-shadows of the carriages, others were indifferent, as though they had no idea what was waiting for them. . . . From the carriage that stood next to ours came a heavy smell, the specific smell of Jewish filth, magnified by the hot summer day. And suddenly I noticed in the gap of the window a Jewish hand pushing forward in a folded tube a violet paper. Other passengers noticed it too: "O, the Jew is showing money! Hungarian pengös!" This paper from the gap was flicking backward and forward like a snake's tongue. This was significant! The Jew was tempting . . . in the same Jewish manner learned through the ages, with the same gold, on account of which this savage, bloody war was being fought, in which he was dying mercilessly. And the Jew dropped the tube; it fell on the sand, opened partially, writhing like a live snake. Several passengers who were passing by the car glanced at it greedily, looked around to see if the guard was not close by and considered whether to take it or not. A movement toward the car with the Jews could mean a bullet in the head. Finally one simple boy dared to and took it. They say that they often drop pengős and dollars on the track in this way: if they do not cause someone harm, at least they will leave a mark, will force someone to remember them longer. (Ibid., 226.)

The phrases "as though they had no idea what was waiting for them," and "will force someone to remember them longer" indicate that he knew of the crematoria. Shocking is the fact that he withholds any human sympathy, and construes every fact (filth, the desire to attract attention) to indicate evil in Jewish character. In view of his apparent knowledge of the mass murder, the total absence of any further reference to it implies tacit support for what was occurring.

Marko Carynnyk has commented that one of the most disturbing features of the above passage is the writerly skill with which the scene is described. Vivid details like the blue eyes of the young woman, the violet color and writhing of the banknote, the clothing hung out to dry make the description memorable. (Tsarynnyk 1984, 93.) However, while breathing in the scene so fully, the writer's human sympathy is completely absent: he is able to deny the fact that these are fellow human beings with a claim on his emotions.

To confirm that Liubchenko knew of what was happening to the Jews, one might quote a parallel passage from Yurii Shevelov's memoirs. Shevelov found himself in almost the same place at the same time. He also describes "freight trains loaded full of human flesh marked for destruction":

These were "the Jews," probably from Hungary, or maybe from the Balkan countries. They were clearly being conveyed for incineration or gassing in camps in Germany, or perhaps in western Poland. It was impossible to even consider approaching those trains because of the strict guard. This was ideology at the stage of absurdity, even madness. The front was breaking up, Germany was in its death agony and disintegrating, while here the railways were being loaded up with this insane traffic. People who might have been used at the front, were being kept guarding these trains! No doubt any humane behavior was unattainably distant in this torrent of destruction, as the experience of Kharkiv, Kyiv, and Lviv had already taught us, but even a simple calculation of military expediency was absent. It was terrifying to look at this mass traffic of what were today still people, but tomorrow would only be decomposing flesh. (Sherekh 1998, 2:5.)

It has been suggested that the underlying paradigm in racism is the differential assessment and treatment of people according to their "value," where "value" is assessed according to a normative and affirmative model of an organic body of the people as a collective entity. (Peukert 1993, 237.) Liubchenko sees no "value" in Jewish people for the Ukrainian body politic. His thinking is governed by a paradigm of social hygiene which accepts the idea of removing "illness" and "deviance" from the national body. The faith in therapeutic progress and in the practical achievements of medicine led in the twenties and thirties to the idealization of youth and health. Liubchenko's prose from this time reveals an admiration of these qualities. He himself was a product of the cult of vitality that gripped the avant-garde in the twenties, and several of his stories explore the "survival of the fittest" theme. A few discuss physical and sexual prowess, as does his diary. These stories also reveal an optimistic, utopian vision of the nation as it will appear in the future, cleansed of its spiritually weaker and deplorable members. This is one explanation for the diary's obsession with identifying, segregating, and removing individuals who are abnormal or sick. If there is a "positive" racism based on a sense of admired hereditary values, and a "negative" racism which is focused on eradicating deviance and weakness, Liubchenko exhibits both. Behind each concern lies the vision of an immortal, healthy national body, an ideal type. This ideal is embodied in certain women, who represent the qualities the author most admires, and whom he claims to love; others fall short of the ideal and these he despises. He also continually searches for defective personalities—failures, parasites, ne'er-do-wells—on whom he blames the nation's ills. Personal defects, when discovered, are often explained in racial terms. This scheme and the need to eradicate human sickness enable him to see Jews as part of social pathology. As one reads the diary, the appalling machinery of the Holocaust, although never mentioned, can be heard working in the background. It is deeply ironic that this worshiper of pagan health and vigor should have left in this diary a record of his own physical decline, a long struggle with ulcers which ended with his death following an unsuccessful operation.

Liubchenko's earlier works take on a new meaning in the light of this diary. His "Ziama" (1924) describes the transformation of a fearful Jewish boy into a communist fanatic. During the revolution he becomes a close comrade-in-arms of the narrator, but when the two are separated during combat, Ziama suspects that his friend is planning to desert. He prepares to shoot the narrator, and then suddenly realizes that the latter has only stopped at a house in order to bandage a wounded leg. The incident reveals deadly suspicion even between fellow fighters. Liubchenko's world is often a Darwinian one ruled by personal strength and animal instincts. This story ends with Ziama's wounding during a subsequent battle. Knowing that he cannot escape, he asks the narrator to shoot him in order to end his agony and prevent capture by enemy forces, who would treat him cruelly as a Jew. After hesitating, the narrator shoots. The story won the author great acclaim and the transformation of the timid Jewish boy into a brave Bolshevik warrior appealed to many. The contemporary reader will, however, suspect the possibility of a concealed sadistic pleasure in the act of "mercy," which in retrospect appears to condone violence without guilt. The reader learns that the friendship between the two main characters, the Ukrainian narrator and Ziama, began in childhood. Early in the revolutionary period, Ziama had turned to his friend with the words "Let us always be together." The shot that ends this friendship can be read both as a tragic denouement and as a subconscious wish to sever ties.

This is not the only work which, in retrospect, raises disturbing questions about an unforgiving, Darwinian view of existence. A number of Liubchenko's stories from the late twenties show a love of biologically strong natures driven by irrepressible and "amoral" instincts. "Krov" (Blood, 1929) is the story of a starving pack of wolves in which the younger, healthier animals challenge the old, lead wolf and are prepared to kill him if he falters. "Vertep" (1929) is a hymn to the steppe and its ability to produce physically and psychologically healthy, harmonious natures. Liubchenko's prose of the twenties has been praised for this cult of vitality. However, certain aspects of his work, such as the acceptance of violence, the fascination with physical strength, the praise of uninhibited eroticism, and the paeans to youth anticipate both the militant Bolshevik aesthetic and the fascistic cult of virility of the thirties.

Postwar Emigré Narratives

An important postwar literary development took place in emigration. The organization MUR (Artistic Ukrainian Movement) was created from intellectuals and writers who found themselves living as displaced persons in Germany. During the years 1945–48 MUR was able to bring together the most talented writers from both Eastern and Western Ukraine in an endeavor to create a new, modern literature of the highest quality and free of ideological diktats. The immediate public were the two hundred thousand Ukrainians in displaced persons camps, but the organization's influence proved to be much wider. It affected all postwar writing in the massive emigration and today exerts an influence in contemporary Ukraine. The few years of MUR's existence have been called "perhaps the most

interesting period in twentieth-century Ukrainian literature after the 1920s."
(Pavlychko 2003, 191.) Over twelve hundred books and pamphlets were produced at this time, around 250 of which were original works of prose, poetry, and
drama. There were also at least eighteen active theaters in the camps. (Revuts'kyi
1992, 307.) The organization's positions and its publications (the periodicals
MUR and *Arka (Arch)*, as well as individual books) were attacked by hostile
writers who adhered to the old *Vistnyk* ideology. There ensued a polemic between the two camps, which has been described in the memoirs of Yurii Sherekh
(pseudonym of Shevelov), MUR's leading critic. In the late forties and early
fifties, he exposed Dontsov's ideology as contemptuous of democracy and liberal
values. Dontsov's extreme nationalism was for Sherekh not a product of the
Ukrainian tradition, but an outgrowth and mirror image of Russian Bolshevism.
This kind of nationalism "had constructed itself according to the law of opposition—and therefore was incapable of overcoming its opponent." (Sherekh 1948,
19.) As far as Sherekh was concerned, Dontsov's vision of rule by an elite who
shared his ideas was an implicit admission that most contemporaries, and the
entire Ukrainian cultural tradition, disagreed with him. Dontsov's response to
this realization was a demand that the nation and its tradition be violently
transformed. The people were for him "haltered animals" who would have to be
driven "to their appointed place." (Ibid., 30.) The *Vistnyk* philosophy, wrote
Sherekh, might have prepared Ukrainians for strong political organizations and
for drawing a clear demarcation line between Ukrainian and Russian culture.
However, it was gripped by a chauvinism that inflamed hatreds and made impossible any compromises with Russian groups who could have been partners.
The Vistnykites "underestimated the power of reason, placing their bets exclusively on willpower and a feeling of animosity." (Ibid., 36.) Sherekh was aware
that Dontsov's ideas had a hypnotic effect on many people, but he consistently
pointed out their harmfulness. In the postwar world, he argued, the new Ukrainian nationalism required a vision of unity, tolerance toward one's partners,
elaboration of the ideal of a fully developed human being, and a holistic understanding of the Ukrainian tradition. (Sherekh 1948, 38.) This counterposition
was also articulated by Samchuk, Yurii Dyvnych (Lavrinenko), Yurii Kosach,
and others in the MUR camp.

Kosach's literary works often embody these ideas, especially his *Enei i zhyttia inshysh* (Aeneas and the Life of Others, 1946), *Diistvo pro Iuriia Peremozhtsia*
(A Play About Yury the Conqueror, 1947), and *Den' Hnivu: Povist' pro 1648 rik*
(Day of Anger: A Novel of 1648, 1947–48). *Enei* represents a demonstrative
break with Dontsov's ideas, exposing their voluntarism and their tendency to

treat people as a means to an end. The hero Iryn sees common people as cogs on the great wheel of history, one that only he and other "corsairs" are capable of moving. The masses are expected to follow orders. His treatment of women displays his commitment to the primacy of the political struggle: he deceives and uses them in order to further the cause. However, at the novel's end, in the postwar world, he is left doubting his own ideology and recognizing the need for change. The other main character is the narrator Enei. In contrast to Iryn, he respects the individuality of others, and supports the women who have been abandoned by his friend. The novel's structure of characterization implies a rejection of Dontsovian fanaticism, utilitarianism, and tendentiousness. In fact, this book played a programmatic role in Sherekh's attack on the *Vistnyk* ideology. He wrote a long article, "Proshchannia z uchora" (Goodbye to Yesterday, 1952) in which he interpreted *Enei* as just such a parting with Dontsovism: "The people educated by it [*Vistnyk*] are still alive, of course, but if they do not wish to be living corpses, they should in some degree revise their old positions." The "apotheosis of will" and the "ecstasy of faith" are born of "weak reasoning." He sees the novel as indicating the need to reject a wartime past ruled by violence, with all its "bestiality and Machiavellianism." (Sherekh 2003, 212, 220.)

Kosach depicts the cruel treatment of a Jew in his *Diistvo pro Iuriia-Peremozhtsia*. This play, as the author indicates in his foreword, is a meditation on Ukrainian history. It depicts Yurii Khmelnytsky, Bohdan's son, as a demented megalomaniac who is a mere puppet of the Turkish sultan, but continues to embrace wild dreams of regaining Ukraine and then going on to conquer India. Out of touch with reality, he is gradually abandoned by his last supporters. He tortures and kills a Jewish leaseholder, driven by the bizarre idea that Jews are part of a "black weakness" which he also identifies as a "Ukrainian illness." (Kosach 1947, 16.) He no longer believes in God's mercy, nor in the political will of his people, commenting that "the rabble are slitherers, slippery, disgusting slitherers." (Ibid., 51) He believes that only merciless violence will bring political success and is prepared, if necessary, to make a wasteland of the country. One character says: "He wants to scorch the Jew like a cancer. He wants to scorch everything around him. And he will be left alone as though in an Arabian desert." (Ibid., 11.)

The half-mad Khmelnytsky, who has imprisoned the leaseholder, thinks that the man has access to secret powers through his knowledge of Jewish books, signs of the Zodiac, and the Kabbalah. Unable to extract these powers from the prisoner, he has him killed, and then informs Yudyt (Judith), the Jew's grieving daughter: "I killed your father, because he alone could introduce me to the devil.

Orun was a wise Jew. He knew everything under Mars, under the Scorpion. I begged him. . . . Surely not for myself? I craved power for those who are to come." (Ibid., 46.) Yudyt argues that the land of Ukraine also includes the Jewish people: "Our blood is also in this land. All blood has become one . . . Polish and Tatar and Muscovite . . . to give growth, so that terrible new purple shoots can appear in early spring. . . . The sowing will bear fruit. Understand this: with or without us this land will blossom. Eternally." She believes in Ukraine's future: "this is a land given by God . . . Zion." (Ibid., 47.) At the same time, however, she thinks continually of revenge. In the end Yudyt drinks the poison that was meant for Khmelnytsky and was prepared by his own jester. She does so "for everyone," choosing not to act on her urge for vengeance, and leaving the tyrant to go down in history as an agent of evil. (Ibid., 61.) Although the action is set in Ukraine in 1681 during the period of ruin, readers would immediately associate the play's action with the Second World War, perhaps with Hitler's maniacal plans, but most of all with the justification of ruthless means. The killing of Orun can be read as a surrogate for the murder of Jews during the war and Yudyt's final statements can be seen as a comment on the dark cloud that these events would cast on future history.

Den' hnivu is set in 1648. It is a swashbuckling story of personal heroism and wartime victories, but it contains a Jewish subplot. Rabbi Nathan Hannover is portrayed writing his account of the destruction of Jewry. He understands the extraordinary magnitude of the uprising, and also the fact that the Jewish population has been swept up in the overpowering wave. He witnessed the cruel punishment of rebels left impaled on stakes, a slow death that takes days as the stake works its way up through their bodies. But another young Jew, the tailor Berakha, has joined the rebels. He witnesses Prince Yarema Vyshnevetsky's cruel punishment of the rebels, commenting: "who will work on his land, if he murders all the serfs?" In conversation with Hannover, Berakha argues that the revolt is "revenge against the dukes, whether they are Polish or Jewish." He feels that Khmelnytsky has raised the flag for all the poor, including "saddlers, tailors, skinny Jews. Khmel, brother, does not ask what faith you profess, Khmel accepts our people too." (Kosach 1947–48, 2:84.) Berakha joins the uprising which brings together all parts of the country and people from all walks of life. He succeeds in opening the gates of the besieged town of Zaslav. Entering the town through a door behind a synagogue that is used by Jews, he and several Cossacks force open the main gate and allow the infantry to storm the town. The keys to the entrance behind the synagogue are obtained from Rabbi Hannover himself. Berakha has been given assurances that the Jews will not be harmed. In a discussion with Hannover, he makes the point that there are different kinds of people in the rebel army: there is chaff among the wheat. But, he says, the same is true of the Jews: some took Cossack daughters as hostages and corrupted them, and some refused the keys to the churches for funeral services or weddings until people kissed their slippers. Hannover comments that "There is eternal hatred in this land," but Berakha responds angrily: "Since this fat land also satiates us . . . since our bones have also been growing out of this soil for centuries, we must understand finally that we owe this fatherland." Hannover reminds Berakha that Jews have one promised land and that they are chosen, a fact that Berakha does not deny. It is unclear whether he steals the keys from the old rabbi or is allowed to take them. (Ibid., 141–42.)

Kryvonis represents the unreliable element in the uprising, the rebel poor, the *chern*. They owe allegiance only to him and he behaves like a warlord. Khmelnytsky, after the victory at Korsun, is now planning a new state structure and fears the *chern*'s lack of discipline. At one point Kryvonis almost loses control of this fickle mass, which is ready to kill him. However, the tide of war turns in favor of the uprising. At the decisive moment everyone plays their part and victory is assured. The urge to freedom, an impulse that the Ukrainian people have always heeded, wins out. The final picture is of a united people basking in the afterglow of a great and successful struggle. Berakha has performed heroically on the field of battle, as have Greeks and members of other nationalities.

These works of the forties represent a rethinking by Kosach of his own prewar writings. In the thirties he had produced adventure tales that sometimes focused on political assassinations or the hard choices required during times of struggle. It was precisely the man of action, the resolute executor of tasks, that the author admired. Such characters were an implicit rejection of the dreamy, sentimental heroes of the past. In an introduction to Kosach's stories published in 1937, one critic wrote admiringly: "Along with the transformation of the spirit—which from the sentimental-melancholic turned hard as steel, merciless and terrible—there came physical reincarnation. People breathed more freely, their eyes shone with faith in the future, their step sounded ancient, Varangian rhythms." (Zh. 1937, 6.) But in the postwar works Kosach reassesses this cult of the martial, of the hero as a titan and inspirer of the masses.

In *Den' hnivu* the idea of merciless, savage struggle has its ideologists on both sides of the barricades. On the Polish side it is adhered to by Yarema Vyshnevetsky and the monk Dominik; on the Ukrainian side primarily by Kryvonis (also known as Perebyinis). However, the novelist demonstrates that ruthlessness can turn its destructive potential against those who use it. The issue of national unity greatly concerned Kosach in the postwar years, as it did many Ukrainians. Anti-Semitism, and the persecution of minorities generally, was portrayed in the literature of these years as not only morally wrong, but divisive in nation-building terms. In Kosach's works it demoralizes fighters for the national cause and destroys solidarity. The author also deemphasizes the role of the strong leader. Khmelnytsky is not the focus of *Den' hnivu*. Although a wise commander, he does not always control events, nor does he inspire them. The focus is on individual stories of heroism, which all play a part in the common struggle. This was a break with the interpretation of the leader's crucial role, as propounded in the thirties by the conservative Viacheslav Lypynsky and the radical nationalist Dmytro Dontsov. However, Kosach also suggests that a naïve faith in the masses is similarly unjustified. Their mood can be swayed by short-lived passions.

Teodosii Osmachka was another major writer of the MUR period. He survived arrest and imprisonment under Stalin by feigning insanity, and the traumatic experiences of persecution by the Cheka, eviction, arrest, and imprisonment are the subject of his works. It is worth noting that *Plan do dvoru: Povist'* (Yard Plan: A Novel, 1951), which deals with this reality, does not mention Jews at all. The Cheka in this novel, as in his other works, are Ukrainians, who provide more than enough sadistic or cruel types to run the repressive apparatus. *Rotonda dushohubtsiv: Opovidannia* (Murderers' Rotunda: A Tale, c. 1951) is another heavily autobiographical work. Here the main character, Brus, does meet two Jews in the Cheka apparatus, one of whom holds a senior position, but his primary persecutors are all Ukrainians. The prisoner is eventually pronounced insane because he continually claims that his parents were poisoned by "the Jews." When asked by the interrogator why he thinks that his father was poisoned, Brus replies: "I think because he resembled Christ" . . . "And if he did, what of it?" . . . "Well, Christ was a Jew, and loved all people in the world, and was crucified for this, as you know. My father also gave his whole life for his countrymen . . . He cured their cattle and sheep . . . And even them, because he sympathized with their suffering, and not for money. And the Jews poisoned him, because in these actions he resembled Christ, whom they are angry with to this day." When the exasperated interrogator, Partsiuk, who is not a Jew, asks him to what nation the prisoner thinks he, Partsiuk, belongs, Brus classifies him as "a servant of the Jews." These last "belong to no nation." (Os'machka [1956], 258–59.) From that point on, this irrational paranoia and anti-Semitism are the only "explanations" that the prisoner offers for his own troubles and those of his family. This and other strange forms of behavior convince the Cheka that they are indeed dealing with a madman. They commit him to an asylum, where he survives the mass killings. The nightmarish atmosphere, the perverse logic of both persecutors and persecuted, and the pervasiveness of human cruelty make this an unsettling book. Just as disturbing is the autobiographical element that lies behind this novel. Osmachka survived arrest, interrogation, and imprisonment by feigning insanity. The whole experience left him traumatized and, after completing the novel, he suffered a mental breakdown.

It would be wrong to view the MUR camp, the anti-MUR camp, or the writers who contributed to *Vistnyk* as monolithic in their ideological concerns or literary interests. Yurii Klen was one of the leading *Vistnyk* poets in the thirties. On the eve of the war he was drafted into the German army, where he served as a translator in Ukraine during 1941–42. His writings, including his magnum opus, the epic poem *Popil imperii* (Ashes of Empires, 1946), are critical of both Soviet and German imperialist attitudes, and refuse support for ruthless conduct in human affairs. Klen had emigrated to Germany in 1931, a privilege allowed him as a descendant of German colonists. In the twenties he had belonged to the neoclassicist grouping around Mykola Zerov, which viewed the world through the prism of universal themes and the long perspective of art. The unfinished *Popil imperii* is an attempt to provide such a perspective on the rise of fascism in Germany in the thirties and on the horrors of the Second World War. It describes the treatment of Jews and other peoples in the concentration camps. As in Dante's *Inferno*, the narrator is conducted through this hell by a guide. Enei (Aeneas) shows the narrator pictures of Auschwitz, Dachau, Mauthausen, and Buchenwald. The sadistic behavior of German guards and the atrocities against Jews are commented upon by the guide Enei, in much the same way as Virgil supplies the necessary explanations to Dante. The tone is also reminiscent of Dante's poem—contemplation of horror from an epic distance:

> We walked on further and saw
> How onto a minefield
> Hundreds of thousands of Jews were driven
> From all neighborhoods and enclosures.
> And from there a groan was sent
> By the earth, torn apart by dynamite.
> Or grandfathers, women, girls
> Were executed in batches.
> The bodies all were thrown into pits
> To which the infants were added. (Klen 1991, 266.)

Later, in the vicinity of Prague, the narrator witnesses the agony of a great tzaddik, who curses the nation that has brought such suffering upon the Jews and

asks God to punish the perpetrators of such crimes. Klen draws parallels between the behavior of the NKVD and the Gestapo. He ends with a depiction of
Jeremiah's lamentation over the destruction of the world and human cruelty, a
discussion on the nature of evil, and the difficulty of describing horrors of such
magnitude. One of the most explicit condemnations of the Holocaust, this work
is also a rejection of all fanaticisms. Ironically, it was never allowed publication in
the Soviet Union and appeared in Ukraine only in 1991, the year of independence.

The postwar Klen, who was a defender of universal values and a humanist,
differed considerably from the man who in the thirties reported for *Vistnyk* from
Germany under the pseudonym Hordii Yavir. Among his reports was a glowing
account of the impression made by Hitler's pre-election speeches in 1932–33
and their powerful effect on the population; a defense of Germany, Italy, and
Japan in 1937 as the only countries capable of standing up to Bolshevism by using "Bolshevik" methods; and a welcoming of Germany's annexation of Austria
in 1938 as a new dawn for Europe and perhaps the world. (Yavir 1933, 817; 1937,
878; 1938, 289.) These contributions to *Vistnyk* make it clear that Klen was not
only attracted in the thirties to the cult of ancient traditions, but also to the anti-
democratic and anti-Semitic policies of Nazi Germany. Particularly surprising is
his glorification of German expansionism, which, he must have known, held fatal consequences for all of Europe, and for Ukraine. Klen was soon disillusioned
and may have been removed from the front because of his contacts with Ukrainians and attempts to mitigate the cruelty of some officers. (Horodyns'kyi 2004,
367–74.) He began writing *Popil imperii* in 1943, and his adherence to MUR in
the years before his death in 1947, can be seen as a reassessment of the *Vistnyk*
period and a self-critique.

Leonid Mosendz was another prominent contributor to the cult of heroes,
myths, and patriotism for which *Vistnyk* was known. He had fought for the UNR
during the revolutionary years. After demobilization, he obtained a degree in
civil engineering, worked in Bratislava until the end of the Second World War,
and died of tuberculosis in Switzerland in 1948. Mosendz's writings of the thirties are a call to break with a submissive, obedient spirit and instead to cultivate
rebelliousness and a staunch, unbending attitude. Dokia Humenna described
his *Liudyna pokirna* (Submissive Person, 1937) in her diary entry of February
22, 1942 as "Ukrainian fascism." (Humenna 1990, 254.) Yet his major novel *Ostannii prorok* (The Last Prophet, 1960) demonstrates a rethinking of his prewar
attitudes. The novel describes the life of John the Baptist. Mosendz worked on it
from 1935 until his death, studying the Bible, Hebrew texts, and Jewish history.

Only three of four parts were completed, but it is clear that the reader is being prepared for a change of heart on the part of John (identified as Yehokhanan, namely Yohanan, in the text), who will leave the Zealots and will work for a moral transformation of the people, not for an armed uprising. The book is remarkable for being set in Judea during Herod's reign, but even more so for the strong resemblance that the Zealots bear to the OUN. The Zealots, moreover, are mostly from Galilee, the most rebellious and ungovernable land of the Jews. Most readers would see in this an allegorical reference to Galicia, or to Western Ukraine as a whole. The allegorical interpretation can be extended: the Roman empire can be seen as the USSR, Jerusalem as Kyiv, the Pharisees and Sadducees as leading Soviet Ukrainian circles. If such a reading is accepted, the hero's discovery that the Zealots are not interested in social equality or the welfare of the population can only be seen as a strong disavowal of OUN "zealotry." In fact, the Zealots are determined to destroy a large number of their own people, who might be hostile or indifferent toward them. They view their task as recalling the military exploits of Samson and the Maccabees, and arousing hatred for Rome and Herod. However, no broader education is to be provided for the masses; they are to obey the leader's decisions unquestioningly. The leader alone knows and decides everything. (Mosendz 1960, 382–33) This leader, in turn, believes that John "thinks too much" and for this reason is to be treated with suspicion. It is clear from the third section of the book, written in 1947, and from Mosendz's correspondence in the last years of his life, that the author had become disillusioned with the ideology of nationalist parties and with the moral behavior of their leaderships. (Kravtsiv 1960, xxx.)

Awaking from History, 1953–2005

I n the late fifties and early sixties a coordinated antireligious campaign in the Soviet Union closed many churches and synagogues. The number of Jewish communities in Ukraine dropped from forty-one to fifteen. Out of five hundred synagogues in the USSR at the time of Stalin's death, only one hundred remained in 1963. (Khiterer 2001a, 146.) From 1945 to 1985 there were no legal Jewish schools, no books or newspapers published in Hebrew or Yiddish, and only one magazine, *Sovietish heimland.* This period also witnessed a campaign against Zionism and the imprisonment of those who demanded the right to emigrate to Israel.

The government sanctioned anti-Semitic publications that linked Jews, Judaism, and Israel, such as Trokhym Kychko's *Iudaizm bez prykras* (Judaism Without Embellishments, 1963). Ironically, Kychko had been expelled from the party over allegations of collaboration. It is thought that this publication may have been his attempt to "redeem" himself. A measure of the acceptance his ideas received in high party circles can be gleaned from the fact that even after the book's international condemnation (it was criticized in the *New York Times* on February 27 and March 14, 1964) the Supreme Soviet of Ukraine awarded him a diploma in 1968 "for his work for atheist propaganda." (Weiner 2001, 201.)

Dissent

In the mid-sixties "dissident" Jewish and Ukrainian writers found themselves cooperating in the struggle for human and civil rights. Leading Ukrainian intellectuals like Ivan Dziuba, Ivan Svitlychny, and Yevhen Sverstiuk made powerful statements of support for the Jewish community. In the 1960s and until the early 1980s meetings organized by activists took place at Babyn Yar. Here, an important turning point occurred on September 29, 1966, on the twenty-fifth anniversary of the mass executions. About five hundred people were present to hear speeches by Dziuba, Viktor Nekrasov, Borys Antonenko-Davydovych, and others. Dziuba's speech in particular made an enormous impression. Taped and transcribed, the text circulated widely in *samvydav* ("self-publishing," or underground publication). In later years he continued to speak out in favor of better mutual relations, defining the Ukrainian-Jewish relationship as a search for mutual understanding between two victims of the historical process and of regimes hostile to freedom. The critic urged both peoples to consider their mutual relations without shifting their sins and hatreds onto one another.

Activists from both nations served prison terms together for their views. Yevhen Sverstiuk, Yakiv Suslensky, and Mykhailo Kheifets have described the good relations and close collaboration between Jewish and Ukrainian prisoners in the camps during the 1970s. Based on shared principles and goals, their joint activities included acts of protest against the government, the publication of underground literature, and mutual support for each other's causes. Both groups clashed with some Russian nationalists in the camps who were hostile to national demands. (Korohods'kyi 1994, 117.) Kheifets has left a moving memoir of the intellectual and spiritual understanding that developed between individuals of different backgrounds. It is a powerful tribute in particular to the Ukrainian poet Vasyl Stus and describes the dialogue between the author and Stus over Jewish and Ukrainian issues, and how each grew to understand and sympathize with the other. Kheifets writes:

> The Jews, in spite of their external sensitivity to universal ideas, as a people have a monologic character. They are so capable of becoming carried away by the world created by their own imaginations, their own ideas and thoughts, that sometimes they fail to see how surrounding objects and subjects react to them. This *self-immersion* into their own internal world aided them to survive as a community without merging with any other through two thousand years of exile, a situation almost unheard of in human history! However, the same qualities of the national character that gave it such a powerful stability—the ability to converse without listening to one's partner, to communicate while not noticing the object of one's communication, to live alongside one's neighbor, trading, greeting, joking and at the same time living on a different planet, on a different plane that does not intersect with the neighbor's—probably these qualities above all provoked the core anti-Semitism of all tribes and peoples who have cast a shadow over the Jewish community in all its wanderings. (Kheifets 1994, 154–55.)

It is difficult to know how to interpret Kheifets's comments. They perhaps reflect his discovery of an intellectual world whose existence he had not anticipated. Stus had been cautious in his initial contacts, fearing that Kheifets was another "universalist" deaf to Ukrainian concerns, but their relationship soon blossomed. In the camps members of persecuted national minorities often exhibited an inferiority complex and a compensatory tendency to defend the unique qualities and the achievements of their peoples. Stus, however, assessed the Ukrainian past soberly, never justifying evil actions. Kheifets reports that the poet characterized Dontsov's attempt to graft racism onto the national psyche as a reaction to national humiliation, and saw the pogroms as part of a long chain of national tragedies. The 1918–19 pogroms, in his view, made most Jews turn to Moscow and in this way created "a mass base for imperial conquest" behind the national movement's lines, while Ukrainian participation in the destruction of the Jews in 1941 did "more than anything else to isolate the Ukrainian national movement in the postwar years."(Ibid., 205.) This narrative, which weaves together Ukrainian and Jewish history, is one that Kheifets accepts and is anxious to communicate to readers.

Helii (Yevhen) Sniehirov has described the life of dissidents in the 1970s in *Roman-donos* (A Novel-Denunciation, 1977, which was also published under the Russian version of his name, Gelii Snegurov). The memoir deals with his arrest, imprisonment, and persecution for trying to discover the truth about the SVU show trial, after he learned late in life that his mother had been implicated in the trial because of her association with several writers. As with Khiefets, the sudden revelation of an unsuspected personal connection to Ukrainian history had a transforming effect. He began to research events surrounding the SVU trial, becoming in the process a strong Ukrainian patriot. Sniehirov had directed a film studio and in the sixties had written prose in both Ukrainian and Russian. His dissident circle included Russians, Jews, and Ukrainians, who all worked together in Kyiv and other cities, especially after the major wave of arrests that took place in 1972 created the phenomenon of *samvydav*. Sniehirov's second wife was Jewish and the possibility of emigration to Israel was available to him, but he chose to stay in Kyiv. His manuscript was prepared in both Ukrainian and Russian. A copy was smuggled to the West in 1976. The author died two years later after being arrested by the KGB.

Sniehirov was shocked to discover the enormity of the SVU affair, and the fact that all the accusations against the defendants, and indeed the very existence of this and a plethora of "fascist" or "bourgeois nationalist" organizations, had been dreamed up at the time by the secret police. He was particularly interested

in two questions: the way in which the police used the trial to discredit the national movement, and why all the defendants pleaded guilty. An analysis of the
trial's mechanism provided answers. Sniehirov was able to establish that almost
all the investigators were Jewish—Bruk, Yuzhny, Grozny, Pravdin, Bronievoi,
Goldenberg—and that there was a conscious policy to link the defendants to
Petliura and Western powers, while simultaneously accusing them of fascism,
pogroms, and anti-Semitism. Four years later the investigators were themselves
arrested and killed, and the leading procurator, Panas Liubchenko, shot himself
on August 30, 1937, after first shooting his wife and son. As for why the defendants pleaded guilty, Sniehirov offers a couple of reasons. Until 1932 a confes-
sion had been legally sufficient to assure a guilty verdict, as it had been under the
tsars, who had often used torture to obtain such admissions. The "producers" of
the spectacle had worked long and hard to extract the required confessions. The
trial "screenplay" had been carefully scripted by the secret police, in particular
by Valerii Gorozhanin, who coordinated the investigations. The prisoners had
been selected from a large number of arrested individuals, and were coached until the secret police decided upon the forty-five defendants whom, they felt, they
could compel to play the required role. Prisoners were told that they could either
admit their guilt at the trial or be killed and disappear without trace. Vasyl Matu-
shevsky, one of only two survivors whom Sniehurov was able to interview, described the questioning. Three interrogators—Bruk, Pravdin, and Goldberg—
took turns, while a revolver lay on the table: "Goldberg takes the gun and checks
the bullets. Bruk says: 'Leave off, you'll have time, one of these bullets will get
him.' Well, they led me to execution. In the night: 'Get ready, quickly!' And they
lead me across a dark garden with the gun barrel in my back, then stop me. 'Hold
it!' Then they lead me again, doors open, stairs lead down to a light—a cell,
where they are going to shoot me. It turned out to be another prison cell."
(Sniehirov 1983, 174.) At one point, Solomon Bruk stated: "We must bring the
Ukrainian intelligentsia to its knees; this is our task and it shall be fulfilled; those
whom we cannot bring to their knees we will shoot!" (Ibid., 110, 174.) Throughout the trial, the newspapers abused the prisoners and whipped up hysteria.
Some defendants harbored hopes of making a final speech that would sway the
judges, or may have been promised lighter sentences if they went along with the
proposed "screenplay." They were, in any case, mostly members of the intelligentsia of the "Chekhov" type, namely "normal people of the late nineteenth
and early twentieth century, that romantic century, when people lived according
to the rules of decency, honor, and conscience, when struggle was without fail
conducted according to the rules of fine, sentimental codes. They were educated

in the spirit of high morals—and now the new epoch crushed them, an epoch of proletarian revolution with its iron, bloody morality based on the absence of all morality, a complete disregard for conscience and honor." (Ibid., 223.) Shell-shocked by events around them, the defendants appeared to sleepwalk through the trial. The SVU and the many smaller trials of students, academics, medical personnel, and other that took place at the time constituted only the first wave of kangaroo courts—dress rehearsals for later show trials and similar publicly conducted prosecutions.

Other nonconformists were going through similar transformative experiences. Yosyf Zisels, who worked closely with Ukrainian intellectuals in defending political prisoners and disseminating underground literature, ascribes the development of his own sense of Jewish identity to meetings with Mykhailo Horyn. (Zisel's 2000, 37.) Arrested and imprisoned in 1975 for joining the Ukrainian Helsinki Monitoring Group, the main human rights defense group in Ukraine, Zisels continued to work closely with other Ukrainian dissidents. After independence, he became the leading figure in the Ukrainian Jewish community.

An extensive dialogue took place between Ukrainian and Jewish intellectuals in the years leading up to the USSR's disintegration. Among other prominent participants were Moisei Fishbein, Myroslav Marynovych, Oksana Zabuzhko, Izrail (Israel) Kleiner, and Yakiv Suslensky. The last-named created an Association for Jewish-Ukrainian Contacts and published the journal *Diialohy* (Dialogues) in Jerusalem. It provided a forum in which both Ukrainian and Jewish viewpoints could be voiced, and succeeded in challenging and correcting a number of prejudices and misconceptions. The same period saw an intensification of the dialogue between Jews and Ukrainians in North America. (Asper and Potichnyj 1983, 14–15.)

Postwar Literature and Memory

The postwar Ukrainian emigration was relatively silent on the Jewish question, but, as the writings by MUR members indicate, it attempted to overcome authoritarian and racializing attitudes. Leonid Poltava (Yensen) eulogized the life of a Ukrainian Jew, Semen Yakerson, based on reminiscences that the author heard from Yevhen Malaniuk in 1963. The poem "Pro zhyda S. Iakersona—Sotnyka armii Ukrains'koi Narodnoi Respubliky" (The Jew S. Yakerson—Captain in the Army of the Ukrainian National Republic, 1966) describes his courageous service in the UNR army. Yakerson then obtained a degree from the Ukrainian Academy of Economics in Poděbrady in Czechoslovakia and during the Nazi oc-

cupation of Prague risked his life entering and leaving the Jewish ghetto, bringing food from his Ukrainian friends. He was eventually killed by the Nazis.
(Poltava 1998, 214–15.) The younger generation of Ukrainians writing in the
West also raised the issue of the Holocaust. Bohdan Boichuk, a leading figure in
the New York Group of poets, in his "Podorozh z uchytelem" (A Trip with
Teacher, 1968) describes the destruction of a ghetto by the Gestapo and the
death of a Jewish woman.

Dokia Humenna's wartime novel *Khreshchatyi iar (Kyiv 1941–43): Roman-
khronika* (The Cross-shaped Ravine (Kyiv 1941–43): A Novel-chronicle, 1956)
gives a vivid account of the German occupation. It is exceptional because of her
frank observations and unique viewpoint. In the thirties she had been banned
from the Soviet Writers' Union. The reasons had to do with her egalitarianism,
and in particular her complaints that a large part of the population, including
members of the Writers' Union, were living the life of a privileged caste. The
main protagonist in the novel, Mariana, is Humenna's alter ego. She is anti-Soviet, but also anti-Nazi, critical of various nationalisms, and sympathetic toward
feminism. Humenna herself remained an enemy of all forms of inequality, authoritarianism, and racism throughout her life, and maintained a strong commitment to personal integrity and outspokenness. A remarkable feature of her
prose is the fascination with ancient cultures, such as the Trypillian (Trypolian)
and Scythian, and with matriarchal traditions that have deep roots in Ukraine.
She read widely on these subjects, attended conferences on archeology, and participated in the excavation of prehistoric sites. In the novel these interests are im-
parted to Mariana, who considers herself a "citizen of the millennia." The long
view of history gives her a distancing perspective on the tragedies unfolding
around her, and allows her to keep her faith in humanity.

The novel follows the lives of several characters and in this way presents
events through the prism of different personal experiences. It chronicles the
population's response to the Soviet retreat, the arrival of the Nazis, the massacre
at Babyn Yar, and the return of the Red Army. In describing relations between
Ukrainians, Russians, Jews, and returning émigrés from Western Ukraine and
Central Europe, it demonstrates the fluctuation of public opinion—particular
of attitudes toward the Jews. At the same time it is a rich source of information on
various historical figures, among them Olena Teliha, Ulas Samchuk, Arkadii
Liubchenko, and Leonid Pervomaisky, who appear under fictional names.

In the early weeks of the war, many Jews escape the city. They often feel like
foreigners among the local people, who resent their relative affluence and their
abandonment of the capital. This is sometimes phrased as a criticism of non-

combatants, but there are other disquieting notes that suggest deeper animosity and the imminence of anti-Jewish violence. Mariana picks up these attitudes from conversations overheard in the streets and through contact with friends. She saves the manuscripts of a rabbi friend by delivering them to another location, and helps her Jewish friend Roza hide her identity when news of Babyn Yar spreads through the city, but she cannot bring herself to recount all that she has heard from rumors in the street:

> Lvivska Street was full of people on the day that Kyiv's Jews were summoned there by the order in the azure-colored notice. They all believed that they were to be transferred, some brought an enormous amount of food with them, purchased little carts for this purpose, or hired baggage handlers. And no one thought that there were so still many of them in Kyiv! There, on the corner of Diohtiarivska and Dorohozhytska, their passports were taken away and thrown into a fire. Those who did not have the word "Jew" registered in their passports were pushed aside, in spite of protests and intentions of sharing a husband's or a wife's fate. Mariana told Roza this. No one comes back from there—she told her this too. But then, about how they were stripped to their underwear, how their things were thrown over the fence, how they were led to Babyn Yar beyond the cemetery, how there above the ravine the machine gun sprayed them with bullets, sweeping them into the ravine, how the Germans threw a couple of grenades and the earth covered thousands who were perhaps only wounded, perhaps still alive, how they were killed by an electrical current—all those rumors that made one's hair stand on end—Marian could not tell Roza this. (Humenna 1956, 194–95.)

Babyn Yar becomes a turning point. When people discover what has happened to friends and colleagues of whose Jewish background they were often unaware, their petty resentments toward the Jewish population turn to an uncomprehending horror. Some characters, who associate the cause of independence with the German invasion and the killing of Jews, become violently antinationalistic. In one climactic scene an altercation takes place between Mariana and Vasanta, a childhood friend, whose family had been arrested and exiled during Stalin's collectivization of agriculture. Vasanta has now adopted anti-Ukrainian, pro-Soviet positions. Mariana, on the other hand, continues to oppose both regimes in the name of a sane political order that must come in the future. The novel is perhaps the most thoughtful attempt to grapple with the Holocaust and with Jewish-Ukrainian relations in Ukrainian fiction of the postwar years, and raises issues that only entered wider public discourse in later decades: political conformism, guilt felt by silent witnesses, responses to limit experiences, and the need to construct a narrative for even the most traumatic events.

A comparison of Humenna's novel with the diary she kept in the years 1941–

43 shows that the fictional account was a deliberate attempt to introduce a narrative of Jewish suffering, which the author tried to interweave with the story of Ukrainian suffering. This was a response to the Holocaust, and the need to recognize the tragedy. The inclusion of both stories of victimization is also part of the author's attempt to broaden the idea of the Ukrainian nation. Mariana's spiritual family includes Ukrainians and Jews, and the loss of Jewish friends is mourned as a loss of family members. After Babyn Yar, Mariana spends time in the deserted apartments of these Jewish friends, contemplating their lives and mourning their fate. Roza has been murdered by the Nazis. However, so has her friend Vasanta the communist sympathizer, and Olena Teliha the nationalist. Both have been tortured to death by the Gestapo. Mariana's spiritual family, her imagined nation, includes all these, indeed all who have throughout the millennia lived on the land and suffered its "ruins, colonizations, fusions, cross-pollinations, subjugations." (Ibid., 281.) She insists that the basic inhabitant, who has always been rooted in the land, has survived past catastrophes and will survive the present horrors. In this way, the novel grapples with the issue of who constitutes "family," what an inclusive identity should look like, and how a narrative of inclusiveness can be constructed. The writer's concept of community stretches racial and national categories to the point of dissolving them. She invokes the Trypillians, the Scythians, the Polovtsians, the Jews, and other peoples, who have all blended into or left their mark on the people and culture of today's Ukraine. It is a view of nation and *patria* that differs from the uncomplicated concept of one homogeneous ethnos to which some contemporary nationalists subscribed.

Humenna does not idolize a romantic or abstract image of the "folk." She well knows what the common people with their wonderful traditions are capable of. The following remarkable scene in the novel is an eyewitness account by the character Hnat:

> One day two very well brought-up young men came to the house—courteous, rosy-cheeked, with innocent blue eyes . . . obviously from a nice family. They asked very modestly for permission to have breakfast. They were so polite and modest that they asked for nothing; they had everything they needed. During breakfast all men in the small town were ordered to immediately gather in the square, so that the old man had to run off without eating anything. The polite young men offered to help the people of the house by taking breakfast to their father. You can immediately tell the old, time-honored culture with its respect for elders.
>
> They went, and then the women and children were also told to gather. In the middle of the square all the men of the small town and village were standing in

line surrounded by SS platoons. Every tenth man was selected and told to stand aside. The father was among them. These selected men were to be hanged. Ukrainian policemen were to do this, but they shook with fear; their hands trembled; one fainted; another began to cry. They were unable to do it. Then the two polite young men with innocent blue eyes, well-bred specialists in hanging, pushed aside the incompetent, useless policemen and expertly, professionally, quickly hanged those who had been selected, including the old man. The people, women and children, were surrounded to prevent them from running away and to force them to watch their relatives being hanged. There were cries to the heavens, sobbing; they went mad; turned gray.

How do you like my story? It is true, because that old man hanged by the sentimental-romantic youths was my father." (Ibid., 362–63.)

This passage is particularly interesting for the way it exposes instrumental rationality, the technological approach to the machinery of destruction. Mass murder becomes possible once it can be reduced to bureaucratic, technical problems, which become the focus of ordinary people involved in its execution. The passage also, of course, raises many questions concerning human responsibility, motivation, and the capacity for violence. How could these young men act with so little reflection? What had prepared them for such moral indifference? Although the passage does not refer to the killing of Jews, it supports the explanation of the Holocaust as the product of instrumental rationality—an issue that has since been widely debated. The passage undermines any view of violence as redemptive, as a way of galvanizing a debased mass, an idea implied in the writings of Dontsov. Humenna's position is close to that of Sherekh and other MUR writers. Her depiction of violence in the above passage is in fact an indirect critique of Dontsov, a suggestion that innocent, untroubled minds like the two young men described might have taken passages from his writings as a license to kill—one sanctioned by higher goals.

Humenna's writings appear to be some of the first by a Ukrainian eyewitness to describe the Holocaust in Kyiv. They predate by more than a decade Anatolii Kuznetsov's *Babii Yar*, which first appeared in heavily censored form in Russian in the Soviet Union and then caused a sensation when it was published in English translation in 1970, shortly after the author escaped to Britain. She deserves credit for portraying a range of public attitudes toward the Holocaust, for problematizing the issue of violence and the question of who forms part of the nation.

Other notable memoirs that devote attention to Jews and were produced at this time include: Fedir Pihido-Pravoberezhny's *"Velyka vitchyzniana viina"* ("The Great Patriotic War", 1954), which confirms many of Humenna's observations of wartime Kyiv; Semen Pidhainy's *Nedostriliani* (Survivors of Execution, 1949), which describes the author's interaction with Jewish fellow prisoners in the Gulag in the years 1933–37; and Volodymyr Makar's *Bereza Kartuzka (Spomyny z 1934–35 rr.)* (Bereza Kartuzka (Memoirs of 1934–35), 1956), which describes interaction between Ukrainians and Jews in the concentration camp set up by the Polish government in the mid-thirties. Many memoirs produced in the postwar years are scattered through numerous books, pamphlets, newspapers, and other periodicals, and have yet to be analyzed by scholars.

On the three-hundredth anniversary of the signing of the Pereiaslav Treaty (1654) between Muscovy and Ukraine, official Soviet literature produced a discourse around the figure of Bohdan Khmelnytsky and the 1648 uprising. In spite of the fact that the "anticosmopolitan" campaign was still in progress at the time, the literary depiction of Jews was markedly careful. Petro Panch's *Homonila Ukraina: Roman* (Ukraine Roared: A Novel, 1945–54) avoids mentioning them at all, referring only to leaseholders and tavernkeepers without providing any ethnic or national identification. The Cossacks are indignant that they have to bow to the orendar and pay him in order to christen a child. This is portrayed as part of the Polish plan to "uproot Ukraine, take its land, and give its church to the Union [of Brest]." The tavern is owned by Chapa, who is identified only as a Romanian. He is a stock character, a grasping leaseholder who heartlessly takes the Cossacks' fish to cover the rent he owes the lord and to enrich himself. The Cossacks are prevented from distilling their own liquor and must pay him for all their alcohol. He grows rich. His relations with the lord are close and when he suspects that homebrewed liquor is being consumed, he calls on his wife to summon the lord and have the offenders clapped in irons. However, it is the renting of churches that produces the greatest profit, and Chapa's wife Iona urges her husband to work with Pan Vazhynsky, who leases from the lord a small town that includes a church. Chapa fits the stereotype of the snooping, meddling, and duplicitous orendar, who tries to stay in the lord's good books by providing information on the Cossacks, but simultaneously fears the latter and tries to avoid antagonizing them. Although identified as a Romanian, Chapa's association with foreignness, leaseholding, and tavernkeeping recall past portrayals of Jews.

There is similarly almost no mention of Jews in Natan Rybak's *Pereiaslavs'ka rada: Roman* (The Pereiaslav Council: A Novel, 1953). A prominent author of Jewish origin, Rybak began publishing poetry in the thirties before making a reputation as a novelist. He followed the official party line unswervingly, portraying the unity of the Russian and Ukrainian people, and avoiding the intrusion of a Jewish voice. The postwar works that do contain Jewish characters portray them in a way that tries to reflect the regime's current thinking. One of his best-known novels, *Pomylka Onore de Balzaka* (Honoré de Balzac's Mistake, 1959) deals with Balzac's trip to Ukraine in 1847–50. The French writer's mistake consists in turning his back on literary work and marrying the wealthy Evelina Hanska, a Pole with an estate in Ukraine, as a way of escaping his debtors. There is an interesting side-plot that includes the poor innkeeper Leibko, his beautiful daughter Nekhama, and the rich banker Halperin. Rybak is anxious to demonstrate that class divisions exist in the Jewish community. Accordingly, Leibko is portrayed as a good man who is ruined by the unscrupulous banker. The latter is in contact with Rothschild in Western Europe and with the local Polish lord, for whom he procures the innkeeper's daughter. She commits suicide. As a result, her distraught and mentally unhinged father is left wandering from place to place, stopping carriages and asking for her. His agony is viewed with great sympathy by the local Ukrainians, though not by the Polish lords. He becomes known among local people as "the wandering Jew," an embodiment of suffering. After he identifies himself as such to some gendarmes, he is conducted to Berdychiv, where he dies. Jews are blamed by some of the population for epidemics and economic hard times: in Berdychiv several merchants are tarred and feathered, while a number of taverns along the highway are burned with their owners inside. As is evident from this summary, the story rehearses a number of stereotypes such as the indolent and exploitative Polish gentry; the scheming rich Jew who clings to this gentry, even though they despise him; and the wretched poor Jew who loses his only treasure, his daughter. The anti-Polish, anti-Western, and anticapitalist message conforms to Soviet requirements, but the book is perhaps most remarkable for the strong sympathy it expresses for a Jewish tragedy, in particular the destruction of Jewish innocence. A Ukrainian reader could not fail to notice the parallel with Shevchenko's *Haidamaky*. In Rybak's work, the tavernkeeper with the same name as the Jew in Shevchenko's work, is unable to protect his beautiful daughter from the lord, and she suffers the fate of Oksana in *Haidamaky*. Like Shevchenko's Yarema, Leibko is fated to search for the innocent that he is charged with protecting. Unlike Yarema, however, he cannot turn to violence or revenge, but can only lament his loss in a continual importuning of passersby.

These works by Panch and Rybak recapitulate the standard fictional topoi about Jews, but Rybak's book also includes a narrative of Jewish victimization, which can be read as an attempt to escape censorship restrictions. Other historical novels, such as Yurii Mushketyk's *Haidamaky* (Haidamakas, 1957), which is devoted to the 1768 uprising, and Oleksandr Ilchenko's playful *Kozats'komu rodu nema perevodu, abo zh Mamai i chuzha molodytsia: Ukrains'kyi khymernyi roman z narodnykh ust* (The Cossack Breed Continues, or Mamai and the Woman: A Ukrainian Whimsical Novel from Folklore, 1958) avoid any mention of Jews. They follow Soviet ideological prescriptions by extolling the union with Muscovy as an expression of Ukrainian history's teleological drive to fuse with Russia. Although avoidance of the Jewish theme was part of a directive from authorities to avoid particularism, at another level, even subconsciously, it perhaps expressed discomfort and a sense of guilt concerning the tragedy of the Jews during and immediately after the war.

Those who did write about Jews were sometimes criticized. In the less restrictive censorship of the sixties, a number of leading writers turned to the Jewish theme. Bazhan was perhaps the most prominent. His "Debora: Z knyhy umans'kykh spohadiv" (Deborah: From a Book of Uman Recollections, 1968) is a long poem that describes his admiration for a friend of his youth, Debora, a talented pianist and the daughter of a cantor in the synagogue. The poem evokes the lost world of Jewish-Ukrainian interaction that was an everyday feature of life in Uman. This world includes the legacies of the Baal Shem Tov and Skovoroda, both of whom saw the gloriously human "in each note and drop of water," the singing in the synagogue and that of kobzars. Melodies and songs of both Jewish and Ukrainian life are described as two rivers that flow into the complex harmony that fills Debora's soul. The cultural intermingling exists at every level against the architectural backdrop of Uman, which includes the hovels of the poor, a synagogue, a church, a Basilian monastery, icons covered in silver, and a well that was used by haidamakas. The synagogue's cantor has taught his daughter to value and praise all that is deeply human, all that is "hidden in every note, as in every droplet of the world." Her inspired playing captures and celebrates this unique Uman culture, bringing its treasures to the surface for listeners to recognize.

Debora's fate is tragic. During the revolution a pogrom takes place, in which she is raped by the leader of a local detachment of brutish soldiers. In 1920 Les Kurbas's troupe comes to the town and puts on a series of theatrical productions. The stories of the haidamakas, Macbeth, Oedipus, and Gonta come to life in marvelous re-creations. Kurbas sympathizes with the cantor and his daughter, whose talent he admires. He asks her to be the pianist with the Kyiv troupe and she performs brilliantly. Her music interweaves Chopin and Lysenko, the melodies of the steppe and those of Palestine. This daughter of two worlds gives a compelling, unforgettable performance. Later, during the Second World War, Debora, along with the town's other Jews, is herded to a ravine and machine-gunned. The poet now stands over the spot. He notices a solitary sunflower and wonders whether it is drawing from her essence. He muses about the possibility that she also gave it the desire to search for the sun, warmth, light, music, and beauty. The poem exhibits a powerful nostalgic yearning for a lost world. In the final lines the narrator reaches out and asks for Debora to give him her hand, so that they can once more walk through the lost romance that was Uman and relive their youth. A requiem for Jews destroyed in the war, the poem is also a reaffirmation of the politics of the postrevolutionary period, when in joint action Ukrainians and Jews tried not only to spread enlightenment and mutual respect, but also to create a cultural renaissance.

Religious imagery runs through Dmytro Pavlychko's books. His "Pokaianni psal'my" (Psalms of Contrition) are a virtuoso reworking of Hebrew texts, a self-examination and self-discovery, and his verse foreshadows a turn to biblical imagery in the work of many poets who began writing at this time, among them Vasyl Stus, Pavlo Movchan, Iryna Zhylenko, Viktor Kordun, and Lina Kostenko. As in the late nineteenth century, Ukrainian poets used biblical stories of Jewish suffering both to draw attention to anti-Jewish atrocities in the recent past, and also to draw parallels with their own victimization.

Prior to the arrests of 1972, Ukrainian literature showed considerable vitality. A number of excellent novels devoted to the Second World War were produced. They no longer focused on mass heroism or on epic depictions of the collective nation-at-war, as had usually been the case with novels of the fifties. Instead the new fiction examined individual motivation. More attention was paid to negative characters and to those in noncombatant roles, especially women and children. The best war novels, Hryhorii Tiutiunnyk's *Vyr* (Maelstrom, 1962), Leonid Pervomaisky's *Dykyi med* (Wild Honey, 1963), and Yevhen Hutsalo's *Mertva zona* (Dead Zone, 1966), were produced at this time. A powerful aesthetic consciousness is at work in this fiction, absorbing even the most monstrous aspects of human behavior into narratives that try to provide some closure to this past, and that anticipate a future in which human beings can live in peace. *Mertva zona* describes the fate of a village under German occupation, laying bare the appalling cruelty of victimizers, who include both German soldiers and the Ukrainian policeman in their service. The village community, however, knows it will survive and that the troubles of the present will pass. There is no world beyond this community; it is a universe unto itself and appears indestructible. Out of these three novels, only *Dykyi med* explicitly discusses the Jewish theme, which it raises in several ways. The theme resonates in the idea that a human being cannot be happy at the cost of someone else's suffering. "Happiness," as one character muses, "is achieved by everyone being happy. It is not diminished, but augmented, when divided among millions of hearts." (Pervomais'kyi 1966, 113.) The human need for, and right to, happiness is the novel's guiding idea. It pursues all the main protagonists. The way this idea is handled relates it to both the Stalinist past and the Hitlerite present. The novel makes clear that there are crimes in Soviet history that affect the lives of soldiers and citizens as much as does the contemporary war. A number of characters have participated in or been victims of Stalin's terror. They are continually processing this past mentally, relating it to the present, and to the broader issue of how to live a good life. At the end of the book, life continues for the survivors, happiness is rediscovered, even though, like the wild honey of the novel's title, it often has a slightly bitter taste. Many readers, aware of Pervomaisky's earlier work, have appreciated the book's sensitivity to all forms of persecution, and to the sense of guilt many felt at having been accomplices to state crimes.

Mynia is a young Jewish soldier with whom Liuda falls in love. She is denounced by Demian, a Christian who thinks of Jews as betrayers of Christ. But Liuda grasps at the temporary wartime happiness that her affair with Mynia brings, even though she realizes that when he departs and her husband returns from the front she will pay a heavy price. Mynia is handsome and fun-loving, but he is entirely focused on the immediate present. In trying to extract the maximum happiness from the moment, he does not care to scrutinize, or fails to understand, the wider implications of his actions: "Mynia lived his vegetative existence unaware of the difference between good and evil, ignorant of shame, or the tortures and reproaches of conscience. Every minute of his existence he felt himself to be a marvelous boy, who was extraordinarily successful in life: everything flowed into his hands, he had countless friends, women loved him, more than that—they flew to him like moths to a flame, and they forgave him things that they would not have forgiven another." (Ibid., 364.) Although Mynia himself has to deal with a few anti-Semitic comments, this is less important for an understanding of his character than is his unreflecting nature, which does not recognize the line between right and wrong, and is therefore prepared to cross it. Mynia's character is contrasted with that of a front-line soldier, Somo Shraibman. The unassuming Shraibman exemplifies Jewish participation in military action. He and his Armenian companion Aram Guloian are assigned to a machine-gun post. A female photographer arrives to take pictures of a German tank that Shraibman and Guloian have disabled and which is located in the no-man's-land between enemy lines. Shraibman and Guloian, who showed great courage in resisting the last tank attack and risked their lives to destroy this particular tank, are to be decorated for this feat. As the photographer crawls to the tank, takes the required photographs, and returns, she comes under fire. Shraibman sees a German soldier, who is also crawling to the tank in order to shoot the photographer, saves her by killing the German, and loses his own life in the act. His medal cannot even be presented to the Shraibman family because they are all "in occupied territory." Ironically, the photographer does not realize what has occurred until she returns to her base and develops the photographs, at which point she notices the German soldier. Not only does this episode show the courage and self-sacrifice of troops in front-line action, it demonstrates the modest behavior of the countless real heroes, and the often unappreciated and unrecognized nature of their sacrifices.

To underscore this point, an unpleasant press correspondent by the name of Upovaichenkov is introduced. He files "patriotic" reports which present the war in uplifting terms, while avoiding any discussion of ugly, unseemly, and depressing realities. He omits numerous details that he deems unnecessary, and the picture of war he creates loses any sense of authenticity. The correspondent is convinced that "by amending truth, he was making it more truthful." (Ibid., 345.) Among the facts he fails to mention are Shraibman's obviously Jewish name: "Shraibman got in Upovaichenko's way, and he mentioned him only in passing, as Guloian's comrade, without mentioning his surname. 'In any case Shraibman is already dead, and he does not need any glory,' Upovaichenkov thought to himself." (Ibid.) This episode is Pervomaisky's answer to the charge that Jews were not present at the front and his explanation for why they were sometimes omitted from descriptions of wartime action.

Borys Kharchuk's *Volyn': Roman, Knyha chetverta* (Volhynia: A Novel, Book Four, 1966) deals with the Nazi occupation and the Jewish genocide. Villagers react variously to the treatment of their Jewish neighbors by the invading German troops. The Jewish Rezia and the Ukrainian Ilko have planned to marry. As the killing begins, many Jews escape to the woods. Rezia and her family are told by a gun-wielding neighbor to follow him to the ghetto where all Jews have been told to meet. He does not, however, take them all the distance, but allows them the possibility of hiding in the woods. Although the rest of her family is executed, Rezia survives and is found by Ilko in a hut with other Jews. The two decide to escape together from the village, but while Ilko buys clothes in preparation for their journey, his mother, fearing for her son's safety, informs the police in another village of Rezia's presence. Fortunately, Ilko's friends in this village realize what is happening and enable the couple to escape.

One scene describes the expropriation of Jewish property. A villager takes a

horse, though not without a fight, from his Jewish neighbor Hershko, because
the German officer in charge of the village has given instructions that anything
taken from villagers by the former regime may now be taken back twofold from
any Jew. In another subplot an older Jew, Tsal, survives the war by forcing himself on his neighbor. He threatens to inform the Germans that the neighbor was
paid to get him out of the ghetto, which is untrue but cannot be disproved. There
is therefore nothing heroic about the neighbor's decision to shelter Tsal, although he does try to receive some sort of reward for this after the war. Nor is
Tsal an endearing character. Indeed it is largely because of the incongruous and
inconceivable relationship between the two men that Tsal's presence goes unsuspected and undetected. In this way, Kharchuk depicts some complexities of
wartime conduct, and the presence of widely differing responses to the fate of
Jews, which range from active support of German intentions to active opposition.

The treatment of Jews during the war is raised in a cautious, indirect manner
in Yurii Shcherbak's *Likari* (Doctors, 1964) and his *Khronika mista Iaropolia*
(Chronicle of the Town of Yaropol, 1986). (Shcherbak became independent
Ukraine's first ambassador to Israel in 1991.) An episode in the latter novel deals
with the Nazi interest in craniology as a method of establishing the superiority of
one race over another, and with Hitler's obsession with racial purity. In the novel
a dim-witted German officer, Shtiupnagel, is obsessed with what he describes as
the pollution of Arian blood.

Pavlo Zahrebelny's *Ia, Bohdan* (I, Bohdan, 1983) returns to the events of
1648, taking up the issue of the Jewish pogroms in a way that had been avoided
in the novels of the fifties devoted to this period. The orendar Zakharii Saby-
lenko is identified as a Jew. He controls almost half the county, including fields,
meadows, mills, ponds, and woods. However, because he has to turn most of the
money over to the lord, his profits are meager. At the lord's orders, he leases
Khmelnytsky's estate of Subotiv, and this drives Khmelnytsky to challenge the
lord to a duel. The orendar warns Khmelnytsky that the lord, Chaplynsky, will
play foul and advises him to wear a metal vest, a precaution that saves Khmelnytsky's life when the lord sends three armed men to kill him at the appointed spot.
After the uprising, the orendar agrees to give Khmelnytsky restitution. In return
neither the orendar nor his tavern are threatened. Following victories in great
battles, Samiilo, one of the Cossacks, brings Khmelnytsky news of the murder
of Jews: "The old and young are being slaughtered, burned, drowned in rivers
. . . the sacred Jewish books are used to line the streets, torn into long shreds.
The priests consecrate the killings. In their presence orendars are put to the

knife, drawn and quartered to avenge their alleged writing in chalk on the blessed breads which they sold the Orthodox faithful." (Zahrebel'nyi 2001, 352.) The hetman defends himself, saying that he has ordered some tavernkeepers not be touched, and also points out that Jews are exploiters. Samiilo, however, reminds him of the impoverishment of most Jews, and the need for fairness and mercy: "Did the Jews shed blood here? Did they kill? Do they take up arms against the Cossacks? You will say: the leaseholders tortured us, they locked the churches, made old men and women plow the ice. But did all Jews act this way? And did they act alone, or under *szlachta* [Polish gentry] orders? And how many poor Jews are there and how impoverished are they? Are they also guilty in everything?" (Ibid., 354.) Samiilo goes on to express sympathy for the Jews as a diasporic nation who have been driven to certain professions by their situation. They have preserved the memory of their past, and should be admired for this. In spite of the accusations leveled against Jews, this was one of the most outspoken descriptions of anti-Jewish violence in Soviet literature since the 1920s. It broke the taboo on mentioning this aspect of the uprising and, in doing so, presented an entirely different portrait of Khmelnytsky.

The hetman is shown as aware of his powerlessness to entirely control events. He makes a journey to Nestervar on the outskirts of Tulchyn, where he is informed of atrocities that have been committed, in particular of a massacre organized by a Captain Zabusky. Khmelnytsky learns that after having been robbed of their possessions, between one and three thousand Jews, many of whom had fought against the Cossacks, were driven into a cherry orchard and given the choice of conversion or death. After they refused conversion, they were killed, although the Cossacks at first refused to obey the order.

The hetman visits the scene of the atrocity and orders that the captain be put in irons. When a kobzar uses his sword to strum on a *bandura*, Khmelnytsky smashes the instrument with the words: "A sword is for shedding blood, strings are for mourning the bloodshed!" He himself sings a song lamenting the loss of life and delivers an impassioned speech to the gathered troops on the crime of killing the unarmed, the wretched, the old and weak, and the widowed. He then orders the Cossacks to return to the place of the tragedy, to find the survivors, bandage their wounds, feed and clothe them, and conduct them to the border. The hetman is partially motivated by the realization that these events will darken his reputation.

Departing from previous portrayals of Khmelnytsky, the novel shows him as a composer and singer of songs. As a result, he is highly conscious of the way in which lyrics will help to create a historical legacy. In none of his songs is there any echo of the two anti-Jewish dumas that Panteleimon Kulish transcribed. This is clearly an attempt to move away from a harmful stereotype and to challenge the portrayals of the 1648 uprising that drew on them. It can also be seen as a challenge to the weight placed on the two dumas in descriptions of these events. Zahrebelny's portrayal of the massacre has a distinctly contemporary feel to it, and can be read as an oblique reference to the murder of Jews during the Second World War. The concern with controlling historical memory is also revealing in this regard. Not only is this a tacit admission of Khmelnytsky's own damaged reputation, it can be interpreted more broadly as an understanding that any military struggle is tainted by such killings. In this way a subdued reflection on the horrors of the Holocaust and atrocities committed in the forties makes its way into the narrative.

Unlike in the West, where the Eichmann trial made the Holocaust an important part of public discourse after the 1960s, there was no official memory of the Holocaust in the Soviet Union. The memorialization of the Holocaust and the construction of official accounts began only recently. The partial guilt of Ukrainians in the destruction of Jews during the war was recognized by President Kravchuk in 1991. At this time the state began annual commemorations of the Babyn Yar tragedy and built monuments at sites of mass execution and burial of Holocaust victims.

In the late eighties Ukrainian literature began to describe the Holocaust in more explicit terms. Volodymyr Yavorivsky's *Vichni Kortelisy* (Eternal Kortelisy) is set in the Volhynian village of Kortelisy in which 2,892 people were shot by the Germans with the aid of the Ukrainian police in 1942. The account uses eyewitness testimony presented during the postwar trial of a number of the perpetrators. It portrays an SS Major, Golling, who works for one of the extermination brigades, employing a heavily sarcastic tone in describing Golling's ideas about destroying the planet's "lower races." Volodymyr Drozd's *Knyha blukaiuchoi v pusteli* (The Book of a Woman Wandering in the Desert, 1996) depicts the ignorance and political blindness of a woman who worships Stalin. Easily manipulated, she is incapable of understanding the tragic fate of those around her, including the Jews. It is a commentary on the loss of historical memory in an entire generation. Anatolii Dimarov had earlier written an unpublished story dealing with events leading up to collectivization and the famine of 1932–33 entitled "Trydtsiati (Prytcha pro khlib)" (The Thirties: A Parable About Bread, 1966, published 1988). Hryhorii Ginsburg, the secretary of a regional party committee in the Poltava oblast, writes a letter to Stalin questioning the wisdom of forced collectivization. He is denounced at a public meeting, removed from his position, and told to surrender his party card. Ginsburg takes out a gun and shoots himself. Like some other farmers, he chooses to speak out and pays for this with his life. Other characters are quick to denounce Ginsburg and support the party in order to gain promotion. In the late eighties Dimarov published *Symon-riznyk* (Simon the Butcher, 1988), which was made into a film in 1991 and is one of the more powerful stories dealing with the Holocaust. In 1932 Simon moves with his family from Odesa to a village near Kyiv. An excellent butcher, an exemplary family man with five sons, and a great storyteller, he has many friends and lives in peace with everyone. Drafted into the army, he hears about Germans killing Jews, but "for a long time did not in his heart of hearts believe this. After all, how could one aim to destroy an entire people? Even animals are incapable of that, while the Germans, one must accept, are people and not all of them are fascists . . . to destroy all the Jews for nothing, just because they were born Jews—this was impossible to grasp." (Dimarov 1988b, 194.)

As he witnesses atrocities, he goes through a psychological change, becoming gloomy and withdrawn, and thinking constantly about his wife and children, who, he realizes, have probably been killed. He is captured, harnessed to a carriage, and made to pull a German officer who enjoys treating him like an animal, even keeping him locked in a stable. Simon eventually takes his revenge by killing the officer and escaping. When finally captured after a fierce fight in which he kills a number of soldiers, he is hanged. The reader is informed that this remarkable story is still recalled by the villagers. It captures the transformation of a serene rural environment by the brutality of war, and conveys the shock felt by ordinary people at the cruel treatment of Jews by the Nazis.

The Contemporary Jewish Voice: Moisei Fishbein and Naum Tykhy

One of the most prominent contemporary Ukrainian poets is the Israeli citizen and Ukrainian émigré Moisei Fishbein. He represents the generation of Jewish writers who made their debut in literature in the 1970s. Fishbein was born in 1946 in Chernivtsi, a city with a mixture of cultures: German, Ukrainian, Jewish, Romanian, Polish, and Russian. It produced, among others, the German-language writer Paul Celan (Paul Antschel/Ancel). More importantly, it has for centuries had a strong, rooted, and self-confident Jewish population—one that had largely lived on good terms with its Ukrainian neighbors and become Ukrainianized. Fishbein's first collection, *Iambove kolo: Poezii, pereklady*

(Iambic Circle: Poems, Translations, 1974) was published with the help of Mykola Bazhan.

After leaving Soviet Ukraine in 1979, Fishbein lived and worked for a number of years in Germany for Radio Svoboda's Ukrainian section, and then moved to Israel. Although translated into Hebrew, he is widely known as a prominent figure in twentieth-century Ukrainian poetry. His collections include *Iambove kolo* (1974), *Bez nazvy* (Without a Name, 1984), *Apokryf* (Apocryphal Writing, 1996). They are influenced by his Jewish experience, but Fishbein lives with considerable ease in both the Jewish and the Ukrainian worlds, combining identities and patriotisms in a natural, unselfconscious manner. This also comes through in his essays on postwar Chernivtsi, "Povernennia do Merydiana" (Return to the Meridian), and on his interaction with literary figures in the 1970s, "Vidstan' piznannia" (Distance of Recognition), which was published in his *Apokryf.*

The poet does not avoid the tragic experience of the Second World War and the Holocaust: one of his most compelling poems, "Iar" (Ravine), deals with Babyn Yar. Yet he is also moved by a profound respect for the Ukrainian language and culture. Dismay at their forcible marginalization is a strong source of inspiration. In his "Netorkani y gvaltovani" (The Untouched and the Raped) the language is described as a raped child:

> Untouched and raped, used up
> And untouchable, like the field's
> Inexpressible and unblemished melody
> In the rye, the words came to me in dreams.
>
> And the dark thickens wintry
> And sleet drenches our souls.
> Cuddle up to me, my little language, my Language,
> Untouched, raped, and sacred. (Fishbein 1996, 12.)

Petrovsky-Shtern feels that Fishbein borrowed the idea of the language's sanctity from Judaic religious tradition and placed this "at the gravitational centre of his Jewish-Ukrainian symbolism." (Petrovsky-Shtern 2004, 16–17.) In this respect he is a disciple of Lesia Ukrainka, whose verse he greatly admires and who has profoundly influenced him. Like Ukrainka he infuses the power of biblical tradition into Ukrainian sentiments, endowing the language with redemptive and uplifting powers.

Whether residing in Israel or in Kyiv, Fishbein writes almost exclusively in Ukrainian and continually examines aspects of the Jewish Ukrainian identity and its path of development. Significantly, in "Ia vbytyi buv shistnadtsiatoho roku" (I Was Killed in '16) he suggests a return to the failed rapprochement of the prerevolutionary years. In this poem, he portrays himself as having been killed during a pogrom in 1916, a fatal turning point, but also foresees a time when he will be resurrected.

The poet combines and reconciles the two aspects of his identity in a number of ways. One is by mixing New and Old Testament imagery. Another is by marrying the cities of Jerusalem and Kyiv. Although critics have sometimes emphasized Fishbein's borderline position, it would be more accurate to speak about his remarkably successful fusion of identities. He is a Ukrainian poet who happens to be a Jew. In this respect he might be compared to the poets of the New York group, who wrote on various themes and experimented with various forms, considering themselves Ukrainian writers who happened to be Westerners. Skurativsky senses this successful integration of perspectives when he writes: "In the poetry of Moisei Fishbein Judaism speaks, for the first time in its history, in Ukrainian." (Skurativs'kyi 1996, 86.) It is precisely for this reason that Fishbein has become a symbol of pluralism and tolerance in the postindependence period. During the 2004 presidential campaign he even accompanied Victor Yushchenko on a pre-election tour.

Fishbein's best poetry rises above contemporary concerns and transports the reader to a realm of deep serenity, where the mind concentrates on the details of human perception and sensation. Poems like "Zdaleka" (From Afar), "Rika" (River) and "Krym: Lito" (Crimea: Summer) focus on poetry's ability to convey the purely physical experience of living in the moment. His themes are eternity, existence, and nonexistence, the imprint left by a life and a consciousness. A neo-classicist's love of formal restraint (the sonnet, iambic structure, careful selection of imagery, limiting of the colors described to black or white) is combined with an associativeness reminiscent of Celan or Neruda. (Shevelov 1984, 9.) The poetic forms chosen impose order on the world, but leave room for various interpretations and the play of whimsical imagination.

It has been suggested that the creative tension between Jewishness and Ukrainianness has worked its way into the poet's language and characteristic literary devices, such as the imagery of white and black, and the love of rhymes that are homonyms and paronyms. These draw attention to the phonetic similarities of two words while simultaneously revealing their different meanings. Whether one concludes, as does Petrovsky-Shtern, that "in his universe Ukrainian and Jewish identities are similar only on a superficial level but are dramatically incongruent in substance" is debatable. (Petrovsky-Shtern 2004, 19.) One might also argue that the tension between aspects of a single identity is his required stimulus for writing.

Fishbein comes at the end of a century-long discourse on Jewish Ukrainian identity among Jewish writers, who include Kernerenko, Troyanker, Pervomaisky, and Naum Tykhy. Like them he articulates some of the dilemmas faced in the construction of this identity, which might be seen as following an evolutionary dynamic: from orphanhood (Kernerenko) and duality (Troyanker), through the struggle for self-definition as "Soviet" Ukrainians (Pervomaisky), to an almost seamless fusion of Jewish and Ukrainian components (Fishbein, Tykhy). Or, in another way of thinking, this evolution models possible ways that the Ukrainian Jew can be perceived: as an outsider, as a partially visible and uncomfortably positioned insider, or as a fully visible and accepted insider.

Some older writers of Jewish origin went through remarkable changes in the postindependence period, in ways that recalls Pervomaisky's late poetry. Abram Katsnelson, who was born in 1914, published his *Poklyk vysoty: Poezii 1993–1996* (Summons of the Heights: Poems, 1993–1996) and *U nimbi syvyny: Novi poezii, 1997–1998* (In the Halo of Gray Old Age: New Poetry, 1997–1998) in Los Angeles, the city to which he moved after the Soviet Union's collapse. In these poems he looks back on the Soviet period as one of fanaticism and ignorance, and expresses shame for the lies of poets and historians. A similar tone of wistful regret mixed with an acceptance of the need for a full and honest retrospective is assumed by Naum Tykhy (Shtilerman) in his *Smak osinn'oho vitru: Poezii* (Taste of Autumn Wind: Poetry, 1996). In "Molytva za Ukrainu" (Prayer for Ukraine) Tykhy underlines his Ukrainian patriotism in a way that hearkens back to Kernerenko. He says that he has always called Ukraine his mother, because from childhood

> With a grateful heart I have taken the warmth
> Of a mother's bosom and believe
> That in your family I am no stepson.
>
> From the cradle you gave me
> Your soaring language; from your deep sources
> I drank and still drink strength; your spirit
> Is the life of my core . . . (Tykhyi 1996, 7–8.)

Tykhy is also the author of verse dramas dealing with the issues of power, man's inhumanity to man, and the refusal to accept difference. The most outspoken and provocative of these were written between 1988 and 1992. *Peredmova: Dramatychna poema-hipoteza* (Preface: A Dramatic Poem-Hypothesis, 1989–90) and *Pisliamova: Variant 1* (Epilogue: Version 1, 1991–93) depict the re-creation of the human species on another planet by highly evolved descendants of today's humanity. The plays suggest that the new society will relive all human history, with its inevitable conflicts. The domination of one social group over another will be repeated due to the inextricable intermingling in human nature of the ignoble with the beastly. Each one of these plays describes a postapocalyptic situation in which the reader is encouraged to contemplate the roots of human wickedness. *Ahasfer (Dramatychna poema-nahad)* (Ahasuerus: A Dramatic Poem-Reminder), 1988–91) deals explicitly with the tragedy of the Jews. It depicts the arrival of Ahasuerus, the Wandering Jew, in Nazi-dominated Germany shortly before *Krystallnacht*. He convinces an assimilated German Jew called Ferdinand (who refuses to believe that any such barbarity might be possible in the land of Bach and Goethe) that the destruction of the Jews is imminent. Ahasuerus shows him on a screen the Jewish past and future, in this way demonstrating the cyclical recurrence of violence. The history of pogroms and expulsions is reviewed. It covers Spain, France, Germany, Switzerland, Bohemia, and Poland, the accusation of being Christ-killers, and the blood libel from Norwich to the Beilis trial in Kyiv. Ferdinand realizes that even though his parents were not religious and he considers himself German, this will not prevent him from being persecuted, because the current wave of anti-Semitism uses "racial" criteria. His fiancée's father returns from the police station horrified to have unexpectedly discovered that a grandmother in the family was Jewish.

The action then shifts to the Soviet Union during the postwar anti-Semitic campaign. The same Ahasuerus appears here and teaches another character, Feliks, a similar history lesson. He shows Feliks scenes from Auschwitz and Babyn Yar, then local Soviet militiamen who discuss the treatment of Jews. They complain that it is impossible to distinguish Jews from Russians because today Jews all speak the language and have changed their surnames. Nonetheless, the militiamen affirm that Jews are all gradually being identified, and will soon be shipped to Siberia, because of their desire "to hand the Crimea over to Israel." Ahasuerus convinces Feliks that the sufferings and miseries of Jews are continually repeated, and someone has to patiently carry this burden. In the play's brief final scene a couple of contemporary militia officers discuss the fact that all Jews should leave Russia, describe the appearance of the anti-Semitic Pamiat organization in Russia, and mention the murder of a local Jewish woman. Ahasuerus, a witness to the sufferings of Jewry throughout the ages, provides the thread between all these illuminating scenes. The reader learns that his identity is assumed by different individuals in different generations, and the final deed of this particular Ahasuerus is to pass on the torch of memory to the unwilling Feliks.

CHAPTER 9

Postindependence Ironies

On the eve of independence Jews in Ukraine were still predominantly Russian-speaking. In 1989 only 2 percent gave Ukrainian as their mother tongue and initially they showed considerable skepticism towards the new Ukrainian state. During the eighties and in the decade after independence approximately a million left Russia and Ukraine, partly because of the economic crisis and partly because they feared a revival of anti-Semitism. However, the Eastern European successor states did not conduct anti-Semitic politics or prevent emigration. In 1992 the Ukrainian parliament accepted a law that guaranteed national, cultural, and religious rights to minorities. Jewish institutions received government support and a revival of community life occurred. Hundreds of local and national Jewish organizations now exist in Ukraine, where there were none in 1988. There are some seventy-four Jewish communities, about forty-three rabbis and synagogues, many schools, study groups, and a Jewish University (Solomon University in Kyiv). Some synagogues confiscated in Soviet times have been returned. Holy places of Judaism where leading tzaddiks lived are being preserved in Medzhybozh, Hadiach, Berdychiv, and Uman, and have become places of pilgrimage. Monuments have been erected in many places where Jews were murdered during the Holocaust. Jewish scholarly institutions have been created in Kyiv—among them the Department of Jewish History and Culture at the Ukrainian Academy of Sciences, and the Judaica Institute—which have encouraged a renascence of Jewish studies. Through publications and conferences they aim to create the ground for mutual understanding and acceptance in a multicultural society. Many archival and museum collections are once more available for study, such as the National Library of Ukraine's remarkable collection of Jewish musical folklore, which, among other things, has about twelve hundred Edison phonographic cylinders recorded early in the twentieth century. The Museum of Historical Treasures of Ukraine has restored Jewish ritual silverware, which was originally bought from private individuals in the years 1912–14. According to the census of 2001 there were 103,000 Jews living in Ukraine, but since there is no obligation to declare one's nationality the true figure is difficult to estimate. (Zisel's 2000, 218.)

In spite of the improving economic situation, the first years of the twenty-first century saw an increase in incidents of anti-Semitism, including attacks on individuals, and the vandalizing of monuments and synagogues. Anti-Semitic materials have been printed by a number of newspapers including *Za vil'nu Ukrainu* (For a Free Ukraine) and *Vechirnii Kyiv* (Evening Kyiv), and some that represent marginal political groups: *Neskorena natsiia* (Unvanquished Nation), *Nezboryma natsiia* (Invincible Nation), and *Holos natsii* (Voice of the Nation). These last are the organs, respectively, of OUN v Ukraini (OUN in Ukraine), DSU (State Independence of Ukraine), and UNA-UNSO (Ukrainian National Assembly-Ukrainian National Self-Defense). They are only a handful among hundreds of newspapers and their influence on political and cultural life is small. Since 2002, an estimated 70 percent of anti-Semitic publications have emanated from MAUP (Interregional Academy of Personnel Management), a large degree-giving institution that is reported to have received funding from Libya, Palestine, Saudi Arabia, and Iran. (Rudling 2006, 85–86.) Among its publications are Vasyl Yeremenko's *Zhydotriepanie . . .* (Jew-Beating . . . , 2005), an anthology of texts taken mainly from the works of Kulish and Kostomarov, and Olena Pchilka's *Vykynuti ukraintsi* (Rejected Ukrainians, 2006), a collection of her journalism from 1908 to 1914. Yeremenko's introduction to the first collection accuses Jews of ritual murders (mentioning in support the fact that in 1820 the Russian Orthodox Church canonized a boy whom it claimed had been killed by Jews in 1690). The author unequivocally accepts the contents of the two dumas dealing with 1648 as historical evidence, and attributes revolutionary terrorism (including the 1881 assassination of the tsar) to the Jews. Anti-Semitic cartoons from the Russian press of the 1880s are reproduced with comments that provide a contemporary spin in order to send a racist message that Jewish perverseness has remained the same throughout the ages. The second collection is introduced by Valerii Arkhypov. He also refers to folklore as evidence of the widespread despotism of orendars, suggesting that Mendel Beilis was guilty of a ritual killing, and deplores the vigorous protests against this libel by the liberal intelligentsia (including Hrushevsky). Like Yeremenko, Arkhypov draws support from reactionary Russian authors who published anti-Semitic brochures in 1912 and 1917. These attempts to revive long-discredited stereotypes have led to letters of protest in the press.

Zisels has praised the legislature for creating legal conditions that allow cultural communities and minorities to develop, and has commented that the prominence of xenophobia, including anti-Semitism, in the general picture of Ukrainian life has diminished. But he has expressed concern with the lack of re-action to xenophobic publications. He puts it this way: "When in France a few years ago monuments in the Jewish cemetery in Lyon were destroyed, all France, together with the president, came out onto the streets in a demonstration of protest. Therefore, 15 percent of the electorate of France giving their vote to Le Pen worries me less than a hundred times fewer anti-Semites in Ukraine." (Ibid., 182.) Zisels sees the creation of strong Jewish communities with support in Ukrainian society as the best way of removing anti-Semitism to the periphery of social life. The larger issue, as he points out, is not overcoming phobias, but the construction of a civil society that can apply checks and balances, and pre-vent a chain reaction that could lead to mass folly.

The literature written after 1991 has challenged earlier myths and master nar-ratives, often ridiculing them as outdated conventions. Not only Soviet reality but a large range of stereotypes and sacred cows have been presented in an ironic, de-mystifying, and often playful tone. The ironists have been a dominant current. They demonstrate a high degree of comfort with the idea of cultural pluralism, multiple viewpoints, and changing perspectives, and reveal a large capacity for viewing their own national mythologies with a relaxed skepticism. Tamara Hun-dorova considers the Chornobyl disaster of 1986 as the crucial turning point, af-ter which critical attitudes that had been dominant in the underground emerged into the open and took on a mass character. (Hundorova 2005, 29.)

Vasyl Kozhelianko's *Defiliada v Moskvi* (Parade in Moscow, 1998) is an example of this ironic prose. The novel presents a bold alternative history, turn-ing the events of the Second World War upside down. The German blitzkrieg against the Soviet Union has brought victory in a few months. The Germans and their allies, who include the OUN, are to participate in a victory parade planned to take place in Moscow on November 7, 1941. The new Ukrainian president, Stepan Bandera, is to appear there together with Hitler and Mussolini. Ukraine has now become a military power, having supplied a million troops for the war effort, and other nations clamor to ally themselves with this emerging state. Schoolboys compose essays on national history that are full of inflated rhetoric. Jews are only mentioned once in the book: Ukraine's Jewish citizens have expressed loyalty to the country and have even supplied enough volunteers to form a regiment to fight on the eastern front. There is no mention of the Holocaust or of the German policy of racial genocide. Only at the end of the book does the main protagonist realize that Hitler has no interest in aiding Ukraine and that a struggle against the German Reich is inevitable. Although the novel does nothing to present the tragic side of the war, it effectively parodies—even in its hyperboles and silences—a new "national" presentation of history that in the nineties was even making its way into some school textbooks. Travestied through hyperbole are the ideas that the OUN and UPA were the only expression of national identity, and that the entire Ukrainian nation supported this movement. Omitted is the idea that the OUN and UPA fought both the Soviets and the Nazis. The novel's action suggests that, on the contrary, OUN's secret hope was the creation of a Ukrainian state under German protection in return for military support—the height, in fact, of collaborationism. The fantasy that sustains this hope is elaborated in the scenario that has the Ukrainian state within a matter of weeks becoming powerful enough to break with and challenge Hitler. The long-nurtured dream of an independent and powerful Ukrainian state is parodied in the visionary goal of an Empire of the Three Seas. Kozhelianko's purpose may have been to draw out the implications of the politics embraced by some OUN supporters, demonstrating in this way the improbable, indeed irrational, nature of the fantasies that underpinned this politics. His fiction can therefore be seen as an exploration of the wish-fulfillment and self-delusion that influenced many in the wartime and postwar generations.

Kozhelianko has continued to publish novels of alternative history. His *Sribnyi pavuk* (Silver Spider, 2004) places the action in Romanian-ruled Bukovyna on the eve of the Second World War. The two main characters, a German and a Ukrainian, are detectives. The first gradually falls under the spell of Hitlerism, joins the National Socialist Party, and becomes a secret agent of the Reich. He competes with his former Ukrainian colleague in discovering a lost treasure, the thirty pieces of silver thrown away by Judas. When the detectives realize that this treasure brings disaster to anyone who owns it, they melt the coins down and recast the metal into a cross, destroying its evil powers. This final act probably suggests another wish-fulfilling fantasy: the desire to end the evil spell cast over the world by two millennia of Christian-Jewish antagonisms.

When Jewish characters make cameo appearances in the literature of the nineties, they are sometimes a benevolent presence, such as trusted wise men and advisors on existential problems. The surrounding world is usually one in which fundamental values are being questioned, new answers to life's imponderables explored, and no easy solutions to individual dilemmas offered. Such is the case in Oles Ulianenko's *Stalinka* (1994), in which an aged Jew's otherworldliness and religious faith insulate and protect him from the mad environment in which he lives, one that resembles a lunatic asylum. Jewish characters occur in *Adept* (The Adept, 1997) by Volodymyr Yeshkilev and Oleh Hutsuliak. The narrative is purportedly an account written in the ninth century by Oleksii, a Slav from Kyiv who was captured and transported to the land of the Khazars by the Caspian Sea, where his skills as a physician put him in touch with the rulers. (Khazaria appeared in the seventh century and around the year 798 adopted Judaism as the state religion.) The hero describes beginning life as a worshiper of Dazhboh, the sun god and chief pagan deity of the Slavs, and then learning about Judaism, Christianity, and other faiths. This narrator juxtaposes and compares the pagan, Judaic, and Christian worlds that he must negotiate. Khazaria is a tolerant society in which many religions coexist. Although the seventy-two leading families, whose ancestors came from the south, are Jewish, there are Christian (Greek and Armenian) communities, Pechenegs, Northern Bulgars, Muslims, and many other groups. Indeed the state is dependent on this layering of cultures and their continued interaction for political survival. Oleksii learns several languages, reads the holy books of the major religions, and witnesses the great wars that finally bring down the polity. He has been provided with secret, though cryptic information concerning the location of the Ark of the Covenant and of an ancient text written by the prophet Jeremiah. After Khazaria's fall, he travels to Egypt and attempts to discover their hiding place. The novel is not only an imaginative tour de force that integrates a great deal of fascinating historical, religious, and cultural information—much of it about Judaism—but is an implicit argument for the benefits of cultural diversity.

A later book by Yeshkilev, *Pafos* (Pathos, 2002) is set in two places, Stanislaviv (Ivano-Frankivsk) and Jerusalem, and also blends ancient, medieval, and modern faith systems into a syncretism of the pagan, the cabbalistic, and the Christian. Like other writers from Ivano-Frankivsk, Yeshkilev has a strong sense of the layered history of space. His imaginative topography constructs Stanislaviv as a metaphysical and mystical place whose existence has from the first been planned and projected into future centuries by forces of which the local inhabitants are unaware. Among the various belief-systems that have combined to create the history of this space is one fundamental binary opposition-unity: Slavic superstition and folklore on the one side, and Jewish cabbalistic and biblical teaching on the other. Yeshkilev suggests that the city's identity is a fusion of these elements. The novel's plot leads to a pessimistic conclusion: the leading characters discover that whether employed in Jerusalem or Stanislaviv they are exploited by the ruthless mafias that dominate society.

Like Yeshkilev, Yurii Andrukhovych also lives in Ivano-Frankivsk, and also accepts, indeed celebrates, the mixing and mingling, confronting and clashing of different traditions. His works demonstrate a drive for inclusiveness, a refusal to efface stories and histories, voices and memories. This attitude aligns itself with the rejection of any narrow view of the nation. Andrukhovych's prose is intellectually playful, demystifying, and often humorous. It presents various narrative voices in conversation with one another, and delights in ridiculing populist mythology. Concerning his own motivation and that of his fellow writers Viktor Neborak and Oleksandr Irvanets (together they constituted the avant-garde Bu-Ba-Bu group), he has written: "literature directed and tempted us with undomesticated nooks, unpopulated spaces, and outdated taboos that we wanted so much to break." (Andrukhovych 1994, 14.) Theirs was conceived as an "adult" literature that would shatter populist culture's naïve self-image of innocence and purity. Literature, he wrote, attracted them because of its modesty, "which is so becoming in every young miss" but not so becoming in her maturity, "on the eve of aging and drying out." (Ibid., 8.) *Dvanadtsiat' obruchiv* (Twelve Rings, 2003) gives the following sardonic picture of a contemporary nationalist, as seen through the eyes and presented in the voice of a visiting Austrian:

> a former prisoner of conscience and author of *samvydav* poetry . . . tried to convince me that his nation was some ten thousand years old, that Ukrainians have direct contact with cosmic forces for good, that the forms of their skulls and eyebrows are very close to *the Aryan standard*, as a result of which there is a certain world conspiracy against them, the immediate executors of which are their closest geographical neighbors and several *internally destructive ethnic forces*—"you understand whom I have in mind, Mr. Zumbrunnen." Then he spent a great deal of effort demonstrating the complete uselessness of Russian culture, not leaving stone upon stone, as it seemed to him, of Mussorgsky, Dostoevsky, Semiradsky, and Brodsky (and the surnames alone reveal so much, he shouted, falling into ecstasy and spattering me with his blue and yellow foam: Rubinstein! Eisenstein! Mandelshtam! Mindelblat! Rostropovich! Rabinovich!) Most amusingly, he had to formulate all this in Russian, because this *true proto-European* knew no European language, not having taken the trouble to learn one. (Andrukhovych 2003, 23–24.)

Fanatically nationalist and anti-Semitic views are subtly but firmly deflated here, as they are in other works by Andrukhovych, who projects a different cultural and political vision. He sees Ukraine as part of a Europe in which there is a rich and respectful interaction between cultures and peoples. It is suggested, through various nostalgic flashbacks and recollections of the past, that the Austro-Hungarian Empire can serve as a model of a multiethnic society—one that can still be accessed. Populist pieties are undermined in other ways too. For example, the invented portrait of the poet Bohdan Ihor Antonych, who lives a carousing life, has a passionate love affair, and attempts suicide, is calculated to shock expectations of decorous behavior in the lives of the nation's poets and iconic figures.

Maria Matios' acclaimed *Solodka Darusia: Drama na try zhyttia* (Sweet Darusia: A Drama in Three Lives, 2004) depicts the Second World War in the Bukovynian village of Cheremoshne. The tone is somber and tragic, and the action covers successive rule by various powers: Romanians, Soviets, Romanians again, Germans and their Hungarian allies, and then Soviets again. During the first Soviet occupation of 1939–41, the tavern is boarded up and the Jewish Kapetuterov family is told to fend for itself. The mill of another Jew, Hershko, is handed over to the indolent Leso Onufriichuk, who knows nothing about milling. Hershko initially helps him, but gradually stops doing so and retreats into himself. When Hershko's oil-making business is also boarded up, people are forced to make oil for themselves in whatever way they can. The shop of Yuzia Rosenfeld, who has run away, is given to the village priest and his large family, while his own house is made into a school. Ten families are arrested and sent to Siberia. With the outbreak of the German-Soviet war, the Communists disappear, Kapetuter temporarily reopens his tavern, and Hershko reclaims his mill and oil-making business. However, they soon leave for good. As each occupation ends, the homes of Jews and arrested Ukrainians are looted, and the taverns of absent Jews are burned down.

The novel had a great resonance in Ukraine, partly because it rejects the official Soviet war myth that held sway for half a century. It overturns, in particular, the benevolent image of the Red Army, and the demonic image of anticommunist guerrillas. The crushing of local armed resistance to Soviet rule (which lasted until 1950), is described in all its cruelty. Didushenko, a sadistic major of the MGB, is a Ukrainian, and is responsible for the atrocities committed when a resistance fighter, Ivan Ohronnyk, and his girlfriend are captured. Ivan's father is tortured for several months before he discloses his son's hiding place. Matronka, the mother of the nine-year-old Darusia, is raped during three days of interrogation by an unnamed MGB officer. Her husband Mykhailo runs the communal store from which resistance fighters take goods. Eventually, the MGB officer makes Darusia testify against her father. When Matronka commits suicide, Darusia becomes dumb. In this way, the novel depicts the complete collapse of village society and its traditional morality.

Another reason for the story's resonance lies in the exposure of local complicity in the violence and property theft. Villagers are often only too glad to give information to the authorities about the resistance fighters, or about the activity of their neighbors, or to take the goods of those who have been arrested. The reader learns that "people are still silent, they are afraid even today . . . some find it inconvenient to recall the truth. It is easier to talk of the dead, because no one can speak up on their behalf, and tell the real truth about them." (Matios 2005, 167–68.) Darusia's muteness becomes a symbol of a traumatized generation unable, or unwilling, to relate its experiences. An orphan, her fate is to suffer in silence for the sins of all.

Violence pervades the narrative. The worst atrocities are committed by two Ukrainian MGB men, Didushenko and the unnamed officer. Their psychology is analyzed in some depth. They are not monsters, but military men committed to rooting out all opposition. Atrocities are part of a deliberate and effective strategy to terrorize the population into submission. This is why the villagers are herded to view the tortured and mutilated bodies of resistance fighters. The novel in this way indicates the existence of a mechanism of repression and murder. It also raises the issue of silent witnesses: those who quietly collaborate, or who benefit from the violence. But perhaps most poignantly, it raises the issue of silence: the inability to bear witness and repressed traumas. These questions are explored by Matios in a way that encourages readers to consider them in a broader framework, but she does not explicitly raise the issue of the Holocaust.

The Holocaust is only indirectly the focus of Maryna Hrymych's *Frida: Roman* (Frida: A Novel, 2006), which is a nostalgic re-creation of multicultural life in Berdychiv from scraps of memory. The focal point is an old, empty apartment building in which Iryna Revutska, now a highly successful business woman, was raised and to which she returns. The interaction between Jewish, Armenian, Polish, and Ukrainian families throughout the twentieth century is recreated from letters that have remained in the building, and which yield a tangled web of love affairs, betrayals, and adoptions. The building serves in this way as a microcosm of the "real" history of Ukraine, one that could not be written while the insipid Soviet version of national assimilation held sway. The "real" history is one in which family and national histories matter; they are not erased, but interact powerfully with one another. Moreover, the house has rules of its own: all inhabitants help one another in times of need and trust one another even with their family secrets. Iryna is in fact Frida Kats. Born of Ukrainian parents, she was orphaned as a baby during the Second World War and was raised by Berta Kats, a Holocaust survivor. Frida changed her name to Iryna after a life-altering car accident. She has therefore gone through several "births" or "rebirths"—from a Ukrainian child to a Jewish one (Frida), back to a Ukrainian identity (Iryna), and now to a rediscovery of her Jewish history (Frida-Iryna). The identity confusion is, of course, deliberate. Other characters also change their names. One of the Shneiersons takes the Ukrainian name Shostak, a Ukrainian called Vedmid changes his name to the Russian-sounding Medvedev, and another character adopts the Jewish-sounding Shukher. The narrator points out that this in fact represents the story of all Ukraine. It is a history of children who are born into one family and raised in another, or of families that become Ukrainian while retaining links to another culture and tradition. (Hrymych 2006, 153.) Frida combines many qualities and abilities attributed to Jews, Armenians, and Ukrainians. She attributes these to her upbringing in a "multicultural" house.

The discourse of plurality within this novel includes a strong response to the idea of Poles, Jews, Armenians, and other minorities as foreign to Ukraine. The Armenian Madzharian tells Iryna-Frida that the Greek, Jewish, Armenian and other trading families who settled in Right Bank Ukraine from the time of Lithuanian rule were given certain privileges: "But privileges are given for certain services. They have to be earned. Trading people earned them by developing these small towns, transforming them into commercial centers . . . This is a very ancient custom. Later, the Polish *szlachta*, like the Cossack *starshyna*, earned privileges with the blood it shed in battle for the Polish king or the Russian tsar." (Ibid., 168.) This argument undercuts the concept of commerce or business as the root of all evil and the realm of foreign exploitation. In fact, several passages underscore the need for contemporary Ukrainians to develop business acumen and learn from peoples who have developed commercial skills over the centuries. The youngest generation has itself fought the contemptuous Soviet attitude to trade, which was seen as a semicriminal "speculation." (Ibid., 181.) Such conversations in the novel also represent a rebuke to the tradition of resentment by agricultural workers of the money economy. Iryna-Frida is herself a representative of today's successful, risk-taking entrepreneur. She is now in a position to help others by setting up some much-needed manufacturing and commercial outlets. In this way the narrative integrates a defense of market economics with a discourse of plurality.

Traumatic memories (revolution, war, famine, Stalinism, the Gulag, Chornobyl) still haunt Ukrainian consciousness, and much contemporary writing denies any way back to innocence, or in some cases even normalcy. As in other literatures of trauma, one of the strongest impulses has been the urge to testify, to confront those who refuse to examine the past. However, the suffering of European Jewry during the Nazi terror still awaits a fuller literary expression and a more probing intellectual scrutiny. Reluctance to represent the Holocaust more fully in literature and to probe more deeply into its meaning has been typical of most Soviet and postindependence literature. However, the arrival of postmodernism and postcolonialism in literature, and the Orange Revolution of 2004 in politics, opened up greater space for a discussion of previously taboo topics, and some painful issues have recently entered public discourse. For example, a debate in the 2005–6 issues of *Krytyka* (Criticism), one of Ukraine's leading intellectual forums, raised the topic of civilian participation in the killing of Jews in the wake of the German advance in 1941, and in 2008 *Ukraina moderna* (Modern Ukraine), a prominent historical journal, began a serious critique of the historiographical schemes that have dominated approaches to the Second World War. Literature can and perhaps ought to play a leading role in allowing readers to deal with these and similar sensitive or neglected issues.

At stake is, first and foremost, the need to recognize what occurred and to commemorate the victims. This is how Grossman put it in his now famous "The Hell Called Treblinka":

> Terrible torments awaited those who arrived from the Warsaw ghetto. Women and children were separated from the crowd and taken to the places where corpses were burned instead of to the gas chambers. Mothers who went mad with terror were forced to lead their children between the glowing furnace bars on which thousands of dead bodies were writhing in flames and smoke, where corpses were squirming and jerking in the heat as if they had become alive again, where stomachs of dead pregnant women cracked from the heat, and unborn babies burned on the open wombs of the mothers. This sight could render even the strongest person insane.
>
> It is infinitely hard even to read this. The reader must believe me, it is as hard to write it. Someone might ask: "Why write about this, why remember all this? It is the writer's duty to tell this terrible truth, and it is the civilian [sic] duty of the reader to learn it. Everyone who would turn away, who would shut his eyes and walk past would insult the memory of the dead. (Beevor and Vinogradova 2005, 301.)

A more candid examination of the Holocaust, such as is now occurring, will heighten awareness of some significant issues. It is likely, for example, to spur deeper considerations of authoritarian ideologies, the nature of individual responsibility, and the way that historical memory is constructed. Conversely, a refusal to deal with sensitive questions risks making literature a contributory cause to the collective amnesia that characterized much of the Soviet period. It also risks sending a public message that history and literature can choose to dismiss uncomfortable facts and issues as aberrations, and can instead focus only on selective and conformist views.

Ukrainian literature has gradually moved away from the essentialist view of culture that was developed by romantic nationalists—one that subscribed to a myth of purity and homogeneity, and located its wellsprings in village life. Instead, its contemporary writers overwhelmingly acknowledge the need for inclusivity and diversity—regional, religious, ethnic, and gendered. The Jewish theme today—implicitly and explicitly—forms part of a discourse in Ukrainian literature around questions of otherness, diversity, historical memory, national identity, and psychological trauma.

But the past continues to shape contemporary attitudes. The various perspectives present in nineteenth-and twentieth-century texts are continually drawn upon to support ideas of the self and other in contemporary writing. The Jewish theme in fact provides a good example of how various past literary incarnations still feed into current discourses, such as the discourse concerning Jewish-Ukrainian relations, and the much broader one concerning diversity, democratization, and civil rights. Although, as has been seen, a Jewish voice has always played a role in Ukrainian literature, it has frequently been marginalized. Along with other suppressed or ignored voices, this voice is gradually being recovered or reintroduced into literature and critical thought.

The process of recovering voices and perspectives has highlighted the need for new methodologies in scholarship and criticism. Dominick LaCapra's introduction to cultural studies of psychoanalytic concepts such as transference, denial, resistance, repression, acting out, and working through is one avenue that a criticism concerned with reticences can explore. The relative silence of postwar literature concerning issues of violence, and the Holocaust in particular, is likely not simply the result of the Soviet proscription of identifying victims by nationality but also a reaction to the pervasiveness of violence in recent history. The consideration of traumatic violence has been focused (perhaps in some cases even subconsciously transferred) to the depiction of such events as the Khmelnytsky uprising, the Koliivshchyna revolt of 1768, the revolution, and—particularly in émigré accounts—the famine of 1932–33 and the Gulag. Here distance in time and the settling of literary myths has allowed for calmer consideration. But the more salient reason is that the description of this violence fits into the new narrative of national suffering that has been developing since independence. Overall, the analysis of extreme violence and civilian suffering during the Second World War has not been given the kind of attention in literature that one might expect, and the mass murder of Jews far less. Depictions of violence in earlier times may in some cases have acted as surrogate accounts for events of the Second World War, but such deflected narratives may also have impeded a deeper discussion not only of guilt and the role of silent witnesses, but of a range of historical and political issues.

When authors have described the Holocaust in fiction, they have often done so by interweaving parallel narrative threads, telling the story of the Jewish catastrophe alongside that of Ukrainian suffering. The Holocaust, it should be recalled, was one of a number of traumatic events whose discussion was largely suppressed in the Soviet period. As a result, a range of painful issues with powerful claims on collective memory all surfaced simultaneously in the nineties, and compelled writers to work through a long list of difficult historical narratives. Authors were called upon to provide a more adequate representation of the violence of 1917–20, the collectivization and famine of 1932–33, the Gulag, collaboration with Stalinism, and an array of other brutal and disturbing realities. Unconscious transference and repression were just as much at work in the representation of these events, which in many cases also have their still-living perpetrators and silent witnesses. Under these circumstances it is probable that the fixation on one trauma has sometimes served as a way of absorbing suppressed feelings associated with another. The emerging new narratives have had the effect of radically challenging the life-choices that people have made, the myths around which they have built their lives, and therefore of probing the very core of their identities. Working through the many issues involved in such a comprehensive recovery of voices and histories—in both imaginative literature and the broader intellectual discourse—remains a daunting assignment. Oksana Zabuzhko has described the contemporary Ukrainian intellectual who must deal with post-Soviet reality as playing the role of Fortinbras making his appearance at the end of *Hamlet*, removing the dead bodies, registering everything that has occurred, and appropriately characterizing the gravity and tragic nature of the events that have gone before. (Zabuzhko 2001a, 26.) Providing such a narrative is not easy. And yet its importance is obvious, since it contributes to the tasks of cultural reconstruction and healing. A review of the historical evidence, a weighing of all the issues and perspectives, and an apportioning of judgments is now being conducted not only in fiction, but also in scholarship and political life. It will not be the work of one group of writers, scholars, or politicians, but will be a collective, intergenerational effort.

Conclusion

Ukrainian literature's master narrative of national liberation and consolidation has at times included the idea of rapprochement with the Jewish community. This was particularly true of the years 1880–1917 when the national movement was dominated by liberal-democratic currents and the struggle for civil and national rights. After the revolution of 1917–20 and the establishment of Bolshevik rule, a Soviet master narrative developed which described the forging of a new community without national tensions. As a consequence, much Soviet literature denied particularism—whether Ukrainian or Jewish. However, from the late thirties, when the Soviet state began to portray itself as the successor to imperial Russia, new narratives of national history began to appear in both Russian and Ukrainian literatures. These two stories of historical consolidation were difficult to reconcile with the earlier concept of a single Soviet community, or with one another. Moreover, both resisted, or denied, the inclusion of Jewish particularism. Over the last two centuries, therefore, at various times the Jewish story has been integrated into Ukrainian literature, and sometimes even highlighted within it, while at other times it has been marginalized or excluded from it.

Zabuzhko has commented that some images acquire a great power and aura in public consciousness, so much so that they are capable of affecting the mentality of an age. They attract new associations, allowing the growth around themselves of new cultural layers—quotations, paraphrases, and intertextual games. (Zabuzhko 2001a, 176.) Over the last two centuries, the "keys to the church" theme, and the portrayals of Ahasuerus, Marko Prokliaty, the orendar, the tavernkeeper, the commissar or Chekist, the poor Jew, the *vykhrest* or convert, and

the victimized Jewish girl have exhibited this mythic power to imaginatively order experience. The various literary elaborations of these themes and characters
have acted like floating signifiers—an imagery with ever-changing, self-ques-
tioning, and self-adjusting meanings that has reflected and shaped attitudes in
the reading public toward Jews and Ukrainian-Jewish relations. It is of course an
imagery that is still today being contested, reworked, and reinterpreted in literature, criticism, scholarship, and journalism. Many literary texts in which representations of Jews occur deal with historical events that have been of great
significance in the lives of both nations: the Khmelnytsky uprising, the Koliivshchyna, the 1917–20 revolution, the Gulag, and the Holocaust. As a result, the
representations have played a very important role in influencing understanding
of these events and in the construction of national identity. Often readers have
uncritically taken the literary constructs for reality. As the present account has
tried to show, each generation has interwoven received imagery with new perceptions of history and contemporary reality to produce its own representation
of Jews and of Ukrainian-Jewish relations.

The powerful desire to "fix" a signified, to distill an essence, to commit to a
final, settled image that acts as an all-explaining framework—perhaps a normal
urge on the reader's part—tends toward simplification and even stereotyping. It
needs to be complicated by the understanding that any image operates by recalling accumulated examples that have arisen as responses to specific circumstances and pressures. The various images associated with Jewishness, or Ukrainianness, are the products of a complex and continuing evolution. The original
stereotypes that crystallized in Ukrainian literature in the first half of the nineteenth century began, in the late 1880s, to give way to what has been described as
a literature of sympathy and pity, one that depicted the suffering of the ordinary,
poor Jew. During the 1930s and the years of the Second World War a politically
inspired literature often revived earlier stereotypes. Contemporary writers, on
the other hand, have often shown an urge to dismantle the literary concepts of
previous generations and to challenge the idea of original essences. On the other
hand, those who are bent on spreading anti-Semitic prejudices have invariably
appealed to some kind of essentialism in order to justify their claims, and have
republished selected texts from the past, presenting these as evidence of an unchanging Jewish or Ukrainian nature.

Ukrainian literature reveals both philo-Semitic and anti-Semitic tendencies.
The philo-Semitic tendency has its particular Ukrainian characteristics, such
as a tragic portrayal of the *vykhrest* or convert, a Jewish voice, and a concern
with victimization and suffering. The anti-Semitic tendency has analogies with

trends in other countries, but it also has a specific character. Ukrainian anti-Semitism has tended to link Jews to social exploitation and national oppression. The negative images summoned up by the "keys to the church" theme, the orendar, the tavernkeeper, or the Chekist are all strongly associated with social and national injustice. Other resentments have of course become entangled with this dominant idea. Among them one might list the competition for positions in society and economic resources; the traditional Christian view of Jews as Christ-deniers or even Christ-killers; the racist view that Jews constituted an entirely different, and defective, nature or civilization; and the charge that Jewish practices are hostile to non-Jews, even the accusation of ritual murder. However, although examples of these resentments can be found in surveying Ukrainian literature, they constitute a small part of the modern literary tradition. Kostomarov's Russian-language story "Zhidotrepannie" (1883) does mention the charge of ritual murder. Racist forms of anti-Semitism are clearly in evidence in Arkadii Liubchenko's wartime diary and are strongly suggested in the scattered comments on Jews that can be found in the writings of Dontsov, but even here, the national issue dominates. Moreover, Dontsov's views were challenged, as the writings of Sherekh and the MUR authors indicate, in the name of a mainstream literary and intellectual tradition of tolerance and compassion. The fact that Liubchenko's comments on Jews only appeared when the full edition of his diary was published in 1999 itself indicates Ukrainian society's acute embarrassment with his views.

The poor Jew, the *vykhrest* or convert, and the victimized Jewish girl are examples of positive portrayals, or at least of attempts to portray Jews with sympathy, but even the negative stereotypes have been at different times and in the works of different authors "subverted" through the conferral of positive traits. Once a portrayal acquires a level of individualization and complexity, it can no longer be easily put to ideological use. Since a wide range of literary elaborations poses problems for those who wish to enforce the simplified or stereotypical, new literary embodiments of particular characters or themes have generated attempts to "police" the imagery, to realign the new representations with a stereotype. This happened during the relative liberal 1860s when Ukrainians began publishing the journal *Osnova*. Kostomarov's articles on the Jews, including his "Iudeiam" (1862), insisted on reaffirming the accusations of class and national exploitation. The writer's manner was to generalize, to paint a picture of the essential Jew, the Jew in all times and all places. In order to make his case he invoked, for example, Shakespeare's portrayal of Shylock in *The Merchant of Venice,* and nineteenth-century portrayals of the Eternal Jew as the "image of the European banker." (Kostomarov 1862, 46.) This represented an attempt to "modernize" the traditional image of the orendar from Khmelnytsky's time by associating him with the contemporary capitalist financier. Similarly, Kostomarov's "Zhidotrepannie," which was published just after the 1881–82 pogroms, appears to have been an attempt to reinforce the Jewish stereotype precisely at a time when it was being challenged by those who expressed shock at the events and sympathy for the victims. Thirty years later, Olena Pchilka's comments on the "literature of sympathy and pity" was in part a response to this literature's blurring of demarcation lines between the two "types" or "natures"—the Ukrainian and Jewish—in fact to the dissolution of the boundary that maintained this stereotype. Recent MAUP publications appear to be a similar reflex reaction to the perceived loss of control over the representation of identity.

The anxiety and defensiveness that accompany the loss of mastery is one reason for the attraction to stereotypes. Today, when the political context and the public discourse have changed, new and diverse portrayals of Jews have begun to appear. MAUP's republication of texts and cartoons that are over a hundred years old indicates a desire to counter the ironic deconstruction of stereotypes among contemporary writers. Homi Bhabha has suggested that the stereotype can be "a complex, ambivalent, contradictory mode of representation, as anxious as it is assertive." (Bhabha 1994, 70.) Nonetheless, as with any typical encapsulation, a stereotype strives to find unity beyond contradictions and vacillations, or perhaps, as has been suggested, precisely through these vacillations. The new and foreign must be adapted to the known and familiar by viewing it through the already established structure of thought and feeling. In this way the threat of disturbance posed by the new is contained, and familiar values can be reimposed. (Said 1978, 58–59.) This appears to be the strategy of the MAUP publications—to emphasize the images that the editors claim are widely accepted and that appeal to a conservative, unchanging view of culture and human nature.

The often rapid evolution of any representation, even a stereotypical one, can be illustrated with reference to the character of the tavernkeeper in the plays of the ethnographic realist current that dominated popular theater in the late nineteenth century. In spite of the fact that this type of melodrama thrives on simplification, the portrayal of the Jewish tavernkeeper quickly evolved. There were, to be sure, plays that refused this kind of dissolution of the stereotype and reasserted the negative role of the orendar and the tavernkeeper. They were common in the popular dramas of Western Ukraine in the interwar years—a reflection, as has been noted, of the fact that from the late twenties the cooperative movement, the anti-alcohol and teetotaling campaigns, and the spread of Prosvita reading clubs ran into direct conflict with Jewish merchants. The dissemination of Dontsov's ideas and his attempt to draw an absolute boundary between Ukrainians and Jews by mapping a series of oppositions and contrasts was a further attempt to reinforce the stereotype. However, the Ukrainian literary tradition has deconstructed such imaginary boundaries—in the plays of the late nineteenth century, the writings of modernists, the postwar works of MUR writers, and contemporary postmodernist writing.

Although there is no systematic study of popular attitudes toward Jews, the consensus among scholars is that these have been largely negative. Commentators have usually based their observations on collections of popular sayings, proverbs, and stories, as well as memoirs and anecdotal evidence. But even these materials show a variety of attitudes. Yaroslav Hrytsak has shown that the perception of popular attitudes could vary among contemporaries. (Hrytsak 2006, 344–50.) And, of course, the experience in different regions, towns, or even schools could be divergent, and could go through significant changes from period to period. The relationship between popular attitudes and literary creativity is another field that awaits research, but it is clear that writers frequently challenged dominant or widespread views whenever they found them prejudiced or immoral. By popularizing Ukrainian-Jewish solidarity, Franko, for example, placed himself in conflict with prevailing attitudes, and as a result was accused of being a "hireling," or "servant" of the Jews. (Ibid., 350.) More often than not writers have taken such a stance in an attempt to enlighten readers, to open up new perspectives, or to overturn entrenched views.

The current interest in Ukrainian-Jewish relations must contend with this history of representation, with received images, and with the underlying discourses in which the literature is rooted. Postindependence Ukrainian readers are in fact the first to have the full range of these representations available to them. They are currently mapping the contours of their cultural history and grappling with its meaning for future Ukrainian-Jewish relations. A close investigation of the creative literature can illuminate the genesis of many received opinions and indicate the ways in which they have been challenged, transformed, or superseded.

Bibliography

Abramson, Henry. 1991. Jewish Representation in the Independent Ukrainian Governments of 1917–1920. *Slavic Review* 50.3:542–50.

———. 1994. The Scattering of Amalek: A Model for Understanding the Ukrainian-Jewish Conflict. *East European Jewish Affairs* 24.1:39–47.

———. 1999. *A Prayer for the Government: Ukrainians and Jews in Revolutionary Times, 1917–1920*. Cambridge, Mass.: Ukrainian Research Institute and Center for Jewish Studies, Harvard University Press.

Adel'heim, Ievhen. 1947. Poeziia borot'by. *Vitchyzna* 11:148–71.

Aheieva, Vira. 1999. *Poetesa zlamu stolittia: Tvorchist' Lesi Ukrainky v postmodernii interpretatsii*. Kyiv: Lybid.

———, ed. 2003. *Proza pro inshykh: Iurii Kosach, Teksty, interpretatsii, komentari*. Kyiv: Fakt.

Andriewsky, Olga. 1990. "Medved" iz berlogi: Vladimir Jabotinsky and the Ukrainian Question, 1904–1914. *Harvard Ukrainian Studies* 14.3–4:249–67.

Andrukhovych, Iurii. 1994. Ave, "Kraisler"! Poiasnennia ochevydnoho. *Suchasnist'* 5:7–8.

———. 2003. *Dvanadtsiat' obruchiv*. Kyiv: Krytyka.

Antonovich, Vl., and M. Dragomanov. 1874, 1895. *Istoricheskiia pesni Malorusskogo naroda*. 2 vols. Kyiv: Tipografiia M. P. Fritsa.

Antonovych, D. 1925. *Trysta rokiv ukrains'koho teatru*. Prague: Ukrains'kyi hromads'kyi vydavnychyi fond.

Applebaum, Anne. 2003. *Gulag: A History of the Soviet Camps*. London: Allen Lane.

Aronov, H., ed. 1999. *"Shtetl" iak fenomen ievreis'koi istorii: Zbirnyk naukovykh prats'*. Kyiv: Instytut Iudaiky.

———. 2000. *Katastrofa ievropeis'koho ievreistva pid chas druhoi svitovoi viiny, Refleksii na mezhi stolit': Zbirnyk naukovykh prats'*. Kyiv: Instytut Iudaiki.

Aronov, H., and L. Finberh, eds. 2001. *Desiat' rokiv ievreis'koho natsional'noho vidrodzhennia v postradians'kykh krainakh, Dosvid, problemy, perspektyvy: Zbirnyk nauko-*

vykh prats'. Materialy konferentsii 28–30 serpnia 2000 r. Kyiv: Instytut Iudaiky, Natsional'na Biblioteka Ukrainy im. V. I. Vernads'koho.

————. 2002. *Dolia ievreis'koi dukhovnoi ta material'noi spadshchyny v XX stolitti:
Zbirnyk naukovykh prats'. Materialy konferentsii 28–30 serpnia 2001 r.* Kyiv: Instytut
Iudaiky, Natsional'na Biblioteka Ukrainy im. V. I. Vernads'koho.

Aronson, I. Michael. 1992. The Anti-Jewish Pogroms in Russia in 1881. In Klier and
Lambroza, 44–61.

Asper, Howard, and Peter J. Potichnyj. 1983. *Jewish Ukrainian Relations: Two Solitudes.*
Oakville, Ont.: Mosaic.

Averintsev, Sergei. 2001. Opyt sovetskikh let: Solidarnost' v Boge gonimom. *Iegupets*
8:3–8.

B., L. 1942. Homonila Ukraina. *Krakivs'ki Visti.* July 3.

Bartal, Israel. 1988. On Top of a Volcano: Jewish-Ukrainian Co-existence as Depicted in
Modern East European Jewish Literature. In Potichnyj and Aster, 309–26. Edmonton: Canadian Institute of Ukrainian Studies.

Barvinok, Hanna. 2001. Zhydivs'kyi kripak: Uryvok z podorozhzhia. In *Hanna Barvinok: Zbirnyk do 170-richchia vid dnia narodzhennia,* ed. Vasyl Shendrovs'kyi, 25–32.
Kyiv: Rada. (Orig. pub. 1861.)

Batchinsky, Julian, Arnold Margolin, Mark Vishnitzer, and Israel Zangwill. 1919. *The
Jewish Pogroms in Ukraine: Authoritative Statements on the Question of Responsibility for
Recent Outbreaks Against the Jews in Ukraine.* Washington, D.C.: Friends of Ukraine.

Bazhan, Mykola. 1968. Debora: Z knyhy umans'kykh spohadiv. *Vitchyzna* 8:1–8.

Beevor, Antony, and Luba Vinogradova, eds. and trans. 2005. *A Writer at War: Vasily
Grossman with the Red Army, 1941–1945.* Toronto: Alfred A. Knopf.

Berkhoff, Karel C. 2004. *Harvest of Despair: Life and Death in Ukraine under Nazi Rule.*
Cambridge. Mass.: The Belknap Press of Harvard University Press.

Berkhoff, K. C., and Carynnyk, M. 1999. The Organization of Ukrainian Nationalists
and Its Attitude Toward Germans and Jews: Iaroslav Stets'ko's 1941 Zhyttiepys. *Harvard Ukrainian Studies* 23.3–4:149–84.

Bezpalka, O. 1928. *Trahediia dvokh narodiv.* Prague: Vydannia Zakordonnoi delehatsii
USDRP.

Bhabha, Homi K. 1994. The Other Question: Stereotype, Discrimination and the Discourse of Colonialism. In his *The Location of Culture,* 66–84. London: Routledge.

Biela, S. 1926. *Potsilunok Iudy.* Ternopil: Podils'ka teatral'na biblioteka.

Bilets'kyi, Leonid. 1941. *Shevchenko i Gonta.* Prague: N.p.

Bilokin', Serhii. 1999. *Masovyi teror iak zasib derzhavnoho upravlinnia v SRSR (1917–
1941 rr.). Dzhereloznavche doslidzhennia.* Kyiv: Kyivs'ke Naukove Tovarystvo im. Pe-
tra Mohyly.

Bilynkis, Lazar. 1998. Hromadians'ka viina na Ukraini ta ievrei: Fragmenty. *Khronika
2000* 21–22:234–51.

Boichuk, Bohdan. 1968. Podorozh z uchytelem (Uryvky z poemy). *Novi poezii* 10:84–95.

Borduliak, Tymofii. 1958. *Tvory.* Kyiv: Derzhavne Vydavnytstvo Khudozhn'oi Literatury.

Borovoi, S. Ia. 1928. *Evreiskaia zemledelcheskaia kolonizatsiia v staroi Rossii: Politika, ideologiia, khoziaistvo, byt*. Moscow: Izdanie M. i S. Sabashnikovykh.

———. 1993. *Vospominaniia*. Moscow: Gesharim, Evreiskii Universitet v Moskve.

———. 1997. Evrei v Zaporozhskoi sechi (Po materialam sechevogo arkhiva). In *Evreiskie khroniki XVII stoletiia (Epokha "khmelnichiny")*, ed. M. Grinberg, 207–50. Moscow: Gesharim. (Orig. pub. 1930, 1934.)

Boshyk, Yury, ed. 1986. *Ukraine During World War II, History and Its Aftermath: A Symposium*. Edmonton: Canadian Institute of Ukrainian Studies.

Brown, Kate. 2004. *A Biography of No Place: From Ethnic Borderland to Soviet Heartland*. Cambridge. Mass.: Harvard University Press.

Cesarani, David, ed. 1994. *The Final Solution: Origins and Implementation*. London: Routledge.

Cherednychenko, Varvara. 1946. Ia—shchaslyva Valentyna. *Vitchyzna* 2:110–27.

Cherikover, Elias [Tcherikower]. 1923. *Antisemitizm i pogromy na Ukraine 1917–18 gg. (K istorii ukrainsko-evreiskikh otnoshenii)*. Berlin: Ostjüdisches Historisches Archiv.

Cherkasenko, Spyrydon [P. Stakh]. 1931. *Tsina krovy: Drama na 5 dii z prolohom*. Lviv: Novi shliakhy.

———. 1934, 1939. Unpublished Correspondence. Oleksandr Koshets Archive, Ukrainian Cultural and Educational Centre (Oseredok), Winnipeg.

———. 1937. *Vyhadlyvyi bursak: Komediika dlia molodi v 2-kh diiakh z chasiv Khmel'- nychchyny*. Uzhhorod: Svoboda.

———. 1991. *Tvory v dvokh tomakh*. 2 vols. Kyiv: Dnipro.

Childers, Thomas, and June Caplan, eds. 1993. *Reevaluating the Third Reich*. New York: Holmes and Meier.

Choseed, Bernard. 1961. Jews in Soviet Literature. In *Through the Glass of Soviet Literature: Views of Russian Society*, ed. Ernest J. Simmons, 110–58. New York: Columbia University Press.

———. 1968. Categorizing Soviet Yiddish Writers. *Slavic Review* 27.1:102–8.

Chubinskii, P. P., ed. 1872. *Trudy etnografichesko-statisticheskoi ekspeditsii v Zapadno-russkii krai snariazhennoi Imperatorskim russkim geograficheskim obshchestvom, Iugo-zapadnyi otdel: Materialy i izsledovaniia*. Vol. 7. St. Petersburg: Tip. K. V. Trubnikova.

Chuzhbinskii, A. 1861. *Vospominaniia o T. G. Shevchenko*. St. Petersburg.

Danko, Arkadii. 1931. *Srul' natiahailo*. Kolomyia: Rekord.

Derehus, Mykhailo. 2004. *Talant*. Kyiv: Ukrains'kyi portret.

Diakiv-Hornovyi, Osyp. 1968. *Ideia i chyn: Povna zbirka tvoriv*. New York: Tovarystvo Kolyshnikh voiakiv U.P.A.

Dimarov, Anatolii. 1988a. Trydtsiati (Prytcha pro khlib). *Prapor* 6:9–70.

———. 1988b. *Ukrains'ka vendeta: Povisti*. Kyiv: Dnipro.

Dmyterko, Liubomyr. 1949. Sostoianie i zadachi teatral'noi i literaturnoi kritiki na Ukraine. *Literaturnaia gazeta*, March 9.

Dontsov, Dmytro. 1933. Partiia chy orden: obiednannia chy roziednannia? *Vistnyk* 2:116–34.

———. 1936. *Nasha doba i literatura*. Lviv: Nakladom Vistnyka.

———. 1948a. Memento. *Na storozhi* 5–6:10–16. (Orig. pub. 1927.)

———. 1948b. *Khrest proty diavola*. Toronto: n.p.

———. 1967. *Khrestom i mechem*. Toronto: Homin.

Dorfman, Boris. 2001. Natsionalnoe dvizhenie vo Lvove v pervye poslevoennye gody. In Aronov and Finberh 2001, 8–11.

Dostoevsky, Fyodor. 1994. *A Writer's Diary*. Vol. 2. Evanston, Ill.: Northwestern University Press.

Drahomanov, M. P. 1908. Evrei i poliaki v Iugo-Zapadnom kraie. In his *Politicheskiia sochineniia*, vol. 1, 217–67. Moscow: Tipografiia T-va N. D. Sytina.

———. 1970. *Literaturno-publitsystychni pratsi v dvokh tomakh*. 2 vols. Kyiv: Naukova dumka.

Drozd, Volodymyr. 1997. Knyha blukaiuchoi v Pusteli. *Iegupets* 3:107–50.

Dubnov, S. 1923. Tret'ia gaidamachina: Istoricheskoe vstuplenie. In Cherikover, 9–15.

Dubnow, S. M. [Dubnov]. 1946. *History of the Jews in Russia and Poland from the Earliest Times until the Present Day*. Vol. 2. Philadelphia: Jewish Publication Society of America. (Orig. pub. 1918.)

Dudakov, Savelii. 1993. *Istoriia odnogo mifa: Ocherki russkoi literatury XIX–XX vv.* Moscow: Nauka.

Dziuba, Ivan. 2004. Shevchenkovi "Haidamaky" z vidstani chasu. *Suchasnist'* 6:67–92.

Edelshtein, Mikhail. 2005. Istoriia odnogo stereotipa. Zelenina, 384–91. Moscow: Mosty kultury—Gesharim.

Erenburg, Ilia. 1966. *Liudi, gody, zhizn'*. Vol. 8 of *Sobranie sochinenii v deviati tomakh*. Moscow: Khudozhestvennaia literatura.

Estraikh, Gennady. 2005. *In Harness: Yiddish Writers' Romance with Communism*. Syracuse, N.Y.: Syracuse University Press.

Fal'kivs'kyi, Dmytro. 1989. *Poezii*. Kyiv: Radians'kyi pys'mennyk.

Fedenko, Panas. 1942. *Homonila Ukraina: Epopeia z doby Bohdana Khmel'nyts'koho.* Prague: Vydavnytstvo Iuriia Tyshchenka.

Fedysiv, Petro. 1903. *Selo Tyndyrivka*. Kolomyia: Z pechati Mykhaila Bilousa.

Feller, Marten. 1994. *Poshuky, rozdumy i spohady ievreia, iakyi pamiataie svoikh didiv, pro ievreis'ko-ukrains'ki vzaiemyny, osoblyvo zh pro movy i stavlennia do nykh*. Drohobych: Vidrodzhennia.

———. 1998. *Poshuky, spohady, rozdumy ievreia, iakyi pamiataie svoikh didiv, pro ukrains'ko-ievreis'ki vzaiemyny, osoblyvo pro neliuds'ke i liudiane v nykh*. Drohobych: Vidrodzhennia.

———. 2001. *Pro nashykh velykykh dukhom: Esei z ukrainoiudaiky*. Lviv: Spolom.

Fialkova, Larysa. 1996. Oleksa Dovbush i ievreis'ka kultura. *Suchasnist'* 10:66–71.

Finberh, Leonid. 1992. Pro deiaki liuds'ki ta antyliuds'ki tendentsii v suchasnomu sviti. *Suchasnist'* 12:50–56.

Finberh, Leonid, and Volodymyr Liubchenko, eds. 2005. *Narysy z istorii ta kul'tury ievreiv Ukrainy*. Kyiv: Dukh i litera.

Fishbein, Moisei. 1984. *Zbirka bez nazvy: Poezii, pereklady*. [Munich]: Suchasnist'.

———. 1996. *Apokryf*. Kyiv: Dovira.

Franko, Ivan. 1883. Pytanie zhydovske. *Dilo*, 20 August (1 September).

————. 1887. Semityzm i antysemityzm w Galicji. *Przegląd Społeczny* 3.5:431–44.

————. 1896a. Panstwo zydowskie. *Tydzien'*, literary supplement to *Kurjer Lwowski*. March 9.

————. 1896b. Review of H. M. Barats, *Sledy iudeiskikh vozzrenii v drevnerusskoi pis'-mennosti: Slovo Kirilla-Filosofa* (Odesa, 1894). *Zapysky Naukovoho Tovarystva im. Shevchenka* 11.3:2–4.

————. 1898. Khmel'nyshchyna 1648–1649 rokiv u suchasnykh virshakh. *Zapysky Naukovoho Tovarystva im. Shevchenka* 23–24:1–114.

————. 1906. Do istorii ukrains'koho vertepa XVIII v. *Zapysky Naukovoho Tovarystva im. Shevchenka* 15.4:9–79, 15.5:5–64.

————. 1976–86. *Zibrannia tvoriv u p'iatdesiaty tomakh*. 50 vols. Kyiv: Naukova dumka.

————. 1984. Lykhvarstvo v Halychyni. In his *Zibrannia tvoriv*, vol. 44.2:373–91. (Orig. pub. 1893.)

————. 1986. Khmel'nychchyna (Dumy, pisni ta virshi). In his *Zibrannia tvoriv*, vol. 43:7–193. (Orig. pub. 1910.)

Friedman, Phillip. 1958–59. Ukrainian-Jewish Relations during the Nazi Occupation. *YIVO Annual of Jewish Social Science* 12:159–96.

Galai, Shmuel. 1974. Early Russian Constitutionalism: "Vol'noe Slovo" and the "Zemstvo Union." A Study in Deception. *Jahrbücher für Geschichte Osteuropas* NF 22.1:35–55.

Galan, Yaroslav. 1950. L'vivs'ki narysy. *Vitchyzna* 5:109–12.

Galant, I. 1909. *Arendovali li evrei tserkvi na Ukraine?* Kyiv: Elektro-pechatnia "Rabotnik."

————. 1928. Vyselennia zhydiv iz Kyiva roku 1835-ho. In *Zbirnyk istorychno-filolohichnoi komisii 73. Zbirnyk prats' zhydivs'koi istorychno-arkheohrafichnoi komisii*, vol. 1., ed. I. V. Galant, 149–97. Kyiv: Vseukrains'ka Akademiia Nauk.

Gitelman, Zvi. 1988. *A Century of Ambivalence: The Jews of Russia and the Soviet Union, 1881 to the Present*. New York: YIVO Institute.

————, ed. 1997. *Bitter Legacy: Confronting the Holocaust in the USSR*. Bloomington: Indiana University Press.

Gitelman, Zvi, Lubomyr Haida, John-Paul Himka, and Roman Solchanyk, eds. 2000. *Cultures and Nations of Central and Eastern Europe: Essays in Honor of Roman Szporluk*. Cambridge, Mass.: Ukrainian Research Institute, Harvard University.

Glaser, Amelia. 2004. The Marketplace and the Church: Jews, Slavs and the Literature of Exchange, 1829–1929. Ph.D. dissertation. Stanford University.

Goldelman, Solomon. 1921. *Lysty zhydivs'koho sotsial-demokrata pro Ukrainu: Materialy do istorii ukrains'ko-zhydivs'kykh vidnosyn za chas revoliutsii*. Vienna: Zhydivs'ke vydavnytstvo "Hamoin" na Ukraini.

————. 1967. *Zhydivs'ka natsional'na avtonomiia v Ukraini 1917–1920*. Zapysky Naukovoho Tovarystva im. Shevchenka, vol. 182. Munich: Dniprova khvylia.

Gon, Maksym. 2003. Ukraintsi ta ievrei zakhidnoi Ukrainy druhoi polovyny 1930-kh rokiv: latentna viina. *Suchasnist'* 9:94–103.

Grabowicz, George. 1988. The Jewish Theme in Nineteenth and Early Twentieth-Century Ukrainian Literature. In Potichnyj and Aster, 327–42. Edmonton: Canadian Institute of Ukrainian Studies.

Hadus, O. 1929. *U kozhnoho rozum ie, iak horivky vin ne p'ie.* Lviv: Rusalka.

Hai, O. 1942. Proshchannia z Kyievom. *Nashi dni* 1.6:12.

Haidabura, Valerii. 2004. *Teatr mizh Hitlerom i Stalinym: Ukraina, 1941–1944. Doli myttsiv.* Kyiv: Fakt.

Haievs'kyi, Stepan.1929. "Aleksandriia" v davnii ukrainskii literaturi. *Zbirnyk istorychno-filolohichnoho viddilu* 98. Kyiv: Vseukrains'ka Akademiia Nauk.

Halii, M., and B. Novyts'kyi. 1934. *Het' Masku! Natsional'na polityka na Rad. Ukraini v svitli dokumentiv.* Lviv, n.p.

Hamm, Michael F. 1993. *Kyiv: A Portrait, 1800–1917.* Princeton, N.J.: Princeton University Press.

Hatnenko, A. 1995. Vid Khortytsi do Apollinera. *Khronika 2000* 2–3:270–75.

Hellebust, Rolf. 2001. *Flesh to Metal: Soviet Literature and the Alchemy of Revolution.* Ithaca, N.Y.: Cornell University Press.

Hertz, Aleksander. 1988. *The Jews in Polish Culture.* Evanston, Ill.: Northwestern University Press.

Himka, John Paul. 1988. Ukrainian-Jewish Antagonism in the Galician Countryside During the Late Nineteenth Century. In Potichnyj and Aster, 111–58. Edmonton: Canadian Institute of Ukrainian Studies.

———. 1997. Ukrainian Collaboration in the Extermination of the Jews During the Second World War: Sorting Out the Long-Term and Conjunctural Factors. In *The Fate of the European Jews, 1939–1945: Continuity or Contingency,* ed. Jonathan Frankel, 170–89. Studies in Contemporary Jewry, vol. 13. New York: Oxford University Press.

Hnatiuk, Volodymyr. 1897. Legendy z Khitars'koho zbirnyka. *Zapysky Naukovoho Tovarystva im. Shevchenka* 16.2:19–39.

Holovanivs'kyi, Sava. 1988. *Memorial: spohady.* Kyiv: Radians'kyi pys'mennyk.

Hordyns'kyi, Sviatoslav. 1942. Pro odnoho Argonavta (Leonid Chernov-Maloshyichenko). *Nashi dni* 1.8:3.

Horodyns'kyi, Orest. 2004. Iurii Klen—voiakom. In Kravchenko, 360–77.

Hrabjanka, Hryhorij. 1990. *The Great War of Bohdan Xmel'nyc'kyj.* Cambridge. Mass.: Distributed by Harvard University Press for the Ukrainian Research Institute of Harvard University. (Orig. pub. 1854.)

Hrabovs'kyi, Pavlo. 1964. *Tvory v dvokh tomakh.* 2 vols. Kyiv: Dnipro.

Hrachova, Sofiia. 2005. Vony zhyly sered nas? *Krytyka* 9.4:22–26.

Hrushevs'ka, Kateryna. 1927, 1931. *Ukrains'ki narodni dumy.* 2 vols. Kharkiv: Vseukrains'ka Akademiia Nauk.

Hrushevs'kyi, Mykhailo. 1956. *Istoriia Ukrainy-Rusy.* Vol. 8, part 2. New York: Knyhospilka. (Orig. pub. 1922.)

———. 1993. *Istoriia ukrains'koi literatury.* Vols. 1–5. Kyiv: Lybid'. (Orig. pub. 1923–67.)

———. 1995. *Istoriia ukrains'koi literatury.* Vol. 6. Kyiv: Instytut literatury im. T. H. Shevchenka Natsional'na Akademiia Nauk Ukrainy.

———. 1999. *History of Ukraine-Rus'.* Vol. 7. Edmonton: Canadian Institute of Ukrainian Studies. (Orig. pub. 1909.)

Hrymych, Maryna. 2006. *Frida: Roman.* Kyiv: PP Duliby.

Hrytsak, Iaroslav. 1996. Ukraintsi v antyievreis'kykh aktsiiakh v roky Druhoi svitovoi viiny. *I* 8:60–9.

———. 2004a. Franko's Boryslav Cycle: An Intellectual History. *Journal of Ukrainian Studies* 29.1, 29.2:169–189.

———. 2004b. *Strasti za natsionalizmom: Istorychni esei.* Kyiv: Krytyka.

———. 2005. Shcho nam robyty z nashoiu ksenofobiieiu? *Krytyka* 9.4:27–28.

———. 2006. *Prorok u svoii vitchyzni: Franko ta ioho spil'nota (1856–1886).* Kyiv: Krytyka.

Hulyk, Vasyl. 1937. *Het' z lykhvoiu, p'ianstvom i temnotoiu.* Stanislaviv: Nakladom avtora.

Humenna, Dokia. 1941–43. Materiial do povisty Hnizdo nad bezodneiu. Dokia Humenna Archive, Ukrainian Cultural and Educational Centre (Oseredok), Winnipeg.

———. 1956. *Khreshchatyi iar (Kyiv 1941–43): Roman-khronika.* New York: Slovo.

———. 1990. Shchodennyk, 1923–49. Dokia Humenna Archive, Ukrainian Free Academy of Sciences in the United States (UVAN), New York.

Hundorova, Tamara. 2005. *Pisliachornobyl's'ka biblioteka: Ukrains'kyi literaturnyi postmodern.* Kyiv: Krytyka.

Iaroslavych, I. 1932. *Pavuky.* Kolomyia: Rekord.

Iavorivs'kyi, Volodymyr. *Vichni Kortelisy: Povist'.* 2d ed. Kyiv: Vyd. TsK LKSMU "Molod," 1988.

Iefremov, Serhii. 1997. *Shchodennyk, 1923–1929.* Kyiv: Hazeta Rada.

Iendyk, Rostyslav. 1940. *V kaidanakh rasy.* Krakiv: Ukrains'ke vydavnytstvo.

———. 1942. Biodynamichni chynnyky v buval'shchyni Ukrainy. *Nashi dni* 1.9:6.

———. 1957. Rozpovid' odnoho zhyda. In his *Zhaha: Noveli,* 235–64. Munich: Ukrains'ke vydavnytstvo.

Ieremenko, Vasyl, comp. 2005. *Zhydotriepaniie: Panteleimon Kulish, Mykola Kostomarov, Ivan Franko.* Kyiv: Mizhrehional'na Akademiia Upravlinnia Personalom.

Ierofeiev, Ivan. 1910. Ukrains'ki narodni dumy i ikh redaktsii. *Zapysky Ukrains'koho naukovoho tovarystva u Kyievi* 7:17–64.

Ieshkiliev, Volodymyr. 2002. *Pafos.* Lviv: Kalvariia.

Ieshkiliev, Volodymyr, and Oleh Hutsuliak. 1997. *Adept: Svidotstvo Oleksiia Sklavyna pro skhodzhennia do triokh imen. Roman znakiv.* Ivano-Frankivsk: Lileia.

Iohansen, Maik. 1929. *Podorozh liudyny pid kepom (Ievreis'ki kolonii).* Kharkiv: Derzhavne Vydavnytstvo Ukrainy.

Isajiw, Wsevolod, Yury Boshyk, and Roman Senkus, eds. 1992. *The Refugee Experience: Ukrainian Displaced Persons after World War II.* Edmonton: Canadian Institute of Ukrainian Studies.

Istoriia Rusov ili Maloi Rossii: Sochinenie Georgiia Koniskago, Arkhiepiskopa Beloruskago. 1991. Kyiv: Dzvin. (Orig. pub. 1846.)

Jabotinsky. *See* Zhabotinskii

Kabanets', Ie. 1998. Ievreis'ki reministsentsii v spadshchyni davn'oho Kyieva. *Khronika 2000* 21–22:29–43.

Kachurovs'kyi, I. 1998. Pro Hryts'ka Kernerenka. *Khronika 2000* 21–22:174–76.

———. 2008. Otse tvoia, poeziie, doroha! *Ukraina moderna* 13:202–10.

Kalik, Judith. 2003. The Orthodox Church and the Jews in the Polish-Lithuanian Commonwealth. *Jewish History* 17.2:229–37.

Kappeler, Andreas, Zenon E. Kohut, Frank E. Sysyn, and Mark von Hagen, eds. 2003. *Culture, Nation, and Identity: The Ukrainian-Russian Encounter (1600–1945)*. Edmonton: Canadian Institute of Ukrainian Studies Press.

Karpenko-Karyi, I. [I. K. Tobilevych]. 1960. *Tvory*. Vol. 5. Kyiv: Khudozhnia literatura.

Katz, Elena M. 2008. *Neither With Them, Nor Without Them: The Russian Writer and the Jew in the Age of Realism*. Syracuse: Syracuse University Press.

Katsnel'son, Abram. 1996. *Poklyk vysoty: Poezii 1993–1996*. Los Angeles: Patmos.

———. 1997–98. *U nimbi syvyny: Novi poezii*. Los Angeles: n.p.

Kaushanskii, Pavel. 1999. Tragediia ukrainskogo evreistva vremen Bogdana Khmel'nitskogo. In Aronov, 46–52.

Kazovskii, Hillel. 2003. *Khudozhniki Kultur-Ligi*. Moscow: Mosty kultury—Gesharim.

Kazovsky, Hillel, ed. 2007. *Artistic Avant-Garde of the 1910s and the 1920s*. Kyiv: Dukh i litera.

Kedrovs'kyi, Volodymyr. 1994. Borot'ba z pohromamy v Ukraini. In Korohods'kyi, 20–70. (Orig. pub. 1930.)

Kellogg, Michael. 2005. *The Russian Roots of Nazism: White Emigrés and the Making of National Socialism, 1917–1945*. Cambridge: Cambridge University Press.

Kenez, Peter. 1992. Pogroms and White Ideology in the Russian Civil War. In Klier and Lambroza, 293–313.

Kernerenko, Hryts'. 1900. I znov na Vkraini. *Literaturno-naukovyi vistnyk* 12:116–17.

———. 1902. Monopoliia. *Literaturno-naukovyi vistnyk* 18:1.

———. 1908. Novyi rik. *Literaturno-naukovyi vistnyk* 41:187.

———. 2005. Ne ridnyi syn. *Ab imperio* 1:241. (Orig. pub. 1908.)

Kheifets, Mikhail. 1978. *Mesto i vremia (evreiskie zametki)*. Paris: Tretia volna.

Kheifets, Mykhailo. 1994. Ukrains'ki syliuety. In Korohods'kyi, 137–392.

Khiterer, Viktoria. 1992. The October 1905 Pogrom in Kiev. *East European Jewish Affairs* 22.2:21–37.

———. 1999. *Dokumenty sobrannye Evreiskoi istoriko-arkheograficheskoi komissiei Vseukrainskoi Akademii Nauk*. Kyiv: Institut Iudaiki-Gesharim.

———. 2001a. *Dokumenty po evreiskoi istorii XVI–XX vekov v Kievskikh arkhivakh*. Kyiv: Institut Iudaiki, and Moscow: Mosty kultury.

———. 2001b. Izuchenie istochnikov po evreiskoi istorii v Kievskikh arkhivakh. In Aronov and Findberh 2001, 222–32.

———. 2002. Konfiskatsiia evreiskikh dokumentalnykh materialov i evreiskoi sobstvennosti v Ukraine v 1919–1930 gg. In Aronov and Findberh 2002, 8–13.

———. 2005. Arnold Davidovich Margolin: Ukrainian-Jewish Jurist, Statesman and Diplomat. *Revolutionary Russia* 18.2:145–67.

Khonigsman, Ia. S., and A. Ia. Naiman. 1992. *Evrei Ukrainy (Kratkii ocherk istorii)*. Pt. 1. Kyiv: Ukrainsko-Finskii Institut Menedzhmenta i Biznes.

Khoroshunova, Irina. 2001. Pervyi god voiny. Kievskie zapiski. *Iegupets* 9:5–110.

Khrystiuk, Pavlo. 1969. *Zamitky i materiialy do istorii ukrainskoi revoliutsii, 1917–1920 rr.* Vol. 4. New York: Vydavnytstvo Chartoryiskykh. (Orig. pub. 1922.)

Kleiner, Israel. 2000. *From Nationalism to Universalism: Vladimir (Ze'ev) Jabotinsky and the Ukrainian Question.* Edmonton: Canadian Institute of Ukrainian Studies.

Klen, Iurii (Osval'd Burhardt). 1991. *Vybrane.* Kyiv: Dnipro.

Klier, John D. 1977. The *Illiustratsiia* Affair of 1858: Polemics on the Jewish Question in the Russian Press. *Nationalities Papers* 5.2:117–35.

———. 1992. Russian Jewry on the Eve of the Pogrom. In Klier and Lambroza, 3–12.

Klier, John D., and Shlomo Lambroza, eds. 1992. *Pogroms: Anti-Jewish Violance in Modern Russian History.* Cambridge: Cambridge University Press.

Kohut, Zenon E. 2000. The Image of Jews in Ukraine's Intellectual Tradition: The Role of *Istoriia Rusov.* In Gitelman et al., 343–53.

———. 2003. The Khmel'nyts'ky Uprising, the Image of Jews, and the Shaping of Ukrainian Historical Memory. *Jewish History* 17:141–63.

Kolessa, Filaret. 1938. *Ukrains'ka usna slovesnist'.* Lviv: Nakladom Fondu "Uchitesia, braty moi."

Kopshtein, Aron. 1941. *Vybrani tvory.* Kyiv: Radians'kyi pys'mennyk.

Korohods'kyi, Roman, ed. 1994. *Pole vidchaiu i nadii: Al'manakh* No. 1. Kyiv: n.p.

Korolivs'k, S. 1961. Tse bulo v 1914-mu . . . Dvi proklamatsii kharkivs'kykh studentiv. *Prapor* 5:90–2.

Kosach, Iurii. 1937. *Trynadtsiata chota: Opovidannia.* Stanislaviv: Dnipro.

———. 1947–48. *Den' hnivu: Povist' pro 1648 rik.* 2 vols. Regensburg: Ukrains'ke slovo.

———. 1947. *Diistvo pro Iuriia-Peremozhtsia: Trahediia.* Regensburg: Ukrains'ke slovo.

Kostomarov, N. I. 1862. Iudeiam. *Osnova:* 38–58.

———. 1967a. *Sobranie sochinenii: Istoricheskie monografii i isledovaniia.* Book 4, vols. 9–11: *Bogdan Khmel'nitskii.* The Hague: Europe Printing. (Orig. pub. 1904.)

———. 1967b. *Sobranie sochinenii: Istoricheskie monografii i isledovaniia.* Book 8, vol. 21: *Istoricheskoe znachenie iuzhnorusskago narodnago pesennago tvorchestva.* The Hague: Europe Printing. (Orig. pub. 1905.)

———. 1967. *Tvory v dvokh tomakh.* Vol. 1. Kyiv: Dnipro.

———. 2005. Zhidotrepannie v nachale XVIII veka. In Ieremenko, 146–225. (Orig. pub. 1883.)

Kotliarevs'kyi, Ivan. 1969. *Eneida.* Kyiv: Dnipro.

Kozych-Umans'ka, A. 1919a. *Pimsta zhydivky.* New York: Ukrains'ka knyharnia im. T. Shevchenka.

———. 1919b. *Vykhrest (V chadu kokhannia).* New York: Nakladom Ukrains'koi knyharni im. T. Shevchenka.

Kravchenko, Les', ed. 2004. *Tvorchist' Iuriia Klena v konteksti ukrains'koho neoklasytsyzmu ta visnykivs'koho neoromantyzmu: Zbirnyk naukovykh prats'.* Drohobych: Vidrodzhennia.

Kravtsiv, Bohdan. 1960. Leonid Mosendz i ioho *Ostannii prorok.* In Mosendz 1960, v–xxx.

Krevets'kyi, Ivan. 1904. Ukrains'ka virsha pro umans'ku rizniu. *Zapysky Naukovoho Tovarystva im. Shevchenka* 15.4:145–6.

Kryms'kyi, A. E., ed. 1929. *Zbirnyk prats' ievreis'koi istorychno-arkheohrafichnoi komisii.* Zbirnyk Istorychno-filolohichnoho Viddilu VUAN, vol. 2. Kyiv: Vseukrains'ka Akademiia Nauk.

Kudriavtsev, P. 1929. Ievreistvo, ievrei ta ievreis'ka sprava v tvorakh Ivana Franka. In Kryms'kyi, 1–81.

Kulish, Panteleimon. 1856. *Zapiski o Iuzhnoi Rusi*. Vol. 1. St. Petersburg: V tipografii Aleksandra Iakobsona.

———. 1858. Letter in *Russkii Vestnik* 18:245–47.

———. 1861a. Drugoi chelovek (iz vospominanii bylogo). *Osnova* 2:64–67.

———. 1861b. Peredovyie zhidy. *Osnova* 9:135–38.

———. 1862. Deshcho pro zhydiv. *Osnova* 1:71–75.

———. 1908. Ukraina od pochatku Vkrainy do Bat'ka Khmelnyts'koho. In his *Tvory*, vol. 1, 13–78. Lviv: Z drukarni Naukovoho Tovarystva im. Shevchenka.

Kunitz, Joshua. 1929. *Russian Literature and the Jew: A Sociological Inquiry into the Nature and Origin of Literary Patterns*. New York: Columbia University Press.

Kuznetsov, Anatoli. 1970. *Babi Yar: A Document in the Form of a Novel*. London: Jonathan Cape.

LaCapra, Dominick. 1994. *History, Theory, Trauma: Representing the Holocaust*. Ithaca, N.Y.: Cornell University Press.

———. 1998. *History and Memory after Auschwitz*. Ithaca, N.Y.: Cornell University Press.

———. 2001. *Writing History, Writing Trauma*. Baltimore: Johns Hopkins University Press.

Lambroza, Shlomo. 1992. The Pogroms of 1903–1906. In Klier and Lambroza, 195–247.

Laslo-Kutsiuk, Mahdalyna. 1987. Ievreis'ka tematyka v tvorchosti Lesi Ukrainky. *Diialohy* 13–14:228–34.

Leskov, Nikolai S. 1986. *The Jews in Russia: Some Notes on the Jewish Question*. Princeton, N.J.: The Kingston Press. (Orig. pub. 1884.)

Levyts'kyi, V., and D. Doroshenko. 1967. *Spohady pro Modesta Levyts'koho*. Winnipeg: Volhyn Institute.

Lewin, Kurt I. 1994. *A Journey Through Illusions*. Santa Barbara, Calif.: Fithian Press.

Liubchenko, Arkadii. 1999. *Shchodennyk Arkadiia Liubchenka*. Lviv: Vydavnytstvo M. P. Kots'.

Liubchenko, V. 2005. Ievrei u skladi Rosiis'koi imperii. In Finberh and Liubchenko, 60–96.

Lower, Wendy. 2005. *Nazi Empire-Building and the Holocaust in Ukraine*. Chapel Hill: University. of North Carolina Press.

Lukoms'kyi, Stefan. 1972. Sobranie istoricheskoe. In *Letopis' samovidtsa: The Eyewitness Chronicle*, 322–72. Munich: Wilhelm Fink Verlag. (Orig. pub. 1878.)

Lulu, L. 1926. Pantsyrnyi zhyd. In *Istorychnyi kaliendar-almanakh Chervonoi kalyny, 1927*, 112–14. Lviv: Chervona kalyna.

Lunachars'kyi, A. 1984. *Vohnenne slovo Kobzaria: Literaturno-krytychni statti pro T. H. Shevchenka*. Kyiv. (Orig. pub. 1912.)

Lvov-Rogachevsky, V. 1979. *A History of Russian Jewish Literature*. Ed. and trans. Arthur Levin. Ann Arbor: Ardis. (Orig. pub. 1922.)

M., D. 1987. Zhydivs'kyi kurin'. *Diialohy* 13.4:159–60.

Mace, James, and Leonid Heretz, eds. 1990. *Investigation of the Ukrainian Famine 1932–1933: Oral History Project of the Commission on the Ukraine Famine.* 3 vols. Washington, D.C.: United States Government Printing Office.

Makar, Volodymyr. 1956. *Bereza Kartuzka (Spomyny z 1934–35 rr.).* Toronto: Liga Vyzvolennia Ukrainy.

Makaryk, Irena R. 2004. *Shakespeare in the Undiscovered Bourn: Les Kurbas, Ukrainian Modernism and Early Soviet Cultural Politics.* Toronto: University of Toronto Press.

Maksymenko, Svitlana. 2006. Iosyp Stadnyk, Director and Actor of the Ukrainian Theatre of the City of Lviv in 1941–42. *Journal of Ukrainian Studies* 31.1–2:117–34.

Margolin, Arnold. 1946. *From a Political Diary: Russia, the Ukraine, and America, 1905–1945.* New York: Columbia University Press.

———. 1977. *Ukraina i politika Antanty (Zapiski evreia i grazhdanina).* Berlin: S. Efron. (Orig. pub. 1922.)

Markish, David. 1991. *Poliushko-pole. Donor: Romany.* Moscow: Izvestiia.

Marples, David R. 2006. Stepan Bandera: The Resurrection of a Ukrainian Hero. *Europe-Asia Studies* 58.4:555–66.

Martin, Terry. 2001. *The Affirmative Action Empire: Nations and Nationalism in the Soviet Union, 1923–1939.* Ithaca, N.Y.: Cornell University Press.

Martynets', V. 1938. *Zhydivs'ka probliema v Ukraini.* London: n.p.

Marynovych, M., and L. Finberh, eds. 2000. *Iudeo-khrystyians'kyi diialoh v Ukraini: Stenohrama seminaru (19–20 kvitnia 1999 roku, m. Lviv).* Lviv: Lvivs'ka Bohoslovs'ka Akademiia, Instytut Iudaiky.

Marx, Karl. 1990. *Selected Writings,* ed. David McLellan. Oxford: Oxford University Press.

Matios, Maria. 2005. *Solodka Darusia: Drama na try zhyttia.* 3 ed. Lviv: Piramida.

Mazepa. I. 1950–51. *Ukraina v ohni y buri revoliutsii, 1917–1921.* 3 vols. Np: Prometei.

McLean, Hugh. 1973. Theodore the Christian Looks at Abraham the Hebrew: Leskov and the Jews. *California Slavic Studies* 7:65–98.

Metelnyts'kyi, P. 2001. *Deiaki storinky ievreis'koi zabudovy Luts'ka.* Kyiv: Dukh i litera.

Michlic, Joanna Beata. 2006. *Poland's Threatening Other: The Image of the Jew from 1880 to the Present.* Lincoln: University of Nebraska Press.

Mishkinsky, Moshe. 1992. "Black Repartition" and the Pogroms of 1881–1882. In Klier and Lambroza, 62–92.

Mitsel, Mikhail. 2004. *Evrei Ukrainy v 1943–1953 gg.: Ocherki dokumentirovannoi istorii.* Kyiv: Dukh i litera.

Mnykh, Roman. 2000. Lirychnyi tsykl Ivana Franka "Iz Knyhy Kaaf" iak symvolichna forma ta ioho iudeis'ki konteksty. In *Jews and Slavs,* ed. Wolf Moskovich, vol. 7: *Jews and Eastern Slavs,* 110–29. Jerusalem: Hebrew University of Jerusalem.

Monolatii, Ivan. 1998. Zabutyi svit—kolomyis'ki ievrei. *Khronika 2000* 21–22:145–52.

Montefiore, Simon Sebag. 2003. *Stalin: The Court of the Red Tsar.* London: Weidenfeld and Nicolson.

Mosendz, Leonid. 1937. *Liudyna pokirna (Homo lenis): Opovidi.* Lviv: Ivan Tyktor.

———. 1960. *Ostannii prorok.* Toronto: Dilovym komitetom dlia vydannia tvoriv L. Mosendza v Toronto.

Moskovich, Wolf. 1996. Ukrainoznavstvo v Izraili. In *Jews and Slavs*, vol. 5: *Jews and Ukrainians*, ed. Wolf Moskovich, 9–12. Jerusalem: Hebrew University of Jerusalem.

———, ed. 1999. *Jews and Slavs*. Vol. 6: *Jerusalem in Slavic Culture*. Jerusalem: Hebrew University of Jerusalem.

Mydlovs'kyi. I. 1910. *Kapral Tymko abo scho nas hubyt'?* Kolomyia: Z pechatni Mykhaila Bilousa.

Myrnyi, Panas [P. Ia. Rudchenko]. 1968. *Zibrannia tvoriv u semy tomakh*. 7 vols. Kyiv: Naukova dumka.

Myrs'kyi, R. Ia., and O. Ia. Naiman. 2000. *Iudofobiia proty Ukrainy*. 2d ed. Kyiv: Akademiia istorii ta kul'tury ievreiv Ukrainy im. Shymona Dubnova.

Mytsiuk, O. K. 1933. *Agraryzatsiia zhydivstva Ukrainy na tli zahal'noi ekonomiky*. Prague: Nakladom avtora.

Mytsyk, Iurii. 1998. Ievrei–kozaky. *Khronika 2000* 21–22:72–76.

Naiman, O. Ia. 1995. Evreiskoe zemledelenia na Ukraine v 1930-e gody. *Vestnik evreiskogo universiteta v Moskve* 1:217–221.

———. 1998. *Ievreis'ki partii ta ob'iednannia Ukrainy (1917–1925)*. Kyiv: Natsional'na Akademiia Nauk Ukrainy, In-t Politychnykh i Etnonatsional'nykh Doslidzhen'.

Nakhmanovich, Vitalii. 1999. Evrei v ukrainskikh narodnykh pesniakh serediny—tret'ei chverti XIX v. In Aronov, 328–36. Kyiv: Instytut Iudaiky.

Nalyvaiko, Dmytro. 1992. *Kozats'ka khrystyians'ka respublika (Zaporoz'ka Sich u zakhidnoievropeis'kykh literaturnykh pam'iatkakh)*. Kyiv: Dnipro.

Nazaruk, Osyp. 1920. *Rik na Velykii Ukraini: Konspekt spomyniv z ukrains'koi revoliutsii*. Vienna: Vydavnytstvo "Ukrains'kyi prapor."

Nechui-Levyts'kyi, Ivan. 2001. *Povisti*. Kyiv: Dnipro.

Noll, Viliam. 1999. *Transformatsiia hromadians'koho suspilstva: Usna istoriia ukrains'koi selians'koi kul'tury, 1920–30 rokiv*. Kyiv: Rodovid.

Nomys, M. 1864. *Ukrains'ki prykazky, pryslivia y take yishe*. St. Petersburg: Drukarnia Tyblena i komp. I. Kulisha.

Oblychchia soviets'koi zhurnalistyky. 1942. *Nashi dni* 1.3:13–14.

Obzor dokumentalnykh istochnikov po istorii evreiskoi literatury v fondakh arkhivokhranilishch Kieva. http//www.jewish-heritage.org/sea6.htm.

Oles', Oleksandr. 1990. *Tvory v dvokh tomakh*. 2 vols. Kyiv: Dnipro.

Opalski, Magdalena, and Israel Bartal. 1992. *Poles and Jews: A Failed Brotherhood*. Hanover, N.H.: Brandeis University Press.

Orlians'kyi, V. S. 2000. *Ievrei Ukrainy v 20–30 roky XX storichchia: Sotsial'no-politychnyi aspekt*. Zaporizhzhia: Zaporiz'kyi derzhavnyi universytet, Zaporiz'ke mis'ke viddilennia tovarystva "Ukraina-Izrail."

Os'machka, T[eodosii]. [1956] *Rotonda dushohubtsiv. Opovidannia*. N.p., n.d.

Osnova i vopros o natsional'nostiakh. 1861. *Sion* 10, September 10.

Pachovs'kyi, Vasyl'. 1914. *Sfinks Evropy: Drama v 3-okh Diiakh*. Lviv: Z druku Dila.

———. 1935. Probliemy ukrains'koi literatury. *Dzvony* 4:182–187, 5:256–263.

———. 1984. *Zibrani tvory*. 2 vols. Philadelphia: Slovo.

Paniotto, Volodymyr. 2000. The Levels of Anti-Semitism in Ukraine. *International Journal of Sociology* 29.3:66–75.

Paustovskii, K. 1967. *Sobranie sochinenii v vos'mi tomakh*. 8 vols. Moscow: Khudozhnaia literatura.

Pavlychko, Solomia. 2003. MUR iak epokha i iak dyskurs. In Aheieva, 189–208.

Pchilka, Olena. 2006. *Vykynuti ukraintsi*. Kyiv: Mizhrehional'na Akademiia Upravlinnia Personalom.

Pervomais'kyi, Leonid. 1927. *Zemlia obitovana*. Kharkiv: Derzhavne Vydavnytstvo Ukrainy. (Also in *Molodniak* 1 [1927]: 11–35, 2 [1927]: 3–18.)

———. 1928. U paliturni. *Molodniak* 4:71–80.

———. 1944. *Zhyttia: Opovidannia ta narysy*. Moscow: Spilka Radians'kykh Pys'mennykiv Ukrainy.

———. 1946. *Ataka na Vorskli: Opovidannia ta narysy*. Kyiv: Radians'kyi pys'mennyk.

———. 1947. *Poezii, 1924–1935*. Kyiv: Derzhavne Vydavnytstvo Ukrainy.

———. 1966. *Dykyi med: Suchasna balada*. Kyiv: Dnipro.

———. 1968. *Uroky poezi: Virshi ostannikh rokiv*. Kyiv: Radians'kyi pys'mennyk.

———. 1971. *Drevo piznannia: Poezii*. Kyiv: Radians'kyi pys'mennyk.

———. 1976. *Suzir'ia liry: Poezii*. Kyiv: Dnipro.

———. 1985. *Tvory v semy tomakh*. Kyiv: Dnipro.

Petliura, Symon. 1907. Peredmova: Uvahy pro zavdannia ukrains'koho teatru. In *Ievrei: p'esa na 4 dii*, by Ievgenii Chirikov, iii–xvii. Kyiv: S. A. Borysov.

Petrov, Viktor. 1929. *Panteleimon Kulish u p'iadesiati roky: Zhyttia, ideolohiia, tvorchist'*. Vol. 1. Kyiv: Vseukrains'ka Akademiia Nauk.

Petrovskii, Miron. 1996. Lev Kvitko v krugu ukrainskikh pisatelei. In *Jews and Slavs*, vol. 5, *Jews and Ukrainians*, ed. Wolf Moskovich, 238–54. Jerusalem: Hebrew University of Jerusalem.

Petrovsky-Shtern, Yohanan. 2004. The New Moses: A Ukrainian-Jewish Poet in the Making. *East European Jewish Affairs* 34.1:12–28.

———. 2005. *The Construction of an Improbable Identity: The Case of Hryts'ko Kernerenko. Ab imperio* 1:191–240.

———. Forthcoming. Being for the Victims: Leonid Pervomaiskyi's Ethical Responses to Violence. In *The Anti-Imperial Choice: the Making and Unmaking of the Ukrainian Jew*. New Haven, Conn.: Yale University Press.

Peukert, Detlev J. K. 1993. The Genesis of the "Final Solution" from the Spirit of Science. In *Reevaluating the Third Reich*, Childers and Caplan, 234–52. New York: Holmes and Meier.

Pidhainyi, Semen. 1949. *Nedostriliani*. 2 vols. N.p.: Ukraina.

Pihido-Pravoberezhnyi, Fedir. 1954. *"Velyka vitchyzniana viina."* Winnipeg: Novyi shliakh. (Rpt. Kyiv: Smoloskyp, 2002.)

Pipes, Richard. 1964. *The Formation of the Soviet Union: Communism and Nationalism, 1917–1923*. Rev. ed. Cambridge, Mass.: Harvard University Press. (Orig. pub. 1954.)

———. 2002. Alone Together: Solzhenitsyn and the Jews, Revisited. *New Republic*. November 25.

Plokhy, Serhii. 2001. *The Cossacks and Religion in Early Modern Ukraine*. Oxford: Oxford University Press.

————. 2005. *Unmaking Imperial Russia: Mykhailo Hrushevsky and the Writing of Ukrainian History.* Toronto: University of Toronto Press.

Polianker, H., and M. Talalaevs'kyi. 1947. Pro odne shkidlyve opovidannia. *Literaturna hazeta,* September 18.

Polishchuk, Klym. 1921a. *Chervone marevo: Narysy y opovidannia z chasiv revoliutsii.* Lviv: Novi shliakhy.

————. 1921b. *Skarby vikiv: Ukrains'ki legendy.* Lviv: Rusalka.

————. 1922a. *Manivtsiamy: Narysy y opovidannia z chasiv revoliutsii.* Lviv: Nakladom Semena Fodchuka.

————. 1922b. *Otaman Zelenyi: Suchasnyi roman v dvokh chastynakh.* Lviv: Rusalka.

————. 1923. *Zhertva: Narysy i opovidannia z dniv suchasnykh.* Lviv: Nakladom Knyharni A. Bardakha.

Poltava, L. 1998. Sotnyk Semen Iakerson. *Khronika 2000* 21–22: 214–20. (Orig. pub. 1985.)

Poltava, P. 1959. *Zbirnyk pidpil'nykh pysan'.* Munich: Ukrains'kyi samostiinyk.

Potichnyj, Peter J., and Howard Aster, eds. 1988. *Ukrainian-Jewish Relations in Historical Perspective.* Edmonton: Canadian Institute of Ukrainian Studies.

Potichnyi, Petro. 1985. Ukraintsi i ievrei. *Diialohy* 9–10:93–94.

Rabinovych, Ia. I. 1998. *Na zlami vikiv: Do 1000-richchia prozhyvannia ievreiv v Ukraini.* Kyiv: Ia. Rabinovych.

Raduts'kyi, Victor. 2000. Vid "Psalmiv Davydovykh" do "Zapovitu": Deiaki aspekty vplyvu Knyhy Psalmiv na poeziiu T. Shevchenka. In *Jews and Slavs,* vol. 7: *Jews and Eastern Slavs,* ed. Wolf Moskovich, 88–109. Jerusalem: Hebrew University of Jerusalem.

Rafes, M. G. 1920. *Dva goda revoliutsii na Ukraine (Evoliutsiia i raskol "BUNDA").* Moscow: Gosudarstvennoe izdatel'stvo.

Rayfield, Donald. 2005. *Stalin and His Hangmen: The Tyrant and Those Who Killed For Him.* New York: Random House.

Redlich, Shimon. 1992. Ievreis'ko-ukrains'ki stosunky v mizhvoiennii Pol'shchi u vysvitlenni ukrains'koi presy. *Suchasnist'* 8:76–88.

————. 1995. *War, Holocaust and Stalinism: A Documented History of the Jewish Anti-Fascist Committee in the USSR.* Luxembourg: Harwood Academic Publishers.

————. 1998. Jewish-Ukrainian Relations in Inter-War Poland as Reflected in Some Ukrainian Publications. *Polin* 11:232–46.

————. 2002. *Together and Apart in Brzezany: Poles, Jews, and Ukrainians, 1919–1945.* Bloomington: Indiana University Press.

Revuts'kyi, Valerian. 1985. Zustrich z Iaremoiu Aizenshtokom. *Diialohy* 9–10:164–65.

————. 1992. Theatre in the Camps. In Isajiw et al., 292–310.

Romanovskaia, Tatiana. 2001. "Sovershenno sekretno . . .": Istoriia kollektsii iudaiki Muzeia istoricheskikh dragotsennostei Ukrainy. *Iegupets* 8:398–406.

Roth, Joseph. 2001. *The Wandering Jews.* Trans. Michael Hofmann. New York: Norton.

Rudling, Per Anders. 2006. Organized Anti-Semitism in Contemporary Ukraine: Structure, Influence and Ideology. *Canadian Slavonic Papers* 48.1–2:81–118.

Rudnytsky, Ivan L. 1987. Mykhailo Drahomanov and the Problem of Ukrainian-Jewish

Relations. In *Essays in Modern Ukrainian History*, ed. Peter L. Rudnytsky. Edmonton: Canadian Institute of Ukrainian Studies.

———. 1988. Ukrainian-Jewish Relations in Nineteenth-Century Ukrainian Political Thought. In Potichnyj and Aster, 69–84. Edmonton: Canadian Institute of Ukrainian Studies.

Rudnyts'ka, Milena. 1957. Pomer dr. Emil Zomershtein, kolyshnii lider halyts'kykh zhydiv. *Svoboda* (Jersey City, N.J.), July 5.

———. 1998. *Statti, lysty, dokumenty*, ed. Marta Bohachevs'ka-Khomiak. Lviv: Misioner.

Rybakov, M. O., ed. 2001. *Pravda istorii: Diial'nist ievreis'koi kul'turno-prosvitnyts'koi orhanizatsii "Kul'turna Liha" u Kyievi,1918–1925. Zbirnyk dokumentiv i materialiv.* Kyiv: Kyi.

Rybyns'kyi, Volodymyr. 1928. Do istorii zhydiv na Livoberezhnii Ukraini v polov. XVIII st. In *Zbirnyk istorychno-fililohichnoi komisii* 73. Zbirnyk prats' zhydivs'koi istorychno-arkheohrafichnoi komisii, vol. 1., ed. I. V. Galant, 1–15. Kyiv: Vseukrains'ka Akademiia Nauk.

———. 1929. Protyievreis'kyi rukh r. 1881 na Ukraini. In Kryms'kyi, 139–82.

Safran, Gabriella. 2000a. Ethnography, Judaism, and the Art of Nikolai Leskov. *Russian Review* 59.2:235–51.

———. 2000b. *Rewriting the Jew: Assimilation Narratives in the Russian Empire.* Stanford, Calif.: Stanford University Press.

Said, Edward. 1978. *Orientalism.* London: Routledge and Kegan Paul.

Schaberg, Jane. 1987. *The Illegitimacy of Jesus: A Feminist Theological Interpretation of the Infancy Narratives.* San Francisco: Harper and Row.

Schapiro, Leonard. 1988. *Russian Studies.* New York: Viking. (Orig. pub. 1961.)

Segel, Harold B. 1996. *Stranger in Our Midst: Images of the Jew in Polish Literature.* Ithaca, N.Y.: Cornell University Press.

Serbyn, Roman. 1988. The *Sion-Osnova* Controversy of 1861–1862. In Potichnyj and Aster, 85–110.

Serge, Victor. 1967. *Memoirs of a Revolutionary, 1901–1941.* London: Oxford University Press.

Shapoval, Iurii. 1994. *Liudyna i systema (Shtrykhy do portretu totalitarnoi doby v Ukraini).* Kyiv: Instytut natsional'nykh vidnosyn i politolohii NANU.

———. 2001. *Ukraina XX stolittia: Osoby ta podii v konteksti vazhkoi istorii.* Kyiv: Heneza.

———. 2003. The GPU-NKVD as an Instrument of Counter-Ukrainization in the 1920s and 1930s. In Kappeler et al., 325–44.

Shapoval, Iurii, V. Prystaiko, and V. Zolotareva. 1997. *ChK-GPU-NKVD v Ukraini: Osoby, fakty, dokumenty.* Kyiv: Abrys.

Shapoval, Iurii, and Vadym Zolotarov. 2002. *Vsevolod Balyts'kyi: Osoba, chas, otochennia.* Kyiv: Stylos.

Shapoval, M[ykyta]. 1910. Novyny nashoi literatury (*Menty natkhnennia* Hryts'ka Kernerenka). *Literaturno-naukovyi vistnyk* 4:124–29.

Shcherbak, Iurii. 1986. *Khronika mista Iaropolia: Povist'.* Kyiv: Dnipro.

Shchurat, Vasyl'. 1963. *Vybrani pratsi z istorii literatury.* Kyiv: Vydavnytstvo Akademii Nauk Ukrains'koi RSR.

Sherekh, Iurii [Iurii Shevel'ov]. 1948. *Dumky proty techii: Publitsystyka.* N.p.: Ukraina.

———. 1998. *Porohy i Zaporizhzhia: Literatura. Mystetstvo. Ideolohiia.* Vol. 3. Kharkiv: Folio.

———. 2003. Proshchannia z uchora ("Koly zh pryide spravzhnii den?"). In Aheieva, 209–53. (Orig. pub. 1952.)

Shestopal, Matvii. 2002. *Ievrei na Ukraini: Istorychna dovidka.* Kyiv: Mizhrehionalna Akademiia Upravlinnia Personalom.

Shevchenko, Taras. 1983. *Kobzar.* Kyiv: Radians'kyi pys'mennyk.

Shevel'ov, Iurii. 1984. U sprobi nazvaty. In *Zbirka bez nazvy: Poezii, pereklady,* by Moisei Fishbein, 4–14. [Munich]: Suchasnist'.

Shkandrij, Myroslav. 1992. *Modernists, Marxists and the Nation. The Ukrainian Literary Discussion of the 1920s.* Edmonton: Canadian Institute of Ukrainian Studies Press.

Sholem Aleichem. 1985. *From the Fair: The Autobiography of Sholom Aleichem.* New York: Viking.

Shpytko, Osyp. 1901. Novomodnyi spivanyk: Perespivy Hrytsia Shchypavky. *Literaturno-naukovyi vistnyk* 15.8:8.

———. 2000. *Vyrid.* Lviv: L'vivske viddilennia Instytutu literatury im. T. H. Shevchenka, Natsional'na Akademiia Nauk Ukrainy.

Shrayer, Maxim D. 2000. *Russian Poet/Soviet Jew. The Legacy of Eduard Bagritskii.* Lanham, Md.: Rowman and Littlefield.

Shul'hin, Oleksander. 2001. *Ukraina i chervonyi zhakh: Pohromy v ukraini.* Kyiv: Vydavnytstvo im. Oleny Telihy. (Orig. pub. 1927.)

Shvarts, S. M. 1952. *Antisemitizm v Sovetskom Soiuze.* New York: Izd. im. Chekhova.

Sicher, Efraim. 1995. *Jews in Russian Literature after the October Revolution: Writers and Artists between Hope and Apostasy.* Cambridge: Cambridge University Press.

"Sion" i "Osnova" pred sudom russkoi zhurnalistiki. 1862. *Sion* 37:581–88.

Skurativs'kyi, Vadym. 1996. Na perekhrestiakh dushi. *Suchasnist'* 12:86–89.

———. 1998. Do ievreis'ko-ukrains'kykh literaturnykh zviazkiv: Poperedni notatky. *Khronika 2000* 21–22:44–57.

Slezkine, Yuri. 2004. *The Jewish Century.* Princeton: Princeton University Press.

Slyvka, Iurii, ed. 1996. *Deportatsii: Zakhidni zemli Ukrainy kintsia 30-kh—pochatku 50-kh rr. Dokumenty, materialy, spohady u trokh tomakh.* Vol. 1: *1939–1945 rr.* Lviv: Natsional'na Akademiia Nauk Ukrainy, Instytut Ukrainoznavstva im. I. Krypiakevycha.

Smolych, Iurii. 1972. *Tvory v shesty tomakh.* Vol. 5. Kyiv: Dnipro.

———. 1990. Z "Zapysiv na skhyli viku." *Prapor* 9:160–78.

———. 2004. Raia. Z "Intymnoi spovidi." *Komentar* 3:15.

Snegirov, Gelii. 2000. Roman-donos. *Iegupets* 7:12–100.

Sniehirov, Helii (Ievhen) [Gelii Snegirov]. 1983. *Naboi dlia rozstrilu ta inshi tvory.* New York: Vydannia Hromads'koho komitetu i Novykh dniv.

Snyder, Timothy. *Sketches from a Secret War: A Polish Artist's Mission to Liberate Soviet Ukraine.* New Haven, Conn.: Yale University Press.

Soloviova, Tetiana. 1990. Memuaryst—Intelihent, humanist. *Prapor* 9:175.

Solzhenitsyn, A. I. 2001–2. *Dvesti let vmeste (1795–1995).* 2 vols. Moscow: Russkii put'.

Spackman, Barbara. 1996. *Fascist Virilities: Rhetoric, Ideology, and Social Fantasy in Italy.* Minneapolis: University of Minnesota Press.

Stambrook, Fred. N.d. *The Golden Age of the Jews of Bukovina, 1880–1914.* Working Papers in Austrian Studies 03-2, Center for Austrian Studies, University of Minnesota.

Staryts'kyi, Mykhailo. 1968. *Ostanni orly: Istorychna povist' iz chasiv haidamachchyny.* Kyiv: Dnipro. (Orig. pub. 1901.)

Stebun, I., and A. Isachenko. 1947. Poetychna tvorchist' Leonida Pervomais'koho. In Pervomais'kyi 1947, 5–45.

Stone, Dan. 1991. Jews and the Ukrainian Question. *Slavic Review* 50.3:531–41.

Streit, Christian. 1994. Wehrmacht, Einsatzgruppen, Soviet POWs and Anti-Bolshevism in the Emergence of the Final Solution. In Cesarani, 103–17.

Stsibors'kyi, M. 1930. Ukrains'kyi natsionalizm i zhydivstvo. *Rozbudova natsii* 3.9–10:266–73.

Sukhodol's'kyi, A. L. 1919. *Khmara: V 5-ty diiakh, z spivamy, khoramy i tantsiamy.* New York: Nakladom Knyharni sichovoho bazaru.

Sulyma, Vira. 1998. *Bibliia i ukrains'ka literatura.* Kyiv: Osvita.

Surmach, Roman. 1923. *Peshchena dytyna.* Winnipeg: Ukrains'ka knyharnia.

Suslens'kyi, Iakiv. 1993. *Spravzhni heroi: Pro uchast hromadian Ukrainy u riatuvanni ievreiv vid fashysts'koho henotsydu.* Kyiv: Tov. Ukraina.

———. 1994. Spil'na borot'ba v Gulaz'kykh umovakh. In Korohods'kyi, 71–136.

Sysyn, Frank, E. 1998. The Jewish Massacres in the Historiography of the Khmelnytsky Uprising: A Review Article. *Journal of Ukrainian Studies* 23.1:83–89.

———. 2003. The Khmel'nyts'kyi Uprising: A Characterization of the Ukrainian Revolt. *Jewish History 17:* 115–39.

Syvoshapka, M. 1940. Spyrydon Cherkasenko. *Svoboda.* April 6.

Szczurat, Wasyl. 1937. Wówczas była to jeszcze mrzonka . . . *Chwila.* August 5.

Tohobochnii [also Tohobichnyi, pseud. of Ivan Shchoholiv]. 1922. *Zhydivka Vykhrestka: Drama v V diiakh.* Lviv: Drukarnia Naukovho Tovarystva im. Shevchenka. (Orig. pub. 1909.)

Trembyts'kyi, Izydor. 1915. *Its'ko-Svat.* Scranton, Penn.: Vydavnytstvo Ukrains'koi knyharni v Skrentoni.

Tsarynnyk, Marko. 1984. Til'ky i iest u nas voroh—nashe sertse. *Suchasnist'* 10:91–99.

Tsymbal, Iaryna. 2004. Raisa Troianker iz dvokh zbirok. *Komentar* 3:14.

Tychyna, Pavlo. 1976. *Tvory v dvokh tomakh.* 2 vols. Kyiv: Dnipro.

Tykhyi, Naum. 1995. *Sedmytsia: Sim dramatychnykh poem.* Kyiv: Dovira.

———. 1996. *Smak osinn'oho vitru: Poezii.* Kyiv: Dovira.

Ukrainka, Lesia. 1979. *Zibrannia tvoriv u dvanadtsiaty tomakh.* Vol. 12. Kyiv: Naukova dumka.

Vaksberg, Arkady. 1994. *Stalin Against the Jews.* New York: Knopf.

Vasyl'chenko, Stepan. 1959–60. *Tvory v chotyr'iokh tomakh.* 4 vols. Kyiv: Akademiia Nauk Ukrains'koi RSR.

Veidlinger, Jeffrey. 1998. Let's Perform a Miracle: The Soviet Yiddish Theater in the 1920s. *Slavic Review* 57.2:372–97.

Veselova, O. M. et al., comp. 1996. *Holod v Ukraini, 1946–1947: Dokumenty i materialy.*
Kyiv: M. P. Kots'.

Veselovs'ka, Hanna. 1998. Zabuti storinky z istorii ukrains'koho teatru. *Khronika 2000*
21–22:177–85.

Vichnyi Zhyd rodom iz Ierusalyma imenem Ahasverii. 1907. Kolomyiia: Nakladom M.
Bilousa.

Vincenz, Stanislaw. 1955. *On the High Uplands: Sagas, Songs, Tales and Legends of the
Carpathians.* Trans. H. C. Stevens. London: Hutchinson.

———. 1980–84. *Na wysokiej połoninie.* Warszawa: Pax. 4 vols. (Orig. pub. 1936–52.)

V kikhtiakh rozpusty abo Nad bezodneiu propasty. 1921. Waterloo, Ont.: Tov. im. Iv.
Franka.

Volkogonov, Dmitri. 1999. *The Rise and Fall of the Soviet Empire: Political Leaders from
Lenin to Gorbachev.* London: Harper Collins.

Vozniak, Mykhailo. 1921. *Istoriia ukrains'koi literatury.* 3 vols. Lviv: Prosvita.

Vynnychenko, Volodymyr. 1907. *Dysharmoniia: P'iesa na chotyry kartyny.* Kyiv: Vik.

———. 1913. Talisman. *Literaturno-naukovyi vistnyk* 4–5:229–56.

———. 1919. *Mizh dvokh syl: Drama na chotyry dii.* Kyiv: Dzvin.

———. 1920. *Vidrodzhennia natsii.* Vol. 1. Kyiv.

———. 1929. *Tvory.* Vol. 9. Kyiv: Rukh.

———. 1930. *Pisnia Izrailia (Kol-Nidre): P'iesa na 4 dii.* Kharkiv: Rukh. (Orig. pub.
1922.)

———. 1998. Do ievreis'koho pytannia na Ukraini. *Khronika 2000* 21–22:153–165.
(Orig. pub. 1923.)

Weinberg, Robert. 1992. The Pogrom of 1905 in Odessa: A Case Study. In Klier and
Lambroza, 248–89.

Weiner, Amir. 2001. *Making Sense of War: The Second World War and the Fate of the Bolshevik Revolution.* Princeton, N.J.: Princeton University Press.

Wilcher, Asher. 1982. Ivan Franko and Theodor Herzl: To the Genesis of Franko's *Moj-
sej. Harvard Ukrainian Studies* 6.2:233–43.

Yavir, Hordii [Iurii Klen]. 2004. Amaliekytiany, amorytiany i gibeonity (Dopys z Nimechchyny). *Vistnyk* 12:877–78.

———. 1933. Z nimets'kykh vrazhin' (Reportazh z Nimechchyny). *Vistnyk* 11:813–17.

———. 1938. 12 bereznia (Dopys z Nimechchyny). *Vistnyk* 4:287–89.

Yekelchyk, Serhy. 2000. *Diktat* and Dialogue in Stalinist Culture: Staging Patriotic Historical Opera in Soviet Ukraine, 1936–1954. *Slavic Review* 59.3:597–624.

———. 2001. The Nation's Clothes: Constructing a Ukrainian High Culture in the
Russian Empire, 1860–1900. *Jahrbücher für Geschichte Osteuropas* 49:230–39.

———. 2002. Stalinist Patriotism as Imperial Discourse: Reconciling the Ukrainian
and Russian "Heroic Pasts," 1939–45. *Kritika: Explorations in Russian and Eurasian
History* 3.1:51–80.

———. 2004. *Stalin's Empire of Memory: Russian-Ukrainian Relations in the Soviet Historical Imagination.* Toronto: University of Toronto Press.

Zabuzhko, O. 2001a. *Khroniky vid Fortinbrasa: Vybrana eseistyka 90-kh.* Kyiv: Fakt.

———. 2001b. *Shevchenkiv mif Ukrainy: Sproba filosofs'koho analizu.* Kyiv: Fakt.

Zahrebel'nyi, Pavlo. 2001. *Ia, Bohdan, Spovid u slavi: Roman.* Kharkiv: Folio. (Orig. pub. 1983.)

Zelenina, G. S., ed. 2005. *Evrei i zhidy v russkoi klassike.* Moscow: Mosty kultury—Gesharim.

Zh., B. Peredmova. 1937. In Kosach 1937, 5–8.

Zhabotinskii, Vladimir (Zeev) [Jabotinsky]. 1905. *Evreiskoe vospitanie.* Odesa.

———. 1922. *Fel'etony.* 3d ed. Berlin: Izdatelstvo S. D. Zaltsman. (Orig. pub. 1913.)

———. 1982. *Vybrani statti z natsional'noho pytannia.* [Munich]: Suchasnist'.

Zhydy v U.H.A. 1922. *Kalendar chervonoi kalyny,* 132. Zhovkva: Red. O. Vasyliian. Rpt. in *Pryiatel' ukrains'koho zhovnira,* 132. Lviv: Chervona kalyna, 1923.

Zipperstein, Steven J. 1999. *Imagining Russian Jewry: Memory, History, Identity.* Seattle: University of Washington Press.

Zisel's, Iosif. 2000. *Iesli ia tolko dlia sebia . . .* Kyiv: Instytut Iudaiky.

Index